Autism

Autism

An Integrated View from Neurocognitive, Clinical, and Intervention Research

Edited by
Evelyn McGregor, María Núñez, Katie Cebula,
and Juan Carlos Gómez

Blackwell
Publishing

© 2008 by Blackwell Publishing Ltd

BLACKWELL PUBLISHING
350 Main Street, Malden, MA 02148–5020, USA
9600 Garsington Road, Oxford OX4 2DQ, UK
550 Swanston Street, Carlton, Victoria 3053, Australia

First published 2008 by Blackwell Publishing Ltd

1   2008

Library of Congress Cataloging-in-Publication Data

Autism : an integrated view from neurocognitive, clinical, and intervention research / edited by Evelyn McGregor ... [et al.].
    p. ;   cm.
Includes bibliographical references and index.
ISBN 978-1-4051-5695-0 (hardback : alk. paper) — ISBN 978-1-4051-5696-7 (pbk. : alk. paper)
    1. Autism. I. McGregor, Evelyn.
[DNLM: 1. Autistic Disorder—psychology. 2. Autistic Disorder—diagnosis. 3. Autistic Disorder—rehabilitation. 4. Brain—physiopathology. 5. Models, Theoretical. WM 203.5 A9363 2008]
    RC553.A88A828 2008
    616.85'8820072—dc22
    2007030474

A catalogue record for this title is available from the British Library.

Set in 10/13 pt Minion
by The Running Head Limited, www.therunninghead.com
Printed and bound in Singapore
by Markono Print Media Pte Ltd

The publisher's policy is to use permanent paper from mills that operate a sustainable forestry policy, and which has been manufactured from pulp processed using acid-free and elementary chlorine-free practices. Furthermore, the publisher ensures that the text paper and cover board used have met acceptable environmental accreditation standards.

For further information on
Blackwell Publishing, visit our website:
www.blackwellpublishing.com

Contents

Preface

Research on autism has flourished in the last 20 years. A natural part of this exciting growth has been specialization within specific research areas across the neurocognitive, clinical, and intervention fields of inquiry. As specialization has increased, however, research lines have become isolated. In order to fully understand this complex developmental condition, these different perspectives now need to be shared among the wide variety of academics and professionals who work in the field of autism.

This book is the outcome of a two-year inter-university seminar series, hosted by the Scottish Autism Research Group (SARG), funded initially by the British Psychological Society, which aimed to respond to this need. These seminars provided an ideal platform for sharing some of the most recent neurocognitive, clinical, and intervention research findings within an integrated context. Only a small selection of the presentations from this first series could be included as a final contribution to this volume; these collectively provide a range of perspectives within neurocognitive, clinical, and intervention areas and the authors have very willingly participated in the process of integrating them. During the five seminars of this first series, however, more than 30 speakers from the UK, other countries in Europe, and the USA discussed their research in this forum, enthusiastically sharing and exchanging their thoughts and doubts with a welcoming, participative audience. Their contributions have been an indispensable part of the development of this forum during its early years. We trust that at least a portion of the same excitement and enthusiasm that brought all of the participants and speakers together in this series will be conveyed through the pages of this book.

Acknowledgments

We would like to thank the British Psychological Society, the University of Edinburgh Development Trust, and the Scottish Hospital Endowments Research Trust for providing the financial support to the Scottish Autism Research Group for a first seminar series. This book is the tangible outcome of that series. We would also like to thank the members of the SARG for their regular seminar attendance that made continuing funding possible, and for their thoughtful contributions to discussions with the guest speakers. Their attendance and their participation in the debate, which drew on a range of research and practitioner backgrounds, was an important step toward an integrated view of autism. More recent Economic and Social Research Council (ESRC) support (grant RES-451–26–0227) has allowed a regular continuation of the seminars and meetings of this discussion forum. The Universities of Edinburgh, Glasgow Caledonian, and St Andrews kindly provided their facilities, which helped us to host the seminar series. Our thankful acknowledgment, too, to St John's College, Oxford, for the visiting scholarship awarded to María Núñez that facilitated the editorial work during the summer of 2006. We also wish to thank Elizabeth-Ann Johnston for her attentive editorial support in the preparation of this book.

Finally, we are most grateful to the artist Zoe Kakolyris and her family for giving us permission to use the painting *All Aboard* for the cover of this book. We got to know her work thanks to Eva Loth, who had organized the exhibition by artists with autism at which Zoe exhibited her work; George Hanrahan, Zoe's representative, kindly facilitated the process of gaining permission. Inspired by this colorful, optimistic painting, we trust this book has made an appealing journey into bringing everyone on board in the process of integrating perspectives in autism.

List of Contributors

Simon Baron-Cohen, Autism Research Centre, Departments of Experimental Psychology and Psychiatry, Cambridge University, Cambridge, UK

Katie Cebula, Moray House School of Education, University of Edinburgh, UK

Aline-Wendy Dunlop, National Centre for Autism Studies, Faculty of Education, University of Strathclyde, Glasgow, UK

Fiona Gibbon, Speech and Hearing Sciences, Queen Margaret University College, Edinburgh, UK

Ofer Golan, Department of Psychology, Bar-Ilan University, Ramat-Gan, Israel, and the Autism Research Centre, Department of Psychiatry, University of Cambridge, UK

Juan Carlos Gómez, School of Psychology, University of St Andrews, UK

Richard P. Hastings, School of Psychology, University of Wales Bangor, UK

Elisabeth L. Hill, Department of Psychology, Goldsmiths, University of London, UK

Glenys Jones, School of Education, University of Birmingham, UK

Warren Jones, Yale Child Study Center, Yale University, New Haven, CT, USA

Rita Jordan, School of Education, University of Birmingham, UK

Ami Klin, Yale Child Study Center, Yale University, New Haven, CT, USA

Fiona Knott, School of Psychology and Clinical Language Sciences, University of Reading, UK

Susan Leekam, School of Psychology, University of Durham, Durham, UK

Beatriz López, School of Psychology, University of West Midlands, UK

Eva Loth, Department of Experimental Psychology, Cambridge University, UK

Tommy MacKay, National Centre for Autism Studies, University of Strathclyde, Glasgow, UK

Sandra Maestro, Division of Child Neuropsychiatry, University of Pisa, Italy

Joanne McCann, Speech and Hearing Sciences, Queen Margaret University College, Edinburgh, UK

Evelyn McGregor, School of Psychology, University of St Andrews, St Andrews, UK

Peter Mitchell, School of Psychology, University of Nottingham, UK

Filippo Muratori, Division of Child Neuropsychiatry, University of Pisa, Italy

María Núñez, Department of Psychology, Glasgow Caledonian University, Glasgow, UK

Anne O'Hare, Royal Hospital for Sick Children, Edinburgh, and University of Edinburgh, UK

Sue Peppé, Speech and Hearing Sciences, Queen Margaret University College, Edinburgh, UK

Danielle Ropar, School of Psychology, University of Nottingham, UK

Marion Rutherford, Royal Hospital for Sick Children, Edinburgh, UK

Elizabeth Sheppard, School of Psychology, University of Nottingham, UK

Bruno Wicker, Institut de Neurosciences Cognitives de la Méditerranée, CNRS, Marseille, France

Joanna G. Williams, Cambridge University and Bath & NE Somerset Primary Care Trust, UK

Justin H. G. Williams, Department of Child Health, University of Aberdeen Medical School, UK

1

Introduction

Seeking Coherence in Autism: From fMRI to Intervention

Evelyn McGregor, María Núñez, Katie Cebula, and Juan Carlos Gómez

Introduction

In Kanner's classic paper describing the developmental phenomenon now known as autism, two statements in particular stand out as distilling the essence of the condition. The first statement describes the quality of interpersonal and social relating, while acknowledging its natural or biological origin:

> The outstanding "pathognomic," fundamental disorder is the children's inability to relate themselves in the ordinary way to people and situations from the beginning of life (Kanner, 1943, p. 242).

The second statement, urging the reader to think about how the person with autism experiences the world, captures the remarkable struggle to cope with change in routine or context:

> Their world must seem to them to be made up of elements that, once they have been experienced in a certain setting or sequence, cannot be tolerated in any other setting or sequence; nor can the setting or sequence be tolerated without all the original ingredients in the identical spatial or chronological order. Hence the obsessive repetitiousness (p. 249).

The descriptions of these apparently disparate behaviors, so elegantly and meticulously expressed, create compelling images of what autism is. They note in the process its origins from the beginning of life—that is, its biological root—and the sense of a fixed, yet fragmented world that is unnervingly unpredictable. Kanner's influence has been profound and enduring: These two aspects of behavior are still represented today in the diagnostic criteria for autism—the first in the impairments in social interaction and communication and the second in the repetitive behaviors and desire for sameness.

Autism is a newly discovered syndrome, relatively speaking, and the contribution of Kanner and of other outstanding researchers and clinicians notwithstanding, it is marked as much by what professionals do not know as by what they do know. Despite rapid advances in neuropsychology, epidemiology, etiology, diagnosis, cognition, and, recently, genetics, the research community continues to wrestle to identify biological causes and developmental processes, at the neural, cognitive, and affective levels. It is, however, an exceptionally vibrant research environment, which is producing an outstanding number of new findings and approaches within its individual specialisms. The challenge is to develop a fuller understanding within these highly productive, specialized, research areas while, increasingly, considering how new findings fit into and even alter the whole knowledge base. The ultimate goal is to integrate research findings fully in order to map out the boundaries and the landscape of autism. This would be a substantial aid to early and precise diagnosis, provide a guide to the most effective remediation, and, in the process, add considerably to our understanding of both atypical and typical development at the levels of brain and behavior across the lifespan.

Autism is not a unitary concept. It consists of a miscellany of features, some of which have no obvious relationship. It appears to varying degrees in different individuals and coexists with a variety of medical conditions. Academic researchers have made continuing efforts in the last 25 years to establish whether these apparently disparate features can be the outcome of a set of simpler core features underlying the condition (Leslie, 1991; Morton & Frith, 1995). Much effort has been made to discover a pattern of cause and effect or association, initially at a relatively simple level, either by demonstrating how features might be linked directly (for example, atypical affect leading to difficulty in social cognition (Hobson, 1993)), or by showing how they could be incidentally related at the neurological level (for example, through linked pathways in the brain (Baron-Cohen & Ring, 1994)). Recent hypotheses are more complex. One posits that the two dominant characteristics of autism, the social and non-social behaviors, may be coexistent but not genetically co-dependent (Ronald, Happé, & Plomin, 2005). Another identifies no fewer than six candidate broader phenotype autism traits (Dawson et al., 2002), while functional magnetic resonance imaging (fMRI) studies propose connectionist models of brain function that indicate atypical modulation of activity and incorporate compensatory mechanisms (see Wicker, Chapter 2). How to rationalize all these? Considerable progress has been made, but it seems that, paradoxically, still further expansion is needed, both within and between research fields, before a fully coherent account can be achieved.

The Challenge of Integration

The reference to seeking coherence in the title of this chapter relates first to the longstanding goal of seeking a coherent explanation for the constellation of behavioral features that comprise autism. However, of no less importance, it relates to the process by which that will eventually be achieved, by referring more specifically to the need for coherence among or across different fields of inquiry. Over time, research areas have become increasingly specialized, with very limited inter-area collaboration or "cross-talk." Yet, ultimately, a coherent account of autism can be created only by a process of integration of research perspectives and findings. It is tempting to use the analogy of a jigsaw puzzle in stressing the need to integrate across research fields, but this would be simplistic, as the task is not merely to join up information from different specialisms, but to merge it. This is no small challenge and there are two obvious difficulties inherent in that process. First, the sheer volume of published work makes the task of keeping pace with all aspects of research daunting. In the years since Kanner's publication, and particularly in the past decade, research on autism has grown exponentially. Volkmar, Lord, Bailey, Schultz, and Klin (2004) observe that almost 3,000 articles have been published on autism between 1994 and 2004. This is, they note, equal to the number published between 1943 and 1989. High-quality reviews of specific research areas at key points do reduce the problem, though they do not remove it. To review the complete literature is now impossible, although two systematic overviews have eased the situation by providing highlights and main achievements across research fields (Bailey, Phillips, & Rutter, 1996; Volkmar et al., 2004).

The second difficulty is the greater of the two. As recognition of the complexity of the condition has increased, the growth of research has not followed a narrowly defined route in the predictable areas of medicine and clinical psychology, but has expanded into many others. Autism research is now represented in several areas of psychology, including developmental and biological psychology, ethology, and comparative cognition, cognitive neuroscience, and, of course, clinical and educational psychology. It is also researched within medicine, in neurology, genetics, and child psychiatry, and in other professional areas such as education and speech and language, music, and art therapy. Beyond the obvious medical/psychological areas it has attracted the interest of academic researchers in philosophy, computer science, and linguistics (Carruthers & Smith, 1996; Moore & Taylor, 2000; Stirling & Barrington, in press). Each specialism has an understanding of the condition within a certain model of functioning, with its own circumscribed knowledge base and terminology and even its own academic culture (in particular, the medical model and the educational model are very different and not always compatible: see Chapter 16). These have resulted in a range of perspectives on autism and could produce quite different answers to the questions "How should autism be defined?" and "What are the fundamental processes through which it develops?" To merge these perspectives would require a decision or agreement about employing a broadly comprehensible terminology, a willingness to explain one's own field, while striving to comprehend another, and a consideration of autism as it is represented in two or more research contexts. Moreover, the answers might be multilayered. After all, it is some time since Goodman (1989) observed that there might not be one overarching mechanism that explains autism. The temptation is to ask, "Is it unrealistic to talk about integrating perspectives?" Is there another way?

The response to these concerns is a growing recognition that effective progress from now on will, in fact, rely on integration. A number of major contributors to research in autism have considered the issue and reached similar conclusions on the need for integration, despite its potential complexity. More than a decade ago, Bailey et al. (1996) first mooted the idea that integration of perspectives should be the way forward, at the same time acknowledging that any attempt needs to recognize that a range of causal models has to be considered. More recently, Dawson et al. (2002), reviewing the cognitive neuroscience of social and language impairments in autism, made a compelling case for integration across genetic, cognitive neuroscience, animal, and clinical studies, of not only research findings, but also approaches and concepts. They maintained that this is a requirement if there is to be progress in understanding. Volkmar et al. (2004) have observed that the full benefit of isolated breakthroughs will actually depend on connections between different fields of inquiry. In fact, they go further, proposing that mandates for future research should include the building of an integrated model of the constructs and mechanisms involved in the pathogenesis of autism. There is little dispute, then, that this is the next rational research step, and that there is a need to merge.

We have outlined the two most obvious difficulties. But there is also a less obvious, although very important problem nested within the second. Any reference to integration usually occurs within the context of integrating aspects of research within medicine (or the clinical diagnostic area), within psychology (or social and neurocognition), or between these two. However, the third main strand of research, that of education/intervention is almost invariably overlooked. Rarely has an explicit reference been made to incorporating this aspect within the integrated frame, though some authors have broached the matter briefly (see, e.g., Sigman, Spence, & Wang, 2006).

Yet one would expect that intervention should be highly dependent on the other two areas, and, in addition, that the outcome of research on intervention would offer considerable insights into the nature of autism. With regard to the first point, Volkmar et al. (2004) comment:

> A major concern is the large, and possibly growing, gap between what science can show is effective, on the one hand, and what treatments parents actually pursue. Another concern is the extent to which the full benefit of scientific research is translated into best practice in actual classroom settings (p. 155).

Sigman et al. (2006) endorse that view. There is, therefore, support for the argument that research and intervention programs should be connected; however, it is not in the context of a move toward integration more broadly. A restricted conception of the role of intervention within any explanatory model has implications for understanding autism: It is undervaluing the contribution that research in intervention might make; additionally, it is distancing the work and potential contributions of the practitioner from those of the researcher: a loss to both. Consequently, the outcomes of both research and practice in intervention could and should be part of any integration framework. In Chapter 16, Leekam and McGregor propose an explanation for this gap: partly an historical outcome of the way in which research in autism evolved such that the general framework has emphasized the causal rather than the developmental; partly a consequence of the dominant role of medicine in the initial characterization of autism.

Those advocating integration have been responding to a perceived need for a common framework to explain autism focused predominantly on causation—or at least causal mechanisms. However, there is a risk that considering theoretical models only in terms of causal mechanisms might underplay the essential contribution of development. Yet autism is defined as a developmental disorder; there is no question that the developmental aspect is intrinsic to the condition, and any explanatory framework must account for this fact. If it has been overlooked in earlier models, an integration of perspectives provides the opportunity needed to incorporate development as it deserves.

There has, certainly, been an increase in awareness of the need for longitudinal data in order to track developmental trajectories, an encouraging shift (Hale & Tager-Flusberg, 2005; Hazlett et al. 2005; Landa & Garret-Mayer, 2006; Lord, Shulman, & DiLavore, 2004; Munson et al., 2006). These studies are predominantly diagnostic, however, and generally look at change over time on one or two measures. Some do refer to developmental trajectories, though they are not designed for any elaborated modeling of interactive developmental processes. A developmental perspective is certainly emerging. For example, Klin, Jones, Schultz, and Volkmar (2003) locate their discussion of the "enactive mind" in autism within a clear developmental context; and although they do not explicitly advocate a wider-ranging, integrated approach to autism research, they do indicate a need to increase the range of methodologies to study social adaptation (see also Jones & Klin, Chapter 4). During the past decade, a developmental approach has been proposed for other developmental disorders, arguing that the necessary frame of reference should be a dynamic construct that encompasses the process of change (Bishop, 1997; Goswami, 2003; Karmiloff-Smith, 1997). The ground, therefore, is being prepared. Starting from such fertilized ground, Leekam and McGregor expand on these issues in the final chapter; throughout this volume, the argument for integration is developed whenever there is an opportunity to cite, draw together, and elaborate on examples from the other chapters of the book

Toward Achieving Integration

The next question for this chapter is, how might the process of integration of research in autism be achieved? There are two possible ways: first, by applying or overlaying models of autism, or aspects of autism from one area to that of another, and assessing, or at least speculating about, the degree of "fit." In this way, reassessment can be made about the likely accuracy of the model and scope offered for the construction of a more complex representation. Second, cross-area collaboration can offer a direct way of testing the degree of fit, or of filling gaps in an incomplete or simple model. With regard to the first, there has always been some interest in, for example, mapping a cognitive model onto a neurological one, matching behaviors characteristic of autism to specific brain areas (e.g., associating impairments in social cognition with atypical functioning of the frontal cortex (Baron-Cohen & Ring, 1994), and this continues at a more sophisticated level with improving technology (see Wicker, Chapter 2). Ideas have been incorporated from developmental psychology that have helped broaden the range of diagnostic instruments, some of which now incorporate the assessment of joint attention and imitation (e.g., the ADOS-G, Lord et al., 2000). These are natural spill-over effects of a subject area that is researched in different disciplines where useful links will naturally be made from time to time. Nevertheless, they do not constitute integration.

With regard to the second way of achieving integration, cross-area collaboration, a growing number of studies are taking an interdisciplinary approach to answering research questions. For example, genetics and cognition have combined in phenotype studies of cognitive profiling in families with autism (e.g., Nurmi et al., 2003). Advances in neurological technology have opened up new possibilities, as performance on cognitive tasks is highly suitable for combination with fMRI scanning studies. These do indicate a distinct move toward a more collaborative approach to research in autism; but they, too, still fall far short of a truly integrated approach. In addition, collaboration has rarely involved more than two topic areas. This method of integrating would provide a very limited and presumably rather protracted merging of models in a prolonged process of pairing collaborations.

The Three Areas of This Book's Focus

This section gives an outline and brief history of each of the three areas of the book's title: neurocognitive, clinical/diagnostic, and intervention. The three areas identified have generally followed strongly independent research paths. Historically, autism was first the preserve of medicine, originally located within psychiatry and later extending into pediatrics, neurology, and genetics. Education/intervention has operated in parallel, responding to behavioral difficulties rather than underlying cognitive anomalies, although, gradually, it has acknowledged the diagnostic criteria in its rationale for intervention (see Jones & Jordan, Chapter 14), and cognitive interventions have been explored (see Golan & Baron-Cohen, Chapter 12). Psychology's interest in autism emerged in the 1960s, initially at a low level, then exploding into a dominant topic of research interest from the 1980s. In one sense psychology occupies the space between the medical and the educational, and has the potential to serve as a powerful facilitator in the process of integrating research in these three areas. Each content chapter in this book covers a major topic from at least one of the three main areas of the book title, and all chapters elaborate on one or more aspects of the core information that follows here.

Clinical/diagnostic area

Diagnostic markers

As yet, there is no identifiable biological marker for autism although there are thought to be atypical patterns of development in certain brain areas (Courchesne, Townsend, & Saitoh, 1994; DeLong, 1992; and see Chapter 2); abnormalities of neurotransmitter function (McDougle, 1997; and see Chapter 3); genetic predispositions (Bailey et al., 1995; Curran et al., 2006; Ronald, Happé, Price, Baron-Cohen, & Plomin, 2006); and co-morbid medical conditions such as epilepsy (Danielsson, Gillberg, Billstedt, Gillberg, & Olsson, 2005). Consequently, autism is identified at the level of behavior, so that diagnosis relies on interpretation and professional judgment. Within medical research, there are two main sub-areas: in diagnosis and in epidemiology (Volkmar et al., 2004). These sub-areas are interdependent, in that epidemiological study requires some kind of diagnostic instrument. At the same time, screening programs have resulted in refinements to instruments as questions were raised about milder or borderline cases.

Diagnosis

Clinicians assess a child by interviewing parents and observing the child's behavior. Current diagnostic criteria are the product of international efforts (Gillberg, 1992; Rutter & Schopler, 1992; Volkmar, et al., 1994) and development of diagnostic tools continues. Williams (Chapter 10) provides more detail on these. Autism was recognized as an official class of disorder in 1980 and is listed in the American Psychiatric Association's *Diagnostic and statistical manual* (1994) and in the World Health Organization's ICD-10 (1993) classification of mental and behavioral disorders (under pervasive developmental disorders). To be given a diagnosis of autism, an individual has to have displayed: (a) a number of proscribed qualitative impairments in social interaction; (b) a number of qualitative impairments in communication; and (c) restricted repetitive and stereotyped patterns of behavior, interests, and activities. Beyond the listed criteria, some children have abnormal eating behavior, disrupted sleeping patterns, or abnormalities of mood or affect. Around 50% have a coexistent general intellectual disability.

Epidemiology

More than 30 epidemiological studies have been conducted (e.g., Fombonne, 2003; Lotter, 1966; Wing & Potter, 2002). Reported prevalence varies substantially (see Chapter 10 for rates and an explanation for variation) but does not appear to vary geographically or ethnically. Genetic influences are considered to have a dominant role in etiology (Bailey et al., 1996). Twin and family studies indicate an autism phenotype, with some family members of normal intelligence showing mild characteristics (Bacchelli et al., 2003; Nurmi et al., 2003; Parr, Lamb, Bailey, & Monaco, 2006). Although autism criteria are listed in psychiatric manuals, it is neither a disease nor a psychiatric condition. It is characterized by disordered or atypical development of the behaviors listed above.

Educational/interventionist area

With the recognition of the condition in the 1940s and 1950s came an accompanying understanding that there was a need for intervention or support. Intervention could take a number of routes. First, it might seek to reduce or remove the behaviors that were considered inappropriate or excessive, such as repetitious behaviors or echolalia. Second, it might aim to introduce or enhance behaviors that seemed to be missing or underdeveloped, such as social interaction or understanding of affect. Third, it might seek to identify the fundamental cause, and by intervening alter the behavioral consequences (see Williams, Chapter 10; Jones & Jordan, Chapter 14). Although a great diversity of interventions is available for both children and adults with autism spectrum disorder (ASD), a common challenge lies in enabling participants to generalize the skills learnt to other contexts (see Golan & Baron-Cohen, Chapter, 12; Dunlop, Knott, & MacKay, Chapter 13). Volkmar et al. (2004) report that "even with the most ecologically valid treatments, generalization needs to be specifically addressed or it will very rarely happen" (p. 151), an echo of Kanner's observation on the need for elements to be re-experienced in the same setting or sequence with all the original features in the same order.

Neurocognitive research areas

As in medicine, psychology too is exploring autism from a range of perspectives. Its interest was slower and later to emerge but has made up for that in the past two decades. It had focused initially on linguistic and symbolic aspects, helping shift the perception of autism from the psychiatric to the developmental (Hermelin & O'Connor, 1970). From the mid-1980s, research in developmental psychology mushroomed as three dominant cognitive theories were proposed in quick succession, replicated, and refined: the theory of mind (ToM) theory (Baron-Cohen, 1993; Baron-Cohen, Leslie, & Frith, 1985; Leslie, 1987), the weak central coherence theory (Happé & Frith, 1996) and the executive function deficit theory (Ozonoff, Pennington, & Rogers, 1991; Pennington & Ozonoff, 1996).

Theory of mind theory

The theory of mind (ToM) theory proposed that people with autism have a deficit or delay in understanding mental states. This was elaborated to include difficulties in emotion recognition (Boucher, 1996; Davies, Bishop, Manstead, & Tautama, 1994; Mitchell, 1997). Precursors were identified, including joint attention, imitation, the ability to pretend, and the ability to relate oneself to others (Charman, 1997; Hobson, 1993; Jarrold, Smith, Boucher, & Harris, 1994; Libby, Powell, Messer, & Jordan, 1997). Theory of mind abilities are often tested using short experimental tasks in story form which most typical 4-year-olds can pass but the majority of people with autism fail. The minority who pass are likely to fail more complex tasks and/or tests of subtler mentalizing phenomena, such as irony, sarcasm, or double bluff (Happé, 1994), or tests of reading subtle signs of complex emotions in the eyes

(Baron-Cohen, Jolliffe, Mortimore, & Robinson, 1997). Task success is associated with verbal mental age (Yirmiya, Solomonica-Levy, Shulman, & Pilowski, 1996) and chronological age (Steele, Joseph, & Tager-Flusberg, 2003). Even those who pass these formal tasks are still challenged in social functioning in daily life (e.g., Klin, Jones, Schultz, Volkmar, & Cohen, 2002 a & b; see Chapters 4 and 5). Thus theory of mind tasks are a useful indicator, but not a comprehensive measure of social understanding or even the everyday understanding of mental states.

Weak central coherence theory

Chapters 6 and 7 together give a comprehensive account of the literature on weak central coherence (WCC) theory, so it is sufficient here merely to give a definition. The original theory, proposed by Frith (1989), states that people with autism "do not tend to integrate incoming information in its context, but instead, preferentially attend to local information" (López, Chapter 6). Thus, people with autism would demonstrate strength in processing detail but weakness in global processing. Refinements to the original theory make a distinction between processing of perceptual and conceptual information and explore the assumption of dissociation between local and global processing abilities implicit in the original theory. Linked to research in both WCC and theory of mind is an important sub-topic—exploring difficulties with configural processing of faces, processing of expression and of emotion (see also Wicker, Chapter 2, and López, Chapter 6).

Executive function theory

Within the cognitive-developmental field, the impact of atypical cognitive profiles in attention, memory, planning, and reasoning has been another area of interest (Shah & Frith, 1993; Russell, Jarrold, & Henry, 1996). Ozonoff et al. (1991) first proposed that the central difficulty in social cognition in autism might be due to more general problems in executive functions, opening the way to a wave of research into executive deficits themselves and their potential impact on the understanding of all areas of impairment in autism. Chapter 8 provides a full account of this aspect of functioning in autism and its links to theory of mind.

Language

From the time of its first description (Kanner, 1943), the unusual use of language has been recognized in autism and language, and communication impairments are a diagnostic feature. There is considerable variety in language use across the spectrum, so the tendency to echolalia and pronoun reversal is commonly observed in less able people, but for more able people, a pedantic style and atypical prosody are more characteristic. The area of language may have been somewhat neglected by research in recent years (though see Tager-Flusberg, 2000), with a tendency to contemplate language impairments as a sub-product of more central impairment (such as theory of mind). However, as McCann et al. (Chapter 11) show, there are important aspects of language, such as prosody, that continue to deserve attention, and an appropriate consideration of language should be part of an integrated view of autism.

Neuroscience

At the outset, neuroscience was expected to have powerful explanatory power, as there was an expectation of identifiable atypicalities. However, it initially provided an inconsistent picture of differences in size of specific brain areas in autism relative to the typical population. Although anatomical differences were evident, it was not easy to map such information onto what was known from other research areas. The only clear message was that there was no obvious, simple anomaly that would offer an explanation. But advances in brain imaging techniques and, recently, electrophysiological studies are enabling researchers to adopt more sophisticated approaches, such that neuropsychology should, after all, ultimately make a major contribution to explaining autism. fMRI studies are the most predominant (Bock & Goode, 2004; McAlonan et al., 2005; Salmond, De Haan, Friston, Gadian, & Vargha-Khadem, 2003), conducted more commonly with adult and adolescent participants than children. For the study of brain function in young children or those with limited verbal ability the use of electroencephalograms (EEGs) and measurement of event-related brain potentials (ERPs) may be a simpler option methodologically, and perhaps ethically (e.g., Chantal & van Engeland, 2006; Lepisto et al., 2005; McPartland, Dawson, Webb, Panagiotides, & Carver, 2004). Recent studies in brain voluming offer potential clues to developmental puzzles, indicating that the brain in autism may be subject to an increase in neuronal growth or a lack of neuronal "pruning," which would have an impact on the specialization of the developing brain (Courchesne, 2002; Frith, 2004). However, longitudinal studies are needed to confirm or disconfirm this hypothesis (see Wicker, Chapter 2, for a fuller account).

Volkmar et al. (2004) observe that the recent neuroimaging studies, suggesting that broader neural systems rather than discrete brain areas underlie autism, challenge the notion of discrete core deficits proposed in the cognitive theories of the 1980s and 1990s. Instead, they prompt a reconsideration of an earlier model involving social motivation processes that in turn influence orientation preference (see Jones & Klin, Chapter 4).

The Perspective of Those With Autism

Those who have a severe coexistent intellectual disability are not usually aware that they fall into a clinical category, that they are different from the norm. However, able adolescents and adults with autism are aware of this categorization. As autism has gained increasing attention—clinical, educational, and from the media, in recent years—able people with autism have begun to comment on their status and how others see them. They may be very sensitive to the repeated use of terms such as "disorder," "abnormality," or "deficit," conscious of being "objectified" by the research process.

As a counteraction to this tendency, the growing community of able people with a diagnosis of ASD have asserted that they are not deficient, but neurologically atypical. In a reverse of the usual diagnostic process, they label the rest of the population "neurotypicals" or NTs. This nicely reminds researchers and clinicians that, certainly for able people with ASD, the impairment exists only in the context of social functioning in the general population. A further counteraction has come from some members of the research community (e.g., the Autism Research Centre in Cambridge) who prefer the term Autism Spectrum Condition (ASC) to Disorder, indicating difference rather than pure deficit. Some of the chapters of this book may refer to "deficits" or "impairments" or "disorder" as this is the conventional language of clinical writing. However, it should be recognized that the terms are context-dependent and relative to "neurotypical" behavior.

The Origins of This Book

In this chapter we have identified the difficulties in integrating research in autism, but pointed out that there is a general consensus that it is nonetheless the only way to proceed. We have then proposed that there are two methods by which we could proceed: first, through mapping findings from one area with those of another and assessing the degree of fit; second, through active collaboration across research areas to test any elaborated models. The latter option would, in general, rely on first carrying out the former. The starting point, however, would be the creation of opportunities to share perspectives across diverse areas in order to encourage cross-talk, not only between two, but among three or more areas. This book is the product of such an opportunity, created by the inter-university seminar series. The seminars encouraged dialogue across a growing network of members with the goal of promoting a coherent program of future research integrating psychological, clinical, and educational perspectives. Following the presentation of research perspectives from different areas, the next stage in the integration process was to produce a book that would provide a representative sample of such perspectives with a view to supporting their integration. The chapters collectively offer a balanced representation of topical research, from fMRI studies to naturalistic intervention, reflecting the range of current research output from teams of international repute. Contributors provide contents based upon their own expertise, but shape their chapters for an interdisciplinary audience. Earlier efforts at integration elsewhere have taken the form of pairing across two research areas. We considered that such an approach is too limited. A more elaborate method of exploring the fit of different models would be to map out a network of connections or, indeed, disconnections and implications of findings across a number of research areas. The book makes a starting point in this direction. It goes beyond a series of independent presentations of recent research, by explicitly cross-referencing chapter findings, noting the implications of one for another. Each chapter ends with an integration section in which authors were asked to identify links with other chapters, not only in their own but also in other areas and discuss the theoretical, conceptual, and practical implications. Finally, in a broader debate about approaches to research in autism and the role of development, a concluding chapter draws examples from these chapter sections, considering theoretical links and, in addition, the practical opportunities and potential challenges to integrating research perspectives. Thus, the book follows the first method or stage toward integration identified in this chapter, by mapping findings, theories, and concepts. It is to be hoped that through this process, the ground has been prepared for the second stage—that of active collaboration to test elaborated and integrated models.

Contents

Content chapters are divided into two main sections—a neurocognitive section and a clinical and intervention section.

Part I Neurocognitive research

Part I begins with two chapters covering aspects of the brain basis of behaviors that characterize autism (Chapters 2 and 3). The first of these reviews the literature on the neural basis of social understanding, argues for a connectionist model, and looks at atypical patterns of connectivity among brain areas in autism during social processing. It identifies novel patterns of spared and affected behaviors and areas. The following chapter presents a theoretical argument for allocentrism as an explanation of the atypical social processing of autism. Evidence from research on neurotransmitter function in autism is presented to support the proposition.

The next two chapters (4 and 5) explore social understanding at the cognitive level. The starting point for both is the "theory of mind" impairment in autism, but they present aspects of processing that are not accounted for by the main theories of the impairment. In Chapter 4, eye-tracking studies identify the relative salience of the mouth and eye regions and of non-social stimuli for people with autism when viewing others engaged in social interaction. Adding a developmental dimension, it takes a microanalytic approach to the topic, using data on physical and social salience from a toddler with autism. Chapter 5 links theory of mind and the theory of Central Coherence to the domain of cultural knowledge, highlighting challenges for individuals with ASD in the flexible processing of social scripts.

Chapters 6 and 7 in this section continue the theme of Central Coherence, proposing theoretical refinements based on the identification of areas of strength and weakness in visuo-spatial abilities with regard to perceptual and conceptual knowledge. The former chapter differentiates also between global and contextual processing in autism, noting the implications for social processing. The final chapter of this grouping reviews executive function in autism, how it relates to autistic symptomatology, adaptive behavior and theory of mind accounts of ASD, and integrates these into a causal modeling framework of the condition.

Part II Clinical and intervention research

Part II begins with three chapters relating to diagnosis (Chapters 9–11). A number of tools have now been established which reliably diagnose classical Kanner's autism in children aged 3–5 years, but much has still to be done to expand the diagnostic boundaries, encompassing younger children and milder cases. The chapters on diagnosis explore less obvious aspects of identification of ASD. The first chapter in this section outlines research that uses home movies to reveal early indicators of autism in the first year of life, the findings bridging social and non-social aspects of development. The second chapter focuses on mild manifestations of autism that may be identified through primary school screening. This chapter provides information on the diagnostic process and range of tools as well as a summary of evaluated intervention studies, offering insights into the current obstacles to implementing screening programs for ASD. The third chapter considers language development in ASD, focusing in particular on receptive and expressive prosody.

The next two chapters (12 and 13) offer contrasting methods of intervention to aid social interaction in autism. The first is based on neurocognitive research findings suggesting emotion-processing difficulties in ASD and explores the use of a multi-media tool to teach emotion recognition. The second aims to address some of the restrictions to generalization of learning in cognitive interventions, using a naturalistic group learning approach. Chapter 14 has a wider remit, examining the influence of theory and research on interventions in ASD. The authors argue for the need to make use of neurocognitive findings in devising interventions. The final content chapter (15) moves beyond the individual with ASD to tackle the broader issue of the impact of autism on family functioning. This chapter also explores the effects on the family when parents implement home-based intervention programs, such as early intensive behavioral intervention.

Conclusion

We have no illusions about the complexity of any process of integrating research perspectives in this highly varied research area. However, there is a consensus from some of the most prestigious research teams in the field that integration is the only way to proceed. What we do offer in this book is a starting point, in which fourteen contributors or author groups have shown a real willingness to think about the theoretical perspectives and practical applications of their work within a much broader research and practitioner context. We hope that it encourages further dialogue and efforts to see the "bigger picture" of autism. The Scottish Autism Research Group continues to build on this initial effort.

References

American Psychiatric Association (1994). *Diagnostic and statistical manual of mental disorders* (4th ed.). Washington, DC: APA.

Bacchelli, E., Blasi, F., Biondolillo, M., Lamb, J. A., Bonora, E., Barnby, G., et al. (2003). Screening of nine candidate genes for autism on chromosome 2q reveals rare nonsynonymous variants in the cAMP-GEFII gene. *Molecular Psychiatry, 8*(11), 916–924.

Bailey, A., Le Couteur, A., Gottesman, I., Bolton, P., Simonoff, E., Yuzda, E., & Rutter, M. (1995). Autism as a strongly genetic disorder: Evidence from a British twin study. *Psychological Medicine, 25*, 63–78.

Bailey, A., Phillips, W., & Rutter, M. (1996). Autism: Towards an integration of clinical, genetic, neuropsychological and neurobiological perspectives. *Journal of Child Psychology and Psychiatry, 37*(1), 89–126.

Baron-Cohen, S. (1993). From attention-goal psychology to belief-desire psychology: The development of a theory of mind, and its dysfunction. In S. Baron-Cohen, H. Tager-Flusberg, & D. Cohen (Eds.), *Understanding other minds: Perspectives from autism* (pp. 59–82). Oxford, UK: Oxford University Press.

Baron-Cohen, S., Jolliffe, T., Mortimore, C., & Robinson, M. (1997). Another advanced test of theory of mind: Evidence from very high functioning adults with autism or Asperger syndrome. *Journal of Child Psychology and Psychiatry, 38*(7), 813–822.

Baron-Cohen, S., Leslie, A., & Frith, U. (1985). Does the autistic child have a "theory of mind"? *Cognition, 21*, 37–46.

Baron-Cohen, S., & Ring, H. (1994). A model of the mindreading system: Neuropsychological and neurobiolocal perspectives. In C. Lewis & P. Mitchell (Eds.), *Children's early understanding of mind* (pp. 183–207). Hove, UK: Lawrence Erlbaum Associates.

Bishop, D. V. M. (1997). Cognitive neuropsychology and developmental disorders: Uncomfortable bedfellows. *Quarterly Journal of Experimental Psychology Section A., 50*, 899–923.

Bock, G., & Goode, J. (Eds.) (2003). *Autism: Neural basis and treatment possibilities.* Novartis Foundation Symposium 251. Chichester, UK: John Wiley. Online publication available at http://www.netlibrary.com/Details.aspx

Boucher, J. (1996). What could possibly explain autism? In P. Carruthers & P. Smith (Eds.), *Theories of theories of mind* (pp. 223–241). Cambridge, UK: Cambridge University Press.

Carruthers, P., & Smith, P. (Eds.) (1996). *Theories of theories of mind.* Cambridge, UK: Cambridge University Press.

Chantal, K., & van Engeland, H. (2006). ERPs and eye movements reflect atypical visual perception in Pervasive Developmental Disorder. *Journal of Autism and Developmental Disorders, 36*, 45–54.

Charman, T. (1997). The relationship between joint attention and pretend play in autism. *Development and Psychopathology, 9*(1), 1–16.

Courchesne, E. (2002, August). Abnormal early brain development in autism. *Molecular Psychiatry, 7* (Suppl. 2), S21–S23.

Courchesne, E., Townsend, J., & Saitoh, O. (1994). The brain in infantile autism: Posterior fossa structures are abnormal. *Neurology, 44*, 214–223.

Curran, S., Powell, J., Neale, B. M., Dworzynski, K., Li, T., Murphy, D., et al. (2006). An association analysis of candidate genes on chromosome 15 q11–13 and autism spectrum disorder. *Molecular Psychiatry, 11*(8), 709–713.

Danielsson, S., Gillberg, I. C., Billstedt, E., Gillberg, C., & Olsson, I. (2005). Epilepsy in young adults with autism: A prospective population-based follow-up study of 120 individuals diagnosed in childhood. *Epilepsia, 46*(6), 918–923.

Davies, S., Bishop, D., Manstead, A. S., & Tantam, D. (1994). Face perception in children with autism and Asperger's syndrome. *Journal of Child Psychology and Psychiatry, 35*(6), 1033–1057.

Dawson, G., Webb, S., Schellengerg, G. D., Dager, S., Friedman, S., Aylward, E., et al. (2002). Defining the broader phenotype of autism: Genetic, brain and behavioural perspectives. *Development and Psychopathology, 14*, 581–611.

DeLong, F. G. (1992). Autism, amnesia, hippocampus, and learning. *Neuroscience and Biobehavioral Reviews, 16*, 63–70.

Fombonne, E. (2003). Epidemiological surveys of autism and other pervasive developmental disorders: An update. *Journal of Autism and Developmental Disorders, 33*, 365–382.

Frith, C. (2004). Is autism a disconnection disorder? *Lancet Neurology, 3*(10), 577.

Frith, U. (1989*). Autism: Explaining the enigma.* Oxford, UK: Basil Blackwell.

Gillberg, C. (1992). The Emmanuel Miller Memorial Lecture 1991. Autism and autistic-like conditions: Sub-classes among disorders of empathy. *Journal of Child Psychology and Psychiatry, 33,* 813–842.

Goodman, R. (1989). Infantile autism: A syndrome of multiple primary deficits. *Journal of Autism and Developmental Disorders, 19,* 409–424.

Goswami, U. (2003). Why theories about developmental dyslexia require developmental designs. *Trends in Cognitive Sciences, 7*(12), 534–540.

Hale, C. M., & Tager-Flusberg, H. (2005). Social communication in children with autism: The relationship between theory of mind and discourse development. *Autism, 9*(2), 157–178.

Happé, F. (1994). An advanced test of theory of mind: Understanding of story characters' thoughts and feelings by able autistic, mentally handicapped and normal children and adults. *Journal of Autism and Developmental Disorders, 24,* 129–154.

Happé, F., & Frith, U. (1996). The neuropsychology of autism. *Brain, 119,* 1377–1400.

Hazlett, H. C., Poe, M., Gerig, G., Smith, R. G., Provenzale, J., Ross, A., et al. (2005). Magnetic resonance imaging and head circumference study of brain size in autism. *Archives of General Psychiatry, 62*(12), 1366–1376.

Hermelin, B., & O'Connor, N. (1970). *Psychological experiments with autistic children.* Oxford, UK: Pergamon Press.

Hobson, R. P. (1993). Understanding persons: The role of affect. In S. Baron-Cohen, H. Tager-Flusberg, & D. Cohen (Eds.), *Understanding other minds: Perspectives from autism* (pp. 204–227). Oxford, UK: Oxford University Press.

Jarrold, C., Smith, P., Boucher, J., & Harris, P. (1994). Comprehension of pretense in children with autism. *Journal of Autism and Developmental Disorders, 24,* 433–455.

Kanner, L. (1943). Autistic disturbances of affective contact. *Nervous Child, 2,* 217–250.

Karmiloff-Smith, A. (1997). Crucial differences between developmental cognitive neuroscience and adult neuropsychology. *Developmental Neuropsychology, 13*(4), 513–524.

Klin, A., Jones, W., Schultz, R., & Volkmar, F. (2003). The enactive mind, or from actions to cognition: Lessons from autism. *Philosophical Transactions of the Royal Society, London, 358,* 345–336.

Klin, A., Jones, W., Schultz, R., Volkmar, F., & Cohen, D. (2002a). Defining and quantifying the social phenotype in autism. *American Journal of Psychiatry, 159*(6), 895–908.

Klin, A., Jones, W., Schultz, R., Volkmar, F., & Cohen, D. (2002b). Visual fixation patterns during viewing of naturalistic social situations as predictors of social competence in individuals with autism. *Archives of General Psychiatry, 59*(9), 809–816.

Landa, R., & Garrett-Mayer, E. (2006). Development in infants with autism spectrum disorders: A prospective study. *Journal of Child Psychology and Psychiatry, 47*(6), 629–638.

Lepisto, T., Kujala, T., Vanhala, R., Alku, P., Huotilainen, M., & Naatanen, R. (2005). The discrimination of and orienting to speech and non-speech sounds in children with autism. *Brain Research, 1066,* 147–157.

Leslie, A. (1987). Pretense and representation: The origins of "theory of mind." *Psychological Review, 94,* 412–426.

Leslie, A. (1991). The theory of mind impairment in autism: Evidence for a modular mechanism of development? In A. Whiten (Ed.), *Natural theories of mind* (pp. 63–78). Oxford, UK, and Cambridge, MA: Basil Blackwell.

Libby, S., Powell, S., Messer, D., & Jordan, R. (1997). Imitation of pretend play acts by children with autism and Down syndrome. *Journal of Autism and Developmental Disorders, 27*(4), 365–383.

Lord, C., Risi, S., Lambrecht, L., Cook, E. H., Jr., Leventhal, B. L., DiLavore, P. C., et al. (2000). The autism diagnostic observation schedule-generic: A standard measure of social and communication deficits associated with the spectrum of autism. *Journal of Autism and Developmental Disorders, 30*, 205–223.

Lord, C., Shulman, C., & DiLavore, P. (2004). Regression and word loss in autistic spectrum disorders. *Journal of Child Psychology and Psychiatry, 45*(5), 936–955.

Lotter, V. (1966). Epidemiology of autistic conditions in young children. I: Prevalence, *Social Psychiatry, 1*, 124–137.

McAlonan, G. M., Cheung, V., Cheung, C., Suckling, J., Lam, G. Y., Tai, K. S., et al. (2005). Mapping the brain in autism. A voxel-based MRI study of volumetric differences and intercorrelations in autism. *Brain, 1*(28), 268–276.

McDougle, C. J. (1997). Psychopharmacology. In D. J. Cohen & F. R. Volkmar (Eds.), *Handbook of autism and pervasive developmental disorders* (2nd ed., pp. 707–729). New York: Wiley.

McPartland, J., Dawson, G., Webb, S. J., Panagiotides, H., & Carver, L. J. (2004). Event-related brain potentials reveal anomalies in temporal processing of faces in autism spectrum disorder. *Journal of Child Psychology and Psychiatry, 45*, 1235–1245.

Mitchell, P. (1997). *Introduction to theory of mind: Children, autism and apes*. London, UK: Edward Arnold Publishers.

Moore, D. J., & Taylor, J. (2000). Interactive multimedia systems for people with autism, *Journal of Educational Media, 25*(3), 169–177.

Morton, J., & Frith, U. (1995). Causal modelling: A structural approach to developmental psychopathology. In D. Cicchetti & D. J. Cohen (Eds.), *Manual of developmental psychopathology* (pp. 357–390). New York: John Wiley.

Munson, J., Dawson, G., Abbott, R., Faja, S., Webb, S. J., Friedman, S. D., et al. (2006). Amygdalar volume and behavioural development in autism. *Archives of General Psychiatry, 63*(6), 686–693.

Nurmi, E. L., Dowd, M., Tadevosyan, L. O., Haines, J. L., Folstein, S. E., & Sutcliffe, J. S. O. (2003). Exploratory subsetting of autism families based on savant skills improves evidence of genetic linkage to 15q11–q13. *Journal of the American Academy of Child and Adolescent Psychiatry, 42*(7), 856–863.

Ozonoff, S., Penington, B., & Rogers, S. (1991). Executive function deficits in high-functioning autistic children: Relationship to theory of mind. *Journal of Child Psychology and Psychiatry, 32*, 1081–1106.

Parr. J. R., Lamb, J. A., Bailey, A. J., & Monaco, A. P. (2006). Response to paper by Molloy et al.: Linkage on 21q and 7q in autism subset with regression. *Molecular Psychiatry, 11*(7), 617–619.

Pennington, B., & Ozonoff, S. (1996). Executive functions and developmental psychopathology. *Journal of Child Psychology and Psychiatry*, *37*(1), 51–87.

Ronald, A., Happé, F., & Plomin, R. (2005). The genetic relationship between individual differences in social and nonsocial behaviours characteristic of autism. *Developmental Science*, *8*(5), 444–458.

Ronald, A., Happé, F., Price, T. S., Baron-Cohen, S., & Plomin, R. (2006). Phenotypic and genetic overlap between autistic traits at the extremes of the general population. *Journal of the American Academy of Child and Adolescent Psychiatry*, *45*(10), 1206–1214.

Russell, J., Jarrold, C., & Henry, L. (1996). Working memory in children with autism and moderate learning difficulties. *Journal of Child Psychology and Psychiatry*, *37*(6), 903–910.

Rutter, M., & Schopler, E. (1992). Classification of pervasive developmental disorders: Some concepts and practical considerations, *Journal of Autism and Developmental Disorders* [Special issue on classification and diagnosis], *22*(4), 459–482.

Salmond, C., De Haan, M., Friston, K. J., Gadian, D. G., & Vargha-Khadem, F. (2003). Investigating individual differences in brain abnormalities in autism. *Philosophical Transactions of the Royal Society, B., 358*, 405–413.

Shah, A., & Frith, U. (1993). Why do autistic individuals show superior performance on the block design task? *Journal of Child Psychology and Psychiatry*, *34*, 1351–1364.

Sigman, M., Spence, S. J., & Wang, A. T. (2006). Autism from developmental and neuropsychological perspectives. *Annual Review of Clinical Psychology*, *2*, 327–355.

Steele, S., Joseph, R., & Tager-Flusberg, H. (2003). Brief report: Developmental change in theory of mind abilities in children with autism. *Journal of Autism and Developmental Disorders*, *33*(4), 461–467.

Stirling, L., & Barrington, G. (in press) "Then I'll huff and I'll puff or I'll go on the roff!" thinks the wolf: Spontaneous written narratives by a child with autism. In: A. C. Schalley, & D. Khlentzos (Eds.), *Mental states: Language and cognitive structure*. Amsterdam/ Philadelphia: John Benjamins.

Tager-Flusberg, H. (2000). The challenge of studying language development in children with autism. In L. Menn & N. Bernstein Ratner (Eds.), *Methods for studying language production* (pp. 313–332). Mahwah, NJ: Lawrence Erlbaum.

Volkmar, F., Klin, A., Siegal, B., Szatmari, P., Lord, C., Campbell, M., et al. (1994). Field trial for autistic disorder in DSM-IV. *American Journal of Psychiatry, 151*(9), 1361–1367.

Volkmar, F., Lord, C., Bailey, A., Schultz, R., & Klin, A. (2004). Autism and pervasive developmental disorders. *Journal of Child Psychology and Psychiatry*, *45*(1), 135–170.

Wing, L., & Potter, D. (2002). The epidemiology of autistic spectrum disorders: Is the prevalence rising? *Mental Retardation and Developmental Disabilities Research Review, 8*, 151–161.

World Health Organization (1993). *The ICD-10 classification of mental and behavioural disorders: Diagnostic criteria for research*. Geneva: World Health Organization.

Yirmiya, N., Solomonica-Levy, D., Shulman, C., & Pilowski, T. (1996). Theory of mind abilities in individuals with autism, Down's syndrome and mental retardation of unknown aetiology: The role of age and intelligence. *Journal of Child Psychology and Psychiatry*, *37*(8), 1003–1014.

Part I

Neurocognitive Research

2

New Insights From Neuroimaging Into the Emotional Brain in Autism

Bruno Wicker

As it has been already described in the initial chapter, autism is a developmental disorder of neurological origin that occurs in a large variety of forms, from mild to severe. Autism is currently defined by behavioral criteria, which include impairments in social interaction, impairments in verbal and non-verbal communication, and restricted interests and activities. One of the hallmark features of autism is a significant qualitative impairment in social interaction (American Psychiatric Association, 1994). This chapter will mostly focus on socio-emotional processing and its underlying brain correlates in autism.

Behavioral studies have greatly contributed to our understanding of socio-emotional deficits in autism. Some studies suggest that the social defects found in autism result from an inability to process emotional information (Fotheringham, 1991; Hobson, 1991). According to this hypothesis, persons with autism spectrum disorders (ASD) lack the biologically based capacity to appreciate the emotional significance of incoming stimuli and attach motivational value to perceived emotional expressions (Hobson, 1986a & b). The lack of this capacity results in a failure to establish interpersonal connections early in life and certainly impedes the further development of the mental functions needed for interpersonal feeling. Facial expression of emotion is considered as one of the core elements of an individual's publicly observable emotional experience, because it provides universally understandable non-verbal messages broadcasting the individual's emotional state to others. In this context, most of the investigations on emotion perception and recognition in autism spectrum disorders have focused predominantly on the processing of facial expressions. Only a few studies have focused on other aspects of emotional information such as prosody or body language (McCann &

Peppé, 2003; see also Chapter 11). Several reports established that persons with autism are impaired in reading facial emotional expressions (Celani, Battacchi, & Arcidiacono, 1999; Teunisse & de Gelder, 2001). Children and adults with autism displayed poorer performance in matching emotion in a single modality (Celani et al., 1999) and in cross-modality tasks (Hobson, Ouston, & Lee, 1988) than developmentally delayed and typically developing control participants. Similarly, children with autism failed to label emotions (Tantam, Monaghan, Nicholson, & Stirling, 1989) and to recognize various emotional facial expressions from photographs. Another set of data, however, reported that performance of the population with autism is within the normal range for tasks involving facial emotion processing. Persons with ASD performed similarly to control participants in discriminating facial emotional expressions and in rating emotion's intensity (Adolphs, Sears, & Piven, 2001). In an emotion recognition task, the performance of children with ASD does not depart from that of typically developing children (Ozonoff, Pennington, & Rogers, 1990) or from that of children with intellectual disabilities without autism (Hobson et al., 1988). Robel et al. (2004), using the Minnesota Test of Affective Processing, also reported that high-functioning children with autism or pervasive developmental disorders performed just as well as controls matched on chronological age in discriminating between different emotional expressions. Entering into more details to clarify these inconsistencies between studies is not within the scope of this chapter. However, a key aspect of facial emotion processing in autism seems to be linked to attentional processes, as performance level seems to be influenced by the explicit or implicit nature of the task (Begeer, Rieffe, Terwogt, & Stockman, 2006). This suggests that it is the automatic, involuntary processing of emotional information that is impaired in autism. In the same line of thought, authors have suggested that persons with autism may rely on other strategies than typically developing persons in recognizing emotions (e.g., Adolphs et al., 2001; Bormann-Kischkel, Vilsmeier, & Baude, 1995). However, this ability to recognize emotional expression might not be fully associated with a correct appraisal of the emotional valence of the expression, as it was suggested by Hobson's original studies several years ago (Hobson, 1986a, 1986b).

The behavioral discontinuities exposed above, the suggestion that autistic people may use alternative cognitive strategies to perform emotion processing, and the fact that autism is a neurodevelopmental disorder point to the importance of studying cerebral functioning in autism. The recent advent of neuroimaging techniques has allowed researchers to deepen the understanding of the so-called socio-emotional brain, by associating specific cerebral structures with different steps of emotional processing, from perceptual processes to more complex emotional understanding. The aim of this chapter is to focus on the cerebral dysfunction underlying emotional deficits and integrate findings from various fields of research to support the argument for a deficit in functional interactions between brain regions in autism. I will first review some of the neuroimaging studies, either anatomical or functional, both in ASD and control participants, which have led to models of cerebral dysfunction in autism. Following this, I will describe a study undertaken in our lab that aimed at identifying cerebral structures involved in emotional processing in autism. Data from this study form the basis for effective connectivity modeling, which enables the study of abnormal functional *interactions* between brain structures in autism during emotional processing.

Neuroanatomical Studies

In the past 15 years, several magnetic resonance imaging (MRI) studies examined the brain anatomy in children and adults with autism in order to identify structural abnormalities. Several reviews have been published recently (Brambilla et al., 2003; Cody, Pelphrey, & Piven, 2002; Mosconi, Zwaigenbaum, & Piven, 2006; Penn, 2006). Even though findings have often been controversial, results of recent studies that have addressed several of the limitations of previous research have begun to highlight key neuroanatomical abnormalities more consistently. Current understanding of atypical brain development in autism recognizes that while specific neural circuits may be important, the underlying pathophysiology of autism affects numerous brain regions and is not limited to a specific structure. I will briefly summarize the main findings, and how they point to disturbed neural networks.

Post-mortem and MRI research combine to provide converging evidence that autism is associated with increased brain size in childhood, although whether this abnormality persists or not remains unclear. Enlarged total brain area and volume have been reported in juvenile and adult male individuals with autism, after adjusting for height, IQ, and intra-cranial volume. This observation in combination with increased fronto-occipital circumference appears to be one of the most consistent neurobiological findings in autism. However, some studies did not find any abnormal total brain area or volumes in individuals either with or without intellectual disability. Elaborating on these discrepant results, Courchesne and colleagues argue that autism is associated with overgrowth in childhood followed by a period of abnormally slowed growth. More specifically, there is an emerging consensus that larger brain volumes may be due to increased neuronal growth or decreased neuronal pruning (Akshoomoff, Pierce, & Courchesne, 2002; Courchesne, Carper, & Akshoomoff, 2003). Such neuronal growth dysregulation has been suggested by a number of recent studies focusing on abnormal levels of proteins that regulate neuronal migration, or production and elimination of neural synapses (Akshoomoff et al., 2002; Nelson, 2001). However, human brain maturation is a complex, life-long process, and future research, including longitudinal studies, will be necessary to provide additional support for this hypothesis. In this respect, ongoing projects that scan participants longitudinally with structural magnetic resonance imaging (MRI), enabling the time-course and anatomical sequence of development to be reconstructed (Giedd, 2004; Toga, Thompson, & Sowell, 2006), could be of great interest.

At the level of specific cerebral structures, autism has been linked to different abnormalities. Most post-mortem, MRI, and PET studies have linked autism with cerebellar deficits. Nearly all cases involve a loss of granular cells in the cerebellar cortex and a significant loss of Purkinje neurons in the cerebellar vermis and cere-bellar hemispheres (Allen & Courchesne, 2003). It is therefore generally accepted that autism is associated with cerebellar impairment, but the link between cerebel-lar deficits and autistic symptomatology remains unclear. Neuroimaging studies have given evidence that cerebellar abnormalities in autism may be linked to defi-cits in shifting and orienting attention.

Several studies have reported deficits in the size of the corpus callosum (CC) and its sub-regions, particularly when group differences in brain volume were taken into consideration. Reduced total, cross-sectional, callosal areas have been reported in several studies (Boger-Megiddo et al., 2006; Egaas, Courchesne, & Saitoh, 1995; Manes et al., 1999). When the sub-regions of the CC have been exam-ined, however, the results have been inconsistent. Several groups have reported reductions in the size of the body and posterior sub-regions of the CC in autistic individuals (Egaas et al., 1995; Haas et al., 1996; Piven, Bailey, Ranson, & Arndt, 1997), whereas others have found significant differences only in the anterior regions (Hardan, Minshew, & Keshavan, 2000) or in the body of the CC (Manes et al., 1999). Recently, two studies using voxel-based morphometry (VBM) have reported reductions in the area of the splenium and isthmus (Waiter et al., 2005) and the genu, rostrum, and splenium of the CC (Chung, Dalton, Alexander, & Davidson, 2004) in individuals with autism. Statistical maps of the CC revealed callosal deficits in autism with greater precision than traditional morphometric methods have done (Vidal et al., 2006). Taken together, these abnormalities in a major site of cortico-cortical fibres suggest atypical connections between cortical regions, which is consistent with the hypothesis of a functional disconnectivity.

Structures such as the hippocampus and amygdala have also been suggested to be structurally abnormal in people with autism. Amygdala volume may be increased (Abell et al., 1999; Sparks et al., 2002), whereas findings on the hippo-campus are still conflicting. The other available evidence suggests the existence of a disturbed neural network involving cortical and sub-cortical areas, includ-ing temporo-parietal cortex, limbic system, cerebellar, and prefrontal regions. All these brain changes could possibly result from abnormalities in brain development, subsequent to disturbance of brain growth early in life, and could anatomically underlie the cognitive and social impairments of persons with autism.

The recent advent of innovative technologies and analysis methods, such as voxel-based morphometry (VBM), diffusion tensor imaging (DTI), and measures of grey matter volumes and cortical thickness have revealed additional results. Many magnetic resonance studies have used VBM, a technique which gives probabilistic information about grey matter volume. VBM studies have found grey matter abnormalities in the inferior frontal (Abell et al., 1999; McAlonan et al., 2002), parietal (McAlonan et al., 2002), and temporal regions, including the STS (Boddaert et al., 2004), as well as changes in the basal ganglia, the amygdala, and the cerebellum (Abell et al., 1999; McAlonan et al., 2002), and in the right fusiform gyrus, the right temporo-occipital region and the left frontal pole extending to the medial frontal cortex (Waiter et al., 2005). More recently, McAlonan et al. (2005) have shown generalized as well as localized grey matter reduction in the fronto-striatal, parietal, and temporal cortex in high-functioning autistic children, pointing to an early structural abnormality of the "social brain."

Using an automated technique of analysis that accurately measures the thickness of the cerebral cortex, Hadjikhani, Joseph, Snyder, and Tager-Flusberg (2006) found cortical thinning in cerebral areas involved in emotion and social information processing, including the STS, the inferior frontal gyrus, inferior parietal lobule, anterior cingulate and prefrontal cortex. In another study using three-way multidimensional scaling of regionally parcellated fMRI data, Welchew et al. (2005) revealed evidence of abnormal functional connectivity of medial temporal lobe structures—amygdala and parahippocampal gyrus—during fearful processing in people with Asperger syndrome.

Functional Neuroimaging Studies

Functional neuroimaging studies have investigated several aspects of behavioral deficits in autism. Most of these studies have focused on the processing of socioemotional information such as face and emotional expression recognition, theory of mind tasks, and mental state attribution. Some studies have also focused on executive functions such as working memory, motor control, language, and attention. One limitation of neuroimaging research in autism is that cerebral areas engaged in the cognitive processes under study are sometimes not well known in the typical brain. In order to compare between populations and draw conclusions about possible cerebral dysfunctions in an atypical population, it is necessary to fully apprehend normal functioning in the typical brain in the experimental task under

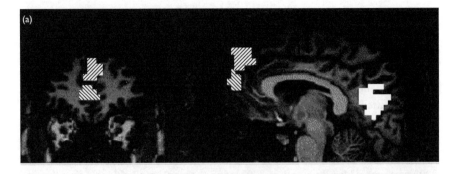

Figure 2.1 Brain regions implicated in human social cognition: (a) Medial regions; (b) Lateral regions. The right temporo-parietal junction selectively recruited when reasoning about others' representation of mental states (vertical stripe). Two nearby but distinct regions are also shown: the posterior right superior temporal sulcus region involved in perceiving intentional action (horizontal stripe) and the right extrastriate body area (checks). In the medial prefrontal cortex, two regions are apparent: ventral MPFC associated with attributing emotion (diagonal downward stripe from upper left) and dorsal MPFC, possibly linked to reasoning about triadic relations (diagonal upward stripe from lower left). The posterior cingulate region, not discussed in this chapter but commonly recruited for social cognitive tasks, is shown in white. Adapted from Saxe, 2006.

study. Regarding socio-emotional processing specifically, functional neuroimaging studies in controls have identified a network of areas coined as the "social brain" in an early paper by Brothers (1990). Brothers's social brain included a restricted set of areas including the amygdala, the orbitofrontal cortex, the temporal poles, and the superior temporal sulcus. Using more and more sophisticated experimental protocols (but see next section), neuroimaging studies have elaborated this social brain, by revealing important roles for the lateral frontal cortex, the anterior cingulate, the dorsomedial prefrontal cortex, and the insula (Figure 2.1).

Although somewhat peripheral to the present paper, I would like here to consider a methodological issue that I think is an important challenge for future studies in socio-emotional cognition. This is the issue of ecological validity. Essentially, all neuroscience data on social cognition come from stimuli that are "social" only in a highly derivative way. Typical examples are static photographs of facial expressions, and the distributed network of brain regions thought to decode social signals has been empirically defined using such static displays of emotional expressions. Participants in the experiments know very well that these are not real people, and although many aspects, especially of perceptual processing, may be shared between such stimuli and the real thing, they clearly lack the interactive and meaningful nature that a real person would provide. In this respect, one neuroimaging study with typical participants suggested that static displays of facial emotional expressions may represent non-canonical stimuli that are processed for emotional content by mental strategies and neural events that are distinct from their more ecologically relevant dynamic counterparts (Kilts, Egan, Gideon, Ely, & Hoffman, 2003). It is important to highlight this issue in the context of studying autism on two grounds: on the one hand, the abnormal sensory perception of participants might make processing even more impaired when stimuli are abstract or far from ecological. On the other hand, this abnormal perception could be the reason why their behavioral performances in laboratory experiments are normal while they still exhibit strong impairments in everyday life contexts. Because real stimuli are experimentally difficult to use, a nice way to overcome this methodological weakness would be to use 3D visual stimuli, combined with eye tracking.

These data from the range of studies outlined above led the scientific community on autism research to the hypothesis that autism might result from abnormal brain connectivity and functional interactions between brain structures. In fact, this concept of autism as a functional disconnection syndrome originates in one of its earliest neurobiological accounts (Damasio & Maurer, 1978) that was later supported by data from Horwitz, Rumsey, Grady, and Rapoport (1988). They reported abnormalities of interregional correlation between frontal, parietal, and neostriatal metabolic rates for glucose measured by positron emission tomography (PET). A few recent studies have thus attempted to explore this connectivity dimension. Abnormally reduced correlation of activity between extrastriate and superior temporal cortices at the temporo-parietal junction, an area associated with the processing of biological motion as well as with mentalizing, was observed during attribution of mental states from movements of animated shapes. This finding suggests a physiological cause for the mentalizing dysfunction in autism: a bottleneck in the interaction between higher-order and lower-order perceptual processes (Castelli, Frith, Happé, & Frith, 2002). Similarly, Just, Cherkassky, Keller, and Minshew (2004) found decreased functional connectivity between Wernicke's and Broca's areas during language processing and Villalobos, Mizuno, Dahl, Kemmotsu, and Muller (2005) found reduced functional connectivity between V1 and inferior frontal cortex in a visuomotor task performed by participants with autism. More recently, abnormally low functional connectivity between frontal and parietal areas was reported in autism during the performance of a Tower of London task (Just, Cherkassky, Keller, Kana, & Minshew, in press). From these studies, several possibilities have been proposed: a bottom-up failure of feed-forward visual signals reaching the superior temporal sulcus (STS) from extrastriate cortices such as the fusiform gyrus; or a top-down failure of feedback signals reaching STS from the anterior components of the mentalizing system, i.e., dorso-medial and lateral prefrontal cortices (DMPFC and LPFC). The theoretical formulation that draws together much of these data is that autism spectrum disorders may be characterized by dysfunctional interactions between networks of distributed brain regions important for socio-emotional cognition.

Unfortunately, neuroimaging studies to date have been unable to address the important question of whether the neurobiological basis of reduced activation of a specific structure resides in the cortex of the region itself, or is the result of a failure in communication between the given region and other brain structures involved in information processing. Indeed, functional connectivity refers only to temporal correlations between remote neurophysiological events and is therefore simply a statement about observed correlations and does not provide any direct insight into how these correlations are mediated.

Neurobiological Models of Autism

A wide range of neurobiological models of autism has been proposed in the last few years. Dawson and colleagues (2005) suggested that the medial temporal lobe and the ventromedial prefrontal cortex make up a brain system specialized for social processing that is deficient in autism, reducing attention to faces, impairing facial processing ability, and leading to difficulties with theory of mind, language, and social skills. Carper and Courchesne (2000) emphasize the role of the cerebellum, and its link to frontal lobe functioning. More recently, models emphasize neural growth dysregulation and decreased or abnormal connectivity of structures in autism. Reviewing current fMRI and neuropsychological data for deficits in face perception and deficiencies in underlying brain systems that mediate face perception and the detection of emotionally salient percepts, Schultz proposed a heuristic model that posits an early developmental failure in autism involving the amygdala, with a cascading influence on the development of cortical areas, specifically the fusiform "face area" (Schultz, 2005). The most recent neurobiological model suggests a connection between autism and a newly discovered class of neurons called mirror neurons (Williams, Whiten, Suddendorf, & Perrett, 2001). As these neurons appear to be involved in abilities such as empathy and the perception of other individuals' intentions, it seemed logical to hypothesize that a dysfunction of the mirror neuron system could result in some of the symptoms of autism. Over the past decade, several studies have provided evidence for this theory, but further investigations are needed (Ramachandran & Oberman, 2006).

The above short list of neurobiological models of autism is not exhaustive. All those models are compelling and clearly point to the hypothesis of abnormal connectivity in the autistic brain. However, there is little concrete evidence linking early pathophysiological abnormalities with neural and behavior correlates. More importantly, those models often take into account only a restricted number of cerebral areas to explain behavioral deficits that are, in the socio-emotional sphere alone, numerous and variegated. Such models might therefore turn out to be simplistic, as they have lacked further tests taking into account other regions of the social brain. New methods of neuroimaging data analysis now enable such tests to be conducted.

Neuroimaging and Effective Connectivity Modeling

In a recent study from our lab, we wished to explore explicit and implicit processing of emotion while overcoming the previous limitation of using static stimuli. Our adult control participants and adult participants with Asperger syndrome or high-functioning autism were scanned while viewing video sequences displaying an actor's face expressing either anger or happiness. Such dynamic stimuli provide visual perceptual inputs that are as lifelike as possible and are thus more sensitive for the study of cerebral activity associated with everyday emotional processing than static stimuli such as photographs. To investigate brain activity related to explicit perception and labeling of facial expressions, we examined the neural substrates of processing dynamic angry and happy faces, of young or older actors, under two different task conditions that employed the same stimuli. In the "Emotion" condition the task was to judge whether the actor was angry or happy, whereas in the "Age" condition the task was to judge whether the actor was old or young. The "Emotion" condition thus forced the participant to pay attention to emotional features of the actor's face. The "Age" condition led to an incidental perception of facial emotional expressions while still requiring participants to carefully examine the stimuli. The simplicity of the task and design ensured that participants with autism would perform as well as controls, removing confounding effects due to difference in behavioral performance between groups. This also allowed us to examine whether specific cerebral structures might underlie a compensatory strategy related to intact explicit emotional labeling by autistic individuals.

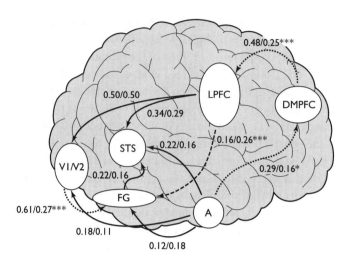

Figure 2.2 Path diagrams from the causal analysis using structural equation modeling. Values of the path coefficients in the control and in the autism group are indicated. Significant differences in these values between groups are shown in dotted lines for Control > ASD and in dashed lines for ASD > Control. * $p<.05$; ** $p<.01$; *** $p<.001$.

Areas of differential activity identified in our control participants during explicit processing of emotional expressions are extremely consistent with the circumscribed activations observed in previous imaging studies of emotional processing (Phan, Wager, Taylor, & Liberzon, 2002) and other aspects of social cognition (Pelphrey, Morris, & McCarthy, 2004). These cortical regions may thus be considered to represent the rudiments of the mentalizing brain network, independent of task or modality (Frith & Frith, 1999). Between-groups, whole-brain analysis of the "Emotion" vs. "Age" conditions revealed three foci, in dorso-medial prefrontal cortex, right lateral prefrontal cortex, and right superior temporal gyrus at the temporo-parietal junction, that showed greater activity in the normal, relative to autism, group. In itself, this fMRI comparison is direct evidence that structures involved in the interpretation of emotional information are functionally abnormal in autism, whereas structures engaged in the earlier perceptual processing of emotional information are spared. Indeed, regions classically involved in the perceptual analysis of facial features and expression, such as STS and fusiform gyrus, seem to be normally engaged in both populations. Thus, participants with ASD would seem to perceive features of the face adequately, but would fail to interpret and associate them correctly with their emotional valence. However, it does not shed light on how the abnormal activity of these brain regions may be related to abnormal functional connectivity in the autistic brain.

For the purposes of effective connectivity modeling, we extracted raw signals acquired during the explicit emotional processing conditions from voxels in six brain regions of interest: namely, superior temporal sulcus in its posterior part, right amygdala, medial prefrontal cortex, right lateral prefrontal cortex, right fusiform gyrus and occipital visual areas. We then tested a hypothesis-driven anatomical model. The design of the structural model incorporated connections between the brain regions of interest, and was constrained by anatomical data (Barbas, 1995), as well as by data from previous functional neuroimaging studies on social-emotional processing, including known functional correlations between brain regions during emotional processing (Castelli et al., 2002; Just et al., 2004; Villalobos et al., 2005). Standardized path coefficients were calculated in both groups, and the fit between this predicted model and the empirical data was tested. The indices of fit indicated that the model adequately fitted the data in both groups.

The comparison between control and autism groups revealed the following significant results (cf. Figure 2.2). First, the highly positive influence of amygdala activity on activity of DMPFC observed in the control group was apparently absent in autistic participants. Anatomically, connections between the amygdala and medial prefrontal areas are robust and bidirectional, and medial prefrontal connections are directly, extensively, and preferentially linked with the expressive and emotional motor system of the amygdala. Functionally, evidence from studies on emotional modulation of sensory and associative cortical activity point to the amygdala as the generator of a "boost" signal, triggered by emotional salience and directed at representational sites of emotional stimuli or events, thus suggesting one likely mechanism of emotionally guided attentional amplification (Taylor & Fragopanagos, 2005). On the other hand, the medial prefrontal region is important in cognitive and affective functions and receives and integrates information from widespread cerebral and sub-cortical systems (Ghashghaei & Barbas, 2002). This intricate network may thus be recruited in cognitive tasks that are inextricably linked with emotional associations, and reduced activation of pathways connecting the amygdala with prefrontal limbic cortices could therefore disrupt a circuit that is likely to have a crucial role in the emotional coloring of events. This may account for the flattening of emotions and inappropriate affect processing typically observed in autism.

Second, the strong influence of DMPFC activity on the LPFC in controls is absent in autism. The prefrontal cortex is heavily interconnected, and so any emotional information registered in the DMPFC could influence executive priorities coded in the LPFC and ultimately alter the direction of attention or, more generally, modify the distribution of processing resources in a given context (Barcelo, Suwazono, & Knight, 2000). The DMPFC can thus be seen as the bridge that conveys emotional information from sub-cortical limbic regions such as the amygdala to the higher cortical executive centers of the prefrontal cortex. As early as 1995, results from anatomical studies on connectivity in the non-human primate brain suggested that feedback projections from limbic cortices may serve to compare the input and output necessary for the interpretation of events, be they emotional or not (Barbas, 1995). The breakdown of massive feedback—originating in limbic areas—observed in the autism group could be related to its role in the integration of distributed pathways associated with sensory perception, associative mnemonic, and emotional processes. The fact that these regions are both phylogenetically and ontogenically late-developing regions (Giedd, 2004) suggests that they may retain some developmental features to a greater extent than other cortices, which would further support the hypothesis of their preferential vulnerability in several neurological and psychiatric disorders such as autism, schizophrenia, and epilepsy.

The third observation from our effective connectivity analysis is an abnormally strong influence of activity in right dorso-lateral prefrontal cortex on the activity of the fusiform gyrus in the participants with autism. LPFC activation has been related to studies focusing on attentional top-down modulation, which have revealed its important role in sustaining emotional representations of stimuli so that attention can be effectively directed in order to achieve task goals (Taylor & Fragopanagos, 2005). An abnormally strong influence of right LPFC on fusiform gyrus could thus represent the neural instantiation of a compensatory cognitive mechanism that would explain the similarly high levels of performance of the explicit emotional task in both groups. By normalizing behavior in explicit contexts, such compensatory processing strategies may mask primary dysfunctions in the emotional information-processing network that normally involves the amygdala–DMPFC axis. Under unconstrained everyday socio-emotional conditions, the compensatory LPFC → Fusiform activity might be less pronounced or unable to be updated as quickly. Consequently, the lack of the boosting signal from the amygdala to DMPFC in participants with autism could then result in uncompensated impairment in automatic face processing, thus generating the typically observed behavioral deficits. Nevertheless, high-functioning autistic or Asperger adults may be able to learn how to explicitly decode social and emotional information and therefore strengthen a compensatory mechanism, providing an encouraging opportunity for therapy, such as teaching recognition of emotion using video clips (Golan & Baron-Cohen, Chapter 12).

Finally, our findings indicate that the activity of the fusiform gyrus is abnormally modulated by the activity of low-level visual areas when participants with autism are explicitly engaged in emotional expression recognition. Given the functional role of the fusiform gyrus in the perception of facial features and its intricate connectivity with other components of the socio-emotional perceptual network, a dysfunction at such an early stage may contribute to the general impairment in social communicative deficits that characterize autism.

By incorporating new data that reveal distinct patterns of effective connectivity, our results provide direct evidence of abnormal, long-range connectivity between the brain structures implicated in the socio-emotional network in autism. This is in line with the idea of reduced long-distance anterior to posterior cortico-cortical connectivity (Courchesne & Pierce, 2005), which impairs the fundamental frontal function of integrating information from widespread and diverse systems (emotional, language, sensory, autonomic, . . .) and providing complex context-rich feedback, guidance, and control to lower-level systems. Furthermore, our data are the first demonstration that this abnormal modulation most likely has its origins in abnormal activity, and effective connectivity, of the medial prefrontal cortex. This adds a functional relevance and value to recent data from histopathological, voxel-based morphometry, MRI volumetric analysis, and diffusion tensor imaging studies suggesting abnormal development, and abnormal local connectivity in the medial part of the prefrontal cortex.

In conclusion, our data firmly corroborate the hypothesis, put forward by several authors, that autism's core deficits in emotional/social behavior result from abnormal modulation of activity within a distributed network of cerebral structures. Future work will be needed to reproduce these results and to test our model of abnormal functioning using other fMRI experimental paradigms of emotional/social processing. Further assistance will also come from new techniques of anatomical analysis, such as DTI imaging, which will allow deeper insight into the physical abnormalities underlying the functional deficits.

Integration

From the point of view of a cognitive neuroscientist whose main research goal is to explore the neural bases of socio-emotional cognition and its dysfunction in autism, a lot of problems related to different aspects of research remain to be addressed. The most prominent problems are the heterogeneity of the population and the diversity of factors—from biological to environmental—involved in the development of this neurodevelopmental condition. Looking for solutions obviously requires taking into account data from a variety of domains including genetics and epigenetics of cerebral development and maturation, the influence of environmental factors, developmental studies in children, etc., all of which means integration of diverse knowledge. This book contributes greatly to this integration by highlighting some crucial aspects of autism research that need to be addressed if one wants to fully apprehend autism as a pathology and propose efficient interventions.

As demonstrated in this chapter and in Williams's (Chapter 3), neuroimaging data suggest that the autistic brain activates alternative neural pathways to process emotional and social information. The presence of a brain dysfunction in autism, be it in the emotional domain or not, opens the way to a wide variety of interpretations. First of all this should be linked to results from other studies reporting, for example, that ASD participants process faces by using neural areas typically engaged in object processing, or that the dynamics of brain electrical activity are different in people with ASD compared to typical individuals when they perceive a face. All in all, however, these data point to the existence of alternative patterns of activity. This is an important conclusion and has to be related to other results and ideas put forward in this book. Results from other studies report, for example, that alternative brain mechanisms may have something to do with the fact that ASD people process information in a different way, as noted by Loth (Chapter 5). This alternative style of information processing might lead to a style of perceptual expertise specific to autism. This expertise could be outside the social sphere, explaining why people with autism may deal with faces as if they were just interesting objects, rather than key sources of information that need privileged processing for appropriate adaptive behavior. This expertise for non-social stimuli in the environment might have shaped the autistic brain in a specific way, e.g., a child with autism who is expert in the recognition of cars might show strong activation of the fusiform face area when he sees a car but not when he sees a face (Gauthier, Skudlarski, Gore, & Anderson, 2000). Abnormal activation found in neuroimaging studies of emotion processing can therefore be regarded as a reflection of the way in which brains with autism process information in their own way. This in turn could explain the good performance of people with autism when they are required to recognize emotional expressions in an experimental setting, but their difficulties in using this same information in everyday life. Importantly, it also means that the teaching of emotion understanding using video clips (Golan & Baron-Cohen, Chapter 12) or other possibilities of interventions using alternative behavioral routes, as reviewed by Jones and Jordan (Chapter 14) are efficient because they are grounded on alternative ways of processing information that make good use of the cerebral circuits that developed atypically in autism.

Second, another often forgotten but crucial set of data comes from the study of attentional processes in autism. These data are important for two main reasons. Gaze tracking enables us to know with great accuracy the attentional focus of tested participants (Jones & Klin, Chapter 4). It helps, therefore, to know exactly what information they perceive at a given time. If this attentional focus is different between typical and ASD populations when they scan a visual scene containing social or emotional interactions, then differences in brain activations should be interpreted with great care. Indeed, attention does influence and modulate brain activity, and many top-down modulations from higher cortical areas toward primary sensory areas are involved when the privileged processing of a particular aspect of a stimulus (e.g., the emotional expression of a face) is required. As hypothesized by Pelphrey, Morris, and McCarthy (2005) the abnormal scanning pattern shown by autistic people when they look at a face or at an emotional context could explain the abnormal activation of the fusiform gyrus.

Finally, and most crucially, to fully address the problem of the origins of abnormal functional connectivity in the brain of the person with autism, we now need more than ever a focus on developmental studies (see, e.g., for developmental studies of behavior, Maestro & Muratori, Chapter 9; and Jones & Klin, Chapter 4). From the perspective of cognitive neuroscience, this means the need to concentrate on carrying out longitudinal studies as an unavoidable step in unraveling the complexity of the atypical network of brain connectivity that characterizes autism.

References

Abell, F., Krams, M., Ashburner, J., Passingham, R., Friston, K., Frackowiak, R., et al. (1999). The neuroanatomy of autism: A voxel-based whole brain analysis of structural scans. *Neuroreport, 10*(8), 1647–1651.

Adolphs, R., Sears, L., & Piven, J. (2001). Abnormal processing of social information from faces in autism. *Journal of Cognitive Neuroscience, 13*(2), 232–240.

Akshoomoff, N., Pierce, K., & Courchesne, E. (2002). The neurobiological basis of autism from a developmental perspective. *Developmental Psychopathology, 14*(3), 613–634.

Allen, G., & Courchesne, E. (2003). Differential effects of developmental cerebellar abnormality on cognitive and motor functions in the cerebellum: An fMRI study of autism. *American Journal of Psychiatry, 160*(2), 262–273.

American Psychiatric Association (1994). *Diagnostic and statistical manual of mental disorders* (4th ed.) (DSM-IV). Washington, DC: APA.

Barbas, H. (1995). Anatomic basis of cognitive-emotional interactions in the primate prefrontal cortex. *Neuroscience and Biobehavioral Reviews, 19*, 499–510.

Barcelo, F., Suwazono, S., & Knight, R. (2000). Prefrontal modulation of visual processing in humans. *Nature Neuroscience, 3*, 399–403.

Begeer, S., Rieffe, C., Terwogt, M. M., & Stockmann, L. (2006). Attention to facial emotion expressions in children with autism. *Autism, 10*(1), 37–51.

Boddaert, N., Chabane, N., Gervais, H., Good, M., Bourgeois, M.-H., Plumet, C., et al. (2004). Superior temporal sulcus anatomical abnormalities in childhood autism: A voxel-based morphometry MRI study. *Neuroimage, 23*(1), 364–369.

Boger-Megiddo, I., Shaw, D. W., Friedman, S. D., Sparks, B. F., Artru, A. A., Giedd, J. N., et al. (2006). Corpus callosum morphometrics in young children with autism spectrum disorder. *Journal of Autism and Developmental Disorders, 36*(6), 733–739.

Bormann-Kischkel, C., Vilsmeier, M., & Baude, B. (1995). The development of emotional concepts in autism. *Journal of Child Psychology and Psychiatry, 36*(7), 1243–1259.

Brambilla, P., Hardan, A., di Nemi, S. U., Perez, J., Soares, J. C., & Barale, F. (2003). Brain anatomy and development in autism: Review of structural MRI studies. *Brain Research Bulletin*, *61*(6), 557–569.

Brothers, L. (1990). The social brain: A project for integrating primate behavior and neurophysiology in a new domain. *Concepts Neuroscience*, *1*, 27–151.

Carper, R. A., & Courchesne, E. (2000). Inverse correlation between frontal lobe and cerebellum sizes in children with autism. *Brain*, *123*, 836–844.

Castelli, F., Frith, C., Happé, F., & Frith, U. (2002). Autism, Asperger syndrome and brain mechanisms for the attribution of mental states to animated shapes. *Brain*, *125*, 1839–1849.

Celani, G., Battacchi, M. W., & Arcidiacono, L. (1999). The understanding of the emotional meaning of facial expressions in people with autism. *Journal of Autism and Developmental Disorders*, *29*(1), 57–66.

Chung, M. K., Dalton, K. M., Alexander, A. L., & Davidson, R. J. (2004). Less white matter concentration in autism: 2D voxel-based morphometry. *Neuroimage*, *23*(1), 242–251.

Cody, H., Pelphrey, K., & Piven, J. (2002). Structural and functional magnetic resonance imaging of autism. *International Journal of Developmental Neuroscience*, *20*(3–5), 421–438.

Courchesne, E., Carper, R., & Akshoomoff, N. (2003). Evidence of brain overgrowth in the first year of life in autism. *Journal of the American Medical Association*, *290*(3), 337–344.

Courchesne, E., & Pierce, K. (2005). Why the frontal cortex in autism might be talking only to itself: Local over-connectivity but long-distance disconnection. *Current Opinion in Neurobiology*, *15*, 225–230.

Damasio, A. R., & Maurer, R. G. (1978). A neurological model for childhood autism. *Archives of Neurology*, *35*(12), 777–786.

Dawson, G., Webb, S. J., Wijsman, E., Schellenberg, G., Estes, A., Munson, J., et al. (2005). Neurocognitive and electrophysiological evidence of altered face processing in parents of children with autism: Implications for a model of abnormal development of social brain circuitry in autism. *Developmental Psychopathoogy*, *17*(3), 679–697.

Egaas, B., Courchesne, E., & Saitoh, O. (1995). Reduced size of corpus callosum in autism. *Archives of Neurology*, *52*(8), 794–801.

Fotheringham, J. B. (1991). Autism: Its primary psychological and neurological deficit. *Canadian Journal of Psychiatry*, *36*(9), 686–692.

Frith, C., & Frith, U. (1999). Interacting minds: A biological basis. *Science*, *286*, 1692–1695.

Gauthier, I., Skudlarski, P., Gore, J. C., & Anderson, A. W. (2000). Expertise for cars and birds recruits brain areas involved in face recognition. *Nature Neuroscience*, *3*, 191–197.

Ghashghaei, H., & Barbas, H. (2002). Pathways for emotion: Interactions of prefrontal and anterior temporal pathways in the amygdala of the rhesus monkey. *Neuroscience*, *115*, 1261–1279.

Giedd, J. (2004). Structural magnetic resonance imaging of the adolescent brain. *Annals of New York Academy of Science*, *1021*, 77–85.

Haas, R., Townsend, J., Courchesne, E., Lincoln, A. J., Schreibman, L., & Yeung-Courchesne, R. (1996). Neurologic abnormalities in infantile autism. *Journal of Child Neurology*, *11*(2), 84–92.

Hadjikhani, N., Joseph, R. M., Snyder, J., & Tager-Flusberg, H. (2006). Anatomical differences in the mirror neuron system and social cognition network in autism. *Cerebral Cortex*, *16*(9), 1276–1282.

Hardan, A. Y., Minshew, N. J., & Keshavan, M. S. (2000). Corpus callosum size in autism. *Neurology*, *55*(7), 1033–6. Erratum in *Neurology*, *55*(9), 1425.

Hobson, R. P. (1986a). The autistic child's appraisal of expressions of emotion. *Journal of Child Psychology and Psychiatry*, *27*, 321–342.

Hobson, R. P. (1986b). The autistic child's appraisal of expressions of emotion: A further study. *Journal of Child Psychology and Psychiatry*, *27*(5), 671–680.

Hobson, R. P. (1991). Methodological issues for experiments on autistic individuals' perception and understanding of emotion. *Journal of Child Psychology and Psychiatry*, *32*(7), 1135–1158.

Hobson, R. P., Ouston, J., & Lee, A. (1988). What's in a face? The case of autism. *British Journal of Psychology*, *79*(4), 441–453.

Horwitz, B., Rumsey, J., Grady, C., & Rapoport, S. (1988). The cerebral metabolic landscape in autism. Intercorrelations of regional glucose utilization. *Archives of Neurology*, *45*, 749–755.

Just, M. A., Cherkassky, V., Keller, T., Kana, R., & Minshew, N. (in press). Functional and anatomical cortical underconnectivity in autism: Evidence from an fMRI study of an executive function task and corpus callosum morphometry. *Cerebral Cortex*.

Just, M. A., Cherkassky, V., Keller, T., & Minshew, N. (2004). Cortical activation and synchronization during sentence comprehension in high-functioning autism: Evidence of underconnectivity. *Brain*, *127*, 1811–1821.

Kilts, C., Egan, G., Gideon, D., Ely, T., & Hoffman, J. (2003). Dissociable neural pathways are involved in the recognition of emotion in static and dynamic facial expressions. *Neuroimage*, *18*, 156–158.

Manes, F., Piven, J., Vrancic, D., Nanclares, V., Plebst, C., & Starkstein, S. E. (1999). An MRI study of the corpus callosum and cerebellum in mentally retarded autistic individuals. *Journal of Neuropsychiatry and Clinical Neuroscience*, *11*(4), 470–474.

McAlonan, G. M., Cheung, V., Cheung, C., Suckling, J., Lam, G. Y., Tai, K. S., et al. (2005). Mapping the brain in autism. A voxel-based MRI study of volumetric differences and intercorrelations in autism. *Brain*, *128*(2), 268–276.

McAlonan, G. M., Daly, E., Kumari, V., Critchley, H. D., van Amelsvoort, T., Suckling, J., et al. (2002). Brain anatomy and sensorimotor gating in Asperger's syndrome. *Brain*, *125*(7), 1594–606.

McCann, J., & Peppé, S. (2003). Prosody in autism spectrum disorders: A critical review. *International Journal of Language and Communication Disorder*, *38*(4), 325–350.

Mosconi, M., Zwaigenbaum, L., & Piven, J. (2006). Structural MRI in autism: Findings and future directions. *Clinical Neuroscience Research*, *6*(3–4), 135–144.

Nelson, C. A. (2001). Neural and behavioral plasticity in the developing brain (Review of the changing nervous system: Neurobehavioral consequences of early brain disorder). *Contemporary Psychology*, *46*, 353–355.

Ozonoff, S., Pennington, B. F., & Rogers, S. J. (1990). Are there emotion perception deficits in young autistic children? *Journal of Child Psychology and Psychiatry*, *31*(3), 343–361.

Pelphrey, K., Morris, J. P., & McCarthy, G. (2004). Grasping the intentions of others: The perceived intentionality of an action influences activity in the superior temporal sulcus during social perception. *Journal of Cognitive Neuroscience, 16*, 1706–1716.

Pelphrey, K. A., Morris, J. P., & McCarthy, G. (2005). Neural basis of eye gaze processing deficits in autism. *Brain, 128*(5),1038–1048.

Penn, H. (2006). Neurobiological correlates of autism: A review of recent research. *Child Neuropsychology, 12*(1), 57–79.

Phan, K., Wager, T., Taylor, S., & Liberzon, I. (2002). Functional neuroanatomy of emotion: A meta-analysis of emotion activation studies in PET and fMRI. *Neuroimage, 16*, 331–348.

Piven, J., Bailey, J., Ranson, B. J., & Arndt, S. (1997). An MRI study of the corpus callosum in autism. *American Journal of Psychiatry, 154*(8), 1051–1056.

Ramachandran, V. S., & Oberman, L. M. (2006). Broken mirrors—a theory of autism. *Scientific American, 295*(5), 62–69.

Robel, L., Ennouri, K., Piana, H., Vaivre-Douret, L., Perier, A., Flament, M. F., et al. (2004). Discrimination of face identities and expressions in children with autism: Same or different? *European Child and Adolescent Psychiatry, 13*(4), 227–233.

Saxe, R. (2006). Uniquely human social cognition. *Current Opinion in Neurobiology, 16*(2), 235–239.

Schultz, R. T. (2005). Developmental deficits in social perception in autism: The role of the amygdala and fusiform face area. *International Journal of Developmental Neuroscience, 23*(2–3), 125–141.

Sparks, B., Friedman, S., Shaw, D., Aylward, E., Echelard, D., Artru, A., et al. (2002). Brain structural abnormalities in young children with autism spectrum disorder. *Neurology, 59*(2), 184–192.

Tantam, D., Monaghan, L., Nicholson, H., & Stirling, J. (1989). Autistic children's ability to interpret faces: A research note. *Journal of Child Psychology and Psychiatry, 30*(4), 623–630.

Taylor, J., & Fragopanagos, N. (2005). The interaction of attention and emotion. *Neural Networks 18*, 353–369.

Teunisse, J. P., & de Gelder, B. (2001). Impaired categorical perception of facial expressions in high-functioning adolescents with autism. *Child Neuropsychology, 7*(1), 1–14.

Toga, A. W., Thompson, P. M., & Sowell, E. R. (2006). Mapping brain maturation. *Trends in Neuroscience, 29*(3), 148–159.

Vidal, C. N., Nicolson, R., DeVito, T. J., Hayashi, K. M., Geaga, J. A., Drost, D. J., et al. (2006). Mapping corpus callosum deficits in autism: An index of aberrant cortical connectivity. *Biological Psychiatry, 60*(3), 218–225.

Villalobos, M., Mizuno, A., Dahl, B. C., Kemmotsu, N., & Muller, R. A. (2005). Reduced functional connectivity between V1 and inferior frontal cortex associated with visuomotor performance in autism. *Neuroimage, 25*, 916–925.

Waiter, G. D., Williams, J. H., Murray, A. D., Gilchrist, A., Perrett, D., & Whiten, A. (2005). Structural white matter deficits in high-functioning individuals with autistic spectrum disorder: A voxel-based investigation. *Neuroimage, 24*(2), 455–461.

Welchew, D. E., Ashwin, C., Berkouk, K., Salvador, R., Suckling, J., Baron-Cohen, S., et al. (2005). Functional disconnectivity of the medial temporal lobe in Asperger's syndrome. *Biological Psychiatry, 57*(9), 991–8.

Williams, J., Whiten, A., Suddendorf, T., & Perrett, D. (2001). Imitation, mirror neurons and autism. *Neuroscience and Biobehavioral Reviews, 25*(4), 287–295.

3

Directedness, Egocentrism, and Autism

Justin H. G. Williams

Sometimes we effect change on the world and the people around us, and sometimes we are subject to the changes the world and its people bring upon us. It is often very important to know what role we played in causing the changes in the world that we experience, and also how other people's actions affect us personally. So, whether we are in professional fields of science or politics, the affairs of friendship, family, or the workplace, allocating blame or adulation is fundamental to social affairs, and a personal sense of a role is most important for self-perception.

One factor that is likely to be important for interpreting the relative personal significance and meaning of actions is the ability to perceive the directions in which actions are executed, whether from me to you, from you to me, or between you and him. However, equally important is the way that we learn to execute actions in a directed manner, learning how our actions will affect others.

In this chapter, I wish to focus on the possible contribution that assessing the directedness of action may have for social development. In particular, how the process of encoding the direction of an action, from its agent to its goal might contribute to what is termed egocentrism. Egocentrism is often considered to be a central feature of Asperger syndrome, but I will argue that, rather than children with autism being egocentric, they suffer from a lack of egocentrism, and this may be a core deficit related to autism.

Autism and Egocentrism

A number of papers have referred to autism as being marked by egocentrism. Frith & de Vignemont (2005) have recently observed that the first person to make this claim was Hans Asperger himself (Asperger, 1944) who described the children he identified as "egocentric in the extreme." They also noted that Gillberg and Gillberg (1989) highlighted extreme egocentrism (or egocentricity) in their diagnostic criteria for AS as a way of characterizing social impairment. Frith and de Vignemont, who support this view, suggest that

> people suffering from Asperger syndrome are likely to represent others predominantly in relationship to themselves . . . They like to talk and write about themselves, as they see themselves, and other people's ideas and opinions are not as interesting as their own. They do not seem to feel the need to compare themselves with others (p. 729).

This view, however, seems to be at odds with the clinical features of autism that are apparent in childhood. Quite often children with autism have preoccupations with interests that are very far removed from themselves and so reflect a distinct lack of self-interest (Lord, Rutter, & Le Couteur, 1994; Lord et al., 2000).[1] They are very different from toddlers who have tantrums when faced with the reality that they are not the center of attention. They may get upset when events do not unfold as they expected, but this is different from being centrally concerned about their own role in these events. Perhaps the most well-known symptom of autism is social withdrawal, a lack of interest in others and a desire to be alone. A child with autism does not demand to be the center of attention. Indeed, a child with autism, sitting in a room on his own, may typically not notice when his mother walks into the room. Even when she speaks, he does not notice that she is referring to him. Far from assuming that everything that is said is directed to them or concerns them, people with autism are more likely to assume otherwise and often do not respond, even when actions are directed specifically at them. Therefore, rather than being egocentric, children with autism appear to be anything but that. The apparent lack of interest in others by individuals with autism is matched by an equal disinterest in whether people pay attention to themselves. And our interest in others ultimately stems from an interest in ourselves. Or, put more gently, an understanding of the way that others' behavior affects us, ultimately gives us an interest in the way our behavior affects them.

Intriguingly, the terms of autism and egocentrism have been juxtaposed before in a social developmental context, and in noticeable contrast to that of the authors identified above. These terms were originally used in developmental psychology by Piaget (1926, particularly pp. 43–49), who made a distinction between autistic thought and egocentric thought. His use of the term "autistic" preceded Kanner's use of the term by almost 20 years (Kanner, 1943). However, both Kanner and Piaget drew from Bleuler's original use of the word in 1912 to describe features of schizophrenia, and thinking that is divorced from logic and reality (Bleuler,

1912). Piaget made a distinction between autistic and egocentric thought based on its directedness and adaptedness to reality. Egocentric thought was described as having an *aim* present in the mind of the thinker, being adapted to reality, and for communication. In contrast, autistic thought was described as "undirected intelligence" that does not pursue conscious aims, and so is not adapted to reality. It serves to satisfy internal desires, is uncommunicated, and is dominated by images. Because it is undirected, it is uncommunicable and is strictly individual.

Interested in its developmental implications, Piaget (1926) studied the spontaneous language of typically developing 6-year-olds and identified two language sub-groupings that he named "socialized" and "egocentric." "Egocentric" language was further classified as echolalia, monologue, and collective monologue. He judged that about half the children's language was "egocentric" and half was socialized. Most of the "egocentric" language was "monologue" and "collective monologue" (which, judging by the descriptions, would probably be classed as "chat" nowadays), and echolalia made up less than 5%. Thus, according to Piaget, it is normal for young children to have language that is highly egocentric.

Piaget observed that just a year later, at 7 years of age, language became much more socialized, and became better adapted for the purpose of communication. Egocentric thought, he argued, is therefore the immature form of socialized thought which is characteristic of intelligence among older individuals. So, within his framework, the distinction between egocentric thought and autistic thought is orthogonal to the difference between egocentric thought and socialized communication, which are developmentally connected. Social, communicated intelligence would not develop from autistic thought as conceptualized by Piaget and Bleuler, as socialization depends upon first engaging in egocentric thought.

Whilst some of the discussion around the meanings of these terms is a little outdated, the separation of the distinctions between autistic and egocentric thought that is concerned with directedness, and between egocentric and socialized thought that is concerned with social adaptation, may still be a very helpful one. The notion of "undirected," rather than self-directed intelligence may apply to autism as we know it today very well, and people with autism may be no more self-interested (and perhaps are even less so) than anybody else.

Egocentrism: Direction Versus Perspective

The apparent contradiction between Piaget, who sees autism as an egocentric deficiency, and other authors who described Asperger syndrome as egocentric excess was perhaps not a problem when autism and Asperger syndrome were regarded as separate conditions. Now that autism and Asperger syndrome are widely regarded as a largely unified clinical entity, the contradiction begs explanation. Resolution may be possible by attending to the variable emphasis on two different aspects of representation in the two forms of egocentrism. Frith and de Vignemont (2005) place an emphasis on perspective and the point of reference. They are concerned with whether an individual is able to see the world only from their own point of view, or whether they are also able to see it from someone else's perspective. In addition is the consideration of whether an individual can take a more independent, third-person perspective. They argue that a difficulty with taking another person's point of view affects individuals with Asperger syndrome, and this difficulty impacts upon their mentalizing ability, as well as other aspects of social function.

In contrast, Piaget (1926) defined egocentrism according to the directedness of speech, action, or thought. Therefore, to suggest that individuals with autism may struggle both with attributing directedness, as well as taking the perspective of another, does not seem to be so problematic. Indeed, it raises the question as to whether attribution of directedness may have any bearing on the development of the ability to see the world from another person's perspective. I will return to this question later, but would first like to consider how more recent evidence addresses the question of whether the development of egocentrism as a form of "directed intelligence" might be impaired in autism.

Directedness and the Clinical Features of Autism

There are many clinical features of autism that indicate an impairment of learning about "directedness," particularly in the way that children with autism execute actions. So, even if these children learn when actions are directed toward them, they do not appear to learn to use these same actions as approaches in obtaining social interaction, and the absence of this aspect of communication is powerfully diagnostic. Children with autism make poor eye contact, and later on in development they modulate it poorly. Another powerful discriminator between children with autism and typical children is that they do not use declarative pointing, descriptive or emphatic gestures in communication. Even when their range of facial expression is good, they do not direct facial expression to their intended recipient. These problems may be especially evident when a child makes a request. Gesture, vocal expression, and eye contact are rarely well coordinated. Pronominal reversal is perhaps one of the few symptoms of autism that is unique to it. They fail to distinguish between "you" and "I" and may even appear to ask with the intonation of a question, "you would like a drink?" when they are actually asking for a drink. Repetitive and stereotyped speech—another feature characteristic of autism—involves the learning and repetitive use of odd language segments that children memorize even though they are not personally relevant.

This pattern of symptoms appears to have in common, not the failure to learn an action per se, but the failure to learn how to modify the actions appropriately for use within a social context where recipients and agents are clearly identified, and an experience of directedness of the action is necessary for it to be understood. My suggestion is that *typical* children develop in an egocentric social context, where they strongly discriminate between actions that are self-directed and other actions, and the self-directed actions tend to be reinforcing. For people with autism or Asperger syndrome, the same actions are learnt, but a lack of discrimination between self-directed and other actions means that self-directedness becomes less relevant to learning.

Directedness, Learning, and Memory in Autism

This raises the question as to whether people with autism have a measurable difficulty in perceiving directedness. Leekam, Baron-Cohen, Perrett, Milders, and Brown (1997) found that children with autism were just as good as other children at judging the direction of gaze when asked. One might expect, therefore, that they should be just as good as other children at judging when it is directed to *them* or not. However, the task of gauging whether social actions are directed specifically toward us, rarely involves simple visuo-spatial discrimination. In a social context such judgments draw upon experience of the context in which the action takes place. An alternative possibility, therefore, could be that direct and averted gaze have differential effects upon learning systems. Associational learning systems are highly dependent upon an orbitofrontal–amygdala system (Kringelbach & Rolls, 2004). This system is also sensitive to eye-gaze, and so it seems possible that for typical infants, stimuli–response associations with direct gaze will be learnt more rapidly than stimuli-response associations with averted gaze. In sum, this means that behaviors that elicit a direct gaze will be highly reinforced compared to those that are associated with averted gaze. The orbitofrontal-amygdala system is likely to be dysfunctional in autism (Bachevalier & Loveland, 2006), and so this would be likely to impact upon differential associational learning in autism, with respect to gaze direction. Adults have been shown to process a face with direct gaze very differently from one with averted gaze (Allison, Puce, & McCarthy, 2000; Haxby, Hoffman, & Gobbini, 2000), and in particular direct gaze impacts upon activity of the amygdala (Adams, Jr., Gordon, Baird, Ambady, & Kleck, 2003; Haxby et al., 2000). This strongly preferential response to direct gaze may be innate. Farroni, Csibra, Simion, and Johnson (2002) found that newborn infants not only show a preference for direct gaze compared to averted gaze, but they also show enhanced occipital processing of direct gaze compared to averted gaze. There is the possibility that this basic process is disrupted or delayed in autism. Grice et al. (2005) found that 3–4-year-old children with autism showed differential EEG responses to direct and averted gaze normally associated with typically developing infants of about 4 months. In 4-year-old children and adults this differential response is lost, perhaps because both types of gaze are processed equally.

Similar thinking may apply to memory. Some of the extraordinary memory skills—for phone numbers, football scores, historical dates, or types of railway locomotive—of individuals with autism are well known. However, people with autism also have some poor memory skills (Minshew & Goldstein, 2001). This includes poor autobiographical skills (a difficulty recalling events as they happened to the individual), and a poor memory for facial identity and emotion recognition (Schultz, 2005). Dalton et al. (2005) showed that this was quite likely to be mediated by amount of eye contact. Individuals with autism were both slower and less accurate for faces where eye-gaze was directed at the viewer, but were just as accurate and fast when the gaze was averted. They found that levels of fusiform hypoactivation were mediated by the time that individuals with autism spent gazing at the face. Most of us would agree that experiences that involve us personally are more meaningful to us and we remember them more vividly than when we are detached observers. In contrast, it seems that for people with autism, when the expression is directed at them, they do not experience an advantage over when it is directed elsewhere. So whilst the relational aspects of a task (whether it is impersonal or personally relevant) are likely to have marked effects on learning in normality, these effects would appear to be less important for people with autism or Asperger syndrome.

Directedness and the Development of Correspondence

A number of researchers have developed theoretical models that explain autism as arising from a deficit in processes that serve specifically the function of relating perceptions of other individuals to those encoded for similar actions by the self—so called "self–other" mapping. Hobson (1990) drew attention to the need for "identification" and socio-emotional connectedness. Rogers and Pennington (1991) drew attention to the possible role of imitation in this developmental process. They offered a comprehensive model for autism suggesting that at the root of autism is "impaired formation/co-ordination of specific self–other representations," manifest first in impaired imitation, followed by a cascade of impairments in emotion-sharing, joint attention, and pretend play (thus including the broad range of social deficits).

The "correspondence" approach places the cognitive problem of matching perceived and executed action at center stage as the linchpin for social development. An alternative approach taken by Peter Hobson (recently expounded in Hobson and Meyer, 2006) is to put "identification" rather than "correspondence" at center stage. An exact definition of identification is elusive, but it is seemingly concerned with expanding one's subjective state to also encompass an awareness of another individual's subjective state (p. 216). It appears to be very similar to joint attention, though perhaps is more dependent on joint affect than joint attention. Here, I am discussing the possibility that the attribution of directedness is central to the development of "self–other mapping," "correspondence," and "identification." One reason is that the development of these functions may depend upon an intrinsically reinforcing process of social interaction that itself depends upon learning how to specifically elicit self-directed actions. If this were the case, one would expect the ability to attribute directedness to impact upon the practice of imitation in autism, simply because it often occurs as part of a social interaction associated with attention directed toward the child. Furthermore, one would predict that imitation more closely associated with social interaction would be more affected. Consistent with this, Williams, Whiten, and Singh (2004) reviewed the literature on imitation in autism and suggested that imitation of gesture may be affected more strongly than the imitation of actions directed toward objects.

Williams, Whiten, Suddendorf, and Perrett (2001) considered the possible role of "mirror neurons" in autism and the process of imitation. These are neurons in parietal and ventral premotor cortex that fire both when an action is perceived (Rizzolatti, Fogassi, & Gallese, 2001) and when that same specific action is executed. Williams et al. suggested that neurons with such a function could possibly serve this process of self–other mapping. Interestingly, an alternative role of directedness attribution for neurons in the ventral premotor cortex has emerged. Kakei, Hoffman, and Strick (2001) identified neurons in this area that were "directionally tuned" in that they fired according to the direction in which an action was executed. Ochiai, Mushiake, and Tanji (2005) found that this activity preceded the actual movements and was more in keeping with activity related to observation of the image of the hand. Therefore, the mirror neuron region may also be important in autism as an area that codes for action direction. This might explain some findings, such as decreased activity of this area in facial imitation (Dapretto et al., 2006) in autism, despite findings that this area does not serve an imitation-specific role (Williams et al., 2006). Also, Theoret et al. (2005) found that decreased activity of this area in individuals with autism was only for actions that were directed away from the observer (they termed this the "egocentric view") but not when directed toward the participants (which they termed the "allocentric" view).

Directedness and Joint Attention

Joint attention, when two individuals both have their attention directed to the same goal, is likely to be an important developmental process that affects the prognosis of autism (Mundy, Sigman, & Kasari, 1990). Whilst its importance for development is usually discussed in terms of the shared experiential context that it generates, less attention is given to the exclusivity of that context. A joint-attention experience can be generated for any number of people (millions of people may watch a football match on the television simultaneously), but it can also be highly exclusive between just two people.

To my knowledge, no studies have so far compared exclusive and all-inclusive joint attention. Arguably, though, the defining characteristic of an exclusive joint-attention experience is direct gaze. One might point out that a speaker addressing an audience may use direct gaze directed to individuals within the audience, but intuitively one might also reflect that when the speaker does this, it gives the member of the audience at the receiving end of that gaze a sense of exclusivity. If direct gaze is reinforcing of an action, it therefore follows that the experience of shared attention, that is associated with gaze directed to the child, will also become reinforcing in itself. Furthermore, the ability to elicit the exclusive joint-attention experience that occurs as an important component of the mother–infant interaction, is an important means of eliciting self-directed action. Children with autism are as likely to show looking, vocalizing, and proximity-seeking behaviors toward their caregivers, but show less attention-sharing behavior (Sigman, Mundy, Sherman, & Ungerer, 1986). This suggests that an impaired capacity for developing a joint attention experience will impact upon the development of egocentrism.

Dawson et al. (2002) suggest that memory may be important for joint attention to function. They found that performance on a task of "delayed non-matching to sample" (DNMS) was a strong predictor of joint-attention abilities in autism. DNMS depends upon visual recognition memory and the ability to associate novelty with reward. Therefore one might expect that a poor DNMS ability would be correlated with poor ability to associate directed gaze with delayed attention to a novel object. Williams, Waiter, Perra, Perrett, and Whiten (2005) investigated the neural substrate of joint attention by comparing brain activity whilst the participant and a figure in a video clip looked at the same object to when they looked in different places. Both non-joint attention and joint attention had the same attentional demands, and yet the experience of the joint attention in the absence of any tangible reward was associated with activity in medial prefrontal cortex, frontal pole, and bilateral caudate nuclei. This suggests that a joint-attention experience in itself facilitates activity within frontostriatal pathways that serve selective attention (Gilbert et al., 2006).

Notably, there was no orbitofrontal cortex or amygdala activation in this contrast, which would be expected during reinforcement of a goal-driven motor action associated with gaze effects (Kringelbach & Rolls, 2004). This might have been because our contrast did not include either action or gaze directed toward the participant, or any self-directed action. This study therefore supports the view that shared experience in itself may influence the development of selective visual attention, which might be served by simple associational learning and the amygdala-orbitofrontal circuit at an earlier stage of development. And poor functioning of joint attention may affect the development of "directed intelligence."

Egocentric Behavior and Mentalizing

Earlier, I queried whether the development of egocentrism in the sense used by Frith and de Vignemont (2005) could be affected by the lack of egocentrism in the sense of Piaget (1926). Frith and de Vignemont (2005) suggest that what they identify as the highly egocentric perspective of a person with Asperger syndrome allows for a well-developed "theory of mind" when it comes to mentalizing introspectively, but poor development of the ability to use a mentalizing ability when looking at relationships that are allocentric to the individual involved (e.g., "what does John think about me" as opposed to "what does John think about Mary"). This is consistent with Piaget's view of autistic thought as "undirected" and introspective thinking. However, it is also likely that attributing directedness to action is important for the development of a "theory of mind." This may be through the attribution of intention (Tomasello, Carpenter, Call, Behne, & Moll, 2005) or through the impact of egocentric learning on the development of joint-attention skills as discussed above. It has been argued by many (e.g., Baron-Cohen, 1997; Mundy, 2003; Williams et al., 2005) that the triadic representation associated with joint attention is a cognitive precursor to the development of "theory of mind." Joint attention involves forming a representation about another individual's attitude toward an object, in relation to one's own attitude toward an object, and this gives rise to an understanding of how another mind relates to one's own. Therefore, a failure to develop joint-attention skills as a result of a lack of egocentricity is likely to impact upon development of a mentalizing ability.

Also, Frith and de Vignemont (2005) discuss how the development of "theory of mind" relates to the ability to shift perspective from the first person to second or third person. It seems likely that appreciating the impact of directedness on experience must be an important component of learning about the effects of different perspectives on the way things appear to different individuals within an interaction. Consequently, appreciating the impact of directedness will also inform the value that one places on taking another's perspective. For an example, think of someone with Asperger syndrome who is held to be behaving in an egocentric fashion when, in a group context, they stand up and talk vociferously about what needs to happen, seemingly with only their own goal in mind, draw heavily on their own personal observations and ideas, and without giving due consideration to other people's views. In this situation, the individual with Asperger's has developed a view from an allocentric stance that is the result of an impersonal analysis. Furthermore, from the perspective of someone with Asperger syndrome, the internal world observed through introspection may provide useful material on which to develop a point of view as does observation of the external world. A lack of egocentricity (in the sense of "undirected intelligence") means that all observations are equally valued whether internal or external. Hence, someone with Asperger syndrome may appear to discuss issues from an egocentric perspective when they are really just trying to communicate it, *"the-way-it-is."* Because of their extreme allocentric perspective, they see *"the-way-it-is"* as independent of the social situation in which they are communicating it.

In contrast, the typical individual who behaved like this in such a situation would be viewing his behavior from the second- and third-person, as well as the first-person perspective. He is bound to be thinking about how his behavior is reflecting on the group's view of him, how it is affecting his social status within the group, and constantly taking this into account in the way he communicates his view. Hence his viewpoint is highly susceptible to the group dynamic, and therefore, were he to hold the floor for an excessively long period, it would most likely be because he thought of himself as more important than others and that his ideas were more valuable. He might justifiably be considered "egocentric."

5-HT Depletion as a Proxy for Autism

I would like to provide some experimental support for my hypothesis by presenting some findings from a study currently under review. The neurotransmitter serotonin (5-HT) has long been implicated in the etiology of autism. Schain and Freedman (1961) first showed blood levels of 5-HT to be high in autism. This has since been a highly replicated finding (e.g., McBride et al., 1998). Autism is thought to show some response to drugs acting on the serotonergic system, and the family histories of people affected by autism are characterized by disorders associated with dysfunctional 5-HT systems such as depression, anxiety, and obsessive-compulsive disorder (McDougle, Erickson, Stigler, & Posey, 2005). Most recently, in a robust study, Devlin et al. (2005) showed that families with autism showed preferential transmission of one type of allele of the gene coding for the 5-HT transporter protein.

If autism does result from impaired 5-HT transmission, then it may be possible to simulate the effects of autism on brain functioning by impairing 5-HT function. Acute tryptophan depletion (ATD) (Young, Smith, Pihl, & Ervin, 1985) is a well-established means of manipulating serotonergic function in humans. Delivering a high amino acid load deficient in tryptophan to a fasting individual excludes serum tryptophan from transport across the blood–brain barrier. As tryptophan is an essential precursor to the manufacture of serotonin, this causes a temporary drop in CNS serotonin production and activity. In an experiment using fMRI to image the effects of dropping serotonin on brain function, we hypothesized that impaired serotonin production would have deleterious effects on the processing of facial emotion in the amygdala, when the faces were viewed from the front compared to being viewed from the side. This is because serotonin has been shown to be an important transmitter in the amygdala and also because variation in the function of the 5-HT transporter gene has been shown to affect amygdala activity during emotion processing (Hariri et al., 2002). We were interested in what other brain regions might be involved in emotion judgment that might be affected by gaze direction and serotonin. We found (Williams et al., 2007) that dropping serotonin function interacted strongly with the view of the face (whether it was directed at or away from the observer). Neuroimaging showed that activity in ventromedial prefrontal cortex, temporal pole, posterior STS, amygdala, and orbitofrontal cortex (as well as insula and Broca's area) was markedly affected by tryptophan depletion. What was quite remarkable about these findings was that a single analysis exploring the interaction between gaze and serotonin deficiency so specifically identified brain areas associated with "theory of mind" and social cognition in previous studies. However, the effects differed according to brain area. In the medial prefrontal cortex, temporal pole, and orbitofrontal cortex, activity during emotional judgment was markedly affected for direct gaze, but there was little activity to speak of for averted gaze, which was consequently little affected by the depletion. In contrast, for STS, activity increased as a result of decreased serotonin when gaze was averted. To complicate matters further, there were also correlations between the extent of tryptophan depletion and activity in areas of cingulate gyrus, particularly an area associated with empathy for pain and emotion (Singer et al., 2004; Lane et al., 1998) thought to code for shared affect. Finally, there were behavioral differences. Lower serotonin was associated with a faster (for all) but less accurate (only for profile) reading of facial emotion. Our interpretation of these results is that direction of gaze plays an important role in determining whether we employ mental state processes when we observe and make sense of behavior. When gaze is directed toward us, it may be adaptive to employ mental state attribution processes. However, when gaze is directed elsewhere, it may be more adaptive to address the goal of the gaze. If I am trying to judge your honesty, it may be worth me "look-

Table 3.1 Clusters of activity identified by Williams et al. (2007) and Baron-Cohen et al. (1999).

	Williams et al.	*Baron-Cohen et al.*
Left STS	−50, −31, 7 (correlation)	−55, −28, 15
Right STS	40, −54, 17 (gp comparison)	40, −28, 15
Right insula	42, −7, 11 (gp comparison)	44, 11, −7
Left Broca's area	−50, 22, 10 (gp comparison)	−46, 22, 9
Left amygdala	−18, −6, −13 (gp comparison)	−23, −11, −7

Note: Coordinates in the Williams et al. study reflect areas where emotional judgment was affected by face direction and serotonin depletion. Coordinates of the Baron-Cohen et al. study reflect areas where emotional judgment was affected by autism.

ing you in the eye," but if your expression is averted and you have an expression of fear on your face because you have seen my enemy approaching with a spear, it is not the time for me to ask about your feelings. It is much more useful in that situation to judge your expression quickly and to look for the goal of your gaze. Our results suggest that serotonin and gaze processing work together to determine whether I employ mental state attribution processes when I look at you or, alternatively, whether I look to see where you are looking, for an external cause of your emotion. We suggest that low serotonin diminishes social engagement involving "social brain" areas. But also, it activates an alternative, quicker but less accurate system for emotion processing involving the right STS. These results are particularly interesting when considered next to the results of the study by Baron-Cohen et al. (1999) as shown in Table 3.1. They studied adults with normal IQ and with autism and asked them to view pictures of eyes expressing different emotions in their gaze. They found group differences in STS, Broca's area, insula, and amygdala just as we found were areas affected by 5-HT depletion. Furthermore, some of the coordinates for these areas affected by autism were very close to those affected by tryptophan depletion. In particular, Baron-Cohen et al. also found higher activity in the autism group in STS when processing gaze. Therefore, both tryptophan depletion and autism seem to be associated with greater activity in STS, and lower activity in insula and amygdala. The picture is more complex because Baron-Cohen's eyes task consisted of a mixture of directed and averted gazes. Furthermore, the similarities of coordinates on that study with ours are with both the serotonin–gaze interaction and the regression analysis, where extent of serotonin depletion correlated with effects on emotional judgment. Nevertheless, the similarities are enough to suggest an important role for serotonin in mediating (a) the processing of emotional expression, (b) the differences between direct gaze and indirect gaze, and (c) the differences between autism and normality in the processing of directed facial emotion. Also the observation that the same area of STS is more active for indirect gaze when processing emotion, and also more active when people with autism process emotion, if taken with our idea that this follows from looking for the external cause of the emotion, supports the idea that people with autism are processing emotion from an allocentric perspective.

Conclusions

The purpose of this chapter was to explore the possible importance of "directedness" in social development and autism, and to challenge the view that autism is a condition of extreme egocentrism. I have argued that children with autism may in fact suffer from a lack of egocentrism, whereas the typical child loves to be the center of attention and relishes the experience of perceiving actions directed toward them. For the typical child the experience of perceiving actions directed toward them is intrinsically interesting and can have a profound effect on attention and learning. Even when parental actions have negative consequences for a child, such as when a parent tells off her toddler for misbehaving, these reprimands can act in such a way to reinforce the undesirable behavior. My suggestion is that children with autism simply lack this egocentricity. The reinforcing effect of a perceived action is similar whether it is directed toward the child or not. Consequently, all actions are experienced "allocentrically" in the sense that effects of an action on learning are similar, irrespective of how they are performed in relation to the observer. A deficit like this may especially affect the development of joint attention, mentalizing ability, and the learning of communicative actions. This means that whereas normal children have an overriding desire to engage in imitation, dyadic interaction, and joint-attention activities, children with autism find these activities less interesting and are not so fussed about being the center of attention. This is different from not requiring security or showing proximity-seeking behavior. It is about the potential of personally directed attention to act as reinforcement. I might seem to be saying that children with autism are unlikely to respond to praise. Through clinical experience (though I don't have systematic data) I have seen this not to be universally true, but I have also seen that children with autism respond to praise in an abnormal way, and some respond in a negative way. My hypothesis is that children with autism may find personally directed attention no more reinforcing than the same sort of attention when it is not personally directed. It is in this sense that they lack egocentrism.

The second part of my hypothesis is that this markedly non-egocentric stance has developmental consequences which may affect the ability to take another individual's perspective, but that egocentrism in this sense actually reflects a selfless attitude. A person with Asperger syndrome may see only one point of view at a time, on which he may ruminate or obsess, or develop to be comprehensive and detailed. This viewpoint may be based on his internal world as much as his external world, for both may provide equally relevant material for consideration. However, this needs to be differentiated from selfishness that is centered on the need for personally directed attention, and preferably adulation, and the egocentricity that emerges from comparing one's self to others, to see one's self as more important, valued, or worthy of reward than others. Piaget may just have got it right when he described "autistic thought" as "undirected intelligence" some years before autism was described as a condition.

Integration Section

The topic of "egocentricity" seems to have had a curious ride within the study of autism. On the one hand, some of the greatest of writers have seen it to be closely related to autism. On the other, however, it appears to have been subjected to little detailed investigation. Differences in the ways that a term such as "egocentrism" is used, and the lack of formality or exploration of its meaning, allow for different understandings of its implications. My objective in writing this chapter was to highlight this knotty and potentially emotive issue, which may be more important than has hitherto been recognized. My suggestion is that there is a fundamental ability to know about whether actions are directed at one's self or elsewhere, and normally, there is also a strong tendency to care about it. What might be the developmental consequences were this capacity or tendency to be diminished? I speculate that it would have many repercussions, some of which are discussed as impairments in autism in other chapters of this book. Also, if such impairment is a feature of autism, it follows that neural functions that contribute to egocentric development may well be impaired in autism.

Wicker (Chapter 2) highlights the roles of the amygdala and the fusiform cortex. Connectivity between these areas seems to be important in determining the greater salience of facial expression directed toward the individual, over expressions directed elsewhere. Wicker also discusses the social brain, which includes superior temporal sulcus (STS) that processes gaze direction and orbitofrontal cortex that serves associative learning. Close connectivity in typical individuals, between amygdala, STS, and orbitofrontal cortex, means that gaze direction is intimately tied to the emotional valence of stimuli. Disruption of connectivity between these structures is likely to mean that associative learning is less dependent on gaze direction, and if this is the case in autism, one would expect that it would adversely affect the development of egocentrism.

Jones and Klin (Chapter 4) have used eye-tracking technology to show that people with autism spend less time looking at people's eyes. They have pursued the likely developmental consequences of this. They point out that attention to objects rather than eyes is likely to result in greater interest, understanding, and expertise in the physical environment, rather than in social objects such as faces and people. However, more specifically, this finding suggests that children with autism are simply not interested in the information available from gaze, such as where gaze is directed. Most of the time, we look at eyes to see where they are looking. Of course, eyes also convey an emotional expression, but this is meaningless if its direction is not first appreciated. My argument is that faces and eyes usually demand so much attention because we have learnt that they convey information about directionality of intention. This is hugely important, because whether someone is looking at us or not is a strong predictor of whether something concerns us as individuals or not. If directionality of intention is not of interest, then other stimuli may become more appealing. So it may be their property of conveying information about directionality that gives faces and eyes such marked salience as stimuli.

In this chapter, I refer to Piaget's conceptualization of autistic thought as a form of "undirected" intelligence. Such a perspective ties in well with Loth's (Chapter 5) exploration of script functioning in autism. Within her analysis, separate events are remembered in isolation from one another, rather than in the context of an ongoing script with beginning, middle, and end that leads toward a goal. One could speculate that such a way of thinking could emerge from a failure to maintain one's self as a single reference point (or "anchor point") for all experiences during development. If events and experiences are remembered egocentrically, according to their differential effects on a single function (the self), then one can see that they are likely to become organized in a hierarchical and sequential fashion. A tendency to organize memory according to more arbitrary and impersonal categories could feasibly result in the sorts of responses shown by the young people with autism in Loth's experiments.

One can of course get carried away with one's theories, twisting them and speculating to make them fit every experimental result. The notion that egocentrism may facilitate the organization of memory during development could easily be extended to develop arguments that this would impact upon the development of conceptual knowledge, weak central coherence, and executive function (see Chapters 6–8 by López; Ropar, Mitchell, & Sheppard; and Hill). Indeed, we could give new meaning to the term "weak central coherence" to see it as "weak self coherence," resulting from poor integration of memories relating to the self. I think this is probably going too far, and just as we need to think of the neural substrate of egocentrism, we also need to think about the cognitive functions that may impinge upon it. The abilities to shift attention between the internal and external world, and selectively attend to objects of relevance, seem likely to be of importance in developing egocentrism. So, I am not arguing that we need to see impaired egocentric development as some sort of primary cause of autism; just that its importance should be considered within the whole scheme.

However, I have suggested in my chapter that the flip-side of failing to attribute directionality to perceived action is that one does not acquire this capacity in one's learning about others. Hence, home movies of children with autism (Maestro & Muratori, Chapter 9) show them to exhibit behaviors which lack directionality as well as a lack of interest in others' directionality. This includes poor communication of affect and "self-absorption." "Aimlessness" is also mentioned, as a characteristic of these home movies, and again the description seems to fit the Piagetian description of autistic thinking. McCann, Peppé, Gibbon, O'Hare, & Rutherford (Chapter 11) discuss prosody in autism, which is perhaps the verbal equivalent of facial expression. Both contain elements that are both universal and learnt according to cultural experience. So, just as with faces, the differentiation between when speech is directed at one's self and when it is directed elsewhere may have a marked effect on the way that it is remembered, and therefore spoken.

The final chapters of the book discuss clinical aspects of autism. Jo Williams (Chapter 10) discusses the use of screening instruments. She reports on a test that is highly sensitive and powerfully predictive, but the use of questionnaires is never likely to be completely effective when even intensive clinical assessments sometimes disagree over diagnosis. The discussion of whether autism is a categorical disorder or a dimensional variant also impinges on their potential, but I should not enter into that issue here. I will simply add that use of a construct such as "egocentrism" could contribute to assessment and the development of a screening tool. Assessment of an infant's tendency toward "directed intelligence" (to use Piaget's term) could provide a single measure that would not seek to be diagnostic but a correlate, which could be used by researchers to investigate its impact on development and its capacity to predict later social functioning.

Similarly, the notion of "egocentrism" may provide a valuable construct for both teaching social skills, and reframing the cognitive capacities of those who have autism. This may be at the level of encouraging eye contact and teaching about the use of faces and gaze for providing information. Or it may influence the way of teaching. In our unit, for example, we use "allocentric" teaching approaches. Some children with autism find it easier to learn if they are shown, "this is how it is done" rather than told, "you must do it this way."

Finally, an allocentric approach may also provide a different cognitive perspective to problems, generating different sorts of analyses that can be hugely beneficial. If this is associated with autism, it may help us to appreciate the importance of autistic thinking for our cultural and intellectual development. To conclude, further exploration of the egocentric/allocentric contrast in child development may provide a very useful approach to understanding the difficulties and skills of children with autism.

Acknowledgments

This study was funded by the National Alliance for Autism Research. I am grateful to Claire Enders for inspiring discussions, and to my colleagues David Perrett, Steve Pechey, and Gordon Waiter with whom I conducted the neuroimaging research.

Note

1   In this chapter I often refer to the clinical features of autism and Asperger syndrome. These are best and most authoritatively described within the Autism Diagnostic Interview and the Autism Diagnostic Observation Schedule. These instruments are the best-validated tools for the diagnosis of autism, and research using them is the best source of information as to which features of autism best discriminate it from other conditions. Hence my emphasis on features such as poorly modulated eye-gaze, a lack of directed facial expression, a lack of declarative pointing or gesture which all stem from use of these clinical features as diagnostically discriminative characteristics to reliably diagnose autism or Asperger syndrome. Therefore, unless otherwise stated, statements about clinical features of autism are based upon their inclusion in the ADI-R or ADOS-G (Lord et al., 1994, 2000).

References

Adams, R. B., Jr., Gordon, H. L., Baird, A. A., Ambady, N., & Kleck, R. E. (2003). Effects of gaze on amygdala sensitivity to anger and fear faces. *Science, 300*, 1536.

Allison, T., Puce, A., & McCarthy, G. (2000). Social perception from visual cues: Role of the STS region. *Trends in Cognitive Science, 4*, 267–278.

Asperger, H. (1944). Die autistischen Psychopathen im Kindesalter. In U. Frith, *Autism and Asperger syndrome*. Archiv für Psychiatrie und Nervenkrankheiten 117 (pp. 76–136. Cambridge, UK: Cambridge University Press. 1991.

Bachevalier, J., & Loveland, K. A. (2006). The orbitofrontal-amygdala circuit and self-regulation of social-emotional behavior in autism. *Neuroscience and Biobehavioral Reviews, 30*, 97–117.

Baron-Cohen, S. (1997). *Mindblindness: An essay on autism and theory of mind*. Cambridge, MA: MIT Press.

Baron-Cohen, S., Ring, H. A., Wheelwright, S., Bullmore, E. T., Brammer, M. J., Simmons, A., et al. (1999). Social intelligence in the normal and autistic brain: An fMRI study. *European Journal of Neuroscience, 11*, 1891–1898.

Bleuler, E. (1912). Das autistiche Denten. In *Jahrbuch für psychoanalytische und psychopathologische Forschungen* (Leipzig and Vienna: Deuticke), *4*, 1–39.

Dalton, K. M., Nacewicz, B. M., Johnstone, T., Schaefer, H. S., Gernsbacher, M. A., Goldsmith, H. H., et al. (2005). Gaze fixation and the neural circuitry of face processing in autism. *Nature Neuroscience, 8*, 519–526.

Dapretto, M., Davies, M. S., Pfeifer, J. H., Scott, A. A., Sigman, M., Bookheimer, S. Y., et al. (2006). Understanding emotions in others: Mirror neuron dysfunction in children with autism spectrum disorders. *Nature Neuroscience, 9*, 28–30.

Dawson, G., Webb, S., Schellenberg, G. D., Dager, S., Friedman, S., Aylward, E., et al. (2002). Defining the broader phenotype of autism: Genetic, brain, and behavioral perspectives. *Developmental Psychopathology, 14*, 581–611.

Devlin, B., Cook, E. H., Jr., Coon, H., Dawson, G., Grigorenko, E. L., McMahon, W., et al. (2005). Autism and the serotonin transporter: The long and short of it. *Molecular Psychiatry, 10*, 1110–1116.

Farroni, T., Csibra, G., Simion, F., & Johnson, M. H. (2002). Eye contact detection in humans from birth. *Proceedings of the National Academy of Science USA., 99*(14), 9602–9605.

Frith, U., & de Vignemont, F. (2005). Egocentrism, allocentrism, and Asperger syndrome. *Consciousness and Cognition, 14*, 719–738.

Gillberg, I. C., & Gillberg, C. (1989). Asperger syndrome: Some epidemiological considerations: A research note. *Journal of Child Psychology and Psychiatry, 30*, 631–638.

Gilbert, S. J., Spengler, S., Simons, J. S., Steele, J. D., Lawrie, S. M., Frith, C. D., et al. (2006). Functional specialization within rostral prefrontal cortex (area 10): A meta-analysis. *Journal of Cognitive Neuroscience, 18*, 932–948.

Grice, S. J., Halit, H., Farroni, T., Baron-Cohen, S., Bolton, P., & Johnson, M. H. (2005). Neural correlates of eye-gaze detection in young children with autism. *Cortex, 41*, 342–353.

Hariri, A. R., Mattay, V. S., Tessitore, A., Kolachana, B., Fera, F., Goldman, D., et al. (2002). Serotonin transporter genetic variation and the response of the human amygdala. *Science, 297*, 400–403.

Haxby, J. V., Hoffman, E. A., & Gobbini, M. I. (2000). The distributed human neural system for face perception. *Trends in Cognitive Sciences, 4*, 223–233.

Hobson, R. P. (1990). On the origins of self and the case of autism. *Development and Psychopathology, 2*, 163–181.

Hobson, R. P., & Meyer, J. (2006). Imitation, identification and the shaping of mind: Insights from autism. In S. J. Rogers & J. H. G. Williams (Eds.), *Imitation and the social mind in autism and typical development* (pp. 198–224). New York: The Guilford Press.

Kakei, S., Hoffman, D. S., & Strick, P. L. (2001). Direction of action is represented in the ventral premotor cortex. *Nature Neuroscience, 4*, 1020–1025.

Kanner, L. (1943). Autistic disturbances of affective contact. *Nervous Child, 2*, 217–250.

Kringelbach, M. L., & Rolls, E. T. (2004). The functional neuroanatomy of the human orbitofrontal cortex: Evidence from neuroimaging and neuropsychology. *Progress in Neurobiology, 72*, 341–372.

Lane, R. D., Reiman, E. M., Axelrod, B., Yun, L. S., Holmes, A., & Schwartz, G. E. (1998). Neural correlates of levels of emotional awareness: Evidence of an interaction between emotion and attention in the anterior cingulate cortex. *Journal of Cognitive Neuroscience, 10*, 525–535.

Leekam, S., Baron-Cohen, S., Perrett, D., Milders, M., & Brown, S. (1997). Eye-direction detection: A dissociation between geometric and joint attention skills in autism. *British Journal of Developmental Psychology, 15*, 77–95.

Lord, C., Risi, S., Lambrecht, L., Cook, E. H., Jr., Leventhal, B. L., DiLavore, P. C., et al. (2000). The autism diagnostic observation schedule-generic: A standard measure of social and communication deficits associated with the spectrum of autism. *Journal of Autism and Developmental Disorders, 30*, 205–223.

Lord, C., Rutter, M., & Le Couteur, A. (1994). Autism Diagnostic Interview–Revised: A revised version of a diagnostic interview for caregivers of individuals with possible pervasive developmental disorders. *Journal of Autism and Developmental Disorders, 24*, 659–685.

McBride, P. A., Anderson, G. M., Hertzig, M. E., Snow, M. E., Thompson, S. M., Khait, V. D., et al. (1998). Effects of diagnosis, race, and puberty on platelet serotonin levels in autism and mental retardation. *Journal of the American Academy of Child and Adolescent Psychiatry, 37*, 767–776.

McDougle, C. J., Erickson, C. A., Stigler, K. A., & Posey, D. J. (2005). Neurochemistry in the pathophysiology of autism. *Journal of Clinical Psychiatry, 66*, 9–18.

Minshew, N. J., & Goldstein, G. (2001). The pattern of intact and impaired memory functions in autism. *Journal of Child Psychology and Psychiatry and Allied Disciplines, 42*, 1095–1101.

Mundy, P. (2003). Annotation: The neural basis of social impairments in autism: The role of the dorsal medial-frontal cortex and anterior cingulate system. *Journal of Child Psychology and Psychiatry, 44*, 793–809.

Mundy, P., Sigman, M., & Kasari, C. (1990). A longitudinal study of joint attention and language development in autistic children. *Journal of Autism and Developmental Disorders, 20*, 115–128.

Ochiai, T., Mushiake, H., & Tanji, J. (2005). Involvement of the ventral premotor cortex in controlling image motion of the hand during performance of a target-capturing task. *Cerebral Cortex, 15*, 929–937.

Piaget, J. (1926). *The language and thought of the child* (M. Warden, Trans.). London: Kegan Paul, Trench, Trubner & Co., Ltd.

Rizzolatti, G., Fogassi, L., & Gallese, V. (2001). Neurophysiological mechanisms underlying the understanding and imitation of action. *Nature Reviews Neuroscience, 2*, 661–670.

Rogers, S. J., & Pennington, B. F. (1991). A theoretical approach to the deficits in infantile autism. *Developmental Psychopathology, 3*, 137–162.

Schain, R. J., & Freedman, D. X. (1961). Studies on 5-hydroxyindole metabolism in autistic and other mentally retarded children. *Journal of Pediatrics, 58*, 315–320.

Schultz, R. T. (2005). Developmental deficits in social perception in autism: The role of the amygdala and fusiform face area. *International Journal of Developmental Neuroscience, 23*, 125–141.

Sigman, M., Mundy, P., Sherman, T., & Ungerer, J. (1986). Social interactions of autistic, mentally retarded and normal children and their caregivers. *Journal of Child Psychology and Psychiatry, 27,* 647–655.

Singer, T., Seymour, B., O'Doherty, J., Kaube, H., Dolan, R. J., & Frith, C. D. (2004). Empathy for pain involves the affective but not sensory components of pain. *Science, 303,* 1157–1162.

Theoret, H., Halligan, E., Kobayashi, M., Fregni, F., Tager-Flusberg, H., & Pascual-Leone, A. (2005). Impaired motor facilitation during action observation in individuals with autism spectrum disorder. *Current Biology, 15,* R84–R85.

Tomasello, M., Carpenter, M., Call, J., Behne, T., & Moll, H. (2005). Understanding and sharing intentions: The origins of cultural cognition. *Behavioral and Brain Sciences, 28,* 675–691.

Williams, J. H. G., Perrett, D. I., Waiter, G. D., Pechey, S. (2007). Differential effects of tryptophan depletion on emotion processing according to face direction. *Social Cognitive and Affective Neuroscience,* doi: 10.1093/scan/nsm021

Williams, J. H. G., Waiter, G. D., Gilchrist, A., Perrett, D. I., Murray, A. D., Whiten, A. (2006). Neural mechanisms of imitation and "mirror neuron" functioning in autistic spectrum disorder. *Neuropsychologia, 44,* 608–619.

Williams, J. H. G., Waiter, G. D., Perra, O., Perrett, D. I., & Whiten, A. (2005). An fMRI study of joint attention experience. *NeuroImage, 25,* 133–140.

Williams, J. H. G., Whiten, A., & Singh, T. (2004). A systematic review of action imitation in autistic spectrum disorder. *Journal of Autism and Developmental Disorders, 34,* 285–299.

Williams, J. H., Whiten, A., Suddendorf, T., & Perrett, D. I. (2001). Imitation, mirror neurons and autism. *Neuroscience and Biobehavioral Reviews, 25,* 287–295.

Young, S. N., Smith, S. E., Pihl, R. O., & Ervin, F. R. (1985). Tryptophan depletion causes a rapid lowering of mood in normal males. *Psychopharmacology, 87,* 173–177.

4

Altered Salience in Autism

Developmental Insights, Consequences, and Questions

Warren Jones and Ami Klin

As researchers and clinicians working with individuals with autism, we face a difficult paradox: the deficits in communication and social interaction cited as defining features of autism necessarily present a central obstacle to the study of autism itself. The struggle of individuals with autism to understand the normative social world is in many ways mirrored by the struggle of researchers and clinicians to understand the remote internal worlds of individuals with autism.

A useful strategy for glimpsing those internal worlds has been to study the point of interaction between an individual and his or her surrounding environment. By measuring a person's selective sampling of that environment, we gain insight into how that sampling impacts upon a person's subsequent understanding. One way to very literally follow an individual's selective sampling of the surrounding world has been to use eye-tracking technology to trace and quantify visual interaction.

This approach has enabled us to ask a series of interesting questions. What does an individual with autism pay attention to (and consequently also not pay attention to) when observing the world at large? How does this selective interaction both reflect and also impact upon the course of an individual's neural and cognitive development? These questions are part of a larger inquiry into how the world is reconstructed in the mind's eye of a child with autism.

Behavioral Relevance and Relative Visual Salience

In considering that reconstruction, the mind's-eye view of the world, there are constraints which limit and guide what is seen. Visual resources themselves are limited. In a complex environment full of relevant and irrelevant information, there are more things to look at than a person has the capacity to see. Facing such a flood of visual information, directing limited visual resources toward areas of greatest behavioral relevance is critical for survival. But what in that environment is most behaviorally relevant? What is or is not salient to any particular individual is a consequence of that individual's survival needs and goals, and consequently varies across species and between individuals. For each, there is a landscape of relative salience, where elements of the world around are weighted unequally in their behavioral importance. The landscape of salience for a bee in search of pollen in a grassy field is different from that of a child playing soccer on that field, just as it is different for a father watching from the sidelines. Each organism will experience his (or her or its) own "peaks" and "valleys" of relative salience (von Uexkull, 1934). This distribution of salience guides our actions, facilitating a species- and individually specific engagement with the most behaviorally relevant aspects of the world around. And because that engagement is selective, understanding of what is seen is also selective: what you see is what you look for (be it flower, team-mate, or daughter).

In the case of typically developing human infants, a good deal is known about their landscape of relative visual salience. Within the first hours of life, typically developing babies attend preferentially to people. They distinguish and prefer their own mother's voice to that of an unknown woman, but prefer the sound of even an unknown woman's voice to that of silence (DeCasper & Fifer, 1980). Human newborns preferentially fixate on faces gazing at them rather than faces looking away (Farroni, Csibra, Simion, & Johnson, 2002), and by 3 months (if not before) they are drawn to the eye region when viewing speaking faces (Haith, Bergman, & Moore, 1977). Infants are also capable of imitating some facial gestures of a person (Meltzoff & Moore, 1977) and by 18 months will imitate more complex behaviors when performed by a person but not when performed by a mechanical device (Meltzoff, 1995). This evidence suggests that typically developing children engage with social and physical aspects of the world differentially, and that they have a predisposition to engage with the social aspects of the world around them: the social dimension is what is highly behaviorally salient and, consequently, is what commands the greatest portion of the typically developing child's attention.

For toddlers with autism, the case is less clear. Children with autism are most often diagnosed at later stages of childhood (Volkmar, Chawarska, & Klin, 2005); as a result, little experimental evidence is available on infants and toddlers with autism spectrum disorders. Despite that lack of experimental measures, clinical evidence—in the form of retrospective (Volkmar, Stier, & Cohen, 1985) and prospective studies (Zwaigenbaum et al., 2005), as well in analyses of home movies made prior to diagnosis—reveals signs of social abnormalities in the first year of life (see Maestro and Muratori's work in Chapter 9 for relevant current work and a thorough review of past studies using home movies). By definition, autism is a disorder marked by deficits in social interaction, deficits in communication, and the presence of repetitive behaviors and restricted interests lacking in social exchange value (American Psychological Association, 2000; Volkmar, Paul, Klin, & Cohen, 2005). In analyses of parents' home movies, the most robust markers for early diagnosis of children with autism center on disruptions of typical engagement with the social world such as reduced interaction with and looking at others (Osterling, Dawson, & Munson, 2002; Werner, Dawson, Osterling, & Dinno, 2000), failure to respond to the calling of one's own name, diminished eye contact, and inability to join in imitative games and reciprocal vocalizations (Dawson, Osterling, Meltzoff, & Kuhl, 2000; Klin, 1991, 1992). From this evidence, a predisposition to preferentially engage with the social world seems absent in children with autism, and the landscape of relative salience—what attracts the attention of these children instead—seems fundamentally altered.

Visual Salience in Autism

In previous research, we explored these alterations in visual salience through the use of eye-tracking technology during naturalistic viewing. Our methods have been driven by an effort to capitalize on the marked discrepancy in performance of individuals with autism spectrum disorders (ASD) in structured/explicit experiments (in which their performance is better) vs. naturalistic/spontaneous experiments (in which their performance reveals greater disability). In several conceptual and empirical papers (Klin, 2000; Klin, Schultz, & Cohen, 2000; Klin, Jones, Schultz, Volkmar, & Cohen, 2002a; Klin, Jones, Schultz, & Volkmar, 2003) we showed that there is a large discrepancy between the performance of individuals with ASD in these two contexts. The effort to emulate natural social situations in the laboratory comes from the knowledge that, in real life, individuals with ASD show the greatest disability when there is no explicit task to solve nor any predefined course of action to take (Klin et al., 2000). Clinically, this is reflected in discrepancies between intellectual capacity and real-life social adaptation. Individuals with ASD with normative IQs still exhibit extreme delays in adaptive functioning. For example, a group of individuals with ASD ranging in age from 8 to 18 years, with a mean verbal IQ of 104.7 (SD = 21.3), had a level of adaptive functioning (in the social domain of the Vineland Adaptive Behavior Scales) corresponding to a standard score of 52.0 (SD = 11.5) and an age equivalent score of 4.5 years (SD = 1.4) (Klin et al., 2007; also Saulnier & Klin, 2007). Taking this discrepancy into account is of critical importance both for understanding autism and

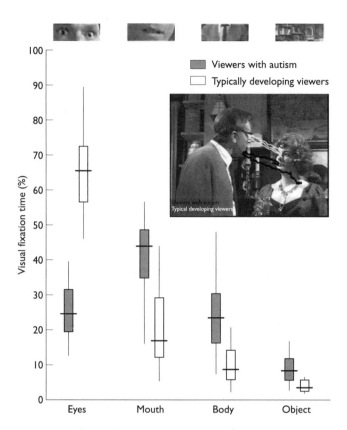

Figure 4.1 Percentage of visual fixation time in adolescents with autism watching natural-istic social situations.

for developing effective treatments. Experimental paradigms that measure social functioning in contexts that most closely resemble social demands in naturalistic situations can in this way be very useful.

Beginning with adolescents and young adults, we have explored spontaneous visual fixation patterns to scenes of social interaction as a means of quantifying altered social engagement in individuals with ASD. In studies of cognitively able individuals with autism and age- and verbal IQ-matched controls, we found marked differences in visual scanning of naturalistic social scenes (Klin et al., 2002a; Klin, Jones, Schultz, Volkmar, & Cohen, 2002b). The experimental paradigm involved having the participants view video clips of complex social situations (Figure 4.1, inset) while wearing a non-invasive eye-tracking device that measured visual scanning and fixations. The fixation data were quantified in terms of percentage of viewing time spent on different areas of the social scenes. The scheme for coding fixation data consisted of four clearly delineated regions-of-interest: eyes, mouth, body, and object. Results revealed significant between-group differences for all viewing areas of interest (Figure 4.1). Relative to age- and verbal IQ-matched controls, individuals with autism focused two times less on the eye region of faces (ASD: 24.6% (8.1) vs. TD: 65.4% (12.8), $p<.000$); two times more on the mouth region of faces (ASD: 41.2% (14.9) vs. TD: 21.2% (12.1), $p<.000$); two times more on the body region (ASD: 24.6% (12.4) vs. TD: 9.7% (5.7), $p<.000$); and two times more on the object region (ASD: 9.6% (6.5) vs. TD: 3.7% (2.4), $p<.003$). Effect size was greatest for fixation on the eye region of faces making it the best predictor of autism group membership (Cohen's $d = 3.19$; for comparison, an effect size of $d = 2$ is at the 97.7th percentile and corresponds to 81.1% segregation of compared samples).

These visual fixation data for adolescents with autism present a direct contrast to the sensitivities and visual preferences toward conspecifics which are evident in typical development from the first months of life. In addition, the presence of analogous visual preferences in newborn chimpanzees (Myowa-Yamakoshi, Tomonaga, Tanaka, & Matsuzawa, 2003) suggests that such sensitivities are highly conserved mechanisms in evolution. Likewise, for humans and for chimpanzees, the importance of mutual gaze both for early social development (Bard et al., 2005; Brooks & Meltzoff, 2002; Trevarthen & Aitken, 2001; van Lawick-Goodall, 1968) and for social adaptation throughout the lifespan (Emery, 2000; Kampe, Frith, Dolan, & Frith, 2001; de Waal, 2003) indicates that fixation on the eyes of others plays a critical role in socialization. Our results lend further support to the notion that these mechanisms are derailed in individuals with autism.

The Developmental Course of Altered Visual Salience

To explore the developmental course of our initial results, we have begun eye-tracking studies of toddlers with autism spectrum disorders. An observation from the case of a 15-month-old girl (called Helen for the purpose of this chapter) is particularly relevant here (Klin et al., 2004). Helen's older brother had been diagnosed with autism some 20 months before. On the day of her evaluation at 15 months, Helen toddled into the playroom behind her father. She engaged enthusiastically with simple cause-and-effect toys but was oblivious to the presence of the clinical examiner. Repeated attempts to engage the child through exaggerated facial gestures and inflected vocalizations—from a distance as close as two inches from her face—did not alter her behavior.

What do Helen's actions reveal about relative salience in the eyes of a 15-month-old child with autism? If a clinical examiner, talking to the child and entreating a response, inches from the child's face, fails to engage her attention, we might be forced to wonder what instead, if anything at all, is salient to this child. In an especially telling incident, despite not looking at the examiner, Helen turned around and, spotting a small piece of candy 5 feet away on the carpet, made her way immediately toward it. Helen thus demonstrated that her visual skills were competent enough to see a small speck of contrast color (on a multi-colored carpet) at a distance. A small red speck captured her attention while a person did not. Thus at 15 months, and despite the fact that she had no cognitive delays in her non-verbal functioning, Helen was not displaying sociability known to be present in very young babies.

After these clinical observations of altered salience, we presented Helen with an experimental paradigm to explore how she might interpret the visual world at large (Klin & Jones, in press). Helen was shown eight-point-light animations (Allison, Puce, & McCarthy, 2000; Johansson, 1973), each with an actor emulating social experiences (e.g., playing peek-a-boo or singing a nursery rhyme) and lasting approximately 30 seconds. The capacity for recognizing this type of point-light animation as an exemplar of "biological motion" (e.g., distinguishing moving dots depicting a walking person from dots moving randomly) has been shown in 3-month-old typical infants (Fox & McDaniel, 1982). The animations appeared on a computer screen with an upright point-light figure on one half of the screen and an inverted (or upside-down) figure on the other (inverting the figure was used to disrupt the perception of its movements as human action; Pavlova & Sokolov, 2000; Sumi, 1984). Presentation was counterbalanced to pre-empt side bias. Each animation was accompanied by the vocal audio track of the social event (e.g., a caregiver playing "peek-a-boo").

While watching these animations, evidence for mental representation of a given social action was measured as a function of the child's viewing patterns: preferential looking toward the upright figure offered evidence of the matching of sound effects with a mental template elicited by the animation (Klin et al., 2003). Helen's pattern of preferential looking was measured with eye-tracking technology. To determine viewing preferences significantly different from chance, we modeled total viewing time as a distribution with two outcomes (looking at the upright or looking at the inverted figure). For the number of "trials" (frames of viewing time) presented, results between 47% and 53% should be considered random viewing at a probability level of $p<.01$.

When summed across all animations, Helen spent 52.8% and 47.2% on the upright and inverted animations, respectively; her preferential viewing results were random. Her viewing evidenced no matching of the social sounds she heard with the ambiguous point-light animations she watched. Instead, she looked randomly back and forth between the upright and the inverted figures. For comparison purposes, a typically developing 15-month-old toddler matched on non-verbal mental age (NVMA) and a typically developing 9-month-old baby matched on verbal age (VMA) completed the same procedure. The NVMA- and the VMA-matched children both showed visual preference for upright relative to inverted animations as follows: 66.1% vs. 33.9% for the NVMA child and 58.8% vs. 41.2% for the VMA child.

The results of viewing all the animations, however, revealed only part of the story. For Helen, one particular animation yielded unusual, outlier results: in that animation, Helen spent 93.9% on the upright figure vs. only 6.1% on the inverted one. Removal of this outlier animation actually made her results "more" random: 48.6% upright vs. 51.4% inverted across all remaining animations. Closer inspection of the outlier animation indicated an interesting experimental confound. That particular animation differed from all others in one way. The animation in question, in which an adult plays "pat-a-cake," provided a physical contingency alongside the social event: points of light colliding on-screen (the "hands" coming together) were accompanied by synchronous sounds (the clapping). In all of the other animations, sounds (primarily speech) occurred contextually rather than as a direct physical consequence of the movement of the point-lights.

During the pat-a-cake animation, Helen's patterns of looking indicate that she was acutely sensitive to the audiovisual synchrony. When watching this animation, she could have looked anywhere: at the inverted figure, at any location on the upright figure, or at the exact location on the upright figure where the physical contingency occurred. The video results attest to the latter. After the onset of clapping in the animation, Helen looked at the exact location where the clapping occurs. Her sensitivity to this audiovisual synchrony shows a rather advanced capacity for cross-modal matching and yet contrasts markedly with her inability to match social contingencies in the other animations. This discrepancy is not unlike her discrepant attention, described earlier, to the clinical examiner vs. a small piece of candy on the carpet. In that case, Helen was sensitive to the small visual signal distinguishing an object on a patterned carpet but insensitive to a visual signal in the social domain (changes in the expression of the clinical examiner).

Following Helen's results when watching the point-light animations, we hypothesized that the dichotomy between her attention to social vs. physical contingencies might also be reflected in atypical visual fixation patterns when looking at people. Typical infants prefer to focus on the eye region of the face from at least the age of 3 months (Haith et al., 1977), consistent with the idea that the eyes most clearly convey social-affective contingencies (Emery, 2000). But where would a child look if, rather than paying attention to social-affective contingencies, she were paying attention to physical contingencies? The landscape of relative salience for such a child should shift toward the area with greatest cross-modal physical contingency: the mouth region, where lip movements and speech sounds come together.

Helen was presented with ten video scenes lasting approximately 20 seconds each. Each scene presented full-screen video and an accompanying audio track showing a female actor playing the role of caregiver: looking directly into the camera at the viewer and entreating the toddler with childhood games (playing peek-a-boo, singing a nursery rhyme, etc.). Visual fixation patterns were measured with eye-tracking technology. On-screen fixations were coded relative to four regions of interest: eyes, mouth, body, and object. The same video scenes were also presented to NVMA- and VMA-matched typically developing children.

In comparison with both these children, Helen, the toddler with autism, showed an overriding preference for looking at the mouth region rather than the eye region of the face. Interestingly, this differed from both the child matched on chronological age and the child matched on verbal abilities. While some fixation on the mouth region was expected in the non-verbal mental age-matched control (due to speech acquisition; Kuhl & Meltzoff, 1982), Helen—despite her delay in language—nevertheless spent far more time looking at the mouth (more than 60% of visual fixation time vs. less than 40% for the NVMA-matched child). The child matched to Helen on language ability (VMA-matched) looked at the mouth of the caregivers less than one-tenth of the time that Helen did. Likewise, in comparison with the NVMA-matched child, Helen spent less than one third of that child's time looking at the eyes, and less than one fourth the looking time on eyes of the VMA-matched child.

These results lend credence to the idea that relative salience in Helen's eyes is very different: she seems to see a world in which physical events—clapping sounds and colliding balls, moving lips and synchronous sounds—are far more salient than strong social cues (the expressive and entreating eye-gaze of a caregiver or a clinical examiner trying to capture her attention). These results suggest that Helen may be watching engaging faces as though they are only a collection of consonant physical properties. A conjecture stemming from these results is that this child with autism may, in effect, be watching a face without seeing a person: she may look at the world around her in terms of its physical causality without fully comprehending the social being behind those physical properties. This would have clear and profound implications for development. It would imply that from an early age, this child's mind would specialize on physical contingencies rather than on social beings. Consequently, it would suggest that later in life her brain and her behavior will also show equally atypical specialization.

While the information presented above is the case of a single individual, it points to interesting directions for future research. In the present chapter, we will make an effort to bridge these initial results from a single toddler with autism to related studies of adolescents and adults by addressing three questions. First, in later life, when looking at a complex visual and social environment, what do individuals with autism find salient? Second, how do individuals with autism make sense of the aspects of the environment with which they do engage? And third, are there any markers of altered relative salience as reflected in the functional specialization of neural systems in individuals with autism?

Salience and Visual Engagement

In one set of studies, adolescents and adults with autism watched scenes of complex social interaction while we recorded their visual fixations and saccades in our eye-tracking laboratory (Klin et al., 2002a; 2002b). As noted above, the individuals with autism showed marked differences in their preferences for looking at the eyes and mouths of on-screen characters, showing a strong preference for looking at the mouth and not the eyes, and also a strong preference for looking at seemingly random objects in the background of the scenes.

These visual fixation patterns revealed cases in which the landscape of relative salience was starkly different between individuals with autism and typically developing viewers. Figure 4.2 shows still images from a 13.5-second conversation in which two characters speak to an off-screen listener.

The young man speaks in frames 1 and 2, while his wife speaks thereafter. The viewer with autism (black crosses) focuses on the speakers' mouths and does not monitor the reactions of the non-speaker. In contrast, for the typically developing viewer, the non-speaker is highly salient during this scene; shifting focus in frames 3, 4, 6, and 8 is critical for understanding the social context. In those frames, the actor's avoidant, downcast eyes show his discomfort and unease. These reactions—his grudging, reluctant acceptance of his wife's storytelling and his embarrassment with her and the way she is acting—tell far more about the relationship of these two people and the meaning of this scene than the actual story the woman is telling. Following the eye-tracking path of the viewer with autism, it is very likely that he was unaware of much of the social meaning of this episode. In contrast, the typical viewer (white crosses) shifted focus six times while watching this conversation, as compared to one shift on the part of the viewer with autism. It is likely that the typical viewer had a fuller appreciation of the social meaning of this scene as a result of his engagement. What a viewer engages with will impact what that viewer subsequently understands.

A related example is shown in Figure 4.3, when competing social and physical cues were presented simultaneously.

What is the relative salience of these cues for each of the two viewers? The figure

Figure 4.2 Visual salience when observing a social situation. Black crosses, viewer with autism. White crosses, typically developing viewer

Figure 4.3 Relative salience of social vs. physical cues. Black crosses and trajectory, viewer with autism. White crosses and trajectory, typically developing viewer.

plots a scene in which a young woman is turning back and forth between two men, her face revealing dismay. The camera pans to the left (in anticipation of the young man's appearance on-screen). Two attentional cues compete: one is a social cue, the emotional expression on the woman's face; the other is a physical cue, the movement of the camera. The figure shows the point of fixation of both viewers in relation to the emotional reactions of the actors and the physical motion of the camera. The viewer with autism (black crosses) is exclusively sensitive to the physical cue, moving fast to the left (following the leading edge of the camera's movement) without glancing at the young woman's eyes. In contrast, the typical viewer (white crosses) is fixated on the woman's emotional expressions: as her head moves back and forth, the typical viewer disregards the camera shift to instead follow the woman's display of emotion. These split-second reactions to relative salience, gathering visual information from the woman's facial expression or from the man's shoulder (where the gaze of the viewer with autism falls), will naturally have an impact on the way each of these individuals interprets what was seen. The effect of these actions will also cycle onwards: what was salient will effect the viewer's interpretation, and the viewer's interpretation will later affect what is deemed salient.

Altered Salience and Its Impact on Understanding

Like the point-light biological motion stimuli shown to Helen, another focus of our past research has involved the use of experimental paradigms that measure viewers' predispositions to interpret ambiguous visual information as having either social or physical underlying causation. In a study of high-functioning adolescents with autism spectrum disorders (Klin, 2000) we demonstrated these individuals' failure to spontaneously view ambiguous animations as human social interaction. Rather than describe a series of animations in terms of social relationships—as their typical, matched peers did—individuals with ASD made frequent attributions of physical causation. In this study, adolescents and adults with autism were presented with the famous Heider and Simmel (1944) cartoon animation in which geometric forms move and act like humans. Typical viewers recognize the social nature of the cartoon and, when asked for an open-ended description of the events, provide narratives that reveal social attributions: typical viewers' descriptions of the event focus on the social relationships portrayed there, for example, describing one "actor" in the geometric animation as a bully, or another as a friend.

In contrast, individuals with autism have difficulty making these attributions (Klin, 2000). Individuals with autism tend to instead make attributions of physical causation. For example, a 38-year-old man with autism, with a high normative IQ, attributed the actions in the Heider and Simmel cartoon to physical forces:

> [The cartoon] starts when a small equilateral triangle breaks out of a square. A small sphere or circle appears and slides down the broken rectangle. The triangles were either equilateral or isosceles. Later the small, I think, isosceles triangle and sphere bounce around each other, maybe because of a magnetic field . . .

The actions of the "actors" are here described in entirely concrete, physical terms.

To test the domain specificity of these results, we created a second animation. This animation involved a "physical attribution task" (in contrast to the social attribution task implicit in the other cartoon) (Klin & Jones, 2006). The physical attribution task was an animation that also depicted geometric shapes. This time, however, rather than depicting the shapes interacting with one another socially, the animation showed the launch of a rocket into space, its lift-off and orbit governed entirely by physical laws of motion. When presented with both this new animation and with the old animation (the social attribution task), a second group of individuals with autism had similar difficulties with social attributions. And yet, on the physical attribution task, these individuals with autism evidenced equal and sometimes superior ability in comparison with typical controls. When looking at the physical attribution task, for instance, the viewer with autism who described the social animation in terms of magnetic forces described the physical animation as follows:

> The rocket is being launched and is in preliminary orbit around the earth, winding around the moon at the appropriate distance so that the satellite can be released. The satellite was launched from the rocket, and it actually landed on the moon. The satellite was actually more like a lunar module . . .

This individual showed an excellent ability to attribute physical meaning to ambiguous visual stimuli, an ability not commensurate with his failure to make social attributions.

From birds to humans, this ability—to discern biological motion from other forms of movement in nature—is critical for survival, so that one can move toward (approach, hunt) or away from (flee, escape) others (Oram & Perrett, 1994; Regolin, Tommasi, & Vallortigara, 2000). Survival in the wild is linked with social adaptation in humans, in that the neural substrate for the perception of biological motion and for the perception of gaze direction and facial expressions, among other social cues, coincide (Allison et al., 2000; Grossman et al., 2000). Also, the ability to detect approaching predators and predict their future actions has been evolutionarily linked to the emergence of the capacity to attribute intentions and motivations to other people (Blakemore & Decety, 2001; Frith & Frith, 1999). Naturally, the results of the studies above suggest that these predispositions may be fundamentally altered in individuals with autism.

Salience and Neural Specialization

Taken together, the observations above suggest that growing up in a landscape of altered salience may lead a person to alternate interpretations of what he or she sees. A related hypothesis is that, for a child like Helen, living in such a world may alter not only the formation of her mind (her cognitive inferences about the world) but also the functional organization of her brain. This prediction is supported by a series of functional neuroimaging studies by Robert Schultz and colleagues (Grelotti et al., 2005; Schultz et al., 2000). In one functional magnetic resonance imaging (fMRI) study, higher-functioning adolescents and adults with autism were presented with pictures of faces and objects, and their patterns of brain activation were compared with those of controls. In contrast to controls—for whom face processing was associated with activation of the lateral fusiform gyrus (a mid-temporal structure specializing in face recognition, Kanwisher, McDermott, & Chun, 1997; and also in perceptual expertise, Gauthier, Tarr, Anderson, Skudlarski, & Gore, 1999)—in individuals with autism face recognition was associated with increased activation of inferior temporal gyrus structures, an activation pattern that was obtained for controls when the controls were processing objects. The conclusion from this study was that individuals with autism processed faces in a manner that was similar neurofunctionally to the way in which typically developing individuals process objects. One interpretation of these results is that they offer an example of the effects of growing up in an environment of altered salience, in which neural specialization leads to a point where faces are seen as little different from the objects used as control stimuli. Rather than developing perceptual expertise for faces, as in typical development, individuals with autism may instead direct their attention elsewhere and consequently develop alternate islets of relative perceptual strengths (e.g., as a special interest or even, in some cases, as a savant skill; Hermelin, 2001; Thioux, Stark, Klaiman, & Schultz, 2006).

The study by Schultz and colleagues (2000), and subsequent studies that corroborated the reported findings of hypoactivation of the fusiform gyrus to face stimuli, generated some speculation that this brain tissue could be at fault in autism and could in fact play a causative role in the syndrome. This idea, however, would run counter to the hypothesis that the brain crystallizes the repeated experiences of the person; that is, counter to the idea that because typical individuals experience, seek, recognize, run away from, and contemplate so many faces in the course of development, activity in the fusiform gyrus reflects that experience and the neural tissue develops its specialization as a consequence thereof. What then is the developmental consequence for infants with autism who grow up in a world of altered relative salience? To explore this question, David Grelotti and colleagues

(2005) conducted an intensive study with one higher-functioning young adult with autism whose main love in life is Digimon characters, which are cartoon figures that appear in computer and video games, TV shows, and movies. This individual was presented with three kinds of stimuli—faces, objects, and Digimon characters—and patterns of brain activation were compared with controls. As expected, the pattern of increased fusiform activity, evidenced in typically developing individuals, was not present in this boy with autism when he viewed faces or objects. But when this boy looked at pictures of the Digimon characters, there was strong activation of the fusiform and associated limbic structures. In this case, it seemed clear that this individual's fusiform and associated circuitry were functioning, but that they had specialized to something other than faces. This specialization can be seen as a reflection of life lived along an alternate course of relative salience, one populated with Digimon characters rather than by people and social interaction.

Implications for Further Study

Understanding of how social and emotional interaction is derailed in autism may benefit from further exploration of what guides the landscape of relative salience in typical development. In particular it would be helpful to understand what draws the focus of typically developing newborns and infants to the eyes of others, and what neural reward systems reinforce that focus so that this interaction in turn becomes a self-reinforcing mechanism for learning about the world. Such a system would seem to be very basic and highly phylogenetically conserved. And while the research mentioned above has primarily utilized the study of visual interaction with the world, one could expect that in autism the landscape of relative salience may be altered across all sensory domains. For children with autism, mapping that terrain of relative salience during the first years of life will hopefully provide an entry point into understanding how such basic mechanisms of socialization become disrupted.

Integration Section

Many of the observations presented above can be seen to overlap with results mentioned in other chapters in this book. For both clinical work and research, a pressing need is to make those points of overlap—research findings which are similar despite different methodological approaches, theoretical models which may be distinct but are hardly mutually exclusive—into sites of active integration. As the theme of this book suggests, alternate approaches need to be knitted together in order to better understand the spectrum of autism and ultimately to produce practicable results which can span the distances that currently exist between neurocognitive, clinical, and educational disciplines.

Some areas of specific overlap with the work in this chapter concern the developmental nature of autism. As in Maestro and Muratori's work in Chapter 9, our own work explores mechanisms of socialization which emerge early in the life of the child. By studying home videos, Maestro and Muratori provide a glimpse into the development of social vs. non-social attention in the first year of life. Interestingly, our own case study results may offer a complementary interpretation of the social attention findings in the 12-month-old children with autism studied by Maestro and Muratori. Their work finds that toddlers with autism exhibit less social attention than typically developing peers at 6 months of age but the same amount of non-social attention. By 12 months of age, the toddlers with autism exhibit an equal amount of social attention but show increased non-social attention. While it may seem surprising that the toddlers with autism exhibit equal social attention at 12 months of age, our own work might call into question what that "social" attention really is: are the toddlers with autism perceiving the same social phenomena as their peers? Or, instead, might they be interacting with the social environment in non-social terms? At both time points, Maestro and Muratori's data can be seen as suggesting an altered landscape of relative salience: at 6 months, that landscape is essentially flat for children with autism, having little distinction between the social and the non-social. By 12 months, engagement with the environment has increased, but non-social attention exceeds social attention. Lacking the structure which an inherent sense of social salience provides, it may that be that children with autism spend much of their first year struggling to make sense of an exceedingly complicated world, a chaotic clutter of light and sound. If the non-social and social succeed equally in gaining attention at 6 months of age, by 12 months these same children may be paying attention largely to those parts of the environment which are most stable and concrete, following physical contingencies in an effort to structure their everyday, and even engaging with people in ways which are not necessarily conventionally social. Both retrospective and also prospective studies of children with autism will be extremely important in pursuing these hypotheses. Maestro and Muratori are already working to fill the gap in knowledge of the earliest years of development in children with autism.

A second area of overlap with our work and other results in this volume concerns the possible consequences of early developmental differences on neural functioning later in life. In Chapter 2, Wicker provides a very interesting account of recent neuroimaging studies in autism. Two points of convergence between that work and our own relate to (1) the need for ecological validity in experimental paradigms exploring the social brain and social development, and (2) the notion

of altered patterns of neural activity in individuals with autism which may reflect
the use of compensatory strategies as well as neurofunctional endpoints of alternate developmental trajectories. Wicker makes a clear argument for ecological
validity, even insofar as the use of dynamic vs. static visual imagery is concerned.
Our own findings support the notion that the use of dynamic imagery may more
closely approximate real-life experience, providing researchers with a useful means
of testing social impairments and better understanding social cognition. The neuroimaging results described by Wicker also present an interesting comparison point
with the neuroimaging results recapped in this chapter. Although the research discussed in the present chapter focuses on differences in relative activation of the
fusiform gyrus, Wicker's results (which find no task-specific differences in activation there) find an intriguing pattern of altered functional connectivity: Wicker's
results suggest that in individuals with autism activity in the fusiform gyrus may
be unusually modulated either by or with activity in the primary visual areas and
activity in the right lateral prefrontal cortex (LPFC). This suggestion of a compensatory mechanism in individuals with autism which is more reliant on explicit
attentional modulation (via the LPFC) and on basic physical properties of the
experimental stimuli (from primary visual cortex and other low-level visual areas)
is compatible with much of the evidence cited in this chapter (in which alternate
experience of the world in physical rather than social terms cycles forward with
alternate neural specialization). Re-entrant inputs from the amygdala to the fusiform gyrus may also play a role in heightening the relative salience of some aspects
of the environment over others, so that a developmental cycle of relative salience,
preferential engagement, and increasing neural/cognitive specialization is tied at
root to basic motivation and reward circuits. The analyses of functional connectivity by Wicker challenges standard assumptions of easily localized differences
in regional activity and make one think instead of how the neural activity measured at one time point is really the result of a life of experiences impacting on brain
activity and growth as a whole. It will be especially exciting for future studies to
explore the developmental paths relating to these findings.

Finally, the work of Jones and Jordan (Chapter 14) reviews intervention research
in autism spectrum disorders and raises, in clearest terms, the need for further
integration: to bring intervention and research practices together for the benefit of
both. In relation to our research on altered salience in autism, the contribution of
Jordan and Jones forces us to consider (at least) two critical questions. First, do our
results offer any insights that might inform intervention efforts? And second, might
our methods have any utility for testing the efficacy of interventions? Relative to
the first question, observations of altered salience in autism, especially during early
and possibly critical periods in development, do suggest strategies for intervention.
But is there a way to alter the landscape of relative salience and to make socially

relevant aspects of the environment more salient to individuals with autism? One can easily imagine alterations to the physical salience of social stimuli, but in order for these to be useful, those newly salient social stimuli would have to be more than physically salient—they would have to be meaningful. As our own case study suggests (with possibly similar findings by Maestro and Muratori), it may not be enough to simply look at a person; the perceptual experience of seeing that person may nevertheless be different. An effective intervention to shift the landscape of relative salience would need to be fundamentally linked to reward drives, so that social interaction might find a motivational underpinning. Such an approach also poses obvious ethical questions. Relative salience is an individual as well as a phylogenetic phenomenon, and each one of us, ASD or not, sees the world in subtly different shades; we are better off collectively for those differences individually.

While considering shifts in the landscape of salience which, while respecting individual differences, might make daily life easier for individuals with ASD, a more immediate use of methods to measure relative salience might be in evaluating intervention strategies. Generalization has long been a key hurdle to intervention efficacy. Using visual scanning patterns or other measures of relative salience to analyze a child's implementation of newly acquired adaptive skills may reveal factors which may either limit or facilitate generalization. This kind of micro-analysis could also shed light on why some interventions are particularly effective for some children but offer little help to others. In addition, this is an excellent site for research into learning processes in children with autism. While our results suggest differences in visual salience for individuals with autism, key questions remain as to how those differences arise.

Overall, neurocognitive, clinical, and educational practices all stand to gain from integration. As is hopefully the case with Helen, the 15-month-old toddler with autism described above, unique viewpoints can at times offer important clues to larger questions. The unique viewpoints of different disciplines and approaches to autism, when brought together, will likely lead to even more beneficial results.

References

American Psychological Association. (1994). *Diagnostic and statistical manual of mental disorders* (4th ed.). Washington, DC: APA.

Allison, T., Puce, A., & McCarthy, G. (2000). Social perception from visual cues: Role of the STS region. *Trends in Cognitive Science, 4*, 267–278.

Bard, K. A., Costall, A., Myowa-Yamakoshi, M., Tomonaga, M., Tanaka, M., & Matsuzawa, T. (2005). Group differences in the mutual gaze of chimpanzees (Pan troglodytes). *Developmental Psychology, 41*(4), 616–624.

Blakemore, S.-J., & Decety, J. (2001). From the perception of action to the understanding of intention. *Nature Reviews Neuroscience, 2*, 561–567.

Brooks, R., & Meltzoff, A. N. (2002). The importance of eyes: How infants interpret adult looking behavior. *Developmental Psychology, 38*(6), 958–966.

Dawson, G., Osterling, J., Meltzoff, A., & Kuhl, P. (2000). Case study of the development of an infant with autism from birth to two years of age. *Journal of Applied Developmental Psychology, 21*(3), 299–313.

DeCasper, A. J., & Fifer, W. P. (1980). Of human bonding: Newborns prefer their mothers' voices. *Science, 208*(4448), 1174–1176.

de Waal, F. X. (2003). Darwin's legacy and the study of primate visual communication. *Annals of the New York Academy of Sciences, 1000,* 7–31.

Emery, N. J. (2000). The eyes have it: The neuroethology, function and evolution of social gaze. *Neuroscience and Biobehavioral Reviews, 24,* 581–604.

Farroni, T., Csibra, G., Simion, F., & Johnson, M. H. (2002). Eye contact detection in humans from birth. *Proceedings of the National Academy of Science USA., 99*(14), 9602–9605.

Fox, R., & McDaniel, C. (1982). The perception of biological motion by human infants. *Science, 218,* 486–487.

Frith, C. D., & Frith, U. (1999). Interacting minds: A biological basis. *Science, 286*(5445), 1692–1695.

Gauthier, I., Tarr, M., Anderson, A., Skudlarski, P., & Gore, J. (1999). Activation of the middle fusiform face area increases with expertise in recognizing novel objects. *Nature Neuroscience, 2,* 568–573.

Grelotti, D. J., Klin, A., Gauthier, I., Skudlarski, P., Cohen, D. J., Gore, J. C., et al. (2005). fMRI activation of the fusiform gyrus and amygdala to cartoon characters but not to faces in a boy with autism. *Neuropsychologia, 43*(3), 373–385.

Grossman, E., Donnelly, M., Price, R., Pickens, D., Morgan, V., Neighbor, G., et al. (2000). Brain areas involved in perception of biological motion. *Journal of Cognitive Neuroscience, 12*(5), 711–720.

Haith, M. M., Bergman, T., & Moore, M. J. (1977). Eye contact and face scanning in early infancy. *Science, 198*(4319), 853–855.

Heider, F., & Simmel, M. (1944). An experimental study of apparent behavior. *The American Journal of Psychology, 57*(2), 243–259.

Hermelin, B. (2001). *Bright splinters of the mind: A personal story of research with autistics savant.* London: Jessica Kingsley Publishers, Ltd.

Johansson, G. (1973). Visual perception of biological motion and a model for its analysis. *Perception and Psychophysics, 14,* 201–211.

Kampe, K. K. W., Frith, C. D., Dolan, R. J., & Frith, U. (2001). Reward value of attractiveness and gaze. *Nature, 413*(6856), 589–590.

Kanwisher, N., McDermott, J., & Chun, M. (1997). The fusiform face area: A module in human extrastriate cortex specialized for face perception. *Journal of Neuroscience, 17,* 4302–4311.

Klin, A. (1991). Young autistic children's listening preferences in regard to speech: A possible characterization of the symptom of social withdrawal. *Journal of Autism and Developmental Disorders, 21*(1), 29–42.

Klin, A. (1992). Listening preferences in regard to speech in four children with developmental disabilities. *Journal of Child Psychology and Psychiatry, 33*(4), 763–769.

Klin, A. (2000). Attributing social meaning to ambiguous visual stimuli in higher functioning autism and Asperger syndrome: The Social Attribution Task. *Journal of Child Psychology and Psychiatry, 41*, 831–846.

Klin, A., Chawarska, K., Paul, R., Rubin, E., Morgan, T., Wiesner, L., et al. (2004). Autism in
a 15-month-old child. *American Journal of Psychiatry, 161*(11), 1–8.

Klin, A., & Jones, W. (2006). Attributing social and physical meaning to ambiguous visual
displays in individuals with higher functioning autism spectrum disorders. *Brain and
Cognition, 61*, 40–53.

Klin, A., & Jones, W. (in press). Altered face scanning and impaired recognition of biological motion in a 15-month-old with autism. *Developmental Science.*

Klin, A., Jones, W., Schultz, R., & Volkmar, F. (2003). The enactive mind—from actions to
cognition: Lessons from autism. *Philosophical Transactions of the Royal Society, Biological Sciences, 358*, 345–360.

Klin, A., Jones, W., Schultz, R., Volkmar, F., & Cohen, D. (2002a). Defining and quantifying
the social phenotype in autism. *American Journal of Psychiatry, 159*(6), 895–908.

Klin, A., Jones, W., Schultz, R., Volkmar, F., & Cohen, D. (2002b). Visual fixation patterns
during viewing of naturalistic social situations as predictors of social competence in
individuals with autism. *Archives of General Psychiatry, 59*(9), 809–816.

Klin, A., Saulnier, C. A., Sparrow, S. S., Cicchetti, D. V., Volkmar, F. R., & Lord, C. (2007).
Social and communication abilities and disabilities in higher functioning individuals
with autism spectrum disorders: the Vineland and the ADOS. *Journal of Autism and
Developmental Disorders, 37*(4), 748–759.

Klin, A., Schultz, R., & Cohen, D. (2000). Theory of mind in action: Developmental perspectives on social neuroscience. In S. Baron-Cohen, H. Tager-Flusberg, & D. Cohen
(Eds.), *Understanding other minds: Perspectives from developmental neuroscience* (2nd
ed., pp. 357–388). Oxford, UK: Oxford University Press.

Kuhl, P. K., & Meltzoff, A. N. (1982). The bimodal perception of speech in infancy. *Science,
218*, 1138–1141.

Meltzoff, A. M., 1995. Understanding the intentions of others: Re-enactments of intended
acts by 18-month-old children. *Developmental Psychology, 31*, 838–850.

Meltzoff, A. N., & Moore, M. K. (1977). Imitation of facial and manual gestures by human
neonates. *Science, 198*, 75–78.

Myowa-Yamakoshi, M., Tomonaga, M., Tanaka, M., & Matsuzawa, T. (2003). Preference for
human direct gaze in infant chimpanzees (Pan troglodytes). *Cognition, 89*, 53–64.

Oram, M. W., & Perrett, D. I. (1994). Response of anterior superior temporal polysensory
(STPa) neurons to "biological motion" stimuli. *Journal of Cognitive Neuroscience, 6*(2),
99–116.

Osterling, J. A., Dawson, G., & Munson, J. A. (2002). Early recognition of 1-year-old infants
with autism spectrum disorder versus mental retardation. *Development and Psychopathology, 14*(2), 239–251.

Pavlova, M., & Sokolov, A. (2000). Orientation specificity in biological motion perception.
Perception and Psychophysics, 62(5), 889–899.

Regolin, L., Tommasi, L., & Vallortigara, G. (2000). Visual perception of biological motion in newly hatched chicks as revealed by an imprinting procedure. *Animal Cognition*, *3*(1), 53–60.

Saulnier, C. A., & Klin, A. (2007). Brief report: Social and communication abilities and disabilities in higher functioning individuals with autism and Asperger syndrome. *Journal of Autism and Developmental Disorders*, *37*(4), 788–793.

Schultz, R. T., Gauthier, I., Klin, A., Fulbright, R., Anderson, A., Volkmar, F. R., et al. (2000). Abnormal ventral temporal cortical activity among individuals with autism and Asperger syndrome during face discrimination. *Archives of General Psychiatry*, *57*, 331–340.

Sumi, S. (1984). Upside down presentation of the Johannson moving light spot pattern. *Perception*, *13*, 283–286.

Thioux, M., Stark, D. E., Klaiman, C., & Schultz, R. T. (2006). The day of the week when you were born in 700 ms: Calendar computation in an autistic savant. *Journal of Experimental Psychology: Human Perception and Performance*, *32*(5), 1155–1168.

Trevarthen, C., & Aitken, K. J. (2001). Infant intersubjectivity: Research, theory, and clinical application. *Journal of Child Psychology and Psychiatry*, *42*(1), 3–48.

van Lawick-Goodall, J. (1968). The behaviour of free-living chimpanzees of the Gombe Stream Nature Reserve. *Animal Behavior Monographs*, *1*, 161–311.

Volkmar, F. R., Chawarska, K., & Klin, A. (2005). Autism in infancy and early childhood. *Annual Review of Psychology*, *56*, 315–336.

Volkmar, F. R., Paul, R., Klin, A., & Cohen, D. (2005). *Handbook of autism and pervasive developmental disorders*. New York: John Wiley & Sons, Inc.

Volkmar, F. R., Stier, D. M., Cohen, D. J. (1985). Age of recognition of Pervasive Developmental Disorder. *American Journal of Psychiatry*, *142*, 1450–1452.

Von Uexkull, J. (1934). A stroll through the worlds of animals and men. In C. Schiller (Ed.), *Instinctive behavior* (pp. 5–80). New York: International Universities Press.

Werner, E., Dawson, G., Osterling, J., & Dinno, H. (2000). Recognition of autism spectrum disorder before one year of age: A retrospective study based on home videotapes. *Journal of Autism and Developmental Disorders*, *30*, 157–162.

Zwaibengaum, L., Bryson, S., Rogers, T., Roberts, W., Brian, J., & Szatmari, P. (2005). Behavioral manifestations of autism in the first year of life. *International Journal of Developmental Neuroscience*, *23*, 143–152.

5

Abnormalities in "Cultural Knowledge" in Autism Spectrum Disorders

A Link Between Behavior and Cognition?

Eva Loth

Introduction

In *An anthropologist on Mars*, Oliver Sacks (1995) recounted a conversation with Temple Grandin, a talented livestock scientist with high-functioning autism. In the following extract, he asked her to reflect upon her social difficulties.

> What is it, then, I pressed her further, that goes on between normal people, from which she feels herself excluded? It has to do, she has inferred, with an implicit knowledge of social conventions and codes, of cultural presuppositions of every sort. This implicit knowledge, which every normal person accumulates and generates through life on the basis of experiences and encounters with others, Temple seems to be largely devoid of. Lacking it, she has instead to "compute" others' intentions and states of mind, to try and make algorithmic, explicit, what for the rest of us is second nature. She herself, she infers, may never have had the normal social experience from which a normal social knowledge is constructed.

Since autism was first identified (Asperger, 1944; Kanner, 1943), this complex and pervasive developmental disorder has been defined based on a profile of behavioral abnormalities. Deficits in social understanding and interaction are most characteristic and defining for individuals with autism, sometimes, as in the case of Professor Grandin, despite intact or even superior intellectual abilities. In addition, successful adaptation is often impeded by a host of repetitive behaviors, such as the need to impose a strict and inflexible order on their own and others' daily routine activities. As a neurodevelopmental brain disorder with a high genetic heritability, autism is being studied at the genetic, neurobiological, neuropsychological, and cognitive levels.

Over the past decades, a central goal for cognitive research has been to identify abnormalities in cognitive functions that are specific and universal to autism. A number of carefully controlled studies have revealed deficits or differences in several cognitive or neuropsychological faculties, in particular in theory of mind (see Baron-Cohen, Tager-Flusberg, & Cohen, 2000, for a review), in executive functions (see Hill, 2004, for a review), and in central coherence (see Happé, 1999 and Happé & Frith, 2006 for reviews; López, Chapter 6). However, more recent studies began to cast doubt on whether impairments or differences in any of these cognitive skills characterize *all* individuals with an autistic condition at *all* stages in development. The notion of individual differences in cognitive profile is in principle compatible with the vast heterogeneity of the behavioral phenotype of Autism Spectrum Disorders (ASD). However, the extent to which severity of abnormalities at the cognitive level can actually predict qualitative or quantitative differences at the behavioral level—which is an important and perhaps *the* essential requirement to inform clinical practice—has been found to be relatively weak or remains untested. For example, while the majority of individuals with autism (who also have mild intellectual disabilities) are impaired in their ability to infer mental states, many individuals with high-functioning autism or Asperger syndrome (with intellectual abilities in the normal range) succeed on relatively complex theory of mind tasks in experimental situations (Bowler, 1992; Dahlgren & Trillingsgaard, 1996) and can, like Professor Grandin, converse about mental states. If theory of mind impairments were the underlying reason for social and communication deficits, as originally proposed, then this sub-group should be more successful in adapting to real-life social demands. This does not seem to be the case. Indeed, as Sack's extract illustrates, for these intelligent individuals, difficulties with open-ended social situations remain a central problem. To address this question, one fruitful recent line of research has moved to study social-perceptual and social-motivational differences. Findings from behavioral and neuroimaging studies show that many cognitively able individuals with ASD have difficulties in attending and responding to subtle social cues or in reading others' facial expressions of emotions, skills which are important to keep track of the to-ings and fro-ings of (often fast-paced) social interactions (Hobson, Ousten, & Lee, 1988; Klin et al., 1999; Klin, Jones, Schultz, Volkmar, & Cohen, 2002a; 2002b; Langdell, 1978; Schultz, 2005; Schultz et al., 2000).

The focus of this chapter is on abnormalities in another area, which I suggest is equally crucial for intuitive social understanding and adaptation—cultural knowledge.

What is cultural knowledge? For the past three or four decades, cognitive anthropologists and cultural psychologists have emphasized that culture not only consists of a set of behavior or material artefacts, customs, and traditions, but that culture is chiefly about shared meanings and shared symbols. Cultural knowledge is socially shared models or meaning systems, beliefs about the world, which influence the way we perceive, construct, think about, define, and interpret the social world and our experiences in it (e.g., Cole, 1996; Quinn & Holland, 1987; Shore, 1996; Shweder, 1991). Here I suggest considering cultural knowledge as an "intermediate level" of analysis, roughly situated between cognition and behavior. On the one hand, cultural knowledge is cognitive, because it is represented by individual minds. On the other hand, cultural knowledge is public, because it is widely shared between members of one culture or community. It is this property which makes it such a valuable tool in modulating social interactions and in establishing "common ground" in communication. Cultural meaning systems, however, not only have a representational function (a system of knowledge and beliefs). They are also *constructive*, as they constitute entities such as football or marriage; they are *directive*, since they often entail certain norms or rules of action; and they are *evocative*, as they contribute to how we *feel* about things, what we like and dislike (D'Andrade, 1984).

This chapter deals with one of the developmentally earliest emerging forms of cultural knowledge: namely, event knowledge. The first part discusses what might be the kind of "normal social experiences" that are foundational for the acquisition of cultural knowledge and that individuals with autism, including intellectually able individuals, might, at least to some degree, miss. In the second part I will consider the role of event knowledge in adaptive, action-oriented cognition, specifically in modulating attention and memory.

Event Knowledge in Typically Developing Children

From early on, many of our social experiences and interactions are embedded in fairly common and routine events, which are more or less ordered and predictable. Events may be characterized as whole scenes or episodes that involve people acting with particular objects and interacting over time and in a particular place in pursuit of a particular goal and subgoals (Nelson, 1986).

Drawing on Schank and Abelson's (1977) script theory, Nelson and colleagues studied event knowledge in preschoolers and school-aged children from around 3 to 6 years (Fivush, 1984; Fivush, Kuebli, & Clubb, 1992; Nelson, 1986; Nelson & Gruendel, 1981). She and her colleagues asked their young participants to provide narratives of experiences with familiar and routine events (e.g., "What happens at playtime?"). These studies revealed that 3-year-olds already had schematic concepts of what usually happens in these events. First, the young children recounted activities in the temporal-causal order in which they normally occur. Secondly, they tended to describe the event in generalized terms rather than recounting a specific past experience. For example, children would state that during playtime, "they play" rather than say "I played." Thirdly, they described the activities at a relatively high level of abstraction, leaving out a great deal of detail unless specifically probed. For instance, they would not spontaneously specify whether "playing" means riding the bike or playing hide-and-seek.

Due to their *generalized* format, event schemas have two important adaptive functions: On the one hand, they offer children (as well as adults) a tool to structure novel experiences. Based on past experiences, one can generate expectations of what is likely to happen next. As a consequence, the event becomes more predictable and less confusing or even frightening than when it was first encountered.

On the other hand, an event episode (e.g., a birthday party) very seldom unfolds in exactly the same way as on a previous occasion. The holistic organization of events (i.e., the tendency to describe activities at a fairly high level of abstraction) allows the accommodation of a great deal of variability between different activities within the event. This way, event knowledge has been suggested to be more oriented to the present and the future, rather than to the recall of the past. However, Nelson and Fivush (2004) also argued that generalized event knowledge plays an important role in preschoolers' development of an episodic memory or, more specifically, an autobiographical memory of one's personal life events (Perner & Ruffman, 1995). Constructing one's own autobiography serves to explain (to oneself and others) why things happened the way they did, and their significance for the present. This requires situating these experiences of one's own life (school, jobs, marriage, etc.) in a frame of place and time, and in the values and expectations of the embedding culture. Without such a cultural frame, the self-history would lack context.

A second research program utilized imitation and re-enactment methods in order to trace the beginnings of event knowledge in pre-verbal infants, and to delineate whether younger children's lower level of event knowledge may be confounded by verbal demands (e.g., Bauer & Dow, 1994; Bauer & Fivush, 1992). In these studies, the young children watch event sequences being acted out using miniature props, on one or multiple occasions. Immediately afterwards, or after a delay period, children are given the props and are encouraged to imitate the model's actions. One and two-year-olds already are sensitive to and remember the correct temporal or causal sequence in which simple 4–6-step events occurred (Bauer & Mandler, 1992). Generalization requires the apprehension that the different objects or "props" (although perhaps physically dissimilar) fulfill the same function in reaching a particular goal. To test generalization, in the re-enactment scenario some of the objects from the original event are replaced with new but functionally equivalent ones that can be used to produce the same event. Already 2- and 3-year-olds began to incorporate the novel objects, provided they had been given the opportunity to explicitly experience variations on at least one or two prior occasions; while from around 4 years of age, children readily did so after only a single experience with a new event (Bauer & Dow, 1994).

In sum, these studies suggest that young children and even pre-verbal infants possess event knowledge in at least rudimentary form and that some of the components of event knowledge are non-verbal. What are the exact mechanisms through which this transition from direct moment-by-moment experience to the formation of conceptual knowledge is achieved? In the next section, I will draw on the literature on social-cognitive development and cultural learning to begin to specify what are the kind of normal social experiences necessary to accrue conceptual event knowledge.

Social-Cognitive Development in Typical Development

From the very beginning, typically developing (TD) infants show a great deal of interest in people. For example, they prefer to look at faces rather than at inanimate objects (Johnson & Morton, 1991); they prefer human movements (biological motion) over physical movements (Slater, 1998); they engage in "protoconversations" with their carers (Trevarthen, 1979).

Most authors agree that something fundamental happens during the last quarter of the first year of life. This period marks the beginning of the development of an arsenal of early social-perceptual and social-cognitive skills. Tomasello (1999; Tomasello Carpenter, Call, Behne, & Moll, 2005) has argued that understanding of intentional action, paired with social motivations, pave the way for the emergence of diverse skills such as joint-attention behaviors, imitative learning, word learning, and pretend (or symbolic) play. Separately and especially in combination, they provide a powerful tool for cultural learning: namely, to learn *through* others (Meltzoff, 1995).

However, with the important exception of language acquisition, research on cultural learning has mainly focused on material aspects of culture, such as tool use. One exception is the observational studies by Nadel and colleagues. In one study, pairs of children between 2 and 4 years were left to their own devices in a room full of identical toys (Nadel, Guérini, Pezé, & Rivet, 1999). The authors observed that the children often spontaneously combined elements of imitation, shared attention, and symbolic play in their activities. Nadel et al. stressed the communicative function of imitation in these dyads, yet their examples also nicely illustrate that in their spontaneous play children frequently enacted and re-enacted common cultural events. It is easy to think of many instances in which, for example, young children let their dolls celebrate pretend tea parties, go shopping, or fry pretend eggs in miniature kitchens. They also imitate others (e.g., mother and father) when they take the "baby" to bed. Examples like these suggest that through their own personal engagement, children learn and "rehearse" a great deal of these events.

A second avenue for young children to "relive" events and organize experiences is through narratives (Bruner, 1986, 1990). Much insight into the role of narratives in consolidating event knowledge has been gained through the meticulous recording of bedtime conversations and monologues of a young girl, Emmy, from when she was 18 months old to her third birthday (Nelson, 1989). This young girl seemed to have a strong *motivation* to "relive" her experiences by talking about them. Her narratives centered around *what* had happened during the day and what she had *felt*. As she became older, she increasingly began to speculate about *why* things happened. In this way, she was not simply reporting, but her monologic narratives had a constitutive function, to make sense of her everyday life.

Third, children learn vicariously about common events through stories. In Western cultures, storybooks for preschoolers often center on familiar events, bedtime routines, school days, birthday presents, holidays, and so on. Frequently, the young children insist on listening to the same story over and over again until they can largely predict what is coming next. This accumulating stock of knowledge of the reliable, or ordinariness, also serves as a background for understanding and interpreting exceptional experiences (Lucariello, 1990).

Early Social-Cognitive Abnormalities and Abnormalities in Event Knowledge in Autism

In the previous section I suggested that young children readily utilize their social-perceptual and social-cognitive skills in their everyday activities, their play, and in narratives, and that one of the functions of this practical application is to acquire event knowledge. To what extent are these early social experiences different in children with autism, and might thus impact (as will be shown in the next section) on the way events are represented?

Earlier retrospective studies using home videos and now prospective studies with young toddlers with autism suggest that diminished social motivations and orientation to social stimuli are amongst the earliest indicators of autism (Dawson, Meltzoff, Osterling, Rinaldi, & Brown, 1998; Klin, Jones, Schultz, & Volkmar, 2003; and see Jones & Klin, Chapter 4; Maestro & Muratori, Chapter 9). These include diminished eye contact and attention to faces more generally (Dawson et al., 1998), and disorganized rhythm and synchrony in social interactions (Trevarthen & Daniel, 2005). In addition, across the lifespan, young children and high-functioning adults with

ASD have been found to show striking abnormalities in social attention. For example, eye-tracking studies illustrate that when observing social situations, the viewers with autism spent a greater proportion of time trying to gather social information from mouths, whereas typically developing viewers intuitively monitored the actors' eyes. The viewers with autism also focused more often on inanimate and irrelevant aspects of the scene (Klin et al., 2002a, 2002b; Jones & Klin, Chapter 4). These findings suggest that individuals with autism appear to experience social events profoundly differently; they miss aspects of the social dimension of the event but may be more likely to notice other, non-social aspects of the environment. If event schemas are built on repeated experiences with the event, then these qualitatively different experiences could be expected to have a cumulative impact on the acquisition of conceptual event knowledge.

Second, profound abnormalities in joint attention, imitation, and pretend play behaviors in autism, in particular across the toddler and preschool years, are well documented (Charman et al., 2003; Rogers, Hepburn, Stackhouse, & Wehner, 2003; Maestro & Muratori, Chapter 9). In addition, abnormalities in all these areas are typically greatest when their spontaneous occurrences rather than instructed competencies are assessed (e.g., Leekam, Baron-Cohen, Perrett, Milders, & Brown, 1993; Lewis & Boucher, 1988). This also reduces their opportunities to rehearse common cultural events, since children with autism are less likely to act out pretend tea parties or to learn about novel aspects of these scenarios by imitating others.

Third, a number of studies document impairments at least in some aspects of narratives. The majority of studies investigated children's ability to retell stories, often elicited by means of wordless picture books. Several studies found that the story narratives produced by children with autism lacked complexity and coherence and showed deficits with the evaluative dimension, and in causal language (Bruner & Feldman, 1993; Capps, Losh, & Thurber, 2000; Diehl, Benetto, & Young, 2006; Loveland, McEvoy, Kelley, & Tunali, 1990; Loveland & Tunali, 1991, 1993; Tager-Flusberg, 1995; Tager-Flusberg & Sullivan, 1995). Meanwhile, two newer studies showed that story narratives of high-functioning children with autism were relatively intact in terms of global structure and evaluation devices (Losh & Capps, 2003; Norbury & Bishop, 2003), but in Losh & Capps's study, these same children had difficulties producing narratives of personal experiences. Interestingly, narrative abilities were related to emotional understanding but not theory of mind or verbal IQ, suggesting that theory of mind abilities did not ensure the successful construction of stories of personal experiences in a more open-ended context.

Following the argument in the preceding section that children's "impulse" to rehearse happenings of the day within a narrative format fosters event knowledge, one might expect abnormalities in *spontaneous motivations* to engage in narrative activities to have the greatest negative impact. To our awareness, this issue has not yet been directly addressed. However, adults with high-functioning autism were found to have diminished motivations to spontaneously impose social meaning on ambiguous visual stimuli, as typically developing adults readily do (Klin, 2000). Unpublished data of a recent questionnaire study (Loth, Gómez, & Happé, in prep.) indicates diminished frequency of talking about personal experiences. In response to the question "Does your son tend to discuss with you or with other people what happens to him during the day?" the majority of parents of boys with Asperger syndrome (AS) indicated that their son did so only rarely or never.

Finally, there are several anecdotal and parents' questionnaire reports that individuals with ASD tend to take less interest in stories, and are instead more interested in factual information (Baron-Cohen, 2003; Briskman, Happé, & Frith, 2001). This might hinder yet another route to the acquisition or consolidation of event knowledge. Taken together, these separate lines of research converge in suggesting that through abnormalities in social attention, social engagement, and social-cognitive skills, the foundations for the formation of conceptual event knowledge, might be compromised in autism spectrum disorders (ASD).

Abnormalities in Event Knowledge in Individuals with Autism

What is the evidence for abnormalities in event knowledge? To date, only a handful of studies have focused on event knowledge in autism, producing mixed results. Loveland and Tunali (1991) reported that participants with autism participated appropriately in a tea-party event involving the experimenter and a confederate. Volden and Johnston (1999) found that when participants with autism and controls were shown videotaped vignettes of familiar events, they were able to indicate what was likely to happen next. In four studies, participants with ASD were asked to provide verbal narratives of common events. In a single case study, a 10-year-old boy with pervasive developmental disorders was unable to provide a generalized account of what happens when people go on holidays (Loveland & Tunali, 1993). Volden and Johnston (1999) reported that participants with autism produced fewer core elements compared to typically developing controls, and instead mentioned more things that were irrelevant, bizarre, or actually not part of the event. Trillingsgaard (1999) divided her ASD sample into groups who had failed versus passed standard theory of mind tasks. She reported that both ASD groups produced significantly impoverished event narratives, relative to matched controls. In addition, while with increasing age and ToM abilities the individuals with autism showed improvements in correctly sequencing activities in their temporal-causal order (mirroring typical development), even the more able and oldest children made little effort to account for options and variations, leaving their scripts more rigid and narrow.

In our study (Loth, Gómez, & Happé, in press) we asked individuals with autism, individuals with intellectual disabilities, and typically developing children to explain to a boy ("Toku," shown in a photograph) who had never been to Britain, what normally happens when people go to a restaurant or celebrate Christmas. Following Trillingsgaard, we also subdivided our participants with ASD into those who failed and those who passed standard false belief tasks and compared both subgroups to typically developing children and people with mild learning disabilities with, respectively, similar verbal abilities. Compared to previous studies, our coding system was finer-grained, since, alongside abnormalities in temporal-causal organization, we also examined differences in the hierarchical organization. This refers to the description of activities and objects related to the situation at different levels of abstraction, where higher-level descriptions entail more generalizations. We reasoned that social-cognitive abnormalities (indexed by level of theory of mind impairment) undermine aspects of generality and temporal-causal order. However, in addition to the social-cognitive abnormalities discussed earlier, autism also entails a preference to process information in a local, detail-focused manner—weak central coherence (Happé & Frith, 2006; see López, Chapter 6, for a review). We predicted that such a local bias might specifically affect the hierarchical organization of events and translate into a tendency to represent activities and objects at the level of individual exemplars rather than in more global/schematic terms.

Our analyses revealed that 62% of participants with ASD who failed standard theory of mind tasks did not demonstrate apprehension of generality, and 87.5% did not structure activities in the temporal-causal order in which they normally occur at all, or made some ordering mistakes. Since a global structure of the event was impaired or altogether lacking, different local bits and activities of a particular event were loosely connected with various unrelated ones in an idiosyncratic chain of linear (but not hierarchical) associations. These deficits were significant relative to the performances of typically developing children and children with intellectual disabilities of similar verbal mental age but who passed standard theory of mind tasks.

By contrast, the high-functioning sub-group of participants with ASD who passed standard and sometimes even complex theory of mind (ToM) tasks showed intact generality and temporal-causal organization of their narratives. However, both ASD groups demonstrated specific abnormalities in the hierarchical organization, and these were related to performance on tasks tapping individual differences in weak coherence. The level of description deserves special attention. For example, when asked what happens when people go to a restaurant, a boy with intellectual disabilities stated "We go in and eat," whereas a boy with autism said "Fish 'n' chips . . . They had beans, sausage and pie for dinner." If a restaurant visit is about "going in and eating," then this helps the structuring of what is likely to happen next time one goes to a restaurant. At the same time expectations are global enough to accommodate various different things that could be eaten. On the other hand, expectations based on the notion that a restaurant visit is about eating "fish and chips" are immediately far narrower, and the ability to accommodate variations between different experiences would be reduced. For example, if a restaurant visit were about fish and chips, going to a restaurant but not having fish and chips would already constitute a considerable deviation from that "script."

In a subsequent study (Loth, 2003; Loth, Gómez, & Happé, in prep.), we further investigated the apprehension of event variability, using a more structured task. Participants read stories about the life of two characters (e.g., Dr Smith on a train to work, in the surgery, and shopping in the supermarket). The stories comprised three types of activities: Activities that were either central and defining for the event (e.g., "In the surgery, Dr Smith examines a patient"), optional (because they were peripheral to the event or described in very specific terms, e.g., "On the train, Dr Smith eats a sandwich"), or inappropriate (e.g., "In the surgery, Dr Smith and his patient are eating sandwiches"). Participants were asked to rate the occurrence of activities on a five-point Likert-type scale ranging from "always," "often," to "sometimes," "hardly ever," and "never." Although the people with ASD made no more mistakes than the control group in rating the occurrences of central and inappropriate acts, they made significantly more mistakes in rating the occurrences of optional acts. In particular, they more often considered activities that might or might not occur as occurring "always."

While this group was mixed in terms of ability levels, the goal of a subsequent experiment was to examine differences in a high-functioning group of boys with Asperger syndrome and to explore relationships with real life features. Consistent with our previous study, these very high-functioning individuals made more errors in rating the occurrence of optional activities relative to the typically developing boys. Interestingly, the number of errors in rating the occurrence of optional acts was related to severity of autistic symptoms, as indicated by parents' responses on the Childhood Asperger Syndrome Test (Scott, Baron-Cohen, Bolton, & Braine, 2002). This suggests that across ability levels, individuals with ASD have specific difficulties apprehending variations between different encounters with familiar events.

The Role of Event Knowledge in Context-Sensitive Cognition

From an event knowledge perspective, the social realm is not only confined to people, but may in fact encompass objects as far as they play a part in the accomplishment of an activity (e.g., reading a menu in a restaurant). Hence, whether something is important or not in a particular situation is not only determined by characteristics intrinsic to the stimuli (e.g., people versus objects) but also depends upon and varies across different contexts. "Context" itself, however, is construed, at least to some extent, by the individual (Kagan, 2002), and, as we argue, often involves drawing on social knowledge. In our recent work we began to examine differences in using event knowledge in the service of context-sensitive cognition. A recent experiment (Loth & Happé, 2005) was inspired by the earlier observation that typically developing adults have a tendency to recall more things that are relevant than irrelevant in a particular situation (Pitchert & Anderson, 1977). We first read participants short story vignettes that established different events. For example, one group read a short story about someone who is about to burgle a house (context A). A second group read instead a brief story about someone who was going to visit a house for a tea party (context B). Participants in both groups were then shown the same colored line drawings (e.g., a living room) for 30 seconds. The scenes contained an equal number of items relevant to context A (e.g., money, pearls, police car outside) and context B (e.g., games, cake, party hat), plus several "neutral" items (e.g., a flower pot, book shelves). Afterwards, they were asked to recall everything they had seen in the picture.

Participants were 28 very high-functioning boys with Asperger syndrome (AS) (aged 8 to 16 years and with IQ in the normal range or above), matched to a group of typically developing boys on age and verbal IQ. Overall, both groups recalled a similar number of items, which rules out an overall memory deficit in the AS group. However, while the typically developing boys recalled significantly more items that were related to and relevant in the present context, the boys with AS did not discriminate between item types. This finding suggests important differences in the way people with and without autism recall events. It seemed that although the memory in the AS group reflected a faithful representation of the world, compared to that of the typically developing boys, it was less context-sensitive and action-oriented.

Since the above study utilized stories in order to manipulate events, participants were also required to keep on-line the mental attitudes of the characters who participated in these situations (e.g., someone *wants* to burgle a house or *wants* to build a kite, etc.). Might individuals with ASD still differ from controls in the extent to which cognitive processes are influenced by schematic expectations of common cultural scenes when this does not involve any form of mental attitude? The goal of a recent, still ongoing study was to examine the role of schematic expectations of different mundane scenes in guiding spontaneous attention. We used a change blindness paradigm, in which participants view, alternating, an original picture A and a modified picture A'. The pictures are interspersed by a very brief grey screen, which evokes the impression of a flicker, similar to an eye-blink. Participants watch the cycle A–A'–A–A' etc. until they have spotted the change or a certain time limit is reached. The notion of "change blindness" relates to the intriguing finding that viewers surprisingly often fail to notice even large changes in a scene if they do not deem the changed object important. On this basis it has been suggested that looking by itself is not enough to see; what we see appears to be modulated by attention, guided on the basis of interest (e.g., O'Regan, 1992).

In our version (Loth, Happé, & Gómez, 2006), participants were presented with photographs of different mundane scenes (e.g., living room, bathroom, kitchen, etc.). We manipulated three types of changes: (1) changes that violated expectations of the things that are usually found in that scene (e.g., a brush in the bathroom was replaced by a frying pan); (2) changes between different kinds of objects, both of which are commonly found in that scene (e.g., a flower vase or a lamp in a living room). The third category of changes related to changes between different exemplars of the same object category (e.g., two different kinds of mugs). (Two different versions of the task were created in order to control for ambient visual cues, changes in contrast, and so on). We predicted that individuals in the control group would find it easiest to detect changes involving something that does not fit into the scene, more difficult to notice changes between two different types of objects that both "belong" to that scene; yet the hardest changes to notice would be those involving different exemplars of the same kind. On the other hand, if attention in ASD were less guided by schematic expectations of conventional scenes, we would expect fewer or no differences in change detection between the three conditions.

Preliminary analyses of this ongoing study from 8 norm-IQ adults with ASD and 10 typically developing controls confirm these predictions. There were no significant overall group differences in the number and speed of changes detected. But, unlike the control group, which performed as expected, the group with autism detected changes between exemplars faster than changes concerning an expectation violation. They were also faster in detecting changes between exemplars relative to the controls. Although these findings are preliminary, they begin to suggest that in ASD spontaneous attention may be less influenced by schematic expectations of common cultural scenes which normally help us to determine which aspects of the environment are ordinary or not, and potentially interesting or not.

Conclusion and Questions for Future Research

This chapter began by highlighting a particular challenge for current cognitive theories of autism: namely, to account for the difficulties in understanding open-ended social situations and adapting to real-life social demands. In searching for answers, we drew on concepts and empirical findings of how typically developing children master this task spontaneously, in particular, the literature on children's acquisition of event knowledge in cognitive development.

Collectively, our studies revealed abnormalities in the way event knowledge is represented and in the way event knowledge is used to guide cognition in an adaptive, context-sensitive manner. These differences may have implications for both social and some non-social features:

First, one sub-group of individuals with ASD, namely those who failed standard theory of mind tasks, showed profound deficits in event knowledge. As such, they may lack a fundamental tool that normally helps to structure experiences, to define a social situation, and anticipate others' actions as well as one's own actions in it.

Second, we found that bright boys with Asperger syndrome remembered *different* things about events, namely fewer things that are socially relevant in a particular situation and more things that are irrelevant.

Third, if abnormalities in the hierarchical organization of event schemas (which we found across the autism spectrum) disturb understanding of variability (that and why specific activities and objects are interchangeable and may not necessarily occur in that form in every encounter), this may help to account for the subjective distress that many individuals with ASD experience in the face of even minute changes to normal routines. It may also shed light on why, from this perspective, the individual insists on the exact repetition of the previous or original incident.

Fourth, our preliminary findings suggest that spontaneous attention is less influenced by schematic expectations of cultural scenes. Instead, our high-functioning adults with ASD were faster in detecting more trivial changes between the same kinds of object, perhaps by attending more to changes in surface features. This finding may open a new window to an often observed though not well understood feature: the tendency to spot minute and trivial changes in the environment.

Integration Section

How might the cultural knowledge approach proposed here contribute to the need for an integrated view on autism, highlighted throughout this volume? And what are the key tasks for future research extending this perspective?

1 Whereas for researchers, the focus is on identifying what is unique and universal to autism by studying group differences, for the clinician, who deals with individuals, the perhaps more pressing need is to know more about how far a particular abnormality (say, at the cognitive or neurobiological level) is related

to and can predict the level or degree of behavioral abnormalities that disrupt adaptation. Therefore, the next task for the cultural knowledge perspective proposed here consists of adopting a dimensional approach to test the above predictions of relatively specific relationships between particular abnormalities in representing and using cultural knowledge and specific social and non-social behavioral features. In the social domain, it will be important to examine relationships with both level of social disability (i.e., level of autistic social symptoms) and level of social adaptive behavior, since these two dimensions have been found to be somewhat unrelated (Klin et al., in press). Furthermore, the cultural knowledge approach predicts associations with some higher-level repetitive behaviors, but not with lower-level manifestations, such as motor stereotypes. Interestingly, these suggestions would be consistent with recent factor-analytic studies suggesting that higher- and lower-level manifestations of repetitive behaviors may be dissociable (Cuccaro et al., 2003) and that higher-level manifestation, such as "narrow interests" or "insistence on sameness may be phenotypically more specific to autism.

2　In the past, researchers have argued for the need to integrate the behavioral, cognitive, neurobiological, and genetic levels of analyses to attain a more comprehensive understanding of the underpinnings of ASD (e.g., Morton & Frith, 1995; Volkmar, Lord, Bailey, Schultz, & Klin, 2004). For example, identification of the nature of abnormalities at the cognitive or neuropsychological levels (e.g., in theory of mind, face perception, executive functions) has helped to specify the search for underlying anomalies at the neurofunctional and neuro-biological levels (Schultz, 2005; Wicker, Chapter 2). What could adding cultural knowledge as another "level" have to offer?

Cultural knowledge, or here more specifically event knowledge, is situated at the interface between the "social" and the "cognitive." On the one hand, the function of event schemas is quintessentially social; on the other hand, event schemas are a key component of cognitive development.

Our preliminary analyses suggest that social-cognitive deficits and characteristic abnormalities in cognitive processes in autism interact in hindering the acquisition of event schemas. This way, studying differences at the level of cultural knowledge offers a new window on the relationship between abnormalities in social-cognitive and cognitive development. Although somewhat speculatively, our work suggests, first, that deficits in social-cognitive/social-perceptual/social-motivational development, which may be primary to this disorder (Jones & Klin, Chapter 4; Maestro & Muratori, Chapter 9) might lead to abnormalities in conceptual development. Second, weak central coherence theory and related accounts addressing cognitive abnormalities in local versus global processing have primarily addressed non-social features of autism, in particular those intriguing areas in which people with autism excel more often than others (see López, Chapter 6, for a review). Here we have begun to import the weak coherence concept in the social domain, finding that distinct differences in the normally adaptive hierarchical organization of activities and props appear to be related to a local processing style.

Moreover, while biases in local/global processing have typically been studied within one domain, abnormalities in the originally proposed tendency to "integrate information in context" also relates to the influence of prior background knowledge in modulating attention, memory, and perception in a particular situation. In cognitive sciences, these processes are often referred to as "top-down modulation" processes. Our findings that recall in intellectually able individuals with AS was less related to what was important in a particular context are, on the one hand, consonant with recent findings of reduced top-down modulation in autism in the perceptual domain (see Ropar, Mitchell, & Sheppard, Chapter 7). On the other hand, they also highlight that, rather than focusing on cognitive abnormalities in autism in ability/deficit terms, the nature of cognitive abnormalities may be, at least partially, better understood in terms of differences in the spontaneous usage of these skills in order to meet the demands of real-life situations. This view has implications for generating hypotheses of abnormalities at the neurodevelopmental and neurofunctional levels. For example, our behavioral findings of reduced "top-down" modulation processes would point, on the neurofunctional level, to the possibility of reduced collaboration between different supra-regional brain areas (including the "social brain" network), which have recently been reported using functional magnetic resonance imaging and diffusion tensor techniques (Belmonte et al., 2004; Just, Cherkassky, Keller, & Minshew, 2004; Wicker, Chapter 2). Theoretically, these suggestions would be consistent with the increasing recognition in social and developmental neurosciences of the impact of real-time, goal-directed interactions between the human being and the environment in developing cognitive processes that meet adaptive demands, and which influence, in turn, the specialization of underlying brain structure and function (e.g., Johnson, 2001).

3   A third priority will be to study abnormalities in event knowledge from a developmental perspective. Virtually all studies discussed earlier investigated event knowledge in older children or adults with ASD, most of whom were relatively high-functioning. Since these individuals can be seen as representing the developmental endpoint, abnormalities are likely to also exist at earlier stages in development. From a practical standpoint, a better understanding of when and why this process of socialization is disrupted is crucial, given the widely agreed notion that the ability to offer early intervention holds the greatest promise to improve chances of positive outcome. Moreover, so far, all existing studies

documented differences in performance results. The lesson learnt from social cognition research (e.g., on theory of mind and face perception) is that performance on social reasoning tasks is only moderately correlated to level of real-life social competence, at least partially, because intellectually able individuals with ASD appear to use atypical, and to some extent compensatory strategies, to solve these tasks. This raises the need to study differences in the underlying learning processes themselves, in an effort to increase the power to predict level of social competence (Volkmar et al., 2004).

In earlier sections of this chapter, I argued that typically developing children accrue event knowledge based on repeated interactive real-life experiences during which they readily apply their emerging social perceptual and social-cognitive skills. I reasoned that abnormalities in these areas in children with autism hinder this (largely uninstructed) route to the acquisition of cultural knowledge. Thus, future work extending this approach will require tracing abnormalities in the transition from experiencing a novel event for the first time to the formation of event knowledge over multiple experiences. In particular, arguments from typical development predict that abnormalities in social attention (Jones & Klin, Chapter 4), social engagement (e.g., imitative learning in an interactive, communicative context, see Williams, Chapter 3), and social motivations (e.g., the propensity to talk about the happenings of the day in narratives) have a *cumulative developmental effect* on the acquisition of cultural knowledge. At the same time, on the moment-by-moment or processing time scale, abnormalities in representing and using cultural knowledge contributes in turn to anomalies in how events are experienced and remembered.

4 Finally, to what extent might the cultural knowledge approach have practical implications? One of the most entrenched challenges for early intervention and educational programs consists of addressing difficulties in *generalizing* social knowledge across different situations. Previous attempts to teach children with autism social scripts have been only moderately successful. Our work suggests that it is necessary to account for characteristic cognitive abnormalities that alter or undermine normal learning processes (Golan & Baron-Cohen, Chapter 12) and is consistent with recent suggestions to foster the understanding of the global meaning of different social situations, rather than targeting isolated skills (Dunlop, Knott, & MacKay, Chapter 13). More specifically, our work highlights the need to include in such programs approaches that specifically target the children's apprehension of event variability related to the hierarchical structure of event schemas, to improve the understanding that different activities and objects come in different forms and shapes, yet fulfill the same function or goal within the event as a whole.

In concluding, the cultural knowledge approach discussed in this chapter offers a novel perspective on social abnormalities in open-ended situations and some non-social features characteristic of individuals with ASD. The suggestion was made to consider cultural knowledge as an intermediate link between cognitive and behavioral abnormalities. We have only begun to test some of several predictions related to this approach experimentally. A more comprehensive program of research is needed, which should include studies examining abnormalities in the underlying learning processes in young children with autism, and the integration of this perspective with social and developmental neuroscience approaches. Ultimately, the usefulness of these suggestions will depend on the extent to which they can inform early intervention and treatment and help children and adults with autistic conditions to cope with real-life social situations.

Acknowledgments

Eva Loth was supported by grants from the ESRC and Nuffield Foundation while writing this chapter. Many thanks to all participants and their families who took part in the studies summarized here. I would also like to thank Juan Carlos Gómez and Maria Núñez for helpful comments and suggestions on an earlier draft of this chapter.

References

Asperger, H. (1944). Die "autistischen Psychopathen" im Kindesalter. *Archiv für Psychiatrie und Nervenkrankheiten, 117,* 76–136.

Baron-Cohen, S. (2003). *The essential difference: Men, women and the extreme male brain.* London: Penguin.

Baron-Cohen, S., Tager-Flusberg, H., & Cohen, D. (Eds.) (2000). *Understanding other minds: Perspectives from cognitive neuroscience.* Oxford, UK: Blackwell.

Bauer, P. J., & Dow, G. A. A. (1994). Episodic memory in 16- and 20-month-old children: Specifics are generalized but not forgotten. *Developmental Psychology, 30,* 403–417.

Bauer, P. J., & Fivush, R. (1992). Constructing event representations: Building on a foundation of variation and enabling relations. *Cognitive Development, 7,* 381–401.

Bauer, P. J., & Mandler, J. M. (1992). Putting the horse before the cart: The use of temporal order in recall of events by 1-year-old children. *Developmental Psychology, 28,* 441–452.

Belmonte, M. K., Allen, G., Beckel-Mitchener, A., Boulanger, L. M., Carper, R. A., & Webb, S. J. (2004). Autism and abnormal development of brain connectivity. *Journal of Neuroscience, 24*(42), 9228–9231.

Bowler, D. M. (1992). "Theory of mind" in Asperger's syndrome. *Journal of Child Psychology and Psychiatry, 33,* 877–893.

Briskman, J., Happe, F., & Frith, U. (2001). Exploring the cognitive phenotype of autism: Weak "central coherence" in parents and siblings of children with autism: II. Real-life skills and preferences. *Journal of Child Psychology and Psychiatry, 42*(3), 309–316.

Bruner, J. (1986). *Actual minds, possible worlds*. Cambridge, MA: Harvard University Press.

Bruner, J. (1990). *Acts of meaning*. Cambridge, MA: Harvard University Press.

Bruner, J., & Feldman, C. F. (1993). Theory of mind and the problem of autism. In S. Baron-Cohen, H. Tager-Flusberg, & D. Cohen (Eds.), *Understanding other minds: Perspectives from autism* (pp. 267–291). Oxford, UK: Oxford University Press.

Capps, L., Losh, M., & Thurber, C. (2000). "The frog ate a bug and made his mouth sad": Narrative competence in children with autism. *Journal of Abnormal Child Psychology, 28*, 193–204.

Charman, T., Baron-Cohen, S., Swettenham, J., Baird, G., Drew, A., & Cox, A. (2003). Predicting language outcome in infants with autism and pervasive developmental disorder. *International Journal of Language and Communication Disorder, 38*(3), 265–285.

Cole, M. (1996). *Cultural psychology: A once and future discipline*. Cambridge, MA: Harvard University Press.

Cuccaro, M. L., Shao, Y., Grubber, J., Slifer, M., Wolpert, C., Donnelly, S., et al. (2003). Factor analysis of restricted and repetitive behaviors in autism using the Autism Diagnostic Interview-R. *Child Psychiatry and Human Development, 34*(1), 3–17.

Dahlgren, S., & Trillingsgaard, A. (1996). Theory of mind in non-retarded children with autism and Asperger's syndrome: A research note. *Journal of Child Psychology and Psychiatry, 37*(6), 759–763.

D'Andrade, R. (1984). Cultural meaning systems. In R. A. Shweder & R. A. LeVine (Eds.), *Culture theory: Essays on mind, self and emotion* (pp. 88–119). New York: Cambridge University Press.

Dawson, G., Meltzoff, A. N., Osterling, J., Rinaldi, J., & Brown, E. (1998). Children with autism fail to orient to naturally occurring social stimuli. *Journal of Autism and Developmental Disorders, 28*(6), 479–485.

Diehl, J. J., Benetto, L., & Young, E. C. (2006). Story recall and narrative coherence of high-functioning children with autism spectrum disorder. *Journal of Abnormal Child Psychology, 34*(1), 83–98.

Fivush, R. (1984). Learning about school: The development of kindergartners' school scripts. *Child Development, 55*, 1697–1709.

Fivush, R., Kuebli, J., & Clubb, P. A. (1992). The structure of events and event representation: A developmental analysis. *Child Development, 63*, 188–201.

Happé, F. G. E. 1999). Autism: Cognitive deficit or cognitive style? *Trends in Cognitive Sciences, 3*(6), 216–222.

Happé, F., & Frith, U. (2006). The weak coherence account: Detail-focused cognitive style in autism spectrum disorders. *Journal of Autism and Developmental Disorders, 36*(1), 5–25.

Hill, E. L. (2004). Executive dysfunction in autism. *Trends in Cognitive Sciences, 8*(1), 26–32.

Hobson, R. P., Ousten, J., & Lee, A. (1988). What's in the face? The case of autism. *British Journal of Psychology, 79*, 441–453.

Johnson, M. H. (2001). Functional brain development in humans. *Nature Reviews Neuroscience, 2*, 475–483.

Johnson, M. H., & Morton, J. (1991). *Biology and cognitive development: The case of face recognition*. Oxford, UK: Blackwell.

Just, M. A., Cherkassky, V. L., Keller, T. A., & Minshew, N. J. (2004). Cortical activation and synchronization during sentence comprehension in high-functioning autism: Evidence of underconnectivity. *Brain, 127*, 1811–1821.

Kagan, J. (2002). *Surprise, uncertainty, and mental structures*. Cambridge, MA: Harvard University Press.

Kanner, L. (1943). Autistic disturbances of affective contact. *Nervous Child, 2*, 217–250.

Klin, A. (2000). Attributing social meaning to ambiguous visual stimuli in higher-functioning autism and Asperger syndrome: The social attribution task. *Journal of Child Psychology and Psychiatry, 41*(7), 831–846.

Klin, A., Jones, W., Schultz, R., & Volkmar, F. (2003). The enactive mind, or from actions to cognition: Lessons from autism. *Philosophical Transactions of the Royal London B Series, 358*, 345–360.

Klin, A., Jones, W., Schultz, R., Volkmar, F., & Cohen, D. (2002a). Defining and quantifying the social phenotype in autism. *American Journal of Psychiatry, 159*, 895–908.

Klin, A., Jones, W., Schultz, R., Volkmar, F., & Cohen, D. (2002b). Visual fixation patterns during viewing of naturalistic social situations as predictors of social competence in individuals with autism. *Archives of General Psychiatry, 59*, 809–816.

Klin, A., Saulnier, C. A., Sparrow, S. S., Cicchetti, D. V., Volkmar, F. R., & Lord, C. (in press). Social and communication abilities and disabilities in higher functioning individuals with autism spectrum disorders. *Journal of Autism and Developmental Disorders*.

Klin, A., Sparrow, S. S., de Bildt, A., Cicchetti, D. V., Cohen, D. J., & Volkmar, F. R. (1999). A normed study of face recognition in autism and related disorders. *Journal of Autism and Developmental Disorders, 29*, 497–507.

Langdell, T. (1978). Recognition of faces: An approach for the study of autism. *Journal of Child Psychology and Psychiatry, 10*, 255–268.

Leekam, S., Baron-Cohen, S., Perrett, D., Milders, M., & Brown, S. (1993). Eye-direction detection: A dissociation between geometric and joint attention skills in autism. *British Journal of Developmental Psychology, 15*, 77–95.

Lewis, C., & Boucher, J. (1988). Spontaneous, instructed and elicited play in relatively able autistic children. *British Journal of Developmental Psychology, 6*, 325–339.

Losh, M., & Capps, L. (2003). Narrative ability in high-functioning children with autism or Asperger's syndrome. *Journal of Autism and Developmental Disorders, 33*(3), 239–251.

Loth, E. (2003). *On social, cultural and cognitive aspects of theory of mind in practice*. Unpublished PhD thesis, University of St Andrews, Scotland.

Loth, E., Gómez, J. C., & Happé, F. (in press). Event schemas in autism: The role of theory of mind and weak central coherence. *Journal of Autism and Developmental Disorders*.

Loth, E., Gómez, J. C., & Happé, F. (in prep.). *Examining the understanding of variations between events in autism*.

Loth, E., & Happé, F. (2005, May 5–7). *Memory for relevant versus irrelevant aspects of the environment: Preliminary evidence for reduced top-down modulation in autism*. Paper presented at the 4th International Meeting for Autism Research (IMFAR), Boston, USA.

Loth, E., Happé, F., & Gómez, J. C. (2006, June 1–3). *Top-down modulation in autism: The influence of prior knowledge on attention and memory.* Paper presented at the 5th International Meeting for Autism Research (IMFAR), Montreal, Canada.

Loveland, K. A., McEvoy, R. E., Kelley, M. L., & Tunali, B. (1990). Narrative story telling in autism and Down's syndrome. *British Journal of Developmental Psychology, 8,* 9–23.

Loveland, K. A., & Tunali, B. (1991). Social scripts for conversational interactions in autism and Down's syndrome. *Journal of Autism and Developmental Disorders, 21,* 177–186.

Loveland, K. A., & Tunali, B. (1993). Narrative language in autism and the theory of mind hypothesis: A wider perspective. In S. Baron-Cohen, H. Tager-Flusberg, & D. Cohen (Eds.), *Understanding other minds. Perspectives from autism* (pp. 247–266). Oxford, UK: Oxford University Press.

Lucariello, J. (1990). Canonicality and consciousness in child narrative. In B. K. Britton & A. D. Pellegrini (Eds.), *Narrative thought and narrative language* (pp. 131–149). Hillsdale, NJ: Erlbaum.

Meltzoff, A. N. (1995). Understanding the intentions of others: Re-enactment of intended acts by 18-month-old children. *Developmental Psychology, 31,* 838–850.

Morton, J., & Frith, U. (1995). Causal modelling: A structural approach to developmental psychopathology. In D. Ciccetti & D. J. Cohen (Eds.). *Manual of developmental psychology, Vol.1: Theory and methods.* (pp. 358–390). New York: John Wiley.

Nadel, J., Guérini, C., Pezé, A., & Rivet, C. (1999). The evolving nature of imitation as a format of communication. In J. Nadel & G. Butterworth (Eds.), *Imitation in infancy* (pp. 209–234). Cambridge, UK: Cambridge University Press.

Nelson, K. (1986). *Event knowledge: Structure and function in development.* Hillsdale, NJ: Lawrence Erlbaum.

Nelson, K. (Ed.) (1989). *Narratives from the crib.* Cambridge, MA: Harvard University Press.

Nelson, K., & Fivush, P. (2004). The emergence of autobiographical memory: A social cultural developmental theory. *Psychological Review, 117*(2), 486–511.

Nelson, K., & Gruendel, J. (1981). Generalised event representations: Basic building blocks of cognitive development. In M. E. Lamb & A. L. Brown (Eds.), *Advances in developmental psychology* (pp. 131–158). Hillsdale, NJ: Lawrence Erlbaum Associates, LEA.

Norbury, C. F., & Bishop, D. V. (2003). Narrative skills of children with communication impairments. *International Journal of Language and Communication Disorders, 38*(3), 287–313.

O'Regan, J. K. (1992). Solving the "real" mysteries of visual perception: The world as an outside memory. *Canadian Journal of Psychology, 46,* 461–488.

Perner, J., & Ruffman, T. (1995). Episodic memory and autonoetic consciousness: Developmental evidence and a theory of childhood amnesia. *Journal of Experimental Child Psychology, 59,* 516–548.

Pitchert, J., & Anderson, R. C. (1977). Taking different perspectives on a story. *Journal of Educational Psychology, 69,* 309–315.

Quinn, N., & Holland, D. (1987). Culture and cognition. In D. Holland & N. Quinn (Eds.), *Cultural models in language and thought* (pp. 3–40). Cambridge, UK: Cambridge University Press.

Rogers, S. J., Hepburn, S. L., Stackhouse, T., & Wehner, E. (2003). Imitation performance in toddlers with autism and those with other developmental disorders. *Journal of Child Psychology and Psychiatry*, *44*(5), 763–781.

Sacks, O. (1995). *An anthropologist on Mars*. London: Picador.

Schank, R., & Abelson, R. (1977). *Scripts, plans, goals and understanding*. Hillsdale, NJ: Lawrence Erlbaum Associates.

Schultz, R. T. (2005). Developmental deficits in social perception in autism: The role of the amygdala and fusiform face area. *International Journal of Developmental Neuroscience*, *23*(2–3), 125–141.

Schultz, R., Gauthier, I., Klin, A., Fulbright, R., Anderson, A., Volkmar, F. R., et al. (2000). Abnormal ventral temporal cortical activity among individuals with autism and Asperger syndrome during face discrimination. *Archives of General Psychiatry*, *57*, 331–340.

Scott, F. J., Baron-Cohen, S., Bolton, P., & Brayne, C. (2002). The CAST (Childhood Asperger Syndrome Test): Preliminary development of a UK screen for mainstream primary-school-age children. *Autism*, *6*(1), 9–31.

Shore, B. (1996). *Culture in mind: Cognition, culture, and the problem of meaning*. Oxford, UK: Oxford University Press.

Shweder, R. A. (1991). *Thinking through cultures*. Cambridge, MA: Harvard University Press.

Slater, A. (1998). *Perceptual development*. Hove, UK: Psychology Press.

Tager-Flusberg, H. (1995). "Once upon a ribbit": Stories narrated by autistic children. *British Journal of Developmental Psychology*, *13*, 45–59.

Tager-Flusberg, H., & Sullivan, K. (1995). Attributing mental states to story characters— a comparison of narratives produced by autistic and mentally-retarded individuals. *Applied Psycholinguistics*, *16*(3), 241–256.

Tomasello, M. (1999). *The cultural origins of human cognition*. Cambridge, MA: Harvard University Press.

Tomasello, M., Carpenter, M., Call, J., Behne, T., & Moll, H. (2005). Understanding and sharing intentions: The origins of cultural cognition. *Behavioral and Brain Sciences*, *28*, 675–735.

Trevarthen, C. (1979). Communication and cooperation in early infancy. A description of primary intersubjectivity. In M. Bullowa (Ed.), *Before speech: The beginnings of human communication* (pp. 321–347). London: Cambridge University Press.

Trevarthen, C., & Daniel, S. (2005). Disorganized rhythm and synchrony: Early signs of autism and Rett syndrome. *Brain Development*, *27*(1), S25–34.

Trillingsgaard, A. (1999). The script model in relation to autism. *European Journal of Adolescent Psychiatry*, *8*(1), 45–49.

Volden, J., & Johnston, J. (1999). Cognitive scripts in autistic children and adolescents. *Journal of Autism and Developmental Disorders*, *29*(3), 203–211.

Volkmar, F. R., Lord, C., Bailey, A., Schultz, R., & Klin, A. (2004). Autism and pervasive developmental disorders. *Journal of Child Psychology and Psychiatry*, *45*(1), 135–170.

6

Building the Whole Beyond Its Parts

A Critical Examination of Current Theories of Integration Ability in Autism

Beatriz López

Introduction

The proposal of weak central coherence theory (Frith, 1989) has had a great impact on the study of autism. Despite its success at explaining aspects of autism that other theories fail to explain, the original notion of central coherence theory suffers from a series of theoretical difficulties, the greatest of which is the over-extension of the definition of central coherence. The aim of this chapter is to reflect on different aspects of the concept of central coherence. In particular, this chapter questions the notion of central coherence as a central mechanism responsible for providing both perceptual and conceptual coherence, the assumption that superior processing for parts is the result of impairment in the ability to integrate visual information (i.e., global processing), and examines the issue of the precise level at which central coherence operates in view of recent empirical evidence and alternative theories such as enhanced discrimination theory (Plaisted, 2001) and enhanced perceptual functioning theory (Mottron & Burack, 2001; revised in Mottron, Dawson, Soulières, Hubert, & Burack, 2006).

It is more than 30 years since Hermelin and O'Connor (1970) made the proposal that children with autism have a cognitive impairment in the ability to integrate information and process information for meaning, yet little is known about the precise nature of this impairment. In an attempt to characterize integration impairments in autism Frith (1989) proposed weak central coherence (WCC) theory. "Central coherence" is the term coined by Frith (1989) to refer to the tendency of the cognitive system to integrate information into meaningful higher-level representations. Her proposal is that central coherence is weak in autism, and thus individuals with autism do not tend to integrate incoming information in its context, but instead preferentially attend to local information. Unlike other theories of autism, this theory attempts to explain not only impairments but also the islets of abilities that have been repeatedly found in autism. For instance, this theory predicts poor performance on tasks requiring the recognition of global meaning but relatively good performance on tasks where attention to local information is advantageous.

The advantage of WCC theory over other theories of autism is that, to date, no other developmental syndrome has been found to have the distinctive cognitive profile identified by WCC theory. Moreover, evidence shows that central coherence is weak even in high-functioning children who are able to pass tests of theory of mind (Happé, 1996). In spite of its advantages, Frith's original proposal suffered from a critical problem—the poor definition of the concept of central coherence. Whilst this may be seen as a criticism, it is important to note that, given the lack of empirical evidence available at the time, Frith's intuition opened a new area of research that has proven to be crucial for our understanding of autism and, more generally, for our understanding of how the cognitive system integrates incoming information.

In the next few sections some of the most controversial issues regarding the concept of central coherence are discussed in relation to recent empirical evidence not available at the time of Frith's (1989) original proposal and in view of two alternative theories: enhanced discrimination theory (Plaisted, 2001) and enhanced perceptual functioning theory (Mottron & Burack, 2001; revised in Mottron et al., 2006).

The Concept of Central Coherence

Despite the widely accepted recognition that the concept of central coherence was "a very slippery concept" (Baron-Cohen & Swettenham, 1997), little research was conducted in the years following Frith's original proposal aimed at developing, and refining, the concept. In the last few years, however, research in this area has advanced at an exponential rate. A first development was Happé's (1999) proposal that central coherence should be understood as a cognitive style that lies within a continuum in the normal population that ranges from strong "global" processing to strong local bias. This reformulation of the concept allowed for the prediction that individuals with autism may not necessarily have a global deficit (i.e., inability to integrate information) but relative poor performance on global tasks. The validity of such prediction, however, as it will be discussed in this chapter, has been contested extensively in view of conflicting empirical evidence regarding global ability in autism.

Another attempt to clarify the concept of central coherence has been the distinction made by Plaisted (2001) of two separate notions of central coherence: namely, conceptual coherence and perceptual coherence. Plaisted (2001) defines conceptual coherence as the ability to extract meaning or process information in its context, and perceptual coherence as the ability to perceive incoming sensory information as a whole rather than as its component parts. The adequacy of separating the conceptual and perceptual domains has, however, been challenged. Some authors argue that it is not possible to separate the two domains (e.g., Shutts & Spelke, 2004); others argue that abstract conception derives from perception (e.g., Goldstone & Barsalou, 1998); and the more traditional approach holds the view that there is a distinct dissociation between perceptual and conceptual processes (Mandler, 2004). This distinction, although questionable, may prove useful in examining the nature of central coherence as it will be discussed later in this chapter.

One of the core assumptions of weak central coherence is that central coherence is a *central* mechanism of the cognitive system, and thus responsible for the integration of information conceptually and perceptually. It has been shown that individuals with autism consistently have difficulty integrating information in context, or weak conceptual coherence (e.g., Frith & Snowling, 1983; López & Leekam, 2003), which is paired with superior local processing of sensory information (Jarrold, Butler, Cottington, & Jiménez, 2000; Morgan, Maybery, & Durkin, 2003; Shah & Frith, 1983). As noted above, however, the evidence of weak perceptual coherence has been contested (e.g., Mottron, Burack, Iarocci, Belleville, & Enns, 2003; Ozonoff, Strayer, McMahon, & Filloux, 1994).

In view of the mixed evidence of a global impairment in autism, Happé and Frith (2006) have proposed a reformulation of the theory, which consists in emphasizing the idea of superior local ability in autism rather than the presence of a global processing deficit. Although this reformulation of the concept allows for the explanation of the mixed evidence regarding global ability, it cannot explain the link between superior processing of sensory information and poor performance in contextual tasks. That is, the theory as it stands does not identify which mechanism or impairment is responsible for superior local processing *and* contextual difficulty in autism; is it an integration impairment or is it a local attentional bias? If it is an integration impairment, why do individuals with autism have difficulty integrating conceptually but not perceptually, and, if it is an attentional local bias, why does it not affect conceptual processing and perceptual processing to the same degree? To answer this question, it is first necessary to establish the extent to which integration deficits appear at both perceptual and conceptual levels in autism.

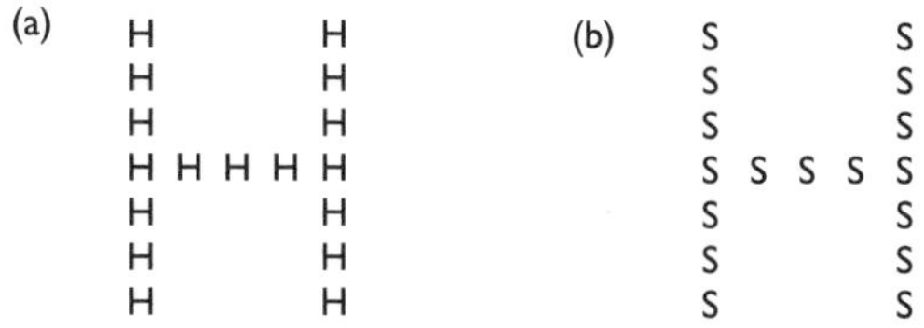

Figure 6.1 Example of stimuli used in the Navon task in the (a) compatible and (b) incompatible conditions.

Is Superior Featural Processing a Reflection of a Global Impairment?

Frith's (1989; 2003) original proposal was that, as a result of having weak central coherence, individuals with autism lack the ability to integrate parts into wholes and consequently present enhanced local processing. Research has demonstrated, with few exceptions (e.g., Brian & Bryson, 1996), that individuals with autism tend to be more accurate and faster (e.g., Jolliffe & Baron-Cohen, 1997; Ropar & Mitchell, 2001a; Shah & Frith, 1983) than comparison samples in tests that require ignoring the global configuration and focusing on parts of visual displays such as the Embedded Figures Test or the Block Design Test (Weschler, 1974; for a review see Happé, 1994). More importantly, evidence shows that this superiority is not due to general superior visuo-spatial abilities (Shah & Frith, 1993). In recent years, studies have also demonstrated superior local processing of auditory stimuli in autism, including superior memory for exact pitch (Heaton, 2003; Heaton, Hermelin, & Pring, 1998), and superior discrimination between melodies (Mottron, Peretz, & Mènard, 2000) and discrimination and categorization of pure tones (Bonnel et al., 2003).

It has been established, therefore, that autism is indeed characterized by superior local processing. The current debate is about whether this superiority is paired with an inability to perceive wholes. Evidence of a global impairment in autism comes largely from studies using the Navon task (Navon, 1977; see Figure 6.1). He designed a task in which stimulus patterns with local letters were nested within a large letter. The identity of the large and small letters could be the same (compatible condition) or different (incompatible). Typical adults were faster at recognizing large rather than small letters ("global advantage"). When participants were asked to report the small letter in the incompatible condition, the identity of the large letter interfered, slowing down reaction times and leading to increased errors. However, when reporting the identity of the large letter, there were no interference effects from the smaller letters in the incompatible condition. This effect is referred to as the "global interference effect."

Several studies have tested global perception in autism with the Navon task with mixed results. WCC theory predicts that a reversal of effects (e.g., "local advantage" and "local interference") would be expected in autism. In contrast, studies in autism have found evidence ranging from typical global advantage and interference effects (Mottron, et al., 2003; Ozonoff et al., 1994), global advantage but no interference effects (Mottron & Belleville, 1993), global advantage but local interference effect (Rinehart, Bradshaw, Moss, Brereton, & Tonge, 2000), or even typical global advantage and interference effects with one procedure, but local advantage and interference effects with another (Plaisted, Swettenham, & Rees, 1999). One other study (Mottron, Burack, Stauder, & Robaey, 1999) even found global advantage and global interference effects in the autism samples but not the comparison samples. Studies using hierarchical auditory stimuli, on the other hand, seem to indicate intact global processing of hierarchical musical stimuli (Heaton, 2003; Mottron et al., 2000).

A different area of research that provides evidence of global processing ability in autism is face perception. Face processing, unlike other types of visual processing, involves both holistic (whole) and featural (parts) processing (Tanaka & Farah, 1993). The most commonly used paradigms to test holistic face processing in autism are inversion paradigms and paradigms in which faces are presented at different angles (Davies, Bishop, Manstead, & Tantam, 1994; Gepner, de Gelder, & Schonen, 1996; Hobson, Ouston, & Lee, 1988; Langdell, 1978). In these paradigms, however, both the holistic configuration *and* features are manipulated, thus it is not possible to determine the individual effect that holistic and featural alterations have on performance.

A paradigm that enables direct comparison of feature and holistic processing of faces is that of Davidoff and Donnelly (1990) in which the ability to recognize a feature in isolation and within a face are compared. This was the paradigm employed in a recent study with ASD adolescents. The results of this study support WCC theory, as the autism sample, but not the comparison sample, failed to use global information of faces, although global processing of faces could be elicited by the provision of cues (López, Donnelly, Hadwin, & Leekam, 2004).

From these data, it is not possible, however, to conclude that there is a general global deficit in autism, as the impairment might be restricted to the social nature of facial stimuli. In a more recent study the same face task was used alongside a condition in which houses rather than faces were presented (López, 2005). The results of the face task study replicated the results of López et al. (2004). In the houses task, however, the same children were able to use global information of houses to recognize parts; this finding suggests that holistic difficulty in autism may be restricted to the processing of facial stimuli (although see Lahaie et al., 2006). The literature reviewed so far indicates that local superior processing in autism might not, after all, be the reflection of a global impairment, as Frith (1989) originally proposed.

Theoretical Explanations of the Relationship Between Local and Global Processing

Three different theories attempt to explain the failure to find global difficulty alongside local processing superiority in autism, enhanced discrimination theory (Plaisted, 2000; 2001), enhanced perceptual functioning theory (Mottron & Burack, 2001, revised in Mottron et al., 2006) and the most recent reformulation of weak central coherence theory (Happé & Frith, 2006). Reacting to recent evidence that global processing might be intact in autism, Happé and Frith (2006) have reformulated the concept of weak central coherence to emphasize the idea of "superiority in local processing rather than deficit in global processing" (p. 21). The proposal, hence, is no longer that superior local processing necessarily stems from a global impairment, but rather that there is a local processing bias which results in local processing strategies in open-ended tasks such as the standard procedure of the Navon task or in face recognition tasks but not in tasks where attention is directed, such as in one version of the Navon task used by Plaisted et al. (1999, Experiment 2). This proposal is further supported by results from a study in which we administered two versions of a face recognition task (López et al., 2004). In one version no cues were provided. In the second version a cue presented prior to the presentation of the face alerted participants to focus on a specific feature. Only in the cued version, but not in the uncued, did participants with autism use holistic information of faces to enhance recognition. These results demonstrate that holistic processing is not impaired in autism but needs to be elicited by means of instructions, as otherwise individuals with autism tend to use local processing strategies.

With the enhanced discrimination theory, Plaisted (2000, 2001) proposes that people with autism have enhanced discrimination of unique features and reduced generalization of common features. This theory is supported by studies showing enhanced feature search regardless of the number of distractors in autism (Jarrold, Gilchrist, & Bender, 2005; O'Riordan, Plaisted, Driver, & Baron-Cohen, 2001; Plaisted, O'Riordan, & Baron-Cohen, 1998) and reduced ability to extract prototypes (Klinger & Dawson, 2001; although see Molesworth, Bowler, & Hampton, 2005). The third theory, enhanced perceptual functioning (Mottron & Burack, 2001; revised in Mottron et al., 2006), states, in contrast, that in autism, perceptual processing overrides higher-control processes and thus the superiority at local processing and absence of global impairments.

Although there are subtle differences between the three theories, all concur in the suggestion that there is enhanced discrimination of features in autism—may this be named local bias, enhanced discrimination, or enhanced perceptual functioning—

B. LÓPEZ

Figure 6.2 Gestalt organizational law of similarity.

and that this superiority in the processing of features is not necessarily the result of, or results in, global processing impairments. There are two issues that need to be taken into consideration when evaluating the validity of these suggestions. First, there is evidence that in certain perceptual tasks individuals with autism do have difficulty integrating information. Second, any theory attempting to explain atypical information processing in autism needs to explain the relationship between the presence of local superiority paired with poor conceptual integration.

Regarding the issue of intact global processing in autism, evidence suggests that individuals with autism require more fragments to identify an object in the Hooper Visual Test (Jolliffe & Baron-Cohen, 2001), and that they are less likely to succumb to visual illusions such as the Titchener circles[1] (Happé, 1996, Figure 1), are less likely to use Gestalt principles (Brosnan, Scott, Fox, & Pye, 2004), are less able to identify impossible figures (Scott & Baron-Cohen, 1996), are not as hindered by the impossibility of a figure (Mottron, Belleville, & Mènard, 1999), or by visual contextual cues when reproducing a slanted circle (Ropar & Mitchell, 2002, and see Ropar, Mitchell,& Sheppard, Chapter 7), and have higher thresholds to detect coherent motion (Bertone, Mottron, Jelenic, & Faubert, 2003; Milne et al., 2002). All these studies indicate that, at some level, individuals with autism fail to integrate parts into wholes, so the issue is no longer as straightforward as the three theories suggest; enhanced local processing in autism does result in (certain) global processing difficulties. Investigating the nature of the integration demands of each might shed some light on which is the precise nature of integration difficulty at the perceptual level in autism (see Ropar et al., Chapter 7).

One plausible explanation for the discrepancy about global processing ability in autism has been suggested by Brosnan et al. (2004), using the distinction between global and Gestalt processing by Kimchi (1990; 1992). In hierarchical tasks, the constituent parts could be replaced without affecting the global configuration (e.g., in the Navon task a large H is perceived whether it is made of small "Ss," small "Ps," or geometrical shapes). In Gestalt figures and illusions, in contrast, the identity of the parts is crucial for the perception of the whole. For instance, in Figure 6.2 replacing one of the dots in the middle row by a different colored dot or by a star shape would no longer produce the illusion of a figure consisting of three rows. This distinction allows for the explanation of impaired performance in certain tasks but not in others in autism. If only Gestalt but not global processing is impaired in autism, then hierarchical tasks should not pose a problem for individuals with autism. Brosnan et al. (2004) found that children with autism indeed used fewer Gestalt principles than children with mild learning difficulty, but crucially, no group differences were found in a hierarchical task.

Currently, this seems to be one of the best explanations available, or at least a proposal worth considering, for the conflicting results found regarding the ability to integrate perceptually in autism, as this distinction can also explain the difficulty people with autism encounter with the Hooper Test, impossible figures, or the use of cues when perceiving a slanted circle, tasks in which it is necessary to process the interconnections between the different parts in order to build the whole.

Enhanced perceptual functioning theory explicitly states that in autism there is "overall superiority in visual processing" (Mottron et al., 2006, p. 14) and thus cannot adequately explain differential patterns of performance dependent on task demands. Enhanced discrimination theory, on the other hand, could explain difficulty with Gestalt principles as stemming from a difficulty to see the commonality between elements. The theory, however, cannot really account for performance in hierarchical or impossible figures tasks where it is not necessary to process similarities between elements.

One of the original criticisms made to WCC was the lack of definition of what precise integration mechanisms were impaired in autism. Brosnan et al.'s (2004) explanation could provide the means to overcome this criticism by offering a refined definition of central coherence as the ability to process Gestalt and not global configuration. It could then be predicted that if central coherence is weak, as it is proposed to be in autism, this would result in difficulty in specific tasks requiring the integration of elements in a particular fashion (e.g., by processing the interconnection between each other and the whole), whilst exhibiting intact performance on hierarchical tasks or any visual task where the identity of the elements is not important for the processing of the whole. This addition to the WCC theory would not interfere with the original proposal that local superiority in autism stems from an inability to integrate information, but this revision would simply specify the type of integration difficulty present in autism. This redefinition of the concept would also fit with Happé and Frith's (2006) conceptualization of central coherence as a cognitive bias that can be overcome by use of cues or training. More importantly, though, this distinction might be useful in explaining contextual difficulty in autism.

Theoretical Explanations for the Relationship Between Conceptual and Perceptual Impairments in Autism

As mentioned earlier, the other requisite a theory must meet to account for information-processing abnormalities in autism is that it explains the relationship between enhanced local processing, impairment in certain types of global tasks, and not in others, and impoverished conceptual processing.

Weak central coherence is based on the assumption that perceptual coherence and conceptual coherence are one and the same thing: that is, that central coherence is a central mechanism that operates at all levels and that, if weak, will result in difficulty on both perception and conception. This assumption has not been formally tested, though, as only two studies to date have explored weak central coherence across levels. The first study (Hoy, Hatton, & Hare, 2004) failed to provide statistical comparison of the perceptual and conceptual tasks, and therefore no conclusion could be drawn. In the second study (López, Leekam, & Arts, submitted) it was found that, contrary to predictions, 75% of the individuals with autism tested did not present difficulty across perceptual and conceptual tasks but instead presented either perceptual (40%) or conceptual integration difficulty (35%). These findings, however, need to be taken with caution, as the perceptual task was a face recognition task and therefore, for the reasons discussed above, might not have been suitable for measuring perceptual central coherence. If confirmed, however, these findings would have important implications for weak central coherence as, first, they question the assumption of a central integration mechanism, and second, the findings indicate the possibility of sub-groups within the autistic spectrum, which, if confirmed, could facilitate the search for neurobiological markers of autism (Tager-Flusberg & Joseph, 2003). The assumption of a central mechanism responsible for the integration of conceptual and perceptual information therefore remains to be tested. More importantly, the underlying integration mechanism common to both types of information processing remains to be identified.

Enhanced perceptual functioning (Mottron et al., 2006) postulates that conceptual difficulty in autism is the result of higher-order control not being mandatory in autism. This is an insightful proposal that is able to account for superior performance on a wide range of perceptual tasks. This theory also allows for the formulation of specific predictions in tasks where perceptual and conceptual information compete. The theory, however, has the same weakness as weak central coherence: namely, the vagueness of the definition of perception which precludes the formulation of specific predictions regarding performance on certain conceptual and perceptual tasks.

An alternative view of the possible relationship between conception and per-ception impairments in autism has been proposed by Plaisted (2001), based on evidence showing that concept formation is closely related to the perception of perceptual similarities (e.g., Allen & Brooks, 1991; Goldstone & Barsalou, 1998). Plaisted (2001) suggests that central coherence difficulties in autism at the concep-tual level stem from abnormalities at the perceptual level. Specifically, she argues that enhanced discrimination at the perceptual level in autism leads to a failure to categorize stimuli as being similar, which in turns leads to limited semantic cate-gorization, consisting of fewer exemplars in each category and fewer links between categories. This proposal, along with those made on the basis of weak central coherence and enhanced perceptual functioning theories, will be examined in the next section in view of evidence of conceptual coherence difficulty in autism.

A New Look at the Evidence of Weak Conceptual Coherence

Despite intact ability in autism to process single words and objects for meaning (Ameli, Courchesne, Lincoln, Kaufman, & Grillon, 1988; Eskes, Bryson, & McCor-mick, 1990; Frith & Snowling, 1983), it has been suggested that "it seems to be in connecting words or objects that coherence is weak [in autism]" (Happé & Frith, 2006, p. 14). A study that has been frequently cited as evidence of difficulty making connections between words is that of Tager-Flusberg (1991) which shows that chil-dren with autism fail to use semantic category information to facilitate recall. In this study, recall from a list of semantically related words (e.g., a list of animals) was compared to recall from a list of unrelated words (e.g., brown, cup, star, . . .). Whilst there was no difference in the number of words recalled from the unrelated list by the different groups, the group of children with autism, in contrast to the comparison samples, failed to show enhanced recall rates for related words.

These results contrast with evidence showing intact use of semantic information to facilitate recall in a visual task very similar in format to that used by Tager-Flusberg (Pring & Hermelin, 1993). In this study, memory for semantically related pictures (i.e., musical instruments) was compared to memory for shape-related objects (e.g., pear, light bulb, etc.). It was found that children with autism, like the comparison sample, tended to remember better the objects from the seman-tically related set than the objects from the structurally similar set. In a second experiment, Pring and Hermelin (1993) also found that children with autism, like the comparison sample, tended to pair together pictures of objects on the basis of semantic information rather than on the basis of the shape, a finding that has been further confirmed (Ropar & Mitchell, 2001b).

A possible explanation for the mixed results is that there is an asymmetry in the ability to conceptually integrate information across domains. Individuals with autism tend to perform better on visual than verbal tasks; thus it would be expected that they would also find it easier to integrate visual rather than verbal information. In order to directly test this possibility, the same semantic memory task used by Tager-Flusberg (1991) was administered to a sample of adolescents with autism (López & Leekam, 2003) who received a new visual condition in which objects rather than words were presented. Also, to enhance the power of the test, the number of lists presented was increased, as Tager-Flusberg's results were based on the comparison of only two word lists. The results showed that the children with autism used semantic information to enhance recall to the same extent as typically developing children, regardless of the modality in which the stimuli were presented. These findings demonstrated that most probably Tager-Flusberg's results are due to a methodological flaw (e.g., the lists used) and not to reduced facilitatory effects of semantic information in autism (López & Leekam, 2003). Furthermore, in this same study children with autism were also as able to use visual and verbal context information as the comparison sample on a semantic priming task, a finding that further supports the presence of intact ability in autism to connect single words and objects on the basis of meaning. Two other studies also confirm the presence of intact semantic priming in autism (Kamio & Toichi, 1998; Toichi & Kamio, 2001).

The results of these studies are quite surprising, as they can be taken as evidence that the ability to make semantic connections between words and objects is intact in autism, a finding in direct contrast to predictions from both the weak central coherence account (Happé & Frith, 2006) and the enhanced discrimination theory (Plaisted, 2001). Enhanced discrimination cannot account for these results, as it specifically predicts reduced semantic priming effects in autism as a result of diminished ability to process common features of objects. Weak central coherence theory, as it stands, cannot account for these results either as it makes a specific prediction about a difficulty to connect words and objects on the basis of meaning (Happé, 2000; Happé & Frith, 2006).

There is, however, vast evidence of weak conceptual coherence in autism in visual and verbal tasks. Individuals with autism show difficulty in sentence tasks (e.g., Frith & Snowling, 1983; Happé, 1997; Hermelin & O'Connor, 1967; Jolliffe & Baron-Cohen, 1999; 2000; López & Leekam, 2003) and in tasks evaluating false memory (Beversdorf et al., 2000). In the visual domain, evidence for difficulty selecting the odd picture out of a series of objects depicting a script (e.g., window-cleaning script = window, bucket, ladder, man, *suitcase*) and spotting an incongruous object in a contextual scene is still uncontested (Jolliffe & Baron-Cohen, 2001).

This evidence supports the notion of weak conceptual coherence difficulty across domains, although, as demonstrated by intact priming effects and use of semantic information in memory tasks (López & Leekam, 2003), the impairment seems to be restricted to higher levels than predicted even by the latest reformulation of the theory (Happé & Frith, 2006). In the absence of specific research directly investigating this issue, it is difficult to suggest which precisely might be the difficulty individuals with autism encounter with conceptual tasks. Brosnan et al.'s (2004) insight into the possible impairments at the perceptual level may be useful to explain the selective difficulty at the conceptual level as well; they argue that perceptual integration difficulty in autism is restricted to tasks where the identity of the elements is crucial for the perception of the Gestalt: that is, tasks where the replacement of any element alters the perception of the whole and where it is necessary to process simultaneously the interconnections between all the elements. This type of integrative processing resembles the type of processing required in higher-level conceptual tasks.

Let's take the window-cleaning script as an example (Jolliffe & Baron-Cohen, 2001). In this script neither window, bucket, ladder, nor man are semantically related. If we were to test the effect of the word or picture "window" on the word or picture "bucket" using a priming paradigm, we would probably fail to find any significant facilitating priming effects, and the same would be found for any of the other possible pairs. Presented together, however, it seems almost obvious that the items have something in common (e.g., being part of the "window-cleaning" script, see Chapter 7). Similarly, the words within a sentence are usually not directly related with each other, but when presented simultaneously, the relation emerges. For instance, in the sentence "*Mary had a tear in her dress*" neither of the possible pairs of words would probably prime any of the other words (e.g., the word "*Mary*" would not prime the word "*had*," nor would the word "*tear*" prime the word "*dress*").

This description of the task demands which are inherent in most conceptual tasks, or at least the tasks described above, is very similar to that of a Gestalt task whereby the replacement of any of the items substantially alters the perception of the whole. This is especially evident in sentence tasks but it is also true for visual tasks such as that used by Jolliffe and Baron-Cohen (2001). That is, in order to appreciate a visual illusion, to spot the odd picture out or to give the correct pronunciation of a homograph, it is necessary to establish the specific type of relationship that links all, and not just some, of the elements.

Landauer and Dumais (1997) propose that language acquisition is not merely the learning of direct associations, or co-occurrence relations, between words (i.e., learning that "*doctor*" and "*nurse*" tend to appear together) but learning of what they called second, higher-order or indirect associations (i.e., associations that go beyond the information presented in the words displayed). This distinction in the type of associations necessary to process, and acquire, language is useful when exploring performance of individuals in contextual and perceptual tasks. It could be argued that what is common to tasks in which individuals with autism present atypical performance is that the relationship between the elements goes beyond the direct associations between the elements. Even if still rather general at this point, this possibility would be worth investigating. More specific predictions could be made for differential performance by people with autism in the ability to detect direct, first-order associations and second-order associations. More importantly, this proposal would allow for the comparison across conceptual and perceptual domains. It would still be open to debate whether the integration impairment was a side effect of a more basic impairment to process information simultaneously, as the ability to establish second-order relationships relies heavily on the ability to hold multiple representations simultaneously.

Conclusions

Frith's (1989) original proposal of weak central coherence in autism has been extensively questioned, especially in the last five years, and as a result two alternative theories have been proposed to account for the wide range of empirical evidence: enhanced discrimination theory (Plaisted, 2001) and enhanced perceptual functioning theory (Mottron et al., 2006). These theories have been proposed in an attempt to explain the finding of spared global ability in autism in certain tasks.

In this chapter it has been argued that any theory attempting to explain atypical information processing in autism needs to adequately explain the link between conceptual and perceptual abnormalities in autism. Whilst enhanced discrimination theory has difficulty explaining the presence of certain conceptual impairments but not others (i.e., intact semantic priming and semantic memory), both weak central coherence and enhanced perceptual processing theories may be able to explain it. For the latter theory it will be necessary, however, to first conceptualize "perception" more specifically, so that predictions and explanations may be drawn to account for differential patterns of performance in perceptual and conceptual tasks. For weak central coherence, it will be necessary to specify the precise mechanism responsible for conceptual and perceptual impairments. This mechanism might be related to the generation of second-order relationships (i.e., connections across multiple stimuli which are not directly related), although more research is needed to prove this suggestion.

Integration Section

The aim of this book is to present an integrative view of theoretical and practical perspectives in autism. This chapter has attempted to provide a comprehensive account of theoretical accounts and empirical research evaluating integration ability in autism. A question that yet remains open is how integration ability/ impairments in autism relate to other areas of functioning and to other impairments in autism. A very interesting proposal on how integration ability may be related to social understanding is that of Eva Loth (Chapter 5). Loth describes a series of experiments which demonstrate that event knowledge is impaired in autism; children with ASD tend to provide idiosyncratic descriptors of events, tend to identify optional acts as central more often, do not use event knowledge to facilitate memory, and do not detect changes in a scene as well as typically developing children when the changes involve an expectation violation.

Loth argues that event knowledge is closely linked to social understanding. In her view, event knowledge typically develops from social skills such as joint attention or shared intentionality which are also precursors of theory of mind and are impaired in autism too. Her proposal is that due to an impairment in these earlier skills, people with autism have a limited understanding of event knowledge, which in turn impacts on their understanding of social situations. This is the best existing proposal of a possible link between social impairments in autism and more basic impairments at perceptual and conceptual levels. Loth talks about the lack of global structure and hierarchization (i.e., integration difficulty) that individuals with autism demonstrate in their description of events. It is possible thus to argue that integration difficulty in autism and social impairments may be related. It is too early to specify the nature or even the direction of this link. Do basic perceptual integration impairments lead to impairments in the understanding of the structure of social situations? Or is it the opposite, i.e., understanding the structure of social situations facilitates and guides perceptual processes later on? More developmental research is needed to explore the interconnections between social and perceptual/integration abilities as, to date, theories on integration impairments have not been linked specifically to the social impairments in autism. Early research in autism aimed to find the core impairment in autism that could explain both social and non-social impairments in autism. More recently, however, theories have been proposed to explain either social or non-social impairments, and hardly any attempt has been made to integrate the two. Loth's proposal is one of the few current theories that attempts to bridge this gap and thus is worth considering if we aim to provide a cohesive view of autism.

In this chapter three theories of integration difficulty in autism have been discussed: weak central coherence theory (Frith, 1989, 2003), enhanced perceptual functioning theory (Mottron et al., 2006), and enhanced discrimination theory (Plaisted, 2001). Despite the extensive empirical research carried out to evaluate these theories, no systematic research has been conducted to date aiming to develop interventions based of these theories.

One of the most cited limitations of interventions in autism is the lack of generalization of any skills learned during intervention sessions to other contexts. This difficulty in autism has been widely documented, yet hardly any links have been made between this difficulty to generalize and cognitive theories such as WCC or enhanced discrimination theory (although see Dunlop, Knott, & MacKay, Chapter 13). Enhanced discrimination theory, for instance, specifically predicts that due to enhanced discrimination of features in autism, individuals with autism will have reduced generalization. Although Plaisted (2001) describes reduced generalization in the context of perception and concept formation, reduced generalization should have an impact on all areas of functioning. Plaisted argues that because individuals with autism have enhanced discrimination of features, they will fail to see what is common between different objects. For instance, children with autism may fail to see what is common between a cat and a dog, and so they will have more difficulty to develop the concept of animals. If this is the case, then it follows that a child who is taught a skill in one intervention context will have difficulty recognizing what is common between the "intervention context" and another context in everyday life, and therefore will fail to produce the learned skill in the new context. Similarly, WCC theory would predict generalization difficulty in autism as stemming from a difficulty to make connections between different situations.

Understanding the precise nature of integration difficulties in autism therefore seems crucial for our understanding of generalization impairments in autism. In this chapter we propose that that all three current theories explaining integration difficulty in autism suffer from a series of theoretical drawbacks. In particular, it is proposed that individuals with autism may have spared integration ability at lower levels and only have difficulty in generating second-order relationships (i.e., connections across multiple stimuli which are not directly related). Jones and Jordan (Chapter 14) argue that interventions in autism do not always reflect changes in cognitive theories. If the proposal made in this chapter is confirmed, then interventions in autism should incorporate this modification to weak central coherence not only to address general problems in integration, but specifically to target the difficulty to make second-order connections and the effects this may have in generalizing skills.

Note

1   Although some studies fail to find differences in performance in visual illusions (e.g., Ropar & Mitchell, 1999; see Chapter 7) evidence shows that there are gamma abnor-

malities during perception of Gestalt-type stimuli even when there are no apparent differences in reaction times or accuracy (Brown, Gruber, Boucher, Rippon, & Brock, 2005).

References

Allen, S. W., & Brooks, L. R. (1991). Specializing the operation of an explicit rule. *Journal of Experimental Psychology: General, 120*, 3–19.

Ameli, R., Courchesne, E., Lincoln, A., Kaufman, A., & Grillon, C. (1988). Visual memory processes in high-functioning individuals with autism. *Journal of Autism and Developmental Disorders, 18*, 601–615.

Baron-Cohen, S., & Swettenham, J. (1997). Theory of mind in autism: Its relationship to executive function and central coherence. In D. J. Cohen & F. R. Volkmar (Eds.), *Handbook of autism and pervasive developmental disorders* (2nd ed., pp. 880–893). New York: John Wiley and Sons, Inc.

Bertone, A., Mottron, L., Jelenic, P., & Faubert, J. (2003). Motion perception in autism: A complex issue? *Journal of Cognitive Neuroscience, 15*, 218–225.

Beversdorf, D. Q., Smith, B. W., Crucian, G. P., Anderson, J. M., Keillor, J. M., Barrett, A. M., et al. (2000). Increased discrimination of "false memories" in autism spectrum disorder. *Proceedings of the National Academy of Sciences, 97*, 8734–8737.

Bonnel, A. C., Mottron, L., Peretz, I., Trudel, M., Gallun, E., & Bonnel, A. M. (2003). Enhanced sensitivity for pitch in individuals with autism: A signal detection analysis. *Journal of Cognitive Neuroscience, 15*, 226–235.

Brian, J. A., & Bryson, S. E. (1996). Disembedding performance and recognition memory in autism/PDD. *Journal of Child Psychology and Psychiatry, 37*, 865–872.

Brosnan, M., Scott, F., Fox, S., & Pye, J. (2004). Gestalt processing in autism: Failure to process perceptual relationships and the implications for contextual understanding. *Journal of Child Psychology and Psychiatry, 45*, 459–469.

Brown, C., Gruber, T., Boucher, J., Rippon, G., & Brock, J. (2005). Gamma abnormalities during perception of illusory figures in autism. *Cortex, 3* [Special issue: *Developmental Neurobiology*], 264–376.

Davidoff, J., & Donnelly, N. (1990). Object superiority: A comparison of complete and part probes. *Acta Psychologia, 73*, 225–243.

Davies, S., Bishop, D., Manstead, A. S. R., & Tantam, D. (1994). Face perception in children with autism and Asperger's syndrome. *Journal of Child Psychology and Psychiatry, 35*, 1033–1057.

Eskes, G., Bryson, S., & McCormick, T. (1990). Comprehension of concrete and abstract words in autistic children. *Journal of Autism and Developmental Disorders, 20*, 61–73.

Frith, U. (1989). *Autism: Explaining the enigma*. Oxford, UK: Basil Blackwell.

Frith, U. (2003). *Autism: Explaining the enigma* (2nd ed.). Oxford, UK: Basil Blackwell.

Frith, U., & Snowling, M. (1983). Reading for meaning and reading for sound in autistic and dyslexic children. *Journal of Developmental Psychology, 1*, 329–342.

Gepner, B., de Gelder, B., & Schonen, S. (1996). Face processing in autistics: Evidence for a generalised deficit? *Child Neuropsychology, 2*, 123–139.

Goldstone, R. L., & Barsalou, L. W. (1998). Reuniting perception and conception. *Cognition*, *65*, 231–262.

Happé, F. (1994). Weschler IQ profile and theory of mind in autism: A research note. *Journal of Child Psychology and Psychiatry*, *35*, 1461–1471.

Happé, F. (1996). Studying weak central coherence at low levels: Children with autism do not succumb to visual illusions: A research note. *Journal of Child Psychology and Psychiatry*, *37*, 873–877.

Happé, F. (1997). Central coherence and theory of mind: Reading homographs in context. *British Journal of Developmental Psychology*, *15*, 1–12.

Happé, F. (1999). Autism: Cognitive deficit or cognitive style? *Trends in Cognitive Science*, *3*, 216–222.

Happé, F. (2000). Parts and wholes, meaning and minds: Central coherence and its relation to theory of mind. In S. Baron-Cohen, H. Tager-Flusberg, & D. J. Cohen (Eds.), *Understanding other minds* (2nd ed., pp. 203–221). Oxford, UK: Oxford University Press.

Happé, F., & Frith, U. (2006). The weak coherence account: Detailed focused cognitive style in autistic spectrum disorders. *Journal of Autism and Developmental Disorders*, *36*, 5–25.

Heaton, P. (2003). Pitch memory, labelling and disembedding in autism. *Journal of Child Psychology and Psychiatry*, *44*, 543–551.

Heaton, P., Hermelin, B., & Pring, L. (1998). Autism and pitch processing: A precursor for savant musical ability. *Music Perception*, *15*, 291–305.

Hermelin, B., & O'Connor, N. (1967). Remembering of words by psychotic and subnormal children. *British Journal of Psychology*, *58*, 213–218.

Hermelin, B., & O'Connor, N. (1970). *Psychological experiments with autistic children.* Oxford, UK: Pergamon Press.

Hobson, P., Ouston, J., & Lee, A. (1988). What's in a face? The case of autism. *British Journal of Psychology*, *79*, 441–453.

Hoy, J. A., Hatton, C., & Hare, D. (2004). Weak central coherence: A cross domain phenomenon specific to autism? *Autism*, *8*, 267–281.

Jarrold, C., Butler, D. W., Cottington, E. M., & Jiménez, F. (2000). Linking theory of mind and central coherence bias in autism and the general population. *Developmental Psychology*, *36*, 126–138.

Jarrold, C., Gilchrist, I. D., & Bender, A. (2005). Embedded figures detection in autism and typical development: Preliminary evidence of double dissociation in relationships with visual search. *Developmental Science*, *8*, 344–351.

Jolliffe, T., & Baron-Cohen, S. (1997). Are people with autism and Asperger syndrome faster than normal on the Embedded Figures Test? *Journal of Child Psychology and Psychiatry*, *38*, 527–534.

Jolliffe, T., & Baron-Cohen, S. (1999). A test of central coherence theory: Linguistic processing in high-functioning adults with autism or Asperger syndrome: Is local coherence impaired? *Cognition*, *71*, 149–185.

Jolliffe, T., & Baron-Cohen, S. (2000). Linguistic processing in high-functioning adults with autism or Asperger's syndrome. Is global coherence impaired? *Psychological Medicine*, *30*, 1169–1187.

Jolliffe, T., & Baron-Cohen, S. (2001). A test of central coherence theory: Can adults with high-functioning autism or Asperger syndrome integrate objects in context? *Visual Cognition, 8,* 67–101.

Kamio, Y., & Toichi, M. (1998). Verbal memory in autistic adolescents. *Japanese Journal of Child and Adolescent Psychiatry, 39,* 364–373. As cited in Toichi & Kamio (2001).

Kimchi, R. (1990). Children's perceptual organisation of hierarchical patterns. *European Journal of Cognitive Psychology, 2,* 133–149.

Kimchi, R. (1992). Primacy of holistic processing and global/local paradigm: A critical review. *Psychological Bulletin, 112,* 24–38.

Klinger, L. G., & Dawson, G. (2001). Prototype formation in autism. *Development and Psychopathology, 13,* 111–124.

Lahaie, A., Mottron, L., Arguin, M., Berthiaume, C., Jemel, B., & Saumier, D. (2006). Face perception in high-functioning autistic adults: Evidence for superior processing of face parts, not for a configural face processing deficit. *Neuropsychology, 20,* 30–41.

Landauer, T., & Dumais, S. (1997). A solution to Plato's problem: The latent semantic analysis theory of acquisition, induction and representation of knowledge. *Psychological Review, 104,* 211–240.

Langdell, T. (1978). Recognition of faces: An approach to the study of autism. *Journal of Child Psychology and Psychiatry, 19,* 255–268.

López, B. (2005). *Global impairments in autism: Global or specific deficit?* Communication at the XIIth European Conference on Developmental Psychology (Tenerife, Spain).

López, B., Donnelly, N., Hadwin, J., & Leekam, S. (2004). Face processing in high-functioning children with autism: Evidence for weak central coherence. *Visual Cognition, 11,* 673–688.

López, B., & Leekam, S. (2003). Do children with autism fail to process information in context? *Journal of Child Psychology and Psychiatry, 44,* 285–300.

López, B., Leekam, S., & Arts, G. (submitted). *How central is central coherence? Preliminary data exploring the link between conceptual and perceptual processing in children with autism.* Manuscript submitted to *Autism.*

Mandler, J. M. (2004). *The foundations of mind: Origins of conceptual thought.* New York: Oxford University Press.

Milne, E., Swettenham, J., Hansen, P., Campbell, R., Jeffries, H., & Plaisted, K. (2002). High motion coherence thresholds in children with autism. *Journal of Child Psychology and Psychiatry, 43,* 255–263.

Molesworth, C. J., Bowler, D. M., & Hampton, J. A. (2005). The prototype effect in recognition memory: Intact in autism? *Journal of Child Psychology and Psychiatry, 46,* 661–672.

Morgan, B., Maybery, M., & Durkin, K. (2003). Weak central coherence, poor joint attention and low verbal IQ: Independent deficits in autism. *Developmental Psychology, 39,* 646–656.

Mottron, L., & Belleville, S. (1993). A study of perceptual analysis in a high-level autistic subject with exceptional graphic abilities. *Brain and Cognition, 23*(2), 279–309.

Mottron, L., Belleville, S., & Mènard, E. (1999). Local bias in autistic subjects as evidenced by graphic tasks: Perceptual hierarchization or working memory deficit? *Journal of Child Psychology and Psychiatry, 40,* 743–755.

Mottron, L., & Burack, J. (2001). Enhanced perceptual functioning in the development of autism. In J. A. Burack, T. Charman & P. R. Zelazo (Eds.), *The development of autism: Perspectives from theory and research* (pp. 131–148). Mahwah, NJ: Lawrence Erlbaum.

Mottron, L., Burack, J., Iarocci, G., Belleville, S., & Enns, J. T. (2003). Locally oriented perception with intact global processing among adolescents with high-functioning autism: Evidence from multiple paradigms. *Journal of Child Psychology and Psychiatry, 44,* 904–913.

Mottron, L., Burack, J. A., Stauder, J. E. A., & Robaey, P. (1999). Perceptual processing among high-functioning persons with autism. *Journal of Child Psychology and Psychiatry, 40,* 203–211.

Mottron, L., Dawson, M., Soulières, I., Hubert, B., & Burack, J. (2006). Enhanced perceptual functioning in autism: An update, and eight principles of autistic perception. *Journal of Autism and Developmental Disorders, 36,* 27–43.

Mottron, L., Peretz, I., & Mènard, E. (2000). Local and global processing of music in high-functioning persons with autism. *Journal of Child Psychology and Psychiatry, 41,* 1057–1068.

Navon, D. (1977). Forest before trees: The precedence of global features in visual perception. *Cognitive Psychology, 9,* 353–383.

O'Riordan, M., Plaisted, K., Driver, J., & Baron-Cohen, S. (2001). Superior visual search in autism. *Journal of Experimental Psychology: Human Perception and Performance Special Issue, 27,* 719–730.

Ozonoff, S., Strayer, D. L., McMahon, W. M., & Filloux, F. (1994). Executive function abilities in autism and Tourette's syndrome: An information processing approach. *Journal of Child Psychology and Psychiatry, 35,* 1015–1032.

Plaisted, K. (2000). Aspects of autism that theory of mind cannot easily explain. In S. Baron-Cohen, H. Tager-Flusberg, & D. J. Cohen (Eds.), *Understanding other minds: Perspectives from autism and cognitive neuroscience* (2nd ed., pp. 222–250). Oxford, UK: Oxford University Press.

Plaisted, K. (2001). Reduced generalization in autism: An alternative to weak central coherence. In J. Burack, T. Charman, N. Yirmiya and P. Zelazo (Eds.), *The development of autism: Perspectives from theory and research* (pp. 149–169). Mahwah, NJ: Lawrence Erlbaum Associates.

Plaisted, K., O'Riordan, M., & Baron-Cohen, S. (1998). Enhanced visual search for a conjunctive target in autism: A research note. *Journal of Child Psychology and Psychiatry, 39,* 777–783.

Plaisted, K., Swettenham, J., & Rees, L. (1999). Children with autism show local precedence in a divided attention task and global precedence in a selective attention task. *Journal of Child Psychology and Psychiatry, 40,* 733–742.

Pring, L., & Hermelin, B. (1993). Bottle, tulip and wineglass: Semantic and structural picture processing by savant artists. *Journal of Child Psychology and Psychiatry, 34,* 1365–1385.

Rinehart, N. J., Bradshaw, J. L., Moss, S. A., Brereton, A., & Tonge, B. J. (2000). Atypical interference of local detail on global processing in high-functioning autism and Asperger's syndrome. *Journal of Child Psychology and Psychiatry, 41,* 769–778.

Ropar, D., & Mitchell, P. (1999). Are individuals with autism and Asperger's syndrome susceptible to visual illusions? *Journal of Child Psychology and Psychiatry, 40*, 1283–1293.

Ropar, D., & Mitchell, P. (2001a). Susceptibility to illusions and performance on visuospatial tasks in individuals with autism. *Journal of Child Psychology and Psychiatry, 42*, 539–549.

Ropar, D., & Mitchell, P. (2001b). Do individuals with autism and Asperger's syndrome utilise prior knowledge when pairing stimuli? *Developmental Science, 4*, 433–441.

Ropar, D., & Mitchell, P. (2002). Shape constancy in autism: The role of prior knowledge and perspective cues. *Journal of Child Psychology and Psychiatry, 43*, 647–653.

Scott, F., & Baron-Cohen, S. (1996). Imagining real and unreal things: Evidence of dissociation in autism. *Journal of Cognitive Neuroscience, 8*, 371–382.

Shah, A., & Frith, U. (1983). An islet of ability in autistic children: A research note. *Journal of Child Psychology and Psychiatry, 24*, 613–620.

Shah, A., & Frith, U. (1993). Why do autistic individuals show superior performance on the block design task? *Journal of Child Psychology and Psychiatry, 8*, 1351–1364.

Shutts, K., & Spelke, E. (2004). Straddling the perception–conception boundary. *Developmental Science, 7*, 507–511.

Tager-Flusberg, H. (1991). Semantic processing in the free recall of autistic children: Further evidence for a cognitive deficit. *British Journal of Developmental Psychology, 9*, 417–430.

Tager-Flusberg, H., & Joseph, R. M. (2003). Identifying neurocognitive phenotypes in autism. *Philosophical Transactions of the Royal Society of London, Series B, 358*, 303–314.

Tanaka, J. W., & Farah, M. J. (1993). Parts and wholes in face recognition. *Quarterly Journal of Experimental Psychology, 46*, 225–245.

Toichi, M., & Kamio, Y. (2001). Verbal association for simple common words in high-functioning autism. *Journal of Autism and Developmental Disorders, 31*, 483–490.

Wechsler, D. (1974). *Weschler Intelligence Scale for Children—Revised*. New York: The Psychological Corporation.

7

The Influence of Conceptual Knowledge on Perceptual Processing in Autism

Danielle Ropar, Peter Mitchell, and Elizabeth Sheppard

The presence of superior perceptual abilities in autism, despite the associated cognitive and social deficits, is a striking contrast which has intrigued teachers, practitioners, and researchers alike. Even individuals with autism who have very low IQ and minimal communication skills can exhibit exceptional performance on tasks which require visual analysis such as drawing (Mottron & Belleville, 1993, 1995). Although some researchers argue over whether perceptual skills in autism are superior to matched controls or merely spared, most agree that it is not an area of deficit. Over the years researchers have tried to explain the uneven profile of abilities which characterizes autism. Although many theories have been proposed, only the theory of "weak central coherence" (WCC) attempts to explain both the strengths and the weaknesses of autism as a single deficit in information processing. The theory which was first proposed by Frith in 1989 includes two aspects of processing. The perceptual aspect states that individuals with autism process information locally rather than globally. That is, they tend to analyze stimuli in terms of their individual components and do not attempt to perceptually integrate these into a larger whole.

The theory also makes predictions about how information is processed at a conceptual level. Frith argues that typically developing individuals process stimuli in context, as they have a natural drive for meaning. This inherent propensity to conceptually integrate information is argued to be lacking in individuals with autism. This second part of the theory is argued to involve higher-level cognition, or what is referred to as "top-down" processing. Although a failure to process global form and meaning was initially characterized as a deficit in autism (Frith, 1989), it has more recently been argued to represent a cognitive style (Happé, 1999; Happé & Frith, 2006).

The theory of WCC has received considerable attention over the years as it is the only theory of autism which attempts to explain both the strengths and the weaknesses of the disorder. Despite its popularity, WCC has been criticized for not specifying the exact level at which coherence is thought to be weak in autism (see López, Chapter 6). This is complicated by the fact that tasks which have been argued to measure WCC can sometimes involve both perceptual and conceptual integration. For instance, Brian and Bryson (1996) argue that good performance on the Embedded Figures Test by individuals with autism (Shah & Frith, 1983) could be interpreted as a lack of integration at a conceptual or perceptual level. The Embedded Figures Task requires an individual to rapidly detect a smaller figure (e.g., a triangle) embedded within a larger design (e.g., a pram). Therefore, good performance on the task could mean that a person is less influenced by their conceptual knowledge linked to the larger design (i.e., being a pram) or that they are less captured by the wholeness. "Less capture by wholeness" simply means that one perceives the figure more in terms of its individual local components rather than as a single global form.

Some versions of the Embedded Figures Test, such as the adult form, involve finding figures in abstract rather than meaningful designs. A number of studies have demonstrated superior performance by individuals with autism using this form of the test (Joliffe & Baron-Cohen, 1997; Ropar & Mitchell, 2001a). In these cases one would be tempted to conclude that good performance by those with autism must be due to weak perceptual coherence. However, findings from these studies raise the possibility that the results could be interpreted at a conceptual level.

The study carried out by Ropar and Mitchell (2001a) demonstrated good performance by individuals with autism on the Adult Embedded Figures Task, despite showing intact perceptual coherence on a different task. Participants were presented with a computer task which measured susceptibility to visual illusions as well as the Embedded Figures Task. Visual illusions are argued to be ideal stimuli for testing perceptual coherence at very low levels, as they require integration of non-meaningful components (Happé, 1996). If one failed to perceptually process the various parts of the illusory stimuli as a whole, then they would not be susceptible to the illusion. The results from Ropar and Mitchell's (2001a) study showed that individuals with autism were just as susceptible to visual illusions as controls, although they outperformed controls on the Embedded Figures Test. Additionally, no correlation between performance on the two tasks was found. In light of these findings, it is important to consider alternative reasons for good performance on the Embedded Figures Test as a failure to integrate at a perceptual level does not seem to be a problem for some individuals with autism.

The study carried out by Joliffe and Baron-Cohen (1997) also demonstrated superior performance by individuals with autism, and the authors proposed that top-down processing (i.e., conceptual coherence) may be involved. They reported that typically developing adults were more likely than those with autism to describe the abstract designs in the Embedded Figures Test in terms of meaning. For example, they described some of the stimuli as a kite or fan. These findings highlight the fact that even when we are presented with stimuli that are assumed to be void of high-level meaning, our top-down processing abilities still operate. The authors suggest that there is a strong possibility that the participants without autism in their study were slower due to their tendency to interpret the stimuli as meaningful. Thus, a failure to search for meaning could explain why individuals with autism performed better than controls even with abstract designs.

In sum, the findings from these studies allow us to draw two important conclusions. First, it is important to explore WCC at both perceptual and conceptual levels within the same individuals, as difficulties may not exist at all levels, and may even vary among those with autism (see López, Chapter 6). Secondly, we should not assume that stimuli which are neither nameable nor identifiable are completely lacking in conceptual meaning. Tasks which may appear to involve processing at a relatively early perceptual stage can in fact involve top-down processing. Therefore, it is important for research into perceptual abilities in autism to explore the role of conceptual knowledge more closely. The aim of the current chapter is to discuss evidence which suggests that perception in autism is less influenced by conceptual knowledge (i.e., top-down processing) than it is in typically developing individuals. Implications of these findings for theories of autism, particularly weak central coherence, will be discussed.

Shape Constancy in Autism

An area where our conceptual knowledge has a definite role in our perception is with shape constancy. The phenomenon of shape constancy involves the perception of an object's real shape regardless of the image it projects onto the retina. A classic study carried out by Thouless (1931) conducted in the early part of the twentieth century investigated perceptual distortion associated with shape constancy. He identified a striking phenomenon surrounding participants' reproductions of a slanted circle: They systematically drew a more circular ellipse relative to the projected image. Thouless concluded that shape constancy exerted its effect by a matter of degree, which caused participants to perceive the ellipse as more circular than actually projected. Importantly, this research identified two factors that might contribute to this kind of shape constancy. One is the prior knowledge that the stimulus is a circle, and the other is ambient perspective cues. In everyday life we have some degree of knowledge about the objects we are viewing, such as their identity (e.g., dish) or associated features (e.g., circular). It could be that our conceptual knowledge about the object's true properties is sufficient to override how it actually appears when viewed at a slant (e.g., elliptical). However, we also view the object in the context of its environment, which is rich with depth and perspective cues. The integration of these cues within our perceptual field conveys that the target is slanted, emphasizing the object's three-dimensional properties (cf. Gibson, 1966). This information would be sufficient to specify the three-dimensionality of the stimulus, according to Gibson. This allows a shape-constancy process to function even if the participant does not regard the stimulus as belonging to the class of objects known as "circles." These alternative explanations can be argued to reflect the two levels of integration proposed by the theory of weak central coherence, the first involving conceptual integration and the second requiring perceptual integration.

If individuals with autism have difficulty integrating information at either of these levels, then we might find that they are more accurate in judging the projected shape of an image than comparison participants. We devised an experiment based on the procedure developed by Thouless (1931) in order to explore the effects of conceptual knowledge on perception independently of perspective cues (Ropar & Mitchell, 2002). Children and adolescents with autism were matched for chronological and verbal mental age with individuals having moderate intellectual disabilities (without autism). Typically developing children (aged 9 years) and adults also took part in the study. All individuals viewed a stimulus they knew was a slanted circle inside a chamber that was either illuminated, so perspective cues were present, or darkened, in which case only the stimulus itself was visible and perspective cues were absent (see Figure 7.1). In both of these conditions the participants' actual knowledge differed from the image projected onto the retina. A third control condition was included where participants were presented with an elliptical shaped stimulus which was positioned upright in the darkened chamber. In this instance, there was no discrepancy between the projected and actual shape, therefore participants were predicted to be fairly accurate when re-creating the shape via the computer. A correct estimation of the projected image in each condition would yield a score of 101 pixels. As expected, typically developing children (aged 9 years) and adults were significantly more accurate in judging shape in the ellipse control condition than the prior knowledge and perspective plus prior knowledge conditions (see Figure 7.2). This effect generalized to participants with moderate intellectual disabilities (without autism) and to individuals with autism. Importantly, however, individuals with autism were unique in exaggerating circularity to a lesser extent in the condition where perspective cues were removed (i.e., prior knowledge condition). In sum, the findings show that individuals with autism are equally affected by perspective cues when estimating shape, but are less

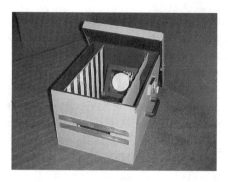

Figure 7.1 The chamber for housing the stimulus.

influenced by their conceptual knowledge than comparison participants. Specifically, whilst integration at a perceptual level appears to be intact, perception in autism may be less top-down or conceptually driven. This evidence emphasizes the value of considering that conceptual and perceptual contexts may influence processes independently.

Drawing Ability in Autism

Is the ability to suppress prior knowledge in autism something that is exploited by those who develop savant artistic ability? There is a general consensus among researchers that our conceptual knowledge proves to be a significant obstacle when attempting to draw an object accurately in typically developing children and adults. Evidence from developmental studies show that children's knowledge interferes with their ability to realistically draw what they see. Typically developing children aged 5–7 years include features in their drawings that form part of the object, but are hidden from their view. For example, a child will include the handle of a mug in their drawing even if it has been turned so that it is no longer visible from their perspective (Freeman & Janikoun, 1972). This phenomenon, which has been referred to as "intellectual realism," characterizes children's drawings until approximately 8 years of age (Luquet, 1913, 1927; Piaget & Inhelder, 1956, 1969). Subsequently, children achieve "visual realism," which allows them to accurately depict what they see (as opposed to what they know) from their own perspective. The difficulty a child experiences in drawing what they *see* correctly has been attributed to the representational knowledge held about the object. Although it is believed that drawing realistically is largely mastered by the age of 8 years, there is evidence of continued difficulty in accurately depicting a stimulus in adult-

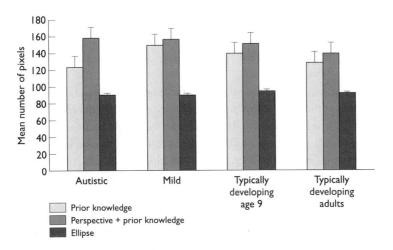

Figure 7.2 Shape estimations made on each condition for each group. The ordinate shows the number of pixels in the vertical axis of the reproduced shape (correct judgment = 101 pixels).

hood. Cohen and Bennett (1997) explored a number of possible causes of drawing errors in adults' depictions of photographs and line drawing. They argued that the major cause of drawing inaccuracies was misperception of an object due to the interference of prior knowledge (although they did not directly test this claim). A study carried out by Mitchell, Ropar, Ackroyd, and Rajendran (2005) provided the experimental evidence needed to confirm Cohen and Bennett's argument. Adult participants showed systematic errors when asked to copy line drawings of tables which where presented from an oblique perspective. Specifically, they made the table tops more rectangular than they actually were in the line drawings, which reflected their knowledge of how tables existed in the real world. Importantly, participants were more accurate when drawing the same table tops presented as parallelograms without the additional context of table legs.

Explanation of drawing abilities in those with autism has mainly been motivated by the existence of savant artists within this population, individuals who possess extraordinary drawing skills but otherwise average or below average cognitive functioning. One of the drawings by Stephen Wiltshire, an autistic savant (see Pring & Hermelin, 1993, p. 1372), is especially pertinent to the topic of the present study. His depiction of the interior dome of the British Library demonstrates, amongst other things, a remarkable talent for reproducing the elliptical projection of a circular feature at the very top of the dome. A study carried out by Mottron and Belleville (1995) also reported greater accuracy in reproducing a drawing of an ellipse that formed the depicted surface of a rotated cylinder. They found that a drawing savant (E. C.) was substantially more accurate than normal draughtsmen. Although unclear from the report, it seems likely that the draughtsmen systematically exaggerated circularity, while this effect was either far weaker or even absent in E. C.

One explanation, proposed by Snyder and Mitchell (1999), is that savant artists perceive visual material with a relative absence of conceptual analysis, enabling high levels of visual accuracy (although see Pring & Hermelin, 1993). They argue that savant artists have minds that are less concept-driven, allowing them to focus more readily on "lower-level" perceptual characteristics. In a further paper, Snyder and Thomas (1997) propose that even for the wider population of individuals with autism, visual perception is less influenced by the mental representations that embody expectations about what is to be seen, than for individuals without autism. Surprisingly, however, accurate depiction in autistic savants appears to occur even in the presence of ambient perspective cues. It could be that autistic savants provide a special case, in that they are less affected by the surrounding depth and perspective cues as well as their conceptual knowledge when drawing. Indeed, Frith (1989) has argued that there may be variation in WCC abilities in typical as well as autistic populations. Autistic savants may represent the lower end of the range of coherence abilities. In support of this suggestion, Pring, Hermelin, and Heavey (1995) provided evidence that autistic savant artists showed WCC to an even greater extent than non-talented individuals with autism. They tested savant artists with autism, gifted artists without autism, and non-talented groups with and without autism on the Wechsler Block Design Task. This task requires an individual to re-create an abstract design using individual blocks, which possess parts of the design on each side. In line with previous studies (Shah & Frith, 1993), the controls with autism were faster than the controls without autism. However, both groups of artists were significantly faster than controls with or without autism. This implies that whilst individuals with autism have a general tendency toward localized visual processing, this tendency is stronger in those that are savant artists. These findings are especially compatible with the more recent formulation of WCC, which posits that weak coherence is a processing style, rather than a deficit, which is also evident in the typical population (Happé & Frith, 2006).

Although it has been suggested that non-savant individuals with autism, as well as those with precocious talents, are less inclined to conceptually analyze visual material (e.g., Milbrath & Siegel, 1996), few studies have systematically investigated whether the drawings of non-savant individuals with autism evidence a lack of conceptual analysis of the subject matter. If perception in autism is less top-down then we might find relatively better drawing performance in non-savant individuals with autism than those without autism. As a result, their drawings could be highly informative, not only about the visual cognition of individuals with autism, but also about the normal processes of visual perception for those without the condition.

Initial studies exploring drawing in non-savant individuals with autism failed to show any signs of advanced or more accurate drawing ability (Charman & Baron-Cohen, 1993; Eames & Cox, 1994). However, drawing is a complex process, and multiple factors will influence success or failure on any particular drawing task (van Sommers, 1989). In these previous studies, participants were asked to draw from real-world three-dimensional models, and various factors could potentially account for failures in accuracy. Difficulties with planning the drawing, an inability to decide which aspects to draw; or failures to understand what kind of drawing was required could all lead to inaccurate drawings. Chen (1985) argues that in order to draw an object (e.g., a cube) from real life, children need to overcome their knowledge about the object and must also have appropriate drawing devices. For example, they must be familiar with the convention of using diagonal lines and foreshortened shapes to create the impression of depth. By contrast, they do not need these drawing devices to copy a cube depicted two-dimensionally, because a solution is already presented. Therefore, any error in drawing the stimulus can be attributed to the interference of one's conceptual knowledge of how the object actually appears in real life. Moreover, when participants are drawing from a real-world model, there is no "ideal" drawing against which to evaluate the success or failure of the drawing produced. A task that involved copying line drawings could allow a more effective examination of the extent to which conceptual analysis of the subject matter has influenced its reproduction.

Research which has explored copying of two-dimensional outline drawings which possess three-dimensional perspective cues have revealed differences between those with and without autism. Mottron, Belleville, and Mènard (1999) reported that individuals with autism were faster than comparison participants in copying impossible geometric figures (e.g., a Penrose triangle), suggesting that they were not perplexed by the oddity of the stimuli. While impossible figures contain contradicting perspective cues on the orientation of various planes, these contradictions are evident only in a comparison between parts of the figure. Perhaps individuals with autism attended successively to different regions of the stimulus in a piecemeal fashion, with the consequence that they remained oblivious to the perspective contradictions in the form as a whole (cf. Frith, 1989). Another possibility, though, is that participants with autism were less influenced by the conceptual knowledge (Ropar & Mitchell, 2002; Shah & Frith, 1983). Perhaps those with autism did not compare the stimuli with prior knowledge of the prototypical form that one expects triangles and forks to take. An absence of influence by prior knowledge would liberate them to attend specifically to the stimulus as presented (cf. Ropar & Mitchell, 2001b).

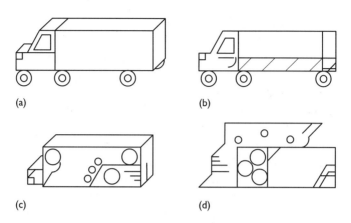

Figure 7.3 Set of four stimuli: (a) meaningful three-dimensional; (b) meaningful two-dimensional; (c) non-meaningful three-dimensional; (d) non-meaningful two-dimensional.

Through most of this chapter we have argued that errors in perception due to our prior knowledge about an object can result in poor performance on judgment and drawing tasks. The term "knowledge" has been used loosely to refer to meaning (in terms of being identifiable) as well as other associated physical properties of an object (i.e., shape/dimensionality). However, there is evidence that different conceptual aspects of a drawn stimulus have independent effects on drawing accuracy. Difficulties with drawing real-world three-dimensional models could be associated with either the meaningfulness of the model (it being a familiar object) or with its three-dimensionality (Sheppard, Ropar, & Mitchell, 2005). Using a copying task, we asked children to copy line drawings where meaningfulness and dimensionality were factorially contrasted (see Figure 7.3 a–d for example stimuli). Typically developing 7-year-olds produced poorer copies of items that depicted the third dimension than items that depicted only two dimensions. This may be because, in order to depict the three-dimensional aspects of the stimuli, it is necessary to overcome a default tendency to draw certain features based on one's knowledge of the true shape. For example, there is an inclination to draw the top of the lorry rectangular, rather than the projected parallelogram shape. For two-dimensional items, where only the frontal plane is drawn, there is no conflict between the individual's knowledge of the true shape and what they are being asked to draw. Typically developing children also produced superior drawings when the item was meaningful than when it was unfamiliar, perhaps because meaning enables individuals to analyze drawings into larger and better-organized chunks. This suggests that children's difficulty may actually arise from their knowledge about the object's physical structure gained from their interpretation of the

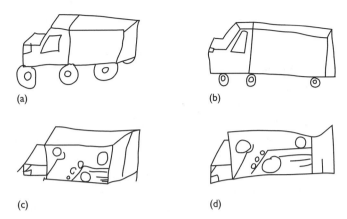

Figure 7.4 Drawings of the three-dimensional (meaningful, a–b; and abstract, c–d) stimuli made by children with and without autism: (a) male with autism, 12 years 2 months; (b) male without autism, 12 years 6 months; (c) male with autism, 9 years, 6 months; (d) female without autism, 9 years, 1 month.

dimensional cues. If meaningfulness and dimensionality can influence drawing accuracy in different ways, it may be useful to consider these two forms of knowledge separately.

Using the methodology developed by Sheppard et al. (2005), we investigated the impact of meaningfulness and dimensionality on drawing accuracy for children and adolescents with and without autism. We predicted that participants without autism would produce superior drawings of meaningful than non-meaningful items, and superior drawings of two-dimensional than three-dimensional items. For participants with autism we predicted that there would be reduced effects of meaningfulness (a smaller difference in accuracy between meaningful and non-meaningful items) and dimensionality (a smaller difference in accuracy between two-dimensional and three-dimensional items). The results showed (Sheppard, Ropar, & Mitchell, in press) that although individuals in both groups produced better drawings of two-dimensional than three-dimensional items, the children with autism were less affected by dimensionality and used more advanced projection systems for drawing cube-shaped items (see Figure 7.4 a–d for examples of participants' drawings). Importantly, there was no evidence that individuals with autism used a localized drawing strategy, such as drawing in a piecemeal or fragmented style, in Sheppard's study, which would be expected according to the theory of WCC (Booth, Charlton, Hughes, & Happé, 2003). These findings could also account for the ease with which individuals with autism draw impossible figures (Mottron et al., 1999). Being less influenced by dimensionality would certainly make an individual more immune to the contradicting depth and perspective cues within impossible figure stimuli.

A surprising finding produced from Sheppard et al.'s work (Sheppard et al., in press) is that children with autism benefited from meaningfulness to the same extent as children without autism. We have previously argued that meaning might allow children to analyze the relevant drawing into larger and better-organized chunks, resulting in better copies (Sheppard, et al., 2005; see also Akshoomoff & Stiles, 1995). It might also lead to the inclusion of small details (based on the expectation of their presence) that might be overlooked if the material is unfamiliar. The finding that those with autism were equally responsive to stimulus meaning as those without autism does not support the broad suggestion that they do not conceptually analyze visual information. Instead, it would seem that they are equally influenced by some conceptual aspects of stimuli but not others. Evidence from research which has not involved drawing also suggests that individuals with autism can be influenced by the meaning of visual material (e.g., Ameli, Courchesne, Lincoln, Kaufman, & Grillon 1988; Brian & Bryson, 1996; López & Leekam, 2003), and use it to their advantage. Conversely, there is research which has shown that individuals with autism often ignore deeper meaningful aspects of stimuli (in favor of attending to visual features) when categorizing stimuli. The following section explores various reasons presented within the categorization literature to explain why individuals with autism might attend to deeper meaningful aspects of stimuli in some tasks but not others.

Do Individuals With Autism Utilize Prior Knowledge When Categorizing?

In order to form conceptual categories, an individual needs to recognize similarities between stimuli. These similarities could exist at either a perceptual or an abstract level. Abstract information in this sense refers to information which cannot be directly perceived but instead must be abstracted from the available input and integrated with previous knowledge. Perceptual categorization, however, can be carried out using a matching strategy solely on the visual information presented. If perception in autism is less top-down, then we might expect a greater tendency to collate items according to perceptual features. Research carried out by Shulman, Yirmiya, and Greenbaum (1995) found that individuals with autism fail to group objects into categories which involve abstract, meaningful representations. In a free sorting task participants were asked to make groups of "things that go together." Individuals with autism were able to successfully associate items of a similar color or shape, but they performed worse than control participants when required to sort items which represented a category such as trees, beds, animals, tools, vehicles, and humans. Shulman et al. (1995) suggest that individuals with autism are more adept at processing concrete features than abstract categories, and this may reflect a more general deficit in processing. Arguably, forming categories based on abstract information is a more difficult skill, as this requires the internal manipulation of representational knowledge.

However, the idea of a general deficit in processing on a representational level is challenged by research showing that individuals with autism can categorize according to meaningful criteria such as function or semantic relatedness (Baron-Cohen, 1991; Ropar & Mitchell, 2001b; Tager-Flusberg, 1985a, 1985b). One might argue that these studies include certain features which help those with autism to attend to abstract criteria. In two studies individuals with autism were explicitly asked to sort according to a pre-fixed category (Tager-Flusberg, 1985b; Baron-Cohen, 1991). Shulman et al. (1995) argue that being provided with the category label is easier than having to infer the category from the stimuli set. The benefit of having a category cue word (e.g., fruit) also was found to assist individuals with autism in recalling a list of thematically related words (Tager-Flusberg, 1991). (See, nevertheless, López, Chapter 6.)

Other studies which have shown that individuals with autism do use abstract information to assist with categorization have used a matching-to-sample paradigm (Ropar & Mitchell, 2001b; Tager-Flusberg, 1985a). Tager-Flusberg's study required participants to match a target picture (e.g., armchair) with either a semantically related (e.g., rocking chair) or non-related alternative (e.g., sedan car). Participants with autism successfully selected the semantic options to match the target items. However, one limitation of the task is that the semantic items were also more structurally similar to the target than to the non-related alternatives. Thus, individuals with autism may have matched the items on the basis of visual similarities rather than abstract relatedness. In Ropar and Mitchell's (2001b) task this problem was avoided by asking participants to match atypically colored stimuli (e.g., blue banana) with either a colored patch that was semantically related (e.g., yellow) or one that was visually similar (e.g., blue). Individuals with autism, like mental age-matched controls, were more likely to select the alternative that was semantically related to the target. Although this supports the view that individuals with autism do process stimuli on an abstract level, the unusual color of the items may have cued attention to the semantically related option. This may have resulted in children responding as if they were being asked to choose the "correct" color. An additional drawback of matching-to-sample paradigms like those used by Tager-Flusberg (1985a) and Ropar and Mitchell (2001b) is that they force participants to use one of two strategies. This could result in an individual picking the correct option by eliminating the alternative. Furthermore, the alternatives act as cues to a particular strategy which an individual might not have generated on their own.

In sum, research which shows that individuals with autism categorize according to abstract criteria has either explicitly provided participants with the category label for sorting, or included certain perceptual features which may have assisted participants to sort in this way. This suggests that they may have a cognitive weakness that results in attention to concrete visual features of the stimuli in the absence of cues toward abstract properties. In an attempt to test out this claim, Ropar and Peebles (2007) devised a task which required participants to sort stimuli according to either concrete visual properties or abstract features. Twenty-four books were created which could be sorted into two groups on the basis of either concrete features (color: orange/green; size: large/small) or abstract criterion (category membership: sports/games). Both concrete and abstract features were fully counterbalanced across the stimuli. Thus, in order to sort using an abstract criterion, one needed to *infer* a relationship between the stimuli which could not be achieved through using a visual strategy. Perceptual features within the pictures representing sports and games were also controlled for. For instance, not all pictures depicting sports included a ball, therefore one could not use a *ball present/ball absent* criterion to distinguish between the sports and games.

Individuals with autism, moderate intellectual disabilities (non-autistic controls matched on mental age), and typically developing 8-year-olds were asked to sort the books into two different boxes. All the typically developing children sorted the items according to category membership, but the two clinical groups used a mixture of strategies. A greater percentage of those with autism sorted according to visual features such as color (52%) and size (9%) than those with moderate intellectual disabilities (color: 15%; size: 6%). Importantly, a significantly smaller percentage of individuals with autism (39%) used category membership as a criterion for sorting than non-autistic matched controls (79%). These results cannot be explained by a lack of knowledge about sports and games as all individuals with autism who sorted visually were able to identify the appropriate category of each book when explicitly asked. Therefore, these findings suggest that individuals with autism are not *incapable* of processing stimuli at an abstract level; they simply do not give this information priority when other alternative, less abstract, information is available.

It seems plausible that the concrete properties of the stimuli, especially color, appeared to be a more salient strategy to those with autism. One might consider that the concrete visual properties detracted attention from the deeper abstract dimension of the stimuli. If the option to sort using a concrete criterion is removed, those with autism may process the stimuli at a deeper level allowing them to sort by category membership. To test this possibility, a further 16 individuals with autism were presented with a set of books which were identical to the first set in terms of the pictures and labels, except that they were all the same size and color (blue). Although all but one were subsequently able to identify each item as a game or sport, only 8 of the 16 participants sorted them according to category membership. Therefore, the removal of salient concrete features was sufficient to allow half of those with autism to use an abstract strategy, while the remaining individuals needed to be provided with the category labels in order to do so.

In sum, these findings suggest that individuals with autism tend not to rely on their prior (abstract) knowledge when sorting stimuli. However, by removing salient visual strategies or by providing them with the category label, individuals with autism were able to sort using an abstract criterion. It might be that any preference to process information that is relevant to abstract criteria is masked by an inability to disengage attention from the more concrete properties of the stimuli (see Hill, Chapter 8; cf. Hughes & Russell, 1993; Ozonoff, Pennington, & Rogers, 1991; Russell, Mauthner, Sharpe, & Tidswell, 1991). If this explanation is correct, then future research might identify an association between a lack of preference for sorting by an abstract criterion and signs of executive dysfunction. Indeed, perhaps those with autism who sorted by category membership had less severe executive impairment than those who sorted according to a concrete criterion. It might be that having autism interacts with having executive dysfunction in militating against using an abstract criterion for sorting (cf. Rajendran, Mitchell, & Rickards, 2005).

Can Less Influence by Conceptual Processing Explain Atypical Perception in Autism?

The aim of this chapter was to review a selection of studies which explored the role of conceptual processing on perception in autism across a range of different tasks. A further aim was to assess the implications of these various findings for the theory of weak central coherence. Is there sufficient evidence to suggest that perception is less top-down, and can the theory of WCC account for this? The study by Ropar and Mitchell (2002) showed that individuals with autism did integrate perceptual cues in their environment, like those without autism, when judging the apparent shape of a slanted circle. However, their prior knowledge of the object's shape does not contaminate their perception and judgment to the same extent. In this respect, individuals with autism might be equipped to inspect a scene more objectively, although they are not completely immune to prior knowledge when processing visual input. It was suggested that less use of top-down processing might enhance drawing performance in non-savant individuals with autism where knowledge can often lead to errors. Evidence from copying outline drawings with three-dimensional properties showed individuals with autism were faster (Mottron et al., 1999) and more accurate in drawing stimuli (Sheppard et al., in press). These findings were attributed to knowledge specifically relating to the three-dimensional properties of the stimuli rather than its meaningfulness (familiar or abstract). In fact, the autism group in Sheppard et al.'s study actually showed better drawing accuracy, as did controls, when the stimuli were familiar and recognizable as objects. Being less affected by certain forms of knowledge that specifically cause distorted perception of stimuli may help explain the increased presence of savant skills in autism. Training programs could be developed which capitalize upon this feature of autism, as, currently, most tend to focus on improving areas of deficit such as social skills (see Dunlop, Knott, & MacKay, Chapter 13). The role of top-down processing in categorization was also discussed. Although individuals with autism are able to classify items according to deeper abstract properties, they may not always use this as a basis for sorting stimuli.

This is the case specifically if they have an alternative way to categorize objects which is more concrete, such as visual similarities (Ropar & Peebles, 2007). It seems that they do not naturally process stimuli in terms of abstract meaning unless their attention is sufficiently directed to this level of processing. These findings may point toward difficulties with executive control such as disengaging and shifting attention (see Hill, Chapter 8). There are also implications for individuals working with autistic populations such as parents, educators, and clinicians. They may need to cue attention to abstract levels of stimuli particularly when they possess salient visual cues.

Although, in general, the evidence shows that perceptual processing in autism may be less top-down than in non-autistic individuals, it would be incorrect to say that they have an extensive problem in *utilizing* knowledge when processing visual input for two reasons. First, the influence of knowledge in perception is attenuated rather than absent. Secondly, individuals with autism do utilize certain forms of knowledge under different conditions.

Do these findings add up to compelling support for the theory of weak central coherence? The findings show that there is something special about autistic visual processing, but it is not necessarily enlightening to explain this by saying they have weak central coherence—on the contrary, this probably would give an incorrect impression of autistic abilities. The theory proposes that individuals with autism are characterized by detail-focused processing such that they do not integrate information at a perceptual or conceptual level. Evidence that individuals with autism do perceptually integrate features has been demonstrated in their susceptibility to visual illusions (Ropar & Mitchell, 2001a), their being equally affected by perspective cues on a shape constancy task (Ropar & Mitchell, 2002), and their lack of a localized drawing style (Sheppard et al., in press). It seems that an ability to integrate information at a perceptual level is intact. However, some individuals with autism may have problems with integrating at a perceptual level, while others have difficulty integrating information at higher levels (see López, Chapter 6). Support for the second part of the theory, which posits difficulty with integrating information to derive higher-level meaning, appears to be mixed. Whilst there is evidence to suggest that those with autism may use top-down knowledge less, this is not always the case. Individuals with autism may utilize some forms of knowledge, but not others (Sheppard et al., in press). Furthermore, characteristics of some tasks may encourage and help an individual with autism attend to deeper conceptual features of stimuli that they would otherwise ignore. If we are to retain the idea that individuals with autism have weak *conceptual* coherence, we need to be able to specify the type of knowledge and circumstances that pose a difficulty for those with autism.

Can features of autism be understood in terms of less influence by conceptual knowledge? There is sufficient evidence to suggest that minimizing the use of top-down processing can be advantageous in some tasks. This can help to explain the superior performance of those with autism on visuo-perceptual tasks and may help to understand savant skills in autism. However, there are instances of atypical perception in autism which cannot be easily explained by a failure to use conceptual processing: notably, superior visual search for a target within an array of distracters (O'Riordan, Plaisted, Driver, & Baron-Cohen, 2001) and interference from local to global levels on hierarchical tasks (Mottron & Belleville, 1993). Therefore, reduced use of top-down knowledge may contribute to atypical perception in autism, but cannot be the only factor involved. Plaisted, O'Riordan, and Baron-Cohen (1998) have suggested that enhanced perceptual processing at low levels may contribute to distinctive perception in autism. Individuals with autism also have a number of social and communication difficulties which need explaining. Relying on our prior knowledge of social norms and rules (i.e., cultural knowledge) is important for us to judge what is and is not appropriate social interaction (see Loth, Chapter 5). It could be that individuals with autism do not utilize this cultural knowledge in the same way as those without autism. In sum, less influence by conceptual knowledge does appear to be a useful avenue to explore to increase our understanding of the non-social and social aspects of autism. Further work will need to be carried out to determine the extent and nature of the difficulty and whether it can be understood in terms of WCC.

Integration Section

Overall, the research discussed in this chapter reveals two important aspects of cognition in autism. First, perceptual processing appears to be intact at lower levels of integration, but less influenced by conceptual knowledge. Secondly, and more crucially, conceptual integration is neither deficient nor is completely absent. Instead, under certain conditions top-down knowledge has relatively little impact on perceptual processing in autism, whereas in other circumstances it appears to be normal. How can these findings be interpreted in light of other current research on cognitive and biological functioning in autism?

As already mentioned in this chapter, the research discussed poses particular difficulty for the theory of WCC. Specifically, there is little evidence for visual perceptual integration difficulties at low levels. If the theory is to maintain credibility, it needs to be able to account for this. López (see Chapter 6) offers a plausible solution by arguing that perceptual integration may be affected only at certain levels, such as Gestalt processing, which could be explicable in terms of difficulties at higher levels. The view appears compatible with the ideas presented in this chapter which emphasize the need to consider the role of higher-level processes in perceptual tasks, such as those exploring shape constancy.

Another challenge that the theory of WCC faces in light of the research reviewed is in explaining the inconsistent findings in relation to conceptual integration. While we found evidence of less influence by top-down knowledge on a shape-constancy task (Ropar & Mitchell, 2002), findings from drawing and categorization studies question the extent to which conceptual integration may be a problem in autism. Results from Sheppard et al. (in press) demonstrate intact processing of meaning in participants with autism, but less influence from dimensional knowledge as evident from their copies of drawings with three-dimensional attributes. This study highlights the importance of exploring how various types of knowledge may be differentially affected in autism. Similarly, López also discusses the need for researchers to consider the specific type of integration required by certain tasks if we are to shed light on the particular difficulties found in autism.

In addition to exploring different forms of integration, we also need to understand why individuals with autism successfully utilize the same type of conceptual knowledge in some circumstances, but not others. This finding is most apparent in the categorization literature, where many inconsistencies exist. Ropar and Peebles (2007) found that the majority of individuals with autism did not sort according to an abstract criterion (i.e., sports/games) when also allowed the option of sorting according to visual features (i.e., color). It was argued that a failure to use an abstract criterion may be due to executive function difficulties in shifting attention away from the more salient visual features of the stimuli. Differences in the visual salience of information in autism have also been reported by Jones and Klin (see Chapter 4). However, they argue specifically for greater salience of non-social than social stimuli. Although the pictures depicting sports and games did not all depict people, it could be argued that these categories hold more social relevance than color. Therefore, it is possible that performance by those with autism in Ropar and Peebles's (2007) task was a result of their preference to attend to non-social over more socially associated features.

When visual strategies were removed, or when those with autism were explicitly asked to sort by sports and games, they were able to do so. This may reflect an inability to generate alternative strategies that require global processing in the presence of possible local strategies such as color (see Hill, Chapter 8). The results of Ropar and Peebles's (2007) study also reflect other findings in the literature of poor implicit but good explicit processing on certain tasks. Loth (Chapter 5) reports that individuals with autism fail to use the relevant context of a situation in order to assist with their recall of a series of objects. This demonstrates that those with autism do not automatically utilize their conceptual knowledge when processing information when not explicitly requested to. Similarly, Wicker (Chapter 2) argues that those with autism perform well on explicit emotion recognition tasks, but poorly on implicit tasks. He proposes that there may be abnormal connectivity of the medial prefrontal cortex in autism based on his functional neuroimaging studies. Specifically, he argues that in explicit tasks, an abnormally strong influence of the right prefrontal cortex may compensate for the dysfunction in the amygdala dorso-medial prefrontal cortex allowing for good performance. However, in everyday life where task demands are less explicit, this compensatory mechanism may be less active, resulting in difficulties. Wicker offers a biological explanation which may help us to better understand the inconsistent use of conceptual knowledge by those with autism in the literature.

In light of the research discussed in this chapter, can the theory of WCC still provide a useful basis for designing interventions to help individuals with autism? While the findings suggest that perceptual integration may be less of a concern, conceptual coherence is still an issue that needs to be addressed by educators and clinicians who work with individuals with autism. Poor integration of conceptual information can impact upon language, memory, categorization, and the ability to generalize information, which are key skills for learning. Even though there is mixed support for conceptual coherence difficulties, recent research appears to be making progress in specifying and understanding the circumstances under which individuals with autism are successful in integrating conceptually. Jones and Jordan point out (see Chapter 14) that established interventions do not always adapt to reflect current findings in research. In order to ensure the most effective learning environments for those with autism, researchers and professionals need to establish better communication. Current knowledge can better equip professionals with the information they need in order to create an appropriate learning plan for a person with autism. For instance, visual attributes may facilitate learning in some circumstances (e.g., TEACCH), but may detract attention away from processing at a conceptual level on other occasions (e.g., categorization). Furthermore, the use of explicit cues (visual or verbal) may help individuals with autism to access their stored knowledge to assist with conceptual integration of material. It is equally important for researchers to take note of what teachers and clinicians report happens in practice, as this can feed into the development of new theories. In sum, by establishing better links between academics and practitioners, more advances can be made in understanding and helping those with autism.

References

Akshoomoff, N. A., & Stiles, J. (1995). Developmental trends in visuospatial analysis and planning: I. Copying a complex figure. *Neuropsychology, 9*(3), 364–377.

Ameli, R., Courchesne, E., Lincoln, A., Kaufman, A. S., & Grillon, C. (1988). Visual memory processes in high-functioning individuals with autism. *Journal of Autism and Developmental Disorders, 18*, 601–615.

Baron-Cohen, S. (1991). The theory of mind deficit in autism: How specific is it? *British Journal of Developmental Psychology, 9*, 301–314.

Booth, R., Charlton, R., Hughes, C., & Happé, F. (2003). Disentangling weak coherence and executive dysfunction: Planning drawing in autism and attention-deficit/hyperactivity disorder. *Philosophical Transactions of the Royal Society of London, B., 358*, 387–392.

Brian, J. A., & Bryson, S. E. (1996). Disembedding performance and recognition memory in autism/PDD. *Journal of Child Psychology and Psychiatry, 37*, 865–872.

Charman, T., & Baron-Cohen, S. (1993). Drawing development in autism: The intellectual to visual realism shift. *British Journal of Developmental Psychology, 11*, 171–185.

Chen, M. J. (1985). Young children's representational drawings of solid objects: A comparison of drawing and copying. In N. H. Freeman and M. V. Cox (Eds.), *Visual order: The nature and development of pictorial representation* (pp. 157–174). Cambridge, UK: Cambridge University Press.

Cohen, D. J., & Bennett, S. (1997). Why can't most people draw what they see? *Journal of Experimental Psychology: Human Perception and Performance, 23*, 609–621.

Eames, K., & Cox, M. V. (1994). Visual realism in the drawings of autistic, Down's syndrome and normal children. *British Journal of Developmental Psychology, 12*, 235–239.

Freeman, N. H., & Janikoun, R. (1972). Intellectual realism in children's drawings of a familiar object with distinctive features. *Child Development, 43*, 1116–1121.

Frith, U. (1989). *Autism: Explaining the enigma*. Oxford, UK: Blackwell.

Frith, U. (2003). *Autism: Explaining the enigma* (2nd ed.). Oxford, UK: Blackwell.

Gibson, J. J. (1966). *The senses considered as perceptual systems*. Boston, MA: Houghton Mifflin.

Happé, F. (1996). Studying weak central coherence at low levels: Children with autism do not succumb to visual illusions: A research note. *Journal of Child Psychology and Psychiatry, 37*, 873–877.

Happé, F. (1999). Autism: Cognitive deficit or cognitive style? *Trends in Cognitive Science, 3*, 216–222.

Happé, F., & Frith, U. (2006). The weak central coherence account: Detailed focused cognitive style in autistic spectrum disorders. *Journal of Autism and Developmental Disorders, 36*, 5–25.

Hughes, H. H., & Russell, J. (1993). Autistic children's difficulty with mental disengagement from an object: Its implications for theories of autism. *Developmental Psychology, 29*, 498–510.

Jolliffe, T., & Baron-Cohen, S. (1997). Are people with autism and Asperger syndrome faster on the Embedded Figures Test? *Journal of Child Psychology and Psychiatry, 38*, 527–534.

López, B., & Leekam, S. R. (2003). Do children with autism fail to process information in context? *Journal of Child Psychology and Psychiatry, 44*, 285–300.

Luquet, G. (1913). *Les dessins d'un enfant*. Paris: Alcan.

Luquet, G. (1927). Le Réalisme intellectual dans l'art primitive. 1. Figuration de l'invisible. *Journal de Psychologie, 24*, 765–797.

Milbrath, C., & Siegel, B. (1996). Perspective taking in the drawings of a talented autistic child. *Visual Arts Research, 22*(2), 56–75.

Mitchell, P., Ropar, D., Ackroyd, K., & Rajendran, G. (2005). How perception impacts on drawings. *Journal of Experimental Psychology Human Perception and Performance, 31*, 996–1003.

Mottron, L., & Belleville, S. (1993). A study of perceptual analysis in a high-level autistic subject with exceptional graphic abilities. *Brain and Cognition, 23*, 279–309.

Mottron, L., & Belleville, S. (1995). Perspective production in a savant-autistic draughtsman. *Psychological Medicine, 25*, 639–648.

Mottron, L., Belleville, S., & Mènard, E. (1999). Local bias in autistic subjects as evidenced by graphic tasks: Perceptual hierarchisation or working memory deficit? *Journal of Child Psychology and Psychiatry, 40*, 743–755.

O'Riordan, M. A., Plaisted, K. C., Driver, J., & Baron-Cohen, S. (2001). Superior visual search in autism. *Journal of Experimental Psychology: Human Perception and Performance, 27*, 719–730.

Ozonoff, S., Pennington, B. F., & Rogers, S. J. (1991). Executive function deficits in high-functioning autistic individuals: Relationship to theory of mind. *Journal of Child Psychology and Psychiatry, 32*, 1081–1106.

Piaget, J., & Inhelder, B. (1956). *The child's conception of space*. London: Routledge & Kegan Paul.

Piaget, J., & Inhelder, B. (1969). *The psychology of the child*. London: Routledge & Kegan Paul.

Plaisted, K., O'Riordan, M., & Baron-Cohen, S. (1998). Enhanced discrimination of novel, highly similar stimuli by adults with autism during a perceptual learning task. *Journal of Child Psychology and Psychiatry, 39*, 765–775.

Pring, L., & Hermelin, B. (1993). Bottle, tulip, and wineglass: Semantic and structural processing by savant artists. *Journal of Child Psychology and Psychiatry, 34*, 1365–1385.

Pring, L., Hermelin, B., & Heavey, L. (1995). Savants, segments, art, and autism. *Journal of Child Psychology and Psychiatry, 36*, 1065–1076.

Rajendran, G., Mitchell, P., & Rickards, H. (2005). How do individuals with Asperger syndrome respond to nonliteral language and inappropriate requests in computer-mediated communication? *Journal of Autism and Developmental Disorders, 35*, 429–443.

Ropar, D., & Mitchell, P. (2001a). Susceptibility to illusions and performance on visuo-spatial tasks in individuals with autism. *Journal of Child Psychiatry and Psychology, 42,* 539–549.

Ropar, D., & Mitchell, P. (2001b). Do individuals with autism and Asperger's syndrome utilise prior knowledge when pairing stimuli? *Developmental Science, 4,* 433–441.

Ropar, D., & Mitchell, P. (2002). Shape constancy in autism: The role of prior knowledge and perspective cues. *Journal of Child Psychology and Psychiatry, 43,* 647–653.

Ropar, D., & Peebles, D. (2007). Sorting preference in children with autism. The dominance of concrete features. *Journal of Autism and Developmental Disorders, 37,* 270–280.

Russell, P. A., Mauthner, N., Sharpe, S., & Tidswell, T. (1991). The windows task as a measure of strategic deception in preschoolers and autistic subjects. *British Journal of Developmental Psychology, 9,* 331–349.

Shah, A., & Frith, U. (1983). An islet of ability in autistic children: A research note. *Journal of Child Psychology and Psychiatry 24,* 613–620.

Shah, A., & Frith, U. (1993). Why do autistic individuals show superior performance on the block design task? *Journal of Child Psychology and Psychiatry, 34,* 1351–1364.

Sheppard, E., Ropar, D., & Mitchell, P. (2005). The impact of meaning and dimensionality on the accuracy of children's copying. *British Journal of Developmental Psychology, 23,* 365–381.

Sheppard, E., Ropar, D., & Mitchell, P. (in press). The impact of meaning and dimensionality on copying accuracy in individuals with autism. *Journal of Autism and Developmental Disorders.*

Shulman, C., Yirmiya, N., & Greenbaum, C. W. (1995). From categorization to classification: A comparison among individuals with autism, mental retardation, and normal development. *Journal of Abnormal Psychology, 104*(4), 601–609.

Snyder, A. W., & Mitchell, D. J. (1999). Is integer arithmetic fundamental to mental processing? The mind's secret arithmetic. *Proceedings of the Royal Society of London B. Biological Sciences. 266,* 587–592.

Snyder, A. W., & Thomas, M. (1997). Autistic artists give clues to cognition, *Perception, 26,* 93–96.

Tager-Flusberg, H. (1985a). Basic level and superordinate level categorization in autistic, mentally retarded, and normal children. *Journal of Experimental Child Psychology, 40,* 450–469.

Tager-Flusberg, H. (1985b). The conceptual basis for referential word meaning in children with autism. *Child Development, 56,* 1167–1178.

Tager-Flusberg, H. (1991). Semantic processing in the free recall of autistic children: Further evidence for a cognitive deficit. *Journal of Developmental Psychology, 9,* 417–430.

Thouless, R. H. (1931). Phenomenal regression to the real object. II. *British Journal of Psychology, 22,* 1–30.

van Sommers, P. (1989). A system for drawing and drawing-related neuropsychology. *Cognitive Neuropsychology, 6*(2), 117–164.

8

Executive Functioning in Autism Spectrum Disorder

Where It Fits in the Causal Model

Elisabeth L. Hill

Introduction

This chapter will provide a selective review of the published literature on executive functions in autism spectrum disorder across the lifespan. In particular, planning, mental flexibility, inhibition, generativity, and multitasking will be considered. The relationship between executive dysfunction, autistic symptomatology, adaptive behavior, and theory of mind will be considered. Findings will be integrated into a causal modeling framework of autism spectrum disorder, and critical directions for future research will be identified.

During the 1980s, a handful of research papers were published in which poor executive function abilities were described in adults with autism spectrum disorder (henceforth referred to as autism). These led to a critical investigation of these skills by Ozonoff and colleagues, who compared the performance of a group of high-functioning individuals with autism to a well-matched clinical control group on a series of tests of emotion perception, theory of mind, and certain executive functions. In this study, executive function deficits were widespread (Ozonoff, Pennington, & Rogers, 1991), and this was true both in those diagnosed with high-functioning autism and those diagnosed with Asperger syndrome (Ozonoff, Rogers, & Pennington, 1991). Moreover, while individuals with high-functioning autism and Asperger syndrome had difficulties on tests of executive function, only those with high-functioning autism showed deficits on tests of theory of mind. The continuing work of this and other research groups has done much to promote the view of executive dysfunction as an important characteristic of autism.

"Executive function" is traditionally used as an umbrella term for abilities such as planning, working memory, impulse control, inhibition, and shifting set, as well as the initiation and monitoring of action. Historically, data from a range of disciplines have linked these functions to frontal structures of the brain, and to prefrontal cortex in particular. Executive functions are typically impaired in patients with acquired damage to the frontal lobes as well as in a range of neurodevelopmental disorders that are likely to involve congenital deficits in the frontal lobes. Such clinical disorders include attention deficit disorder, autism spectrum disorder, obsessive-compulsive disorder, Tourette's syndrome, and schizophrenia (e.g., Sergeant, Geurts, & Oosterlaan, 2002).

As an umbrella term, "executive functions" is rather vague. A range of functions is included, and the term is often confused at different levels of explanation: namely, constructs, operations, and functions (Burgess et al., 2006). Using this structure, a *construct* is a theoretical account such as working memory or theory of mind. This refers to "a change in the brain," "cognitive system," or "mind" (Burgess et al., 2006, p. 195). An *operation* refers to each individual component of a construct that is "experimentally detectable or inferable" (Burgess et al., 2006, p. 195), and accounts for a change in the individual—the mental manipulation of representations, for example. Finally, a *function* is the output of a series of operations that is, itself, directly observable. This describes a change upon the world and might include empathic behavior or verbal rehearsal. While it is standard (and easy) to use "executive dysfunction" as a short-hand way of referring to the putative cause of a specific set of autistic difficulties, this fails to provide the necessary specificity for understanding and interpreting the disorder. A quick look at the literature shows a pattern of strengths and weaknesses in performance on tests assumed to measure different executive functions, and so it is important to clarify this performance profile in order to provide greater clarity when confronted with the complex issue of understanding autism. To this end, the terminology used by Morton and Frith (1995) in their causal modeling approach to neurodevelopmental disorders will be adopted in this chapter. This approach has been outlined in detail recently (Morton, 2004). Before focusing on the performance of individuals with autism on tests of executive function, it is, therefore, important to provide a brief outline of the causal modeling approach, its principles and terminology.

Causal Modeling

The causal modeling approach provides a graphical tool for thinking about neurodevelopmental disorders. This approach can be used to model multiple theories of a disorder, and to model possible similarities and differences between the causes and consequences of different disorders. In this chapter I will use it to discuss one theoretical account of one such disorder: executive dysfunction in autism.

The causal modeling approach has four constituent parts: biology, cognition, behavior, and the environment (see Figure 8.1 later in this chapter). In turn, these factors may themselves be broken down further. In the biological domain membrane proteins, receptors, and neurons, for example, may all play a role. Likewise, cognitive processes will be broken down into their constituent parts: for example, phonological processing, verbal short-term memory, and skill automatization. (These relate to Burgess et al.'s (2006) *constructs* and *operations*.) Behaviors include reading skill, digit span, and word naming, and equate to Burgess et al.'s *functions*. Finally, aspects of the environment may have an influence at any level of the model. These influences may be protective or destructive and might include intra-uterine environment, parenting style, diet, or relationships. Cognition is crucial in the causal modeling approach, as it acts as a mediator between biological and behavioral features. Finally, it is likely that there will be *interactions* between different levels of the model, such that relationships between components will be bi-directional, having a *developmental* impact on one another over time.

Causal Modeling of Executive Functions in Autism

Owing to the complexity of tests that measure executive functions, and to the frequent confusion between behavior and cognition in the literature, it is almost impossible to provide a short but comprehensive review of studies of executive function in autism at the behavioral and cognitive levels separately. In terms of cognition, some of the behavioral difficulties measured and described in autism have been explained by deficits in certain aspects of executive functions, especially difficulties in planning, cognitive flexibility, generativity, and in particular aspects of inhibition. In this chapter, these studies will be reviewed briefly. Further detail and evaluation can be found elsewhere (e.g., Hill, 2004; Russell, 1997). Working memory is often listed as an executive function, and has been found to be particularly sensitive to prefrontal damage (Baddeley, Della Sala, Papagno, & Spinller, 1997), although it will not be the focus of this review. In relation to autism, findings have been mixed, with some reporting little if any impairment (e.g., Ozonoff & Strayer, 1997; Geurts, Verté, Oosterlaan, Roeyers, & Sergeant, 2004) and others reporting decreased activation of prefrontal areas during spatial working memory (Luna et al., 2002) and specific deficits in spatial working memory but not verbal working memory (Williams, Goldstein, & Minshew, 2006).

Behavioral features of executive function in autism

Executive dysfunction can be seen to underlie many of the key characteristics of autism, both in the social and non-social domains. The behavior problems addressed by this theory are rigidity and perseveration, being explained by poverty in the initiation of new non-routine actions and the tendency to be stuck in a given task set. At the same time, the ability to carry out routine actions can be excellent and is manifested in a strong liking for repetitive behavior and sometimes elaborate rituals. Repetitive behaviors are one of the three core diagnostic features of autism. These have been divided into low- and higher-level categories (Turner, 1999). In autism, typical low-level repetitive behaviors include stereotyped movements and self-injurious behaviors, while higher-level repetitive behaviors include insistence on sameness and circumscribed language.

The tests used most commonly to assess executive functions include the Tower of London (where counters must be rearranged in as few moves as possible; conceptualized as a test of planning), the Wisconsin Card Sorting Task (WCST, Nelson, 1976; where cards must be sorted according to an unsaid rule; conceptualized as a test of mental flexibility), the Stroop Task (Stroop, 1935; where the ink color of color words printed in the wrong colors must be read; conceptualized as a test of inhibition), and verbal fluency (produce as many words beginning with the same letter or in the same semantic category as possible in one minute; conceptualized as a test of generativity). Behavioral features relate to the observable performance on these tests, such as the number of moves to complete a Tower puzzle, the number of perseverations made when told to switch sorting rule on the WCST, accurate naming of ink colors on a Stroop Task and number of words produced on a verbal fluency task. Additional behavioral features relate to symptomatology (e.g., repetitive behaviors), adaptive behavior, and skill in activities of daily living. It is these measures that allow us to put forward proposals about the cognitive mechanisms involved in autism. In the following section, some of the behaviors seen in autism that have been taken to indicate cognitive difficulties in specific executive functions will be discussed, with reference to the cognitive constructs and operations that they are thought to reflect.

Cognitive features of executive function in autism

Systematic reviews of the literature reveal mixed evidence for executive dysfunction in autism. Mixed findings may arise from a number of factors, including the nature of the tasks administered as well as the nature of the autism and/or control

Table 8.1 Tasks used to assess planning, mental flexibility, inhibition, and generativity, showing the number of studies in which individuals with autism have been reported to be impaired.

Planning	Mental flexibility	Inhibition	Generativity
BADS Zoo Map; 2/2	Hayling test; 2/2	Day–Night task; 0/1	Category fluency; 1/2
Drawing task; 1/1	ID/ED shift; 2/2	Detour reaching task; 2/2	Design fluency; 2/2
Luria bar task; 1/1	WCST; 11/16	Go/No-Go task; 1/1*	Ideational fluency; 1/1
Milner mazes; 1/1		Stop-Signal; 0/1	Letter fluency; 1/2
Stockings of Cambridge; 2/2		Stroop; 0/5	Pretend play; 1/1
Tower of Hanoi; 4/4		Tubes task; 0/1	Verbal fluency; 0/4
Trail-making; 1/2		Windows task; 3/3	Word fluency; 2/2

* Prepotent inhibition condition only

samples used (Hill, 2004). Overall, however, difficulties on lab-based tasks assessing the cognitive areas of planning, mental flexibility, generativity, the inhibition of a prepotent response, and multitasking have all been well documented (see Table 8.1). Here I will focus on the most consistently reported deficits, starting first with well-controlled, lab-based studies and ending with studies that have linked these results with autistic symptomatology, adaptive behavior and activities of daily living.

Planning

Planning is a complex, dynamic operation in which a sequence of planned actions must be constantly monitored, re-evaluated, and updated. This requires the conceptualization of changes from the current situation, looking ahead by taking an objective and abstracted approach to identify alternatives, making choices, and then implementing the plan and revising it accordingly. Studies of planning in autism have tended to use Tower tasks, revealing autism-specific planning deficits in children, adolescents, and adults with autism in relation to typically developing individuals and those with other disorders not associated with generalized intellectual disability (e.g., Ozonoff & Jensen, 1999; Ozonoff et al., 1991). This impairment remains over time (Ozonoff & McEvoy, 1994). Planning difficulties are also present on other tasks such as Luria's Bar Task (Hughes, 1996). However, tasks such as the Tower Tasks are complex and involve a number of processes over and above planning per se (e.g., working memory, inhibition of prepotent but inefficient sub-goal moves). There is some evidence that these play a role in performance on Tower Tests (Hughes, Russell, & Robbins, 1994; Sykes, 2001). IQ also has a role to play, and continued detailed studies to investigate such influences are required.

Mental flexibility

Perseveration is a widely acknowledged consequence of poor executive functioning that is seen in autistic individuals. Typically, perseveration in autism has been attributed to a deficit in mental flexibility. Mental flexibility is often termed "set-shifting" or cognitive flexibility. These terms refer to the ability to shift to a different thought or action according to changes in a situation. Poor mental flexibility (used here interchangeably with the term "set-shifting") is illustrated by perseverative, stereotyped behavior and difficulties in the regulation and modulation of motor acts. Using the WCST, autism-specific perseverative behavior has been reported in children, adolescents, and adults with autism in relation to normally developing individuals and those with other disorders not associated with generalized learning disability (e.g., Ozonoff & Jensen, 1999; Ozonoff et al., 1991). This deficit is maintained over time (Ozonoff & McEvoy, 1994) and is not restricted to Western cultures (Shu, Lung, Tien, & Chen, 2001). Further insight into the specific nature of autistic perseveration comes from studies of the Intradimensional–Extradimensional shift (ID/ED shift) task of the Cambridge Neuropsychological Test Automated Battery (CANTAB). This task is presented in several stages, providing a more precise identification of the locus of difficulty on a set-shifting task than is possible using the WCST. Both Hughes et al. (1994) and Ozonoff et al. (2004) have reported autism difficulties only in the final stages of the task, when an extra-dimensional shift is required. These studies suggest that it is not that autistic individuals perseverate in a global sense, but rather that they experience an autism-specific "stuck-in-set" perseveration.

The picture, therefore, seems reasonably clear: planning and mental flexibility deficits exist in autism, observed through greater inefficiency when solving Tower puzzles, and difficulty in switching to sort cards using a second rule in the WCST. IQ appears to play some role, however, and thus the choice of control groups warrants careful consideration both when designing a study and when interpreting its results. In the future it will be important to focus on the influence of a number of factors in order to come to reliable conclusions as to the nature of any mental flexibility deficit in autism and the implications of this for a specified theory of executive dysfunction. At present, important issues would appear to include the influence of verbal ability on mental flexibility as well as the impact of intellectual disability, and any additive effect of autism plus intellectual disability.

Inhibition

Inhibition is a further aspect of thought and behavior attributed to executive function that has been investigated in autism. The Stroop Task is a classic example of a test of inhibition. In this task the interference of one input can be measured on the performance of another (e.g., naming the ink color of color words when the word and ink are either congruent—the word "red" printed in red ink—or incongruent—the word "red" printed in green ink). Overall, the evidence indicates that children, adolescents, and adults with autism show equal amounts of interference on this task in comparison to typical control groups. This is in contrast to other neurodevelopmental disorders associated with executive dysfunction such as ADHD (Ozonoff & Jensen, 1999). Furthermore, individuals with autism are unimpaired on other tests of inhibition, in particular negative priming and neutral inhibition trials of a Go/No-Go task (Ozonoff, Strayer, McMahon, & Filloux, 1994). However, certain tests involving prepotent inhibition—such as the Windows Task or the Detour-Reaching Task—cause difficulty for individuals with autism in relation to well-matched typically developing individuals. On the Windows task, for example, a child can win a desired object (a piece of candy) by pointing to one of two windows, one with the candy visible and the other without a candy. In order to win the candy, the child must point to the empty box, something that has been found to be difficult for children with autism. In their study, Hughes and Russell (1993) found that only 15% of children with autism passed most of 20 trials on this task, compared to 70% of well-matched control children. In this study, 50% of the children with autism failed to point to the correct box on any of the 20 trials. None of the children in the control group showed this performance profile. Russell (2002) has explained this performance profile by suggesting that the rules of some executive function tests appear arbitrary to those with autism, and that it is this *arbitrariness* that causes the observed difficulties.

Generativity

Difficulties in the capacity to generate novel ideas and behaviors spontaneously have been argued to underlie the lack of spontaneity and initiative seen in autism, the poverty of speech and action, and the apparent failure to engage in pretence. This impairment may also be related to the high rates of repetitive behavior characteristic of autism as well as avoidance and dislike of change (Turner, 1997). In a comprehensive study of generativity, Turner (1999) asked children, adolescents, and adults with autism, as well as well-matched control groups, to complete tests of verbal fluency, ideational fluency (e.g., produce as many uses for a newspaper as possible within two and a half minutes), and design fluency (e.g., produce as many different designs as possible within five minutes). Responses on the verbal and ideational fluency tests suggested that individuals with autism are impaired in the generation of novel responses and behavior, while the findings of the design fluency tests were equally consistent with an impairment in the regulation of behavior through inhibition and/or monitoring. In this study the presence/absence of an autism diagnosis, rather than IQ, discriminated performance, with those high-functioning individuals with autism showing particularly impoverished performance in some aspects of the analyses. Importantly, Turner (1997) reported a correlational link in autistic individuals between poor performance on ideational and design fluency tasks and high levels of repetitive behavior in daily life. A generativity impairment would have widespread implications. Turner (1999) argued that in addition to disrupting spontaneous behavior, an impaired capacity to generate novel behavior would hinder the execution of routine behavior where changed circumstances occur and some form of trouble-shooting is required. It may also cause early difficulties that have traditionally been associated with a theory of mind deficit, such as initiating pretend play (Jarrold, Boucher, & Smith, 1996).

Evaluating Naturalistic-Like Tasks in the Lab: The Case of Multitasking

While it is essential to break down task components in order to understand the source of any deficit, it is also important to understand how dysfunction can impact on naturalistic tasks. In reality, it is unlikely that day-to-day tasks involve individual executive functions, and thus it is important to assess performance on tasks with ecological validity (see also Chapters 2 and 4 in this volume). Multitasking is a prime example of multiple executive functions at work, and one that is reminiscent of our daily lives. Consequently, it provides an ecologically valid, naturalistic form of task assessment. The study of multitasking has been assessed predominantly in adults with neuroanatomical damage (Burgess, Veitch, De Lacy, Costello, & Shallice, 2000), and has been associated with damage to prefrontal cortex. One recent study of multitasking in children with autism has been published. This paper reported performance on the Battersea Multitask Paradigm in which children had three minutes in which to sort counters and beads, and to color caterpillars. Four rules had to be followed. MacKinlay, Charman, and Karmiloff-

Smith (2006) reported that children with autism showed a deficit in multitasking, being less efficient at planning, organizing, and coordinating the performance of the multiple activities of the task in comparison to gender-, age-, and IQ-matched peers. This was despite the fact that all children were equally aware of the rules. These findings are consistent with the findings of a study investigating the performance of adults with Asperger syndrome on a range of traditional and ecologically valid tests of executive functions in which performance on the Six Elements Task (Wilson, Alderman, Burgess, Emslie, & Evans, 1996), a test of multitasking, was found to be most sensitive to difficulty in a group of adults who did not differ from well-matched controls on other measures (such as the WCST, verbal fluency, and the Stroop Task) (Hill & Bird, 2006). Careful investigations of multitasking will be critical for future autism research, since if carefully thought out, they provide original, ecologically valid, and yet scientific methods to understand the day-to-day difficulties of those with autism. Furthermore, it will be important to understand how cognitive components interact with one another, and the impact that this has on the behaviors observed in those with autism.

The Relationship Between Executive Dysfunction and Symptomatology, Adaptive Behavior, and Activities of Daily Living

In the studies discussed above, clear deficits have been reported in tightly controlled tasks, although there are a number of studies in which no deficit has been seen on such tasks (see Table 8.1). Despite this, there are many anecdotal accounts of the everyday difficulties of individuals with autism that are consistent with executive dysfunction. For example, Channon, Charman, Heap, Crawford, and Rios (2001) reported that, according to parents, a group of adolescents with Asperger syndrome showed significantly more behaviors associated with dysexecutive syndrome than did a typically developing group. Gilotty, Kenworthy, Sirian, Black, and Wagner (2002) reported that the Initiate and Working Memory domains of the BRIEF questionnaire (Gioia, Isquith, Steven, Guy, & Kenworthy, 2000), a parent-report form concerning executive functioning, were negatively correlated with most domains of adaptive behavior measured using the Vineland Adaptive Behavior Scales (VABS; Sparrow, Balla, & Cicchetti, 1984). Furthermore, the Communication and Socialization domains of the VABS were negatively correlated with several areas of executive functioning evaluated using the BRIEF. These data suggest that specific aspects of executive functions are associated with difficulties reported in communication, play, and social relationships in individuals with autism. However, the strongest evidence will come from direct comparisons with both adaptive behavior and autistic symptomatology, and these have been made recently. Ozonoff et al. (2004) reported a correlation between specific planning and cognitive flexibility difficulties in individuals with autism in relation to a measure of adaptive behavior. Interestingly, poor performance on the tests of executive function did not predict autism severity or specific autism symptoms. Lopèz, Lincoln, Ozonoff, and Lai (2005) have reported a positive relationship between cognitive flexibility, working memory, and response inhibition, and restricted, repetitive behaviors, while these behavioral symptoms were not related to planning and generativity. These studies have tended to compare executive functions, as measured through formal tasks, with day-to-day behaviors, and it may be that stronger relationships exist than are measurable in this way. For example, a certain degree of compensation is likely to occur in strictly controlled settings, but when this structure is removed, difficulties may be accentuated (the multitasking studies described above provide some evidence for this, as do anecdotal reports). Such arguments are reflected in other areas of autistic difficulty: for example, in social interactions where individuals may pass lab-based tests of theory of mind, but fail to reveal a true theory of mind in online interactions (see Chapters 4 and 5, this volume).

Executive functions and theory of mind

Since the emergence of the executive dysfunction account of autism, there has been much debate over the potential relationship between this and the theory of mind deficit account of autism.[1] A number of research studies have highlighted the relationship between these cognitive domains. The difficulties experienced by individuals with autism with inhibitory control and attentional flexibility are particularly notable, since these are the two components of executive function that have been shown to predict theory of mind performance in typically developing children (Hughes, 1998a). Moreover, performance on tests of executive function predicts performance on theory of mind tests, while the reverse association is not seen (Hughes, 1998b). These findings suggest that the difficulty that autistic individuals have on theory of mind tests is at least in part attributable to their lack of executive control.

It has been difficult to assess the *developmental* interaction between theory of mind and executive function. One reason for this arises from the fact that most tests of theory of mind may not be "pure" tests of this cognitive capacity, but may also involve an executive component. This has been highlighted, for example, in the false photograph test (e.g., Leslie & Thaiss, 1992), leading some to argue that it is the executive component of theory of mind tests that causes difficulty for those with autism. However, Perner and Lang (2000) reported an association between theory of mind and executive function performance even when theory of mind tasks involve only a low executive component, and therefore argue that we cannot account entirely for associations in this way. Overall, three theoretical positions have been taken. First, that the development of executive functions allows the child's theory of mind to develop (Russell, 2002); second, that the capacity to represent mental states is necessary for the development of executive function (e.g., Perner & Lang, 2000); third, that there are no specific systems for processing mental states, and that performance on theory of mind tasks can be reduced to executive function ability alone (e.g., Frye, Zelazo, & Palfai, 1995). Poor performance on a test of false belief such as the classic Sally-Ann Task, for example, would arise where there is a deficit in the ability to inhibit a prepotent response while holding in working memory some action-relevant information. A further explanation of any interaction between theory of mind and executive function abilities could arise from the anatomical proximity of the brain regions that mediate these cognitive processes, and certainly there is overlap between these brain networks (Frith & Frith, 2006).

Biological features of executive function in autism

With the emergence of increasingly sophisticated methods for evaluating neuroanatomy at both structural and functional levels, as well as other biological techniques such as behavioral genetics, considerable advances in our understanding of the biological contribution to autism will be made. Executive functions are associated with the frontal lobes, and there is increasing evidence of frontal lobe abnormalities in individuals with autism as well as in the neural networks linking the frontal lobes and several brain areas. Evidence is also suggestive of a developmental impact at the biological level, as early damage to one brain area could change the structure and function of another, with cascading effects on further development across connected structures.

The key neuroanatomical studies are outlined in Chapter 2 of this volume, and here I focus on just a couple of studies that paid particular attention to frontal cortex. Using single case voxel-based morphometric analysis, Salmond, de Haan, Friston, Gadian, and Vargha-Khadem (2003) reported that 13 of 14 autistic children and adolescents showed evidence of abnormality in the orbitofrontal cortex. Structural abnormality in this area was seen in far more cases than in the other regions of interest reported (amygdala, cerebellum, hippocampal formation, and superior temporal gyrus). Intriguingly, a recent neuroimaging study has reported increased activation of Brodmann's area (BA) 10 (rostral prefrontal cortex) during correct inhibition of trials on a Go/No-Go Task, in addition to significantly increased grey matter density in BA10 in a group of 10 adults with Asperger syndrome and high-functioning autism in comparison to 12 healthy controls (Schmitz et al., 2006). BA10 might, therefore, be a candidate for future, detailed investigation. This area is the last place in which myelination occurs in normal development (Fuster, 1997) and might be particularly susceptible to slow increases in the frontal lobe white matter described by Carper and Courchesne (2000), or to poor neural pruning. Burgess, Simons, Dumontheil, and Gilbert (2005) have argued recently that BA10 is involved in a variety of functions, including straightforward "watchfulness" to complex activities such as remembering to carry out intended actions after a delay, multitasking, and aspects of recollection. (They have named this the "gateway" hypothesis.) This account predicts poor performance on a task such as the Six Elements Task where the situation is a novel one and where a specific need to switch has been identified (e.g., I must pay special attention to the time that I have left). This need for vigilance on simple tasks and the need to initiate change in behavior relates to thoughts generated internally in the light of external information. In contrast, performance on a Card Sorting Test such as the WCST would not be compromised, as although this task requires switching from one sorting rule to another, this is done in the context of cued switching and feedback. Indeed, this pattern of performance is one that we have identified recently in a comprehensive study of planning, mental flexibility, inhibition, and generativity in adults with Asperger syndrome (Hill & Bird, 2006). In relation to autistic symptomatology, atypical functioning of BA10 might explain some of the oddness in communication documented. Poor monitoring of a social, communicative situation caused by poor watchfulness, monitoring, multitasking, and recollection might lead to a disjointed interaction and/or withdrawal from such situations. It will be important to replicate and extend these findings, and work is ongoing to do this.

In addition to a specific area of frontal lobe abnormality, it is also likely that abnormalities in a brain *network* that includes frontal cortex could be involved in accounting for the profile of executive dysfunction seen in autism (such accounts are described in Chapter 2). For example, Dawson et al. (2002) hypothesized that executive dysfunction is a consequence of abnormalities in medial temporal lobe (MTL) function, with variability in performance on executive tasks arising from the varying severity of MTL brain abnormalities. Impairments in prefrontal function in older individuals with autism are seen as secondary consequences of early MTL dysfunction, consequences that do not become apparent until the frontal lobes mature. Neither a specific nor a network account needs to be mutually exclusive. It is possible that differing degrees of impairment could be seen in the presence of one, rather than both, of these difficulties, although it is likely that there would be a developmental implication of either abnormality for the other. The developmental impact of abnormality in a brain area(s) is likely to have a critical impact on the development of the cognitive functions mediated by that area, as well as on the anatomical development of the interconnected brain areas (see Luna, Doll, Hegedus, Minshew, & Sweeney, 2007). Studies of executive functions of very young children with autism have shed some light on this process.

Executive functions in preschool children with autism

While studies of executive functions in children, adolescents, and adults with autism have found difficulties in areas such as planning, mental flexibility, and the inhibition of a prepotent response, the picture regarding preschool children with autism has revealed much subtler deficits, with the more striking deficits being revealed only in later childhood (e.g., Griffith, Pennington, Wehner, & Rogers, 1999; McEvoy, Rogers, & Pennington, 1993). Such findings have been taken to imply that executive dysfunction cannot be a central part of autism. However, they are consistent with the view that executive dysfunction is an important contributory factor to autism, for a number of reasons. First, the development of the frontal lobes is protracted and continues over the first 20 years of life. Second, executive functions emerge in a multi-stage process, and sub-components of executive functions may possess different developmental trajectories and mature at different rates (e.g., Diamond, 2002). This understanding of normal processes aids in interpreting the autism data. It might be that a well-functioning prefrontal cortex undergoes deterioration in later childhood development or that prefrontal cortex is sufficient to subserve the simplest executive functions but fails to adequately mature past a given level. A further alternative could be that interference from elsewhere (poor pruning, for example) expands over time. Whatever the explanation, the failure of the frontal lobes to follow a normal maturational pattern is likely to have long-term consequences for all development. This abnormality would be reflected differentially over time as the impact of abnormal development on that of other connected systems is seen.

Biology, Cognition, and Behavior

In this chapter, a brief overview of the findings of executive dysfunction in autism has been given. On the whole, autism-specific difficulties in areas of planning, mental flexibility, the inhibition of a *prepotent* response, generativity, and multi-tasking have been identified. However, there are aspects of executive functions that remain intact in autism, and therefore it is important to specify clearly which functions are problematic, rather than using an all-inclusive, non-specific label.

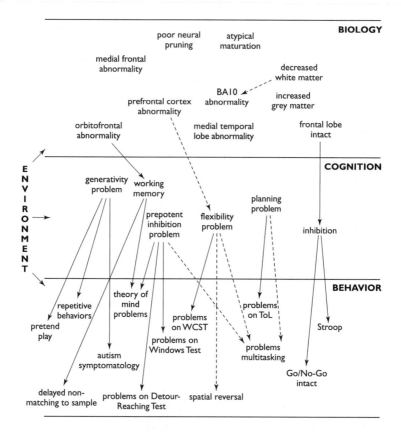

Figure 8.1 Illustration of the relationship between executive functions and autistic behaviors using the notation of the causal modeling approach. Full lines indicate relationships identified in past research (although not all relationships are necessarily indicated); dotted lines indicate speculative relationships; where no arrows are shown, no relationship has yet been suggested. Relationships between items in the model may be bi-directional.

There are many studies of executive functions in autism, and it has only been possible to scratch the surface of these findings in this chapter. There is much debate about the nature and cause of these difficulties, as well as concerning the relationship between executive functions and theory of mind. The causal modeling approach provides a graphic tool for mapping the relationship between directly observable behaviors, inferred cognitions, and the putative biological causes of these. An illustration of the relationship between *executive functions* and autistic behaviors is given in Figure 8.1. In this figure, just some of the many findings have been included, and much more research is needed. However, at this stage, the picture gives an indication of the complexity of the area. Other areas could

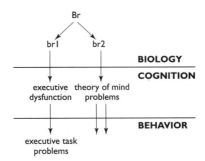

Figure 8.2 One possible model showing how a common brain origin might lead to both executive function and theory of mind deficits (redrawn from Morton 2004, p. 132).

be included using this notation, such as the theory of mind and weak central coherence models, and these can be investigated to see whether they are mutually exclusive or causally related. Figure 8.2 provides a hypothetical illustration of how a common brain origin might lead to both executive function and theory of mind deficits. In this example, there is no causal relationship between these two cognitive domains.

You will notice that I have not discussed environmental influences on executive functions in autism, yet the environmental contribution is highlighted in the causal modeling approach. At this point we know rather little about the potential environmental contributors to difficulties with executive dysfunctions in autism. However, it is worth noting that whatever the cause of, and relationship between, a specific profile of executive difficulties, an environment in which planning, mental flexibility, inhibition, generativity, etc. are essential will place inordinate stress on a non-optimal executive system. Support can be successful in reducing some of the consequences of executive dysfunction in daily life. A good illustration of this comes from Adam, a 44-year-old man with Asperger syndrome. Adam performs poorly on tests of various executive functions, particularly multitasking. He has developed an intricate series of lists, which he creates on a daily basis and refers to every few minutes. These lists categorize the tasks that he must achieve each day, the steps that must be gone through to achieve these, and the time at which each task must be started. As a final step, Adam ticks off each stage as he completes it. This is a clumsy and time-consuming way to plan and monitor one's behavior; however, it works with reasonable success for Adam.

Integration Section

The potential impact of the contribution of individual executive functions to autism spectrum disorder is large, as indicated by the growing number of papers focusing on this area in recent years, and the strength of the debate by proponents for and against executive dysfunction as a causal component in autism. Here, I focus on some of the issues raised in other chapters of this volume: specifically on (i) how understanding of executive dysfunction in autism may relate to attempts to achieve an integrated explanation of the causes of the disorder, (ii) links between the research and clinical literatures in this area, and (iii) the influence of the causal modeling approach to understanding autism. Some of the other links have been noted earlier in this chapter.

One of the arguments pervading the autism literature addresses the parsimony question, with research programs seeking to identify the one explanation that can account for all three components of the autism triad. This has been true of studies investigating behavioral, cognitive, and biological explanations of the disorder. However, it has been difficult to establish much evidence for the priority of one cause over another, although there is plenty of evidence to support many of the explanations that have been proposed. Recently a small but significant handful of studies have pointed to the view that there is no single explanation of autism. Instead, each component that has been identified at the behavioral, cognitive, and biological levels of explanation may be separable. On this account, we are not searching for genes for autism, but for genes for specific traits, with separate genes contributing to the autism triad of difficulties (and, most probably, to the other areas that have been identified as problematic for those with autism). Likewise, at the cognitive level of description, no single cause has emerged, and it is increasingly likely that impairment in different cognitive mechanisms causes the multiple deficits observed. This would be tied to the genetic fractionation proposed. Evidence to support this view comes from population studies, as well as from studies of individuals with autism and of the broader autism phenotype (see Happé, Ronald, & Plomin, 2006).

Earlier in this chapter, the potential relationships between individual executive functions, autistic symptomatology, adaptive behavior, and activities of daily living were discussed. Through this area of investigation, a link can be made between the findings of "academic" research and more clinical questions and applied studies. The concept of executive functions, and their individual definitions, are crucial for those working in health and education. Since it is intuitive to think that the daily life problems that are assumed to relate to executive dysfunction might be ameliorated through intervention techniques, or at least through structured support (cf. the case of Adam, mentioned earlier), it is crucial that clinicians working in these areas have an understanding of this domain. Furthermore, it is important that the relationships between specific components of executive dysfunction and intervention techniques are investigated in detail. A literature search at the time of writing identified only one training study, in which training in either theory of mind or executive functions was given to small groups of children with autism (Fisher & Happé, 2005). No improvement was shown on tests of executive functions in either group, although improvement in theory of mind tasks was seen after training in both groups. (Note that this literature search was in no way exhaustive.) In this volume, Jones and Jordan (Chapter 14) evaluate the research base for intervention in autism. Here, they discuss the theoretical influence of the executive dysfunction debate on intervention studies of autism, highlighting the input that the principles of this approach have had on the development of interventions such as the TEACCH approach. Well-controlled studies assessing the specific association between an individual's executive function skills and the positive improvement seen using techniques such as the TEACCH are necessary.

Finally, the causal modeling approach, which provides a notation for thinking about the impact of, and interaction between, biology, cognition, behavior, and environmental effects on disorders, is one framework within which all the work presented in this book could be conceptualized. The integration of these four areas is picked up nicely in Chapter 4. Here, Jones and Klin highlight their findings with regard to visual salience through illustrations of studies of a young child, adolescents, and adults with autism. They illustrate how a biological difference from birth leads to innate differences in developing cognitive systems. In turn, these lead to behavioral atypicalities. In the longer term, however, these differences do not arise only as a consequence of an innate difference, but also from the consequent changes in the environment in which an individual chooses to interact. These differences will contribute, in turn, to further changes in biology, cognition, and behavior. Thus, an innate difference leads to a different developmental pathway that has long-term implications for both brain and behavior.

Ultimately, the purpose of research into executive functions in autism is driven by the need to understand the theoretical and conceptual causes and consequences of such dysfunction. By obtaining a clear understanding of these areas, it will be possible to provide more sensitive interventions for individuals with autism. The causal modeling approach may be beneficial in this regard. Note that this approach does not favor one theoretical account or another. Rather, it allows us to map out known findings and to hypothesize relationships between different levels of explanation. These hypothetical relationships can then be tested systematically. The process is a reciprocal one: The model will help to clarify directions for future work, and the work will allow our understanding of autism to evolve.

Acknowledgments

The ideas in this chapter have been developed over the years in discussion with a number of colleagues, particularly Jim Russell and members of the Developmental and Executive Functions groups at the Institute of Cognitive Neuroscience, University College London.

Note

1   Theory of mind refers to our intuitive understanding of mental states and our ability to attribute mental states to self and others. It includes understanding of false beliefs, as well as desires, pretence, irony, non-literal language (e.g., double bluff), and deception (e.g., white lies).

References

Baddeley, A., Della Sala, S., Papagno, C., & Spindler, H. (1997). Dual-task performance in dysexecutive and nondysexecutive patients with a frontal lesion. *Neuropsychology, 11*(2), 187–194.

Burgess, P. W., Alderman, N., Forbes, C., Costello, A., Coates, L., Dawson, D. R., et al. (2006). The case for the development and use of "ecologically valid" measures of executive function in experimental and clinical neuropsychology. *Journal of the International Neuropsychological Society, 12,* 194–209.

Burgess, P. W., Simons, J. S., Dumontheil, I., & Gilbert, S. J. (2005). The gateway hypothesis of rostral prefrontal cortex (area 10) function. In J. Duncan, L Phillips & P. McLeod (Eds.), *Speed, control and age: In honour of Patrick Rabbitt* (pp. 217–248). Oxford, UK: Oxford University Press.

Burgess, P. W., Veitch, E., De Lacy Costello, A., & Shallice, T. (2000). The cognitive and neuroanatomical correlates of multitasking. *Neuropsychologia, 38,* 848–863.

Carper, R. A., & Courchesne, E. (2000). Inverse correlation between frontal lobe and cerebellum sizes in children with autism. *Brain, 123,* 836–844.

Channon, S., Charman, T., Heap, J., Crawford, S., & Rios, P. (2001). Real-life-type problem-solving in Asperger's syndrome. *Journal of Autism and Developmental Disorders, 31*(5), 461–469.

Dawson, G., Webb, S., Schellenberg, G. D., Dager, S., Friedman, S., Aylward, E., et al. (2002). Defining the broader phenotype of autism: Genetic, brain, and behavioral perspectives. *Development and Psychopathology, 14,* 581–611.

Diamond, A. (2002). Normal development of prefrontal cortex from birth to young adulthood: Cognitive functions, anatomy and biochemistry. In D. T. Stuss & R. T. Knight (Eds.), *Normal development of prefrontal cortex from birth to young adulthood: Cognitive functions, anatomy and biochemistry* (pp. 466–503). Oxford, UK: Oxford University Press.

Fisher, N., & Happé, F. (2005). A training study of theory of mind and executive function in children with autistic spectrum disorders. *Journal of Autism and Developmental Disorders, 35*(6), 757–771.

Frith, C. D., & Frith, U. (2006). The neural basis of mentalizing. *Neuron, 50*(4), 531–534.

Frye, D., Zelazo, P. D., & Palfai, T. (1995). Theory of mind and rule-based reasoning. *Cognitive Development, 10*, 483–527.

Fuster, J. M. (1997). *The prefrontal cortex: Anatomy, physiology and neuropsychology of the frontal lobe.* Philadelphia: Lippincott–Raven.

Geurts, H. M., Verté, S., Oosterlaan, J., Roeyers, H., & Sergeant, J. A. (2004). How specific are executive functioning deficits in attention deficit hyperactivity disorder and autism? *Journal of Child Psychology and Psychiatry, 45*(4), 836–854.

Gilotty, L., Kenworthy, L., Sirian, L., Black, D. O., & Wagner, A. E. (2002). Adaptive skills and executive function in autism spectrum disorders. *Child Neuropsychology, 8*(4), 241–248.

Gioia, G. A., Isquith, P. K., Steven, C., Guy, S. C., & Kenworthy, L. (2000). *Behavior Rating Inventory of Executive Function™ (BRIEF™).* Lutz, FL: Psychological Assessment Resources Inc.

Griffith, E. M., Pennington, B. F., Wehner, E. A., & Rogers, S. J. (1999). Executive functions in young children with autism. *Child Development, 70*, 817–832.

Happé, F., Ronald, A., & Plomin, R. (2006). Time to give up on a single explanation for autism. *Nature Neuroscience, 9*(10), 1218–1220.

Hill, E. L. (2004). Evaluating the theory of executive dysfunction in autism. *Developmental Review, 24*, 189–233.

Hill, E. L., & Bird, C. M. (2006). Executive processes in Asperger syndrome: Patterns of performance in a multiple case series. *Neuropsychologia, 44*, 2822–2835.

Hughes, C. (1996). Planning problems in autism at the level of motor control. *Journal of Autism and Developmental Disorders, 26*, 101–109.

Hughes, C. (1998a). Executive function in preschoolers: Links with theory of mind and verbal ability. *British Journal of Developmental Psychology, 16*, 233–253.

Hughes, C. (1998b). Finding your marbles: Does preschoolers' strategic behavior predict later understanding of mind? *Developmental Psychology, 34*(6), 1326–1339.

Hughes, C., & Russell, J. (1993). Autistic children's difficulty with mental disengagement from an object: Its implications for theories of autism. *Developmental Psychology, 29*(3), 498–510.

Hughes, C., Russell, J., & Robbins, T. W. (1994). Evidence for executive dysfunction in autism. *Neuropsychologia, 32*(4), 477–492.

Jarrold, C., Boucher, J., & Smith, P. K. (1996). Generativity deficits in pretend play in autism. *British Journal of Developmental Psychology, 14*, 275–300.

Leslie, A. M., & Thaiss, L. (1992). Domain specificity in conceptual development: Neuropsychological evidence from autism. *Cognition, 43*, 225–251.

Lopèz, B. R., Lincoln, A. J., Ozonoff, S., & Lai, Z. (2005). Examining the relationship between executive functions and restricted, repetitive symptoms of autistic disorder. *Journal of Autism and Developmental Disorders, 35*(4), 445–460.

Luna, B., Doll, S. K., Hegedus, S. J., Minshew, N., & Sweeney, J. A. (2007. Maturation of executive function in autism. *Biological Psychiatry, 61*, 478–481.

Luna, B., Minshew, N. J., Garver, K. E., Lazar, N. A., Thulborn, K. R., Eddy, W. F., et al. (2002). Neocortical system abnormalities in autism: An fMRI study of spatial working memory. *Neurology, 59*, 834–840.

MacKinlay, R., Charman, T., & Karmiloff-Smith, A. (2006). High functioning children with autism spectrum disorder: A novel test of multitasking. *Brain and Cognition, 61*(1), 14–24.

McEvoy, R. E., Rogers, S. J., & Pennington, B. F. (1993). Executive function and social communication in young autistic children. *Journal of Child Psychology and Psychiatry, 34*(4), 563–578.

Morton, J. (2004). *Understanding developmental disorders: A causal modelling approach.* Oxford, UK: Blackwell.

Morton, J., & Frith, U. (1995). Causal modeling: A structural approach to developmental psychopathology. In D. Cichetti & D. J. Cohen (Eds.), *Manual of developmental psychopathology* (Vol. 1, pp. 357–390). New York: John Wiley.

Nelson, H. E. (1976). A modified card sorting test sensitive to frontal lobe defects. *Cortex, 12*, 313–324.

Ozonoff, S., Cook, I., Coon, H., Dawson, G., Joseph, R. M., Klin, A., et al. (2004). Performance on Cambridge Neuropsychological Test Automated Battery sub-tests sensitive to frontal lobe function in people with autistic disorder: Evidence from the collaborative programs of excellence in autism network. *Journal of Autism and Developmental Disorders, 34*(2), 139–150.

Ozonoff, S., & Jensen, J. (1999). Specific executive function profiles in three neurodevelopmental disorders. *Journal of Autism and Developmental Disorders, 29*(2), 171–177.

Ozonoff, S., & McEvoy, R. E. (1994). A longitudinal study of executive function and theory of mind development in autism. *Development and Psychopathology, 6*, 415–431.

Ozonoff, S., Pennington, B., & Rogers, S. J. (1991). Executive function deficits in high-functioning autistic individuals: Relationship to theory of mind. *Journal of Child Psychology and Psychiatry, 32*(7), 1081–1105.

Ozonoff, S., Rogers, S. J., & Pennington, B. F. (1991). Asperger's syndrome: Evidence of an empirical distinction from high-functioning autism. *Journal of Child Psychology and Psychiatry, 32*(7), 1107–1122.

Ozonoff, S., & Strayer, D. L. (1997). Inhibitory function in nonretarded children with autism. *Journal of Autism and Developmental Disorders, 27*(1), 59–77.

Ozonoff, S., Strayer, D. L., McMahon, W. M., & Filloux, F. (1994). Executive function abilities in autism and Tourette syndrome: An information processing approach. *Journal of Child Psychology and Psychiatry, 35*(6), 1015–1032.

Perner, J., & Lang, B. (2000). Theory of mind and executive function: Is there a developmental relationship? In S. Baron-Cohen, H. Tager-Flusberg, & D. Cohen (Eds.), *Understanding other minds: Perspectives from developmental cognitive neuroscience* (pp. 150–181). Oxford, UK: Oxford University Press.

Russell, J. (Ed.) (1997). *Autism as an executive disorder.* Oxford, UK: Oxford University Press.

Russell, J. (2002). Cognitive theories of autism. In J. E. Harrison & A. M. Owen (Eds.), *Cognitive deficits in brain disorders* (pp. 295–323). London: Martin Dunitz.

Salmond, C. H., de Haan, M., Friston, K. J., Gadian, D. G., & Vargha-Khadem, F. (2003). Investigating individual differences in brain abnormalities in autism. *Philosophical Transactions of the Royal Society, 358*, 405–413.

Schmitz, N., Rubia, K., Daly, E., Smith, A., Williams, S., & Murphy, D. G. M. (2006). Neural correlates of executive function in autistic spectrum disorders. *Biological Psychiatry*, *59*(1), 7–16.

Sergeant, J. A., Geurts, H., & Oosterlaan, J. (2002). How specific is a deficit of executive functioning for attention-deficit/hyperactivity disorder? *Behavioural Brain Research*, *130*, 3–28.

Shu, B.-C., Lung, F.-W., Tien, A. Y., & Chen, B.-C. (2001). Executive function deficits in non-retarded autistic children. *Autism*, *5*, 165–174.

Sparrow, S. S., Balla, D. A., & Cicchetti, D. V. (1984). *Vineland Adaptive Behavior Scales*. Circle Pines, MN: American Guidance Service.

Stroop, J. R. (1935). Studies of interference in serial verbal reactions. *Journal of Experimental Psychology*, *18*, 643–662.

Sykes, E. D. A. (2001). *Planning in autism: The role of working memory*. Unpublished PhD., University of Cambridge.

Turner, M. (1997). Towards an executive dysfunction account of repetitive behaviour in autism. In J. Russell (Ed.), *Autism as an executive disorder* (pp. 57–100). Oxford, UK: Oxford University Press.

Turner, M. (1999). Annotation: Repetitive behaviour in autism: A review of psychological research. *Journal of Child Psychology and Psychiatry*, *40*(6), 839–849.

Williams, D. L., Goldstein, G., & Minshew, N. (2006). The profile of memory function in children with autism. *Neuropsychology*, *20*(1), 21–29.

Wilson, B. A., Alderman, N., Burgess, P. W., Emslie, H., & Evans, J. J. (1996). *Behavioural Assessment of the Dysexecutive Syndrome*. Bury St Edmunds, UK: Thames Valley Test Company.

Part II
Clinical and Intervention Research

9

How Young Children With Autism Treat Objects and People

Some Insights into Autism in Infancy From Research on Home Movies

Sandra Maestro and Filippo Muratori

Background

Autism represents a spectrum of conditions that affect how people respond in the environment, both in their social and non-social relationships. It disturbs the development of interpersonal sympathy and cooperative action, interferes with cultural learning and sharing a "common sense" of the world (Frith, 1991; Gillberg et al., 1990; Trevarthen & Aitken, 2001). This puzzling and complex disorder poses basic questions about the neurodevelopmental bases of social behavior and human relationships. To understand autism, we must understand how we have come to be social beings and, further, how differences in our biological makeup translate into variations in our social behavior. This is a daunting task that requires collaboration among many scientists from multiple disciplines, each with its own perspective, method of inquiry, and scientific methods (Dawson et al., 2002b). Therefore current efforts to integrate information across multiple levels of analysis are necessary in order to understand the nature, etiology, and effective treatment of autism. In his original description L. Kanner (1943) realized that autism is already evident in infancy in the inability of those affected to develop social relationships with people. Nevertheless, formulating a diagnosis before 2 years of age is still extremely challenging, because of the difficulties in detecting indicators of autism in very young children. First of all, some criteria specified by the DSM-IV for the diagnosis of ASD in older children may not even be present in young children with autism because they have not developed the prerequisite skills to exhibit the behaviors: for example, stereotyped mannerisms and repetitive behaviors need a certain degree of brain development. An additional problem encountered when assessing for ASD is that many children have both ASD and other developmental disabilities (e.g., intellectual disabilities and language disorder), so that it is not clear whether the early signs of deviance are specific to autism or a more general effect of the developmental delay. Finally, obtaining infants with autism as research participants is a daunting task, even if the major diffusion of early screening programs, the increase in cultural awareness, and information on ASD allow better identification of infants at risk, improving our clinical knowledge in this field. In synthesis, extending autism research to its potential origin in infancy requires new paradigms that can bring together both development and psychopathology.

Autism in Infancy: Some Key Issues

There are several key issues to be addressed regarding both development and psychopathology in the description of early features of autism, such as the unanswered questions that follow:

- Which clinical patterns derive from different times of onset of ASD symptoms?
- How is the onset of the disorder influenced by the child's developmental level?
- What is the etiologic basis for such different times of onset?
- What distinguishes very young children with autism from those with typical development?
- Is the impairment in social behaviors (such as difficulty in maintaining eye contact, little response to name, poor motor imitation, and lack of pretend play, verbal, and non-verbal communication) specific to ASD?
- What are the different clinical outcomes for children with different times of onset?
- Are there any tools for clinicians to reduce the period from the "time of onset" of signs to the "time of recognition"?

The chapter will address some of these issues, in particular the ones related to the time of onset, the different courses, and the distinction of ASD infants from infants with typical development.

There are diagnostic criteria for ASD available, not only to specify the accepted features of autism but also to differentiate the different time of onset and course of the disorder. Up to now the information has come mainly from retrospective studies based on parental report.

Parental Report Studies

Among the features that discriminated the children with autism were their isolation, their lack of play, their failure to attract attention to their own activity, their lack of smiling, and their empty gaze. Some studies have noted that parents report a pervasive lack of responsiveness at some point in their child's development. Overall interpersonal engagement is diminished such that the child displays less frequency and intensity of eye contact; he/she uses eye contact less often for referential communication; moreover, he/she is not very cuddly and lacks the range of affective expression, particularly around positive interactions with familiar persons (Wimpory, Hobson, Williams, & Nash, 2000). In some cases, these deficits are reported by parents from early in infancy, and in other cases, the deficits are reported to emerge following some period of normal development.

Indeed, many parental reports noted a feeling of being treated like an object, which is consistent with research by Dawson, Meltzoff and Osterling (1998), providing empirical validation of such a behavior. Some additional social-communicative deficits reported by parents retrospectively are delayed speech, poor imitation abilities, and lack of anticipatory postures. Finally, early parental reports converge on a variety of unusual reactivity patterns such as hypersensitivity to sounds, lack of response to pain, problems with regulating sleep cycles, and feeding disorders. For example, based on the Early Development Interview (a questionnaire about children's behavior from birth through 2 years of age administered to parents of 3- to 4-year-old children) children with autism were reported by Werner, Dawson, Munson, and Osterling (2005) to have elevated symptoms in the regulatory domain (difficult to hold/cuddle; exceptionally fussy or easy baby; sleeping and feeding problems; overly sensitive to noise and/or touch) by 3–6 months. Despite the limitations of the parent report studies, mainly related to the influence of the actual condition of the child on recall ability, parents are still an optimal source of information, especially if their reports are integrated with findings from empirical studies. Therefore researchers have been seeking systematic retrospective ways to identify features that can discriminate the very young child (later diagnosed as having autism) from typical children of the same age. The need has been for an objective source of early information from the parents that was not tinted by current experience or the shortcomings of memory.

Retrospective Research Through Home Movies

Retrospective analysis of home movies provides that potential research source. The home movies are videos taken by parents of children with autism during their children's early years, before the child's problems are diagnosed. They are considered as an excellent option for providing direct observation of the earliest stages of autism development. Currently they are the only instrument available to study the actual course of onset of the disorder in infants with autism. The following section will review those studies and in doing so, explain the rationale for our own work.

Massie (1978) and Massie and Rosenthal (1984) were the pioneers of the home movie method. Through the analysis of ten home movies, they were able to point out early difficulties in the interactions between infants and their mother. These were characterized by diminished affective exchanges and an atypical pattern of cognitive development. Concerning affect, on the basis of the quality of parenting, the rhythm and the synchrony of the mutual exchange, and of the quality of the infant's responsivity, the authors described five configurations of the mother–infant interaction. With regard to the earliest emerging symptoms, most of the specific signs occurred between 6 and 12 months. The five configurations consisted of (i) "self-absorption"; (ii) no visual pursuit of people, looking away from people, avoiding mother's gaze, resisting being held, arching torso away from parents; (iii) rocking and hand flapping; (iv) absence of communicating affect or intention; (v) aimlessness. Concerning cognition, early cognitive development showed three main patterns: (a) slow development but with progression through Piaget's sensorimotor stages; (b) arrest at an early stage with mild or moderate deficit; (c) primitive fixation at lowest level with severe deficit. It is important to note that from the outset the authors emphasized the methodological issues related to the specificity of the signs detected through this methodology and decided therefore to provide a control group of children with typical development.

In Losche's (1990) study, the most significant data consist of the higher presence of "aimless" activity and the lack of the use of means–end actions by 20 months of life in children later diagnosed with autism compared to typical children. Both of these signs were considered by Losche as precursors of stereotypies in autism.

Adrien and colleagues (Adrien et al., 1991a and b, 1992a and b, 1993; Sauvage et al., 1988) focused their research on the severity and frequency of the early symptoms of autism, before and after the first year of life. To achieve this aim, the authors applied the Behavior Summarized Evaluation Scale with 12 home movies. In the first year of life they found five behaviors that significantly differentiated the group of children with autism from the typical group: poor social interaction, lack of social smile, lack of appropriate facial expression, hypotonia, and unstable attention. In the second year of life, seven new additional symptoms were observed: ignoring people, preferring aloneness, no eye contact, lack of appropriate gestures, lack of appropriate postures, too calm, no expression of emotions.

Teitelbaum, Teitelbaum, Nye, Fryman, and Maurer (1998) focused exclusively on early movement patterns. They studied movie footage of 17 children with autism, using the Eshkol–Wachman Movement Analysis System (Teitelbaum, Benton, Shah, Prince, Kelly, et al., 2004) in combination with still-frame videodisc analysis. These showed disturbances of movement that could be detected clearly at the age of 4–6 months and sometimes even at birth. Disturbances were revealed in the shape of the mouth, similar to Moebius syndrome, and in some or all of the milestones of development, including lying (asymmetry), righting from supine to prone (sideways-upward pattern of righting, rather than starting on their side as typically developing children), sitting (difficulties in maintaining sitting stability without using any allied reflexes to protect themselves when falling), crawling (asymmetrical lack of adequate support in the arms; asymmetry in the legs), standing (relative akinesia with a longer standing time), and walking (delayed development, asymmetry in the movements involving the arms and legs, a gait characterized by sequencing, not superimposition, which creates a "goose step" form of walking). All these movement disturbances typically occurred on the right side of the body, and can be interpreted as infantile reflexes "gone astray." Some reflexes are not inhibited at the appropriate age in development, whereas others fail to appear when they should. It is of value that the same group has described the same movement disorders in infants later diagnosed as having Asperger syndrome (Teitelbaum et al., 2004), suggesting that these children too can be diagnosed very early, independent of the presence of language.

Baranek (1999) found differences in both motor and social behavior at a later stage of infancy. The importance of this study lay in the inclusion for the first time of a comparison group with intellectual disabilities (children affected with Down's syndrome). She focused her attention on the 9–12 month periods of three groups of children. Her sample comprised 11 with autism, 10 with developmental disabilities, and 11 typically developing children. She found that those later diagnosed with autism mouthed objects more, had less orientation to visual stimuli, oriented less to name, and showed aversion to social touch.

A few years later Osterling and Dawson (1994; Osterling, Dawson, & Munson, 2002) examined home movies taken by parents at the first birthday parties of 11 children subsequently diagnosed with ASD and of matched control children with typical development. They found significant differences in looking at the face of another and in joint attention (pointing and showing). How often a child looked at the face of another person was the best single predictor of a later diagnosis of autism. A successive study has extended the search for impairments in social attention downwards, and significant failure in "orienting to name" was found in 8- to 10-month-old infants later diagnosed as having autism. A third study of the same group has indicated that autism can be distinguished also from learning disability by 1 year of age on the basis of the deficit in social attention.

Table 9.1 Summary of the atypical behaviors identified by different research groups during the different stages of infancy.

	0–6 months	6–12 months	12–18 months	18–24 months
Massie, 1978; Massie & Rosenthal, 1984; Rosenthal, Massie, & Wulff, 1980		Self-absorption, gaze atypies, rocking, and hand flapping, lack of communicating affect, aimless, cognitive delay		
Losche, 1990			Aimless activity, lack of use of means–end actions	
Sauvage, 1988; Adrien and others, 1991–1993	Poor social interaction, lack of social smile, lack of appropriate facial expression, hypotonia, unstable attention	Poor social interaction, lack of social smile, lack of appropriate facial expression, hypotonia, unstable attention	Poor social interaction, lack of social smile, lack of appropriate facial expression, hypotonia, unstable attention	Poor social interaction, lack of social smile, lack of appropriate facial expression, hypotonia, unstable attention
Teitelbaum et al., 1998, 2004	Disturbances in the shape of the mouth, asymmetry in lying, righting from supine to prone	Disturbances in sitting, crawling, standing	Delayed walking, asymmetry in the movements involving arms and legs	
Baranek, 1999		More mouthing objects, less orientation to visual stimuli, less orienting to name, aversion to social touch		
Osterling & Dawson, 1994, 2000; Osterling, Dawson, & Munson, 2002		Deficit of behaviors of looking at face, pointing, showing, orienting to name		

In considering these latter contributions, it is important to note that the research on early detection of ASD has moved from a search for early pathological signs (such as stereotypies, anomalies of gaze) to marking out those typically developing behaviors that are absent, such as orienting to name, pointing, joint attention, responding to name or to verbal language (see Table 9.1).

In conclusion, following the seminal work of Massie, a growing body of literature has demonstrated that home movies can be an excellent source for research on early autism, identifying both social and motor anomalies. There are, however, a number of limitations to be considered. Home movies provide very spontaneous and naturalistic situations for study, but they don't always allow for a precise discrimination of an infant's ability as accurately as in experimental settings; for example, if we were to explore the infant's capacity for looking at people, we could not define the visual scanning of faces which could allow for a more sophisticated discrimination between typical and atypical gaze directions. In particular, there are five main limitations. First, researchers can explore only those developmental behaviors shown by the movie, without information about other dimensions of a child's early development. Second, spontaneous recording by parents may pre-select pleasant situations and avoid videotaping children during adverse conditions, and this process may obscure certain abnormal behaviors. Therefore subtle signs occurring during the first year of life can be forgotten, overlooked, or denied by the parents, because of difficulty in recall, anxiety, or lack of knowledge of normal child development.

Third, the use of only typically developing comparison groups limits the findings, because they may reflect general developmental delay rather than the effects of autism per se; studies of young infants with autism that include a control group of cognitively delayed children without autism are needed to determine the impact of cognitive impairment on the abilities of children with autism and the specificity of signs related to autism. A fourth problem is related to the instruments utilized for these studies, which are often specifically designed without standardization or validation beyond test–retest.

Finally, most of the studies developed through this methodology have utilized only a small number of home movies due the difficulties in obtaining a large group of long enough videos describing the child in different situations and during different ranges of age.

For these reasons, using this technique necessitates a stringent methodology. This includes accurate participant assessment, procedures for videotape collection and review, control for age of the infants in the videotapes, video editing and video coding procedures, blind observers, and inter-rater reliability, precise definition of behavioral items, and different control groups composed of participants with typical development and with other developmental disabilities such as learning disability.

If such limitations are overcome, retrospective analysis of home movies can be a valid and ecological tool for addressing the issue of early recognition of autism; in fact, the originality of this approach and its advantage lie in the opportunity to obtain data and information that are not influenced by time or by parent's recall. Moreover, the videos of the early periods of life allow us to observe the precursors of the symptoms, anticipating the age of recognition of early deviance in the infants' development.

To conclude, the information obtained from parent reports, early screening, and retrospective research on home movies needs better organization and orientation, to build a new "glossary" for analyzing the child's developmental behaviors in the first two years. Knowledge of the longitudinal course of signs of autism is essential in order to analyze how the emergence of some signs may interfere with the course of developmental abilities in the child. Moreover, better understanding of the reciprocal interference between development of competencies and onset of signs can clarify the core clinical challenge of autism, which is not to make a diagnosis, but to "detect" the first signs indicative of a development at risk for ASD.

Our Experience

We started our research in 1990, asking the families of children referred to consultation for ASD for the videos that they had recorded during the first years of life before they were aware of their child's condition. The aim was to detect the presence of symptoms of autism, on the basis of our knowledge of this disorder in older children. Using the home movies of 26 children diagnosed with autism, we applied the Infant Behavior Summarized Evaluation (IBSE) that was developed by the University of Tours research group (Adrien et al., 1992; Barthélémy et al., 1992) to evaluate the severity of behavioral problems in children with autism.

Which clinical patterns derive from different times of onset of ASD symptoms?

In our first study on early signs of autism (Maestro, Casella, Milone, Muratori, & Palacio-Espasa, 1999) we described two main forms of onset and course of autism, but subsequently added a third, as follows:

Progressive

In the first course that we described, the appearance of symptoms was evident from the first months of life, and the course of the disorder was slow and progressive.

In the observed sequences, starting from 3 months, children do not show progressive increase in vivacity and capacity for modulating the affective states that should appear in normal infants of the same age. Instead, they show a degree of indifference, apathy, and depressive moods. However, these children show the emergence of some primary communicative competence such as exchanging glances, attention to objects, sometimes synchronic reaction to environmental stimuli; nevertheless, the attention of the observer is drawn to the lack of vitality and of interactive exchanges. The emotional and intersubjective relationship fails to develop over time, and by the beginning of the second year of life, the child shows an increased withdrawal. This is the onset most frequently described in the literature.

Regressive

The second course is characterized by a "free period" before the onset unexpectedly of the first signs of autism. The change takes place between 12 and 18 months of life, and it mainly concerns the reaction to environmental stimuli, the appearance of communicative gestures, and interest in people. The increasing social withdrawal takes the child into a "world of his own," with less gaze monitoring and a lack of interest in and response to speech. Between one sequence and the next, even if the time gap is very short, the child passes from a situation of thriving social contacts to one of being withdrawn and isolated. However, during the analysis of the videos, we have recognized a small percentage of cases that we were not able to place in one of these two main courses of onset. We have labeled these cases as "fluctuating onset."

Fluctuating

During the first months of life, these children show a slight delay in postural maturity and a poor motor initiative accompanied by hypo-reactivity to environmental stimuli. Sometimes the child shows more interest in objects, but continuous and exaggerated stimulation from the mother is necessary for this activity. Between 6 and 18 months of life, one can see unexpected communicative competencies and slight improvements in the interest and participation in surroundings. After that, a loss of contact comes to the fore again. Between 12 and 18 months the child can interact, can imitate, can have more lively mimical and verbal exchanges. Then, around 18–24 months, the onset of the disorder appears clearly, and the child becomes isolated, and his play is stereotyped with loss of his social competence. These "problematic" cases prompted us to consider how to study these emerging developmental competencies to understand more deeply the core of this "discontinuity" in the course of the disorder.

Recently (Maestro et al., 2005) we have reviewed these findings by applying BSE to a larger sample of home videos of ASD children, and with a more stringent data analysis. To define the time of onset of ASD in infancy, we have introduced a new cutoff-based criterion, individuating three different ages of onset of ASD symptoms. (i) very early onset (children start to display atypical behaviors within the first semester of life); (ii) early onset (children show developmental abnormalities only within the second semester of life after an apparently typical development); (iii) late onset (children appear completely non-symptomatic during the first year of life).

Moreover we have discovered an additional group of rated items, that constitutes a typical symptom constellation characterized by withdrawal (expressed by item 2: ignores people), poor social interaction with difficulties in making eye contact, hypo-activity, and lack of emotional modulation (which suggests a mood disorder) with an increasing degree of intensity from the first semester of life up to the second year of life.

In our sample 87.5% of the participants have symptoms within the first year of life, and only 12.5% become symptomatic in the second year of life. Comparing this finding with other percentages in the literature, our late onset group results are smaller than the percentage of regressive cases reported elsewhere. One explanation could be related to the particularity of the video material analyzed, which provides direct observations of the earliest stages of development, allowing a more accurate recognition of symptoms compared to retrospective interviews. Moreover, several accurate studies on the development of typical behaviors in autism show subtle and qualitative abnormalities of normal behaviors. Therefore the developmental regression, based on the assumption of a previously normal development, could be only apparent. In fact, many of the infants video-recorded in the home videos analyzed in our research display a repertoire of social abilities (sequences of proto-conversations with adults, looking and smiling at people, gesture imitation), but these skills don't seem to anticipate other forms of social development. For these reasons we began to wonder what happens to these abilities in the later development of the child, and we asked ourselves how we could study these early competencies in a systematic way.

To conclude, knowledge of the longitudinal course of signs is crucial to analyzing how the emergence of some signs may interfere with the course of developmental abilities in the child. Indeed, it is plausible that a better understanding of the reciprocal interference between development of competencies and onset of signs could lead to the illumination of the core clinical problem in autism.

Study of Social and Non-Social Attention: A Paradigm to Understand Early Human Development From Research on Infants With Autism

Infant research has shown that typically developing very young infants regularly engage in behaviors relating to social attention (e.g., use of eye contact or social gaze and orienting to name being called by others), affective responsiveness (i.e: social smiling and prosodic proto-conversation), and emotion discrimination (Stern, 1977). Micro-analytic studies and naturalistic observations have revealed the natural sociability of infants. Human neonates show visual preference for human faces, directing attention to face-like patterns as compared to non-face-like stimuli or to scrambled faces (Dawson et al., 2002b). Infants engage the interest and affection of their caregivers through increasing pro-social coordinated elicitations (Trevarthen, 1979; Trevarthen & Hubley, 1978). The infant's need for communication and the "intuitive parenting" that supports it give rise to self–other awareness, to the emotions, and to shared experiences that shape social relationships through the course of development (Braten, 1998; Reddy, Hay, Murray, & Trevarthen, 1997). Infants' sensitivity to social cues from their mothers and to sudden disruptions of anticipated interactive patterns is evident from studies of contingency disruption in face-to-face interaction (Murray, Cooper, & Hipwell, 2003; Weinberg & Tronick, 1996). A sensitive caregiver responds to subtle signals from the infant indexing a motivation to interact and a need for disengagement and modulates his/her behavior to match and channel the infant's experience. The process of reading or sensing another's state and modulating behavior across sense modalities to match it has been described as affect attunement (Stern, 1977). This mutual matching is built on the infant's perceptual skills and on mutually dynamic anticipation. By 6 months, mothers and infants have well-established patterns for synchrony and attunement; they know each other intimately and are able to predict each other's expressions in time (Stern, 1977).

In the first six months of life, smiling is the most prevalent infant social behavior, and there is a strong correlation between smiling and gazing at the mother. Coordinated facial expression, vocalization, and gaze express positive and negative emotions and have been found to be highly patterned and consistent by the age of 3 months (Yale, Messinger, Cobo-Lewis, & Delgado, 2003). By 9 months infants coordinate smiles, eye contact, and gestures to communicate about objects in episodes of joint attention (Bates, Benigni, Bretherton, Camaioni, & Voltera, 1979).

For many authors the first sign of social deficit is related to the lack of development of joint-attention skill, which is known to be problematic in children with autism over 12 months of age (Baron-Cohen et al., 1996; Sigman, Mundy, Sherman,

& Ungerer, 1986). A number of experimental clinical studies have focused on attention abnormalities in autism (Courchesne et al., 1994; Plaisted, O'Riordan, & Baron-Cohen, 1998) and other studies have demonstrated a specific deficit in attention to social stimuli. Swettenham et al. (1998) have demonstrated that 2-year-old children with autism look less and for shorter duration at people, and more and for longer duration at objects.

The absence of joint attention, and of other typical developmental milestones such as proto-declarative pointing, showing objects, and pretend play have been specifically indicated as clinical markers of ASD in childhood at 18 months (CHAT: Baron-Cohen, Allen, & Gillberg, 1992). Joint attention is considered a pivotal skill in autism identification (Charman, 2003; Dawson et al., 2002a). "Pivotal" can refer both to "acting as a fulcrum" and to "being of crucial importance" or "the thing on which progress depends." In typical development joint-attention behaviors emerge between 6 and 12 months and involve the triadic coordination or sharing of attention between the infant, another person, and an object or event. The term encompasses a complex of behavioral forms, including gaze and point following, showing, and pointing. As far as pointing is concerned, it has been shown that the critical distinction may not be the imperative (where triadic exchanges serve an instrumental or requesting function) versus declarative (where triadic exchanges serve to share awareness of an object or event) level. Rather, the degree to which a child is monitoring and regulating the attention to the other person in relation to objects determines the severity of the deficit seen in autism (Charman, 1998; Mundy, 1995; Mundy & Crowson, 1997). This does not mean that joint-attention impairments cause autism. However, it does suggest that joint attention is a critical "downstream" effect of earlier brain psychopathology (Charman, 2003). Much interest has focused on the role of joint attention as a "precursor" to later theory of mind development in both typically developing children and children with autism (Charman et al., 2000; Tomasello, 1995). Recognition that joint attention is not a starting point but merely a staging post (Tomasello, 1995) for early social communicative development, and hence a "postcursor" of earlier psychological and developmental processes, shifts the focus of research onto which earlier impairments undermine the development of joint-attention skills in autism. The triadic coordination of attention between the infant, another person, and an object represents the base for this ability (Bakeman & Adamson, 1984). Therefore, the knowledge of possible precursors of joint attention is of seminal importance for the comprehension of early social development. In particular, a specific focus on the infant's two types of attention (attention to people and attention to objects) could provide essential data about their different roles as precursors to joint attention. For these reasons we have considered the study of the infant's attention as one of the best predictors of the further development of the joint-attention function.

What Distinguishes Very Young Children With Autism From Others With Typical Development?

How children treat objects and persons

Our first study in this direction was focused on the first six months of life (Maestro et al., 2002). On our hypothesis significant quantitative and qualitative differences between typical and ASD children might be detected at this age. We expected that infants with autism would exhibit a specific deficit of attention to social stimuli and that the distribution of spontaneous attention between social and non-social stimuli would be different compared to that of normal children, such that infants with autism would attend more to non-social than to social stimuli.

We have studied home movies regarding the first six months of life of two groups of children. The first (experimental group) was composed of the home movies of 15 children, 10 males and 5 females, referred to the clinical consultation service for autism spectrum disorder. The diagnosis was reached after a multidimensional five-day assessment inpatient period encompassing direct individual observations, psychological testing, group observation, and biological exams, on the basis of the DSM-IV (American Psychological Association, 1994) criteria. Additionally, the Childhood Autism Rating Scale (CARS) was administered. On this measure (Schopler, Reichler, & Renner, 1988) all 15 children received scores above the cutoff of 30 (mean: 36.6; range: 30–48). The control group was composed of 15 typically developing children, 9 males and 6 females, who were attending a kindergarten.[1]

The home videos of all the sample were comparable in length and in the sequences of normal daily activities. They included familiar routines (breast or bottle feeding, bathing, toileting), special events (siblings' birthdays, infant's baptism, Christmas, Easter, and other holidays), play situations with objects or people. During these activities the infant could be alone, or in interactions with parents or siblings; there was no event in one group favoring social interactions more than the other. For both groups we have included only videos without any editing by the parents, without any selection by the researchers and running for a minimum of 10 minutes.

To analyze the videos, the tapes were reviewed in detail and logged according to the child's chronological age during each scenario and to specific content.

Chronological ages were calculated by full months, based on the child's birthdate, and corresponding dates appearing on the tapes themselves. The films of the two groups were mixed and rated by observers who were blind to group membership. The various scenes of the first six months of life were analyzed and divided, labeling every scene in which the infant was visible and involved in human and object interaction. We coded only the scenes that lasted more than 40 seconds. All available footage was coded in order to prevent selection bias. After a complete description of the study was given to the families, written informed consent was obtained.

For this new research we adapted the grid that we had used in the previous research, which had already demonstrated a high degree of face validity and a good inter-rater reliability. The items have been chosen by the research team to explore the basic behaviors that support the development of the joint-attention ability from 6 months of age, placing at this time the birth of intersubjectivity. Moreover, at this age children show the capacity to attune and to understand the meaning of social experiences, mutual relations with other people respecting the social rules for interaction, as well as the ability to represent another's state of mind. Therefore we have chosen eleven behaviors more representative of the growing infant's social competencies, and we have grouped these behaviors into three developmental areas: social attention; non-social attention, and social behavior. The first two areas are composed of dichotomous items. The area of Social Attention is composed of four items: "Looking at people"; "Orienting toward people"; "Smiling at people"; "Vocalizing to people." The area of Non-social Attention is composed of four items: "Looking at objects"; "Orienting toward objects"; "Smiling at objects"; "Vocalizing to objects." The third area is composed of items referring to more global Social Behaviors such as "Postural attunement," "Seeking contact" and "Anticipating the other's aim" (Table 9.2).

For the first time in this study we have used an interval scoring method, computing the frequencies for each observed behavior. In our previous research, based on the presence/absence coding method, we observed that for typical children we needed only a few minutes of home movies to codify the behavior as present, but for children with autism it was necessary to have much more time; so we expected the frequency method to be more useful to detect differences between typical and autistic infants. At this very early age, infants with autism showed significantly lower interest in social stimuli as compared to typical children. By contrast, we did not find that attention to objects as a behavior was able to distinguish infants with autism from infants with typical development. In short, infants with autism exhibited a specific qualitative pattern of attention, highly consistent with theories predicting that ASD children have a specific deficit in attending to social stimuli (Swettenham et al., 1998). Moreover, these similar results for attention to non-social stimuli seem to indicate that in autism attention is not implicated as a primary function of the condition but as an elective function only toward social stimuli.

After these promising results we decided to extend upward our research on social and non-social attention, studying its developmental pathway during the first year of life. We expected to find a continuity of the differences found in the

Table 9.2 Grid for the analysis of Social and Non-social Attention

1	Looking at people	The child looks at mother or other persons
2	Looking at objects	The child looks at objects, camera, or other things
3	Orienting toward people	The child has a spontaneous gaze direction to persons or human voice
4	Orienting toward objects	The child has a spontaneous gaze direction to objects or non-human sounds
5	Postural attunement	The child shows a tonic aptness to other person's body
6	Seeking contact	The child has spontaneous movements to reach or change the contact with a person
7	Smiling at people	The child smiles at someone
8	Smiling at object	The child smiles at objects
9	Attuning the behaviors	The child has movements or facial expression attuned to other's behaviors
10	Vocalizing to people	The child produces vocalizations, sounds, or babbling toward another person
11	Vocalizing to object	The child produces vocalizations, sounds, or babbling toward objects
12	Anticipating the other's aim	The child shows anticipatory gestures in response to adult actions; the child waits for a specific action of another person
13	Explorative activity with an object	The child explores an object with mouth or hands

first six months of life. We adopted the same methodology as that of our first study, but the results were different from our expectations.

In fact, we found significant group differences in all items in the area of social attention at Time 1 (T1) but not at Time 2 (T2). By contrast, no differences were found in the items regarding non-social attention, either at T1 or T2. In short, we observed a decrease in differences between the two groups as far as attention to social stimuli are concerned, during the second semester of life (Figure 9.1).

This finding was supported by an improvement of social behaviors in the ASD group, while typical children showed a stable trend of the same behaviors. Moreover, we found an increase in behaviors dealing with attention to non-social stimuli present in both groups, but more evident in infants with autism, so that at

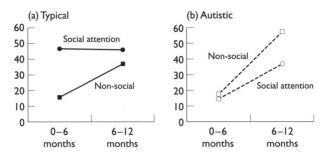

Figure 9.1 Measures of non-social and social attention for typical infants and infants with autism at 0–6 and 6–12 months.

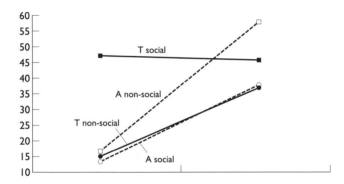

Figure 9.2 An increase of behaviors concerning attention to non-social stimuli present in both groups but more evident in infants with autism, so that at the end of the first year these children were significantly more attracted by objects than typical children. The graph also shows a decrease of differences in social attention between typical and autistic infants at 12 months.

the end of the first year these children were significantly more attracted by objects than typical children (Figure 9.2). Table 9.3 shows that at T1 there is no difference between the two groups concerning non-social attention, while there are significant differences concerning social attention (Typ vs. Aut). At T2, there are no significant differences between the two groups in the area of either social or non-social attention. Further, at T1 within the group of typical children there are significant differences between social and non-social attention (social attention vs. non-social attention), and at T2 we found significant differences within the autistic group between social and non-social attention (non-social attention vs. social attention).

The decrease of differences in social attention between typical and autistic infants

Table 9.3 At T1 there is no difference in non-social attention between the two groups (typical vs. autistic); there are significant differences in social attention. At T2, there are no significant differences between the groups in social or non-social attention. At T1, for typical infants, there are significant differences between social and non-social attention. At T2 there are significant differences for the infants with autism in social and non-social attention.

		0–6 months	6–12 months
Between group	Non-social	ns	ns
	Social	0.001	ns
Within group	Autism	ns	0.05
	Typical	0.001	ns

represents an intriguing and counter-intuitive finding that requires a full commentary. In fact, it may seem somewhat surprising that early significant differences in social attention are not confirmed later on. One explanation could be related to the development, in typical children, of person awareness versus object awareness as an essential precursor to joint attention. As described by Trevarthen and Aitken (2001), an infant was proved to possess an active and immediately responsive conscious interest in adult intentions (which is named primary intersubjectivity); during these earliest stages of postnatal development, faces are highly salient to typically developing infants. Around the middle of the first year, the baby's increasing interest in objects competes with this earlier interest in persons and just before the end of the first year leads, through shared and lively games with objects, to the development of joint attention, which has profound effects on infant development, creating a new form of person–person–object awareness (which is named secondary intersubjectivity). This is shown in our study through the clear rapprochement in typical children between the interest in people and the interest in objects. By comparison, children with autism are seen to mature in their social and non-social abilities, but with a totally different and divergent behavioral organization from that of typical children. We hypothesize that while the rapprochement of interest in people and in objects represents a developmental process that allows joint attention to emerge, the deficit of early social attentional skills we have observed during the first six months of life, and the divergent pathway of social and non-social attention in the second semester of life in children with autism, could prevent joint attention from emerging, even when social contact seems to improve. The very different pathways of social and non-social attention in very young children with autism compared to typical children allow us to recognize joint attention as a "postcursor." Our finding suggests that the early deficit in the tendency to direct attention to social stimuli (together with an excessive developmental progression of attention to objects) may create in infants later diagnosed with autism an atypical developmental gap and a later deficit of integration of social and non-social attention during the second half of the first year of life. Indeed, they add plausibility to the view that autism-specific deficits in joint attention and other aspects of triadic interaction (as well as so-called theory of mind) may arise from developmentally prior abnormalities in the infant's ability to establish and experience primary intersubjectivity with others, as suggested by Rogers and DiLalla (1990; also Rogers, 2004; Wimpory et al., 2000).

The increasing attention to objects between 6 and 12 months also makes exploratory activity with objects, which we see in the home movies of children with autism, no different from the same activity in home movies of typical children. These latter data suggest that stereotypy with objects is not present from the beginning, and that it is not a useful item to be considered in the first year of life. Stereotypy with objects probably becomes more obvious after the second year of life, and we can hypothesize that they are a long-term consequence of the earlier social dysfunctions, which do not allow the child to enlarge the knowledge of objects through interactive social actions. We also suggest that this difficulty in including objects in human relationships could be responsible for the high rating of the item "mouthing objects" found by Baranek (1999) around the first birthday of children with autism.

Conclusion

Dawson and others (2002b), confirming Schultz et al.'s (2000) studies, hypothesized that abnormal social attention or "social orienting" in autism might be related to abnormalities specific to face processing. Neural systems that mediate face processing exist very early in life (Dawson et al., 2002b); hence the impairment in attending to people's faces may be one of the earliest indicators of abnormal brain development in autism. In typically developing infants the visual preference for faces and very rapid face recognition are present at birth (Dawson et al., 2002b). In autistic infants the impairments in face processing might reflect abnormal neural representation of this process in the brain. Morton and Johnson (1991) hypothesize that at birth face-processing abilities are served by a sub-cortical system, which is replaced by a less fragile and experience-dependent cortical system that emerges by 6 months of age. This "experience-expectant development" could be impaired in autistic children. In fact, the deficit of social attention that we have observed in the first six months of life, could be related to an early innate deficit of the sub-cortical system and to a later vulnerable development of the cortical system, only partially corrected by the interaction with the environment. We could also hypothesize that after the first six months, the development of some "human being connecting" behaviors (looking, smiling, vocalizing) may mask the onset of the deficit in joint-attention behavior which can be interpreted as a hierarchically higher integration of the social and non-social systems. Therefore, in infants with autism there is an abnormal development of these two systems, with an atypical developmental gap and a later deficit of integration; the fundamental impairment of joint attention could be considered a consequence of the early disconnection between attention to people and to objects.

The study of the abnormal developmental trajectories for social and non-social attention could help us to understand the relationship between adaptive capacities and symptoms, and sets the stage for creating appropriate early interventions that could limit consequences of the dysfunction of brain regions and help to develop compensatory strategies. Finally, our research could suggest that the deficit in social attention in early autism could be more a sign of vulnerability than a definitive impairment.

Integration Section

Early detection of autism spectrum disorder (ASD) is important because early intervention programs can have a substantial impact on long-term outcome and improve the quality of life of these children and their families. For this reason, to figure out features of ASD before the age of 1 is a priority in the forefront of the scientific community.

Our study describes the developmental trajectory of a very specific function of infants' development: that is, attention to people and attention to objects during the first year of life. The focus is on the way the infant uses some basic abilities, to orient his/her attention toward different environmental solicitations. Our findings indicate that the infant who will develop an autism spectrum disorder displays a deficit in social attention, more evident in the first six months of life, while showing an increase in non-social attention throughout the first year of life. These atypical pathways may create the foundation for the later deficit of integration between social and non-social attention, and provide some support to implement programs aimed at screening autism at a "pre-symptomatic" stage (Williams, Chapter 10), that is, before the emerging of the joint-attention competence. We hypothesize that the fundamental impairment of joint attention in children with autism could be considered a consequence of the early disconnection between the two systems (attention to people and to objects). However, these behavioral indexes should be integrated with other biological parameters related to early brain development (Wicker, Chapter 2). In fact, our clinical observational data are close to the Courchesne finding of two phases of brain growth abnormality in infants with autism: a reduced size at birth and a sudden and excessive increase in head size in the second semester of life (Courchesne, Carper, & Akshoomoff, 2003). This author has suggested that these morphological data could be an expression of a complex disorder involving brain maturation: the excess of neurons, along with the reduced apoptosis and pruning, are so great that during the second semester the brain of children with autism can actually be heavier and larger. It is possible to think that the increasing symptomatology that we have observed in the second semester of life represents a clinical correlate of these neurobiological data. Moreover, detecting these infants at risk could reduce the parents' stress through carefully framed information about the development of their child's atypical attention abilities (Hastings, Chapter 15). In fact, parents might interpret the lack of visual attention of the baby to their faces, voices, and smiling as an active withdrawal or avoidance, developing the unpleasant feeling of being rejected by the child. Sometimes in the home videos it is possible to observe a change in the quality of the interactions between the parents and the child. The parents seem to develop a sense of discouragement before a child who does not react to their solicitations as they might expect. Therefore the child risks being gradually deprived of the kind of stimulation which he needs in a special way, and this could determine a reciprocal (caregiver–infant) withdrawal from the interactions. We propose that this dynamic could be the foundation for the IPP (Mundy) of the relationships. Therefore early intervention programs based on these insights could prevent secondary disorders of the relationships. In fact, it is possible to hypothesize that at this early stage of development the infants display a vulnerability rather than a structured deficit, so that interventions that are designed to develop early social and emotional engagement (Jones & Jordan, Chapter 14) could modify the natural history of the disorder.

Note

1   At this stage of our research we were not yet able to provide a third group of control children with intellectual disability.

References

Adrien, J. L., Barthélémy, C., Perrot, A., Roux, S., Lenoir, P., Hameury, L., et al. (1992a). Validity and reliability of the Infant Behavioral Summarized Evaluation (IBSE): A rating scale for the assessment of young children with autism and developmental disorders. *Journal of Autism and Developmental Disorders, 22*, 375–394.

Adrien, J. L., Fauré, M., Perrot. A., Haumery, L., Garreau, B., Barthélémy, C., & Sauvage, D. (1991a). Autism and family HM: Preliminary findings. *Journal of Autism and Developmental Disorders, 21*, 43–49.

Adrien, J. L., Lenoir, P., Martineau, J., Perot, A., Hameury, L., Larmande, C., et al. (1993). Blind ratings of early symptoms of autism based upon family HM. *Journal of the American Academy of Child and Adolescent Psychiatry, 33*, 617–625.

Adrien, J. L., Perrot, A., Hameury, L., et al. (1991b). Family home movies: identification of early autistic signs in infants later diagnosed as autistic. *Brain Dysfunction, 4*(6), 355–362.

Adrien, J. L., Perrot, A., Sauvage, D., et al. (1992b). Early symptoms in autism from home movies. Evaluation and comparison between 1st and 2nd year of life using IBSE-scale. *Acta Paediatrica, 55*, 71–75.

American Psychiatric Association (1994). *Diagnostic and statistical manual of mental disorders* (4th ed.). Washington, DC: APA.

Bakeman, R., & Adamson, L. B. (1984). Coordinating attention to people and objects in mother–infant and peer–infant interaction. *Child Development, 55*, 1278–1289.

Baranek, G. T. (1999). Autism during infancy: A retrospective video analysis of sensory-motor and social behaviours at 9–12 months of age. *Journal of Autism and Developmental Disorders, 29*, 213–224.

Baron-Cohen, S., Allen, J., & Gillberg, C. (1992). Can autism be detected at 18 months? The needle, the haystack and the CHAT. *British Journal of Psychiatry, 138*, 839–843.

Baron-Cohen, S., Cox, A., Baird, G., Swettenham, J., Nightingale, N., Morgan, K., et al. (1996). Psychological markers in the detection of autism in infancy in a large population. *British Journal of Psychiatry, 168*, 158–163.

Barthélémy, C., Adrien, J. L., Roux, S., Garreau, B., Perrot, A., & Lelord, G. (1992). Sensitivity and specificity of the behavioural summarized evaluation (BSE) for the assessment of autistic behaviors. *Journal of Autism and Developmental Disorders, 22*(1), 23–31.

Bates, E., Benigni, L., Bretherton, I., Camaioni, L., & Voltera, V. (1979). *The emergence of symbols: Cognition and communication in infancy.* New York: Academic Press.

Braten, S. (Ed.). (1998). *Intersubjective communication and emotion in early ontogeny* (pp. 354–371). New York: Cambridge University Press.

Charman, T. (1998). Specifying the nature and course of the joint attention impairment in autism in the preschool years. *Autism, 2*, 61–79.

Charman, T. (2003). Why is joint attention a pivotal skill in autism? In U. Frith & E. Hill (Eds.), *Autism: Mind and brain* (pp. 67–87). New York: Oxford University Press.

Charman, T., Baron-Cohen, S., Swettenham, J., Baird, G., Cox, A., & Drew, A. (2000). Testing joint attention, imitation and play as infancy precursors to language and theory of mind. *Cognitive Development, 15*(4), 481–498.

Courchesne, E., Carper, R., & Akshoomoff, N. (2003). Evidence of brain overgrowth in the first year of life in autism. *Journal of the American Medical Association, 290*, 337–344.

Courchesne, E., Townsend, J., Akshoomoff, N., Saitoh, O., Yeung-Courchesne, R., Lincoln, A., et al. (1994). Impairment in shifting attention in autistic and cerebellar patients. *Behavioural Neuroscience, 108*, 848–865.

Dawson, G., Meltzoff, A. N., & Osterling, J. (1998). Children with autism fail to orient to naturally occurring social stimuli. *Journal of Autism and Developmental Disorders*, 28(6), 479–485.

Dawson, G., Munson, J., Estes, A., Osterling, J., McPartland, J., Toth, K., et al. (2002a). Neurocognitive function and joint attention ability in young children with autism spectrum disorder versus developmental delay. *Child Development*, 73(2), 345–358.

Dawson, G., Webb, S., Schellenberg, G. D., Dager, S., Friedma S., Aylward, E., & Richards, T. (2002b). Defining the broader phenotype of autism: Genetic, brain, and behavioral perspectives. *Development and Psychopathology*, 14, 581–611.

Frith, U. (Ed.) (1991). *Autism and Asperger syndrome.* Cambridge, UK: Cambridge University Press.

Gillberg, C., Ehlers, S., Schaumann, H., Jakibsson, G., Dahlgren, S. O., Linddblom, R., et al. (1990). Autism under age 3 years: A clinical study of 28 cases referred for autistic symptoms in infancy. *Journal of Child Psychology and Psychiatry*, 31, 921–934.

Kanner, L. (1943). Autistic disturbances of affective contact. *Nervous Child*, 2, 217–250.

Losche, G. (1990). Sensorimotor and action development in autistic children from infancy to early childhood. *Journal of Child Psychology and Psychiatry*, 31, 749–761.

Maestro, S., Casella, C., Milone, A., Muratori, F., & Palacio-Espasa, F. (1999). Study of the onset of autism through home-movies. *Psychopathology*, 32, 292–300.

Maestro, S., Muratori, F., Cavallaro, M. C., Pei, F., Stern, D., Golse, B., et al. (2002). Attentional skills during the first 6 months of age in Autism Spectrum Disorders. *Journal of American Academy of Child and Adolescent Psychiatry*, 4, 1239–1245.

Maestro, S., Muratori, F., Cesari, A., Cavallaro, M. C., Paziente, A., Pecini, C., et al. (2005). Course of autism signs in the first year of life. *Psychopathology*, 38(1), 26–31.

Massie, H. N. (1978). The early natural history of childhood psychosis: Ten cases studied by analysis of family home movies of the infancies of the children. *Journal of the American Academy of Child Psychiatry*, 17, 29–45.

Massie, H. N., & Rosenthal, J. (1984). *Childhood psychosis in the first four years of life.* New York: McGraw-Hill.

Morton, J., & Johnson, M. H. (1991). CONSPEC and CONLERN: A two-stage process of infant face recognition. *Psychological Review*, 98, 164–181.

Mundy, P. (1995). Joint attention and social-emotional approach behavior in children with autism. *Developmental Psychopathology*, 7, 63–82.

Mundy, P., & Crowson, M. (1997). Joint attention and early social communication: Implications for research on intervention with autism. *Journal of Autism and Developmental Disorders*, 27, 653–676.

Murray, L., Cooper, P., & Hipwell, A.(2003). Mental health of parents caring for infants. *Archives of Women's Mental Health. 6, Suppl 2S.*, 71–77.

Osterling, J., & Dawson, G. (1994). Early recognition of children with autism: A study of first birthday home videotapes. *Journal of Autism and Developmental Disorders*, 24, 247–257.

Osterling, J., & Dawson, G. (2000), Brief report: recognition of autism spectrum disorder before one year of age: a retrospective study based on home-videotapes. *Journal of Autism and Developmental Disorders*, 30, 157–162.

Osterling, J. A., Dawson, G., & Munson, J. A. (2002). Early recognition of 1-year-old infants with autism spectrum disorder versus mental retardation. *Development and Psychopathology, 14*, 239–251.

Plaisted, K., O'Riordan, M., & Baron-Cohen, S. (1998). Enhanced discrimination of novel, highly similar stimuli by adults with autism during perceptual learning task. *Journal of Child Psychology and Psychiatry, 39*, 767–777.

Reddy, V., Hay, D., Murray, L., & Trevarthen, C. (1997). Communication in infancy: Mutual regulation of affect and attention. In G. Bremner, A. Slater, & G. Butterworth (Eds.), *Infant development: Recent advances* (pp. 247–273). Hove: Psychology Press.

Rogers, S. J. (2004). Developmental regression in Autism Spectrum Disorders. *Mental Retardation and Developmental Disabilities Research Reviews, 10*, 139–143.

Rogers, S. J., & DiLalla, D. L. (1990). Age of symptom onset in young children with pervasive developmental disorders. *Journal of the American Academy of Child and Adolescent Psychiatry, 29*, 863–872.

Rosenthal, J., Massie, H. N., & Wulff, S. (1980). A comparison of cognitive development in normal and psychotic children in the first two years of life from home movies. *Journal of Autism and Developmental Disorders, 10*, 433–444.

Sauvage, D., Faura, M., Adrien, J. L., Hameury, L., Barthélémy, C., Perrot, A. (1988). Autisme et les familiaux. *Annals of Psychiatry, 3*, 418–424.

Schopler, E., Reichler, R. J., & Renner, B. R. (1988). *The Childhood Autism Rating Scale (CARS), Revised.* Los Angeles: Western Psychological Services Inc.

Schultz, R. T., Gauthier, I., Klin, A., Fulbright, R. K., Anderson, A. W., Volkmar, F., et al. (2000). Abnormal ventral temporal cortical activity during face discrimination among individuals with autism and Asperger syndrome. *Archives of General Psychiatry, 57*, 331–340.

Sigman, M., Mundy, P., Sherman, T., & Ungerer, J. (1986). Social interaction of autistic, mentally retarded and normal children and their caregivers. *Journal of Child Psychology and Psychiatry, 27*, 647–656.

Stern, D. (1977). *The interpersonal world of the infant.* New York: Basic Books.

Swettenham, J., Charman, T., Baron-Cohen, S., Cox, A., Baird, G., Drew, A., et al. (1998). The frequency and distribution of spontaneous attention shifts between social and non-social stimuli in autistic, typically developing, and non-autistic developmentally delayed infants. *Journal of Child Psychology and Psychiatry, 39*, 747–753.

Teitelbaum, O., Benton, T., Shah, P. K., Prince, A., Kelly, J. L. & Teitelbaum, P. (2004). Movement notation in diagnosis: The early detection of Asperger's syndrome. *Proceedings of the National Academy of Science, USA, 101*(32), 11909–11914.

Teitelbaum, P., Teitelbaum, O., Nye, J., Fryman, J., & Maurer, R. G. (1998). Movement analysis in infancy may be useful for early diagnosis in autism. *Proceedings of the National Academy of Science, USA, 95*, 1392–7.

Tomasello, M. (1995). Joint attention as social cognition. In C. Moore & P. Dunham (Eds.), *Joint attention: Its origins and role in development* (pp. 103–130). Hillsdale, NJ: Lawrence Erlbaum Associates.

Trevarthen, C. (1979). Communication and co-operation in early infancy: A description of primary subjectivity. In M. Bullova (Ed.), *Before speech: The beginning of human communication* (pp. 321–347). London: Cambridge University Press.

Trevarthen, C., & Aitken, K. J. (2001). Infant inter-subjectivity: Research, theory and clinical applications. *Journal of Child Psychology and Psychiatry, 1,* 3–48.

Trevarthen, C., & Hubley, P. (1978). Secondary inter-subjectivity: Confidence, confiding and acts of meaning in the first year. In A. Lock (Ed.), *Action, gesture and symbol* (pp. 183–229). London: Academic Press.

Weinberg, M. K., & Tronick, E. Z. (1996). Infant affective reactions to the resumption of maternal interaction after the still-face. *Child Development, 67*(3), 905–914.

Werner, E., Dawson, G., Munson, J., & Osterling, J. (2005). Variation in early developmental course in autism and its relation with behavioral outcome at 3–4 years of age. *Journal of Autism and Developmental Disorders, 35,* 337–350.

Wimpory, D. C., Hobson, R. P., Williams, J. M., & Nash, S. (2000). Are infants with autism socially engaged? A study of recent retrospective parental reports. *Journal of Autism and Developmental Disorders, 30*(6), 525–536.

Yale, M., Messinger, D., Cobo-Lewis, A., & Delgado, C. (2003). The temporal co-ordination of early infant communication. *Developmental Psychology, 39*(5), 815–824.

10

Screening for Autism Spectrum Disorders in Primary School-Aged Children

Joanna G. Williams

The identification and diagnosis of autism spectrum disorder (ASD) is a complex process. This is because of the multidimensional nature of the condition, the variety of symptoms, and developmental change occurring within the individuals. Given this complexity, it is not surprising that research is still needed into the best ways to identify and diagnose ASD.

Identification of ASD in the UK is typically through concerns being raised by a parent, teacher, or other professional about a child's development. At this point the diagnostic process begins. Diagnosis is a matter of clinical judgment and is made by assessing whether a child meets the criteria outlined in the International Classification of Diseases (World Health Organization, 1993). The criteria cover social impairments, communication impairments, and repetitive or stereotyped behaviors. Depending on the exact manifestations of clinical symptoms, a variety of diagnoses may be given: childhood autism, atypical autism, Asperger syndrome, or pervasive developmental disorders not otherwise specified (PDD-NOS). Collectively these sub-groups are often referred to as ASD. An alternative approach to the identification of ASD would be to offer population screening universally—for example, at school entry—in order to identify behavioral characteristics which may point to an ASD which has not been previously recognized.

This chapter addresses three questions. First, would population screening be an effective means of achieving earlier diagnosis for children with an ASD? Second, can we develop a high-quality screening test based on behavioral markers of ASD, and specifically, is the Childhood Asperger Syndrome Test (CAST) suitable for use in practice or research? Third, how does the issue of identification and screening relate to other areas of autism research?

A Consideration of Population Screening for ASD

Screening is a public health program offered to a defined population, where the participants or those around them do not necessarily perceive that they have a disease or disorder. The aim of screening is to identify those likely to benefit at an early stage from further tests or interventions (National Screening Committee, 1998). Screening is distinct from the use of tests where concerns have already been raised about a child's development, although it is possible that the same test may be considered for use in both contexts.

Screening for ASD is not currently offered in the UK. This contrasts with the USA, where routine developmental screening has been recommended, which includes identifying possible symptoms of ASD that might merit further investigation (Filipek et al., 2000). A recent survey of 894 members of the American Academy of Pediatrics (Sand et al., 2005) indicated that general developmental surveillance is carried out by most pediatricians (71%), and 23% of respondents reported always or almost always using a standardized screening test.

The possibility of introducing population screening in the UK has been raised by professionals and parents for a number of reasons. Screening might enable earlier diagnosis. ASD tends to be diagnosed relatively late, especially if the manifestations are subtle, and at least two years after parents suspect that their child has developmental problems (Gray & Tonge, 2001). Research indicates that the average age of diagnosis for children with Asperger syndrome is 11 years (Howlin & Asgharian, 1999). Whilst some delay between concerns being raised and diagnosis may be unavoidable, as the diagnostic process may need to take place over a period of time in order to observe a child in different settings and within the context of their development, screening could enable this process to be initiated earlier. This may be desirable to allow for genetic counseling for parents, to implement earlier intervention, to alleviate existing parental concern, to initiate parental support, and to take steps to prevent psychopathology associated with ASD (Baird et al., 2001; Scott, Baron-Cohen, Bolton, & Brayne, 2002). Screening may also serve to reassure parents who have unwarranted anxiety, and to increase awareness and understanding of autism; conversely, it may increase public concern about the condition.

In the UK, any proposed new screening program is scrutinized by the National Screening Committee (NSC). The NSC assesses each program against a set of criteria, to ensure that programs do more good than harm, at a reasonable cost. The National Health Service may not introduce any new screening program until the NSC has reviewed its effectiveness and cost-effectiveness. For this reason, a proposal for population screening for autism must be examined against the NSC criteria.

The NSC has 22 criteria (National Screening Committee, 2003) which cover the condition, the tests to screen and diagnose the condition, treatment options, and the effectiveness, cost-effectiveness, and acceptability of the screening program as a whole. Each of the criteria should be met with robust research evidence.

The current policy position of the NSC states that: "On the basis of current evidence, population screening for ASD cannot be recommended" (July 2006) (National Screening Committee, 2006). This conclusion has been consistently reached previously. In 1996 a working party on child health surveillance (Hall, 1996) noted lack of clarity over case definition, the unpredictability of the natural history of developmental conditions, and the lack of evidence for the effectiveness of interventions. Recent re-examination of these issues indicated that many of these difficulties remained (Hall & Elliman, 2003). Other authors have identified difficulties in developing a screening test with sufficiently high sensitivity for use in the general population (Baird et al., 2001), and have concluded that population screening cannot be recommended (Le Couteur, Baird, & National Initiative for Autism Screening and Assessment, 2003).

Evidence relating to the NSC criteria has been reviewed in detail elsewhere (Williams & Brayne, 2006). Here, key issues, relating to the condition, the screening test, the treatment options, and the screening program, are highlighted to demonstrate why population screening for autism cannot currently be recommended.

The condition

The NSC criteria state that the epidemiology and natural history of the condition should be well understood, a precursor to which is agreement on case definition. The criteria also state that the condition should be an important health problem (National Screening Committee, 2003).

In order to screen, it is necessary to impose a dichotomous classification to distinguish those likely to have or unlikely to have the disorder. Difficulty arises, as autism is often conceptualized as a spectrum, and an arbitrary cut-point must be justified. Alternatively, if ASD is conceptualized as distinct sub-groups, disagreement remains about the composition of these groups (Volkmar, Klin, & Cohen, 1997).

Furthermore, in ASD, case definitions are based on behavioral symptoms, and it is only possible to make a diagnosis once the symptoms are manifest. However, in population screening, the aim would typically be to identify a latent or pre-symptomatic phase of the condition, such that an intervention could be offered to alter the course of the disease.

There are many unresolved questions regarding the epidemiology of autism (Medical Research Council, 2001). In order to plan the resources needed to run a screening program, accurate estimates of the prevalence of the condition are needed. A systematic review of prevalence studies (Williams, Higgins, & Brayne, 2006) has indicated that the true prevalence of autism is likely to be between 1.6 and 30.6 per 10,000, and the prevalence of all ASD between 4.9 and 82.1 per 10,000. The studies have indicated a possible increase in prevalence estimates over time, and prevalence estimates have varied widely. The review showed that much of the variation in reported prevalence estimates can be attributed to the different diagnostic criteria used, the age of the children in the studies, and the study location which may act as a proxy for different diagnostic practices. Other factors may explain the increase in prevalence estimates over time such as an increase in services available, including diagnostic services; increased awareness amongst professionals; a growing awareness that autism can coexist with a range of other conditions; or a possible rise in risk factors for autism (Charman, 2002; Fombonne, 2002, 2003; Wing & Potter, 2002).

Longitudinal studies of the natural history of ASD are needed to act as a baseline to provide an understanding of the developmental trajectories of the condition, against which to compare the effect of screening and subsequent interventions. Whilst many follow-up studies have been published, these comprise referred cases, and in a discussion of population screening the focus of interest is the outcome of cases identified from the general population. Very few population-based longitudinal studies of autism have been published (e.g., Gillberg & Steffenburg, 1987; Lotter, 1974; von Knorring & Hagglof, 1993). These were small-scale studies that included individuals identified at a wide range of ages. It would be valuable to conduct longitudinal studies identifying children in the early years in order to have data against which to assess outcomes following identification by screening.

There is little doubt that ASD is an important condition, both on an individual and a population level. ASD is rare compared to many other childhood diseases and disorders, but, due to the severity and lifelong duration, the public health burden of the disorder is great.

There is currently insufficient information about the condition to justify screening, predominantly because of controversies about case definition, variation in prevalence estimates, and gaps in our understanding of the natural history of these disorders.

The test

For use in a population screening program, a screening test must be validated within that specific context: for example, in a primary care or educational setting, as opposed to a referred population. A screening test's performance is typically assessed against a "gold standard" diagnosis of ASD, which is often based on clinical judgment aided by diagnostic tools designed to collect diagnostic information in a systematic manner once concerns have been raised about a child's development or a child has a positive result on a screening test. Two particular measures are used to describe a screening test's performance, which assess the validity of the test, sensitivity, and specificity. *Sensitivity* is a measure of test performance, and indicates the proportion of cases (i.e., those with a condition) who are correctly identified by the test. *Specificity* indicates the proportion of those who are not cases (i.e., who do not have the condition), who are correctly identified by the test. *Positive predictive value* describes the performance of the test in a particular population, and summarizes the proportion of those who receive a positive result who are found to have the condition at assessment. It is also important to gauge the reliability of a screening test, to assess whether it performs in a consistent manner. In particular, test–retest reliability demonstrates whether the test gives the same results each time it is administered.

A recent review identified 24 screening tests for ASD that have been developed across all age groups (Williams & Brayne, 2006). Of these, only two tests had data on the sensitivity and specificity against a gold standard diagnostic assessment and full validation in the general population: the Checklist for Autism in Toddlers (CHAT: Baird et al., 2000) and the Modified-CHAT (M-CHAT: Robins, Fein, Barton, & Green, 2001). The CHAT and the M-CHAT were designed for preschool-aged children. The M-CHAT study did not include diagnostic follow-up of the children, and measures of sensitivity and specificity were estimated from a discriminant function analysis. Validation is required against a full diagnostic assessment. The CHAT was validated in a large population sample of 18-month-old children. The CHAT showed good specificity (0.99) for those considered to be at high risk for autism, but it had an unacceptably low positive predictive value at only 0.20 for children classified as being at high risk for autism on the basis of the CHAT.

A further four tests had data on sensitivity and specificity, but obtained in a clinical setting: the Autism Screening Questionnaire (ASQ, since renamed the Social Communication Questionnaire, SCQ: Berument, Rutter, Lord, Pickles, & Bailey, 1999; Bölte, Crecelius, & Poustka, 2000), the Asperger Syndrome Screening Questionnaire (ASSQ: Ehlers, Gillberg, & Wing, 1999), the Autism Behavior Checklist (ABC: Krug, Arick, & Almond, 1980), and the Screening Test for Autism in Two-Year Olds (STAT: Stone, Coonrod, & Ousley, 2000). Many of these have shown good test characteristics in a clinical setting. The ASSQ has been used in two studies in the general population (Ehlers & Gillberg, 1993; Kadesjo, Gillberg, & Hagberg, 1999). One of these studies included retrospective validation of the ASSQ in a small sample of 826 children from the general population, indicating that the sensitivity was 100% (Kadesjo et al., 1999). None of these tests is accompanied by published data on all three measures, the sensitivity, specificity, and positive predictive value, based on studies from the general population.

Since this review (Williams & Brayne, 2006) further studies have been published on existing tests in clinical settings: on the SCQ (Eaves, Wingert, Ho, & Mickelson, 2006b; Eaves, Wingert, & Ho, 2006a), the M-CHAT (Eaves et al., 2006a), the Developmental Behavioral Checklist (Gray & Tonge, 2005), and the STAT (Stone, Coonrod, Turner, & Pozdol, 2004). New tests have been evaluated in clinical settings: the Early Screening of Autistic Traits questionnaire (ESAT: Dietz, Swinkels, van Daalen, van Engeland, & Buitelaar, 2006). Existing tests have also been translated and re-evaluated: the AQ (Kurita, Koyama, & Osada, 2005), and the CHAT/M-CHAT (Wong et al., 2004). The new Social and Communication Disorders Checklist (SCDC: Skuse, Mandy, & Scourfield, 2005) showed sensitivity of 0.90, specificity of 0.69, and positive predictive value of 0.75 in a mixed clinical and population sample in discriminating pervasive developmental disorders from other conditions. It would be valuable to have data on validity for the SCDC from the general population only.

These literature searches have shown that there is currently no screening test available that has been fully validated in the general population which could be used in a screening program. This further explains why population screening is not currently recommended.

Treatment options

The NSC criteria (National Screening Committee, 2003) state that there should be effective treatment or interventions, with evidence of early rather than late treatment leading to better outcomes, and that there should be evidence-based policies covering the appropriate treatment to be offered. Typically, systematic reviews of randomized controlled trials (RCTs) are considered as the most robust evidence of effectiveness in this context. Difficulties in applying this type of methodology, originally designed for use in relation to biomedical and pharmacological interventions, to the autism field have been described (Mesibov, Fuentes, Prior, & Wing, 2006). Nevertheless, some researchers have demonstrated that these methodologies can be applied to behavioral interventions (Diggle, McConachie, & Randle, 2002).

To date, six systematic reviews of RCTs of interventions for ASD have been published and included in the Cochrane Library database of systematic reviews. These reviews examined a variety of interventions: vitamin B6 and magnesium supplements (Nye & Brice, 2005), parent-mediated early intervention (Diggle et al., 2002), intravenous secretin (Williams, Wray, & Wheeler, 2005), gluten- and casein-free diets (Millward, Ferriter, Calver, & Connell-Jones, 2004), auditory integration training (Sinha, Silove, Wheeler, & Williams, 2004), and music therapy (Gold, Wigram, & Elefant, 2006). The Cochrane Library currently includes other literature reviews that examine the effectiveness of interventions, but not using the Cochrane methodology. For example, reviews have covered the Lovaas program (Bassett, Green, & Kazanjian, 2000) and social interactive training (Hwang & Hughes, 2000). None of the systematic or other reviews of effectiveness included in the Cochrane Library have demonstrated definitive evidence of superior effectiveness of any particular intervention, and the reviews were often limited by methodological problems in the primary studies.

The Cochrane register of RCTs includes around 100 studies, covering more than 40 different types of intervention. The majority of these studies are of pharmacological interventions, and relatively few are on educational and behavioral programs. There is a need for more high-quality RCTs of the effectiveness of specific behavioral interventions and for research evidence to be synthesized in systematic reviews, to clarify whether there is consistent evidence of effectiveness for any of the approaches.

At an individual level, there are indications of approaches that can be of benefit: "A structured, organized daily program based on each individual's skills, impairments and special interests continues to be the best available approach" (Mesibov et al., 2006). Nonetheless, the current evidence of effectiveness of interventions is not sufficient to meet the criteria of the NSC.

The screening program

The NSC criteria state that evidence is needed relating to the screening program as a whole, and includes questions such as: Does the benefit outweigh any harm caused? Is the program cost-effective? Is it acceptable to the population? Are there sufficient resources to support the program? And have all alternative options for managing the condition been considered? Gaps in the other areas of evidence for screening make it hard to envisage a program as a whole, and therefore to consider these criteria. Here just the area of potential harms is addressed.

No screening test is perfect, and with any test there will be false positive and negative results. False positive results might increase parental and child anxiety, and might lead to delays in the detection of other developmental difficulties. False negative screening results might lead to difficulties in getting access to diagnostic assessments and subsequent interventions when parents continue to raise concerns. Even a correct positive screening test can bring harms: there may be stress or stigma surrounding investigations or a diagnosis. Parents are divided over whether or not they would have preferred to have known about their child's developmental disorder before they noticed any difficulties themselves (Baird et al., 2001).

If the NSC criteria were met concerning the condition, the test, and the treatment, the NSC recommend that a RCT of the screening program as a whole should be carried out prior to any national screening program.

Current practice in the identification of ASD

For the reasons outlined here, population screening for autism is not recommended in the UK. There has, nevertheless, been an acknowledgment that services for identification and diagnosis have not been as effective and efficient as they could be. In the light of this, the National Autism Plan for Children (NAPC) was published (Le Couteur et al., 2003) by the Royal College of Paediatrics and Child Health and the Royal College of Psychiatrists, through the National Autistic Society. Drawing widely from research and expert opinion, these guidelines recommend approaches to improve the identification of developmental difficulties that may point to autism, to ensure swift access to diagnostic services, and ongoing support tailored to each individual.

In the next section, the particular issue of developing a screening test is addressed, and studies are presented that were carried out to develop and evaluate the Childhood Asperger Syndrome Test (CAST). The development of such a test may have applications when concerns are raised about a child's development to indicate whether a full diagnostic assessment for ASD would be appropriate, as in the model outlined in the NAPC. The continued development of screening tests is also valuable to contribute to the body of evidence for screening, and tests may have applications in epidemiological research which can contribute to our understanding of the condition.

The Development and Evaluation of the Childhood Asperger Syndrome Test

When developing a test for use in screening, it is appropriate to consider how best to identify children who have subtler manifestations of ASD, who might otherwise take longer to come to the attention of clinical services. The CAST was designed to identify ASD in primary school-aged children who may not have been identified at an earlier age. The CAST is not specific to Asperger syndrome, but was developed to be sensitive to ASD in the mainstream school population, and therefore for use predominantly among children with cognitive ability within the normal range.

SCREENING FOR ASD IN PRIMARY SCHOOL-AGED CHILDREN 201

The CAST was first published in 2002 by Scott et al., and is available elsewhere in print (J. Williams et al., 2005) and online (ARC, 2006). Studies to develop and evaluate the CAST have examined the discriminative power of the test and the individual test items, the test validity, the test–retest reliability, and the research team has begun to develop a teacher version.

Design and development of the CAST

The CAST is a parental questionnaire, which includes 37 questions about the child's development and behavior. The questions in the CAST are based on a variety of behavioral descriptions from the ICD-10 (World Health Organization, 1993) and DSM-IV (American Psychiatric Association, 1994) criteria for the features of ASD, covering social impairments, communication impairments, and repetitive or stereotyped behaviors. Questions include, for example, "Does s/he come up spontaneously for a chat?" and "Does s/he make normal eye contact?," to which the parent responds "yes" or "no." Thirty-one of the questions are scored, where a score of one represents a behavior that may indicate the presence of an ASD. The remaining six questions are general developmental questions which are not scored.

Two early pilot studies were carried out (Scott et al., 2002). The first study compared scores on the CAST in a sample of 13 children of around 7 years of age previously diagnosed with Asperger syndrome, and 37 typically developing children of similar age. The mean score was significantly higher in the group with Asperger syndrome (mean = 21.08 (sd = 5.51)) than in the group of typically developing children (mean = 4.73 (sd = 3.57)). Individual questions demonstrated good discrimination between the two groups of children. On the basis of these findings, a preliminary cut-point score was set at 15.

The second study drew from a larger sample of 1,150 4–11-year-olds from four mainstream primary schools in Cambridgeshire, UK (Scott et al., 2002). The study had a disappointingly low response rate at 17% (n = 199). As a result, it is unlikely that those responding were representative of the population. 6.5% of children were identified to be above the cut-point of 15 on the CAST, and were invited for a follow-up assessment using the Autism Diagnostic Observation Schedule-Generic, ADOS-G (Lord et al., 2000). At this assessment stage, all four previously diagnosed cases of ASD were found to have been identified by the CAST, and an additional six cases of ASD were identified. These preliminary results indicated that the specificity of the CAST for ASD was 98%, and the positive predictive value was 64%. It was not possible to calculate the sensitivity of the test in this study, because there were no diagnostic assessments of children scoring lower than 15 on the CAST. In this study, scores on the CAST and the SCQ (Berument et al., 1999) were compared, and the CAST was found to be more sensitive in identifying less clearcut cases of Asperger syndrome and related ASD in this general population sample.

Validity of the CAST

The validation study of the CAST (J. Williams et al., 2005) followed on from the pilot studies, to replicate the preliminary findings in a larger population sample of children. The aims were to improve the response rate, to estimate the sensitivity of the test, and to confirm an appropriate cut-point score for the CAST.

Five mainstream schools in Cambridgeshire were selected, representing different geographical areas of the county. Each school was asked to distribute a copy of the CAST to each child between the ages of 5 and 11 years, for completion by their parents. A total of 1,925 questionnaires were distributed. A second batch of questionnaires was distributed to the same sample of parents in order to improve response rates.

Questionnaires were scored, and scores grouped into three bands: at or above 15, 12 to 14, and less than 12. All those scoring at or above 15, and 12 to 14, and a 5% random sample of those scoring less than 12 were invited to participate in a full diagnostic assessment, in order to assess the criterion validity of the CAST.

Assessments were carried out in each child's home. The CAST was completed again at the start of each assessment in order to assess its retest reliability. Two instruments were used as a "gold standard" for diagnostic assessment: the ADOS-G (Lord et al., 2000), and the Autism Diagnostic Interview-Revised (ADI-R: Lord, Rutter, & Le Couteur, 1994). The researcher was blind to the CAST score.

Cases of ASD were defined in two ways. First, an assessment diagnosis was given if a child scored above the cut-point for autism or ASD on both the ADI-R and the ADOS-G, or if they had a previous clinical diagnosis of autism, Asperger syndrome, or another ASD. Second, a consensus diagnosis was given if they received an assessment diagnosis or if they were below the cut-point (≤ 2 points) in only one of the domains covered in the algorithm on either the ADOS-G or ADI-R, and the research team agreed that they met ICD-10 research criteria for a diagnosis of atypical autism, Asperger syndrome, or PDD-NOS.

The second case definition was used for a number of reasons. The ADI-R algorithm includes a cutoff score only for autism, and not for wider spectrum disorders. The ADOS-G and ADI-R algorithms could be considered too stringent to include PDD-NOS. Disagreement between the ADI-R and ADOS-G has been observed using the current algorithms, and this type of consensus approach has also been taken in previous studies (Bishop & Norbury, 2002).

As the study was based on a two-stage sampling strategy, inverse probability weighting using sampling weights was applied in the estimation of indices of test accuracy, reflecting both the sampling procedure and the response rate. Where the proportion was 100%, exact binomial confidence intervals were calculated using the weighted count.

The response rate to the CAST was 29% (552 of the 1925 questionnaires distributed). Scores ranged from 0 to 24, with 5.8% scoring 15 or more before exclusions, and 4.8% scoring 12–14. Fifty-two CAST questionnaires were excluded where whole sections were incomplete, or a child was outside the intended sample. Sixty-five children were invited to participate in the assessment. There were no significant differences between those invited and not invited for assessment in the lowest score group, according to the CAST score, the child's age or gender, parental education, previous concerns, or diagnoses of developmental difficulties.

Eighteen children (72%) scoring 15 or more, 11 (55%) scoring 12 to 14, and 11 (55%) scoring less than 12 agreed to participate in the assessment phase, an overall response rate of 62%. A comparison of responders and non-responders to the assessment invitation showed that there were no significant differences in the ages, gender of children, or parental education. Where teachers or health visitors had expressed concerns over the child's development significantly more children took part than refused. However, when those accepting and refusing assessment were compared within score groups, there was no significant difference, indicating that this is likely to have had only a minimal impact on the study results.

Six children in the assessment sample had a previous clinical diagnosis. All of these children had scored at or above 15 on the CAST. Of these six, four warranted an assessment diagnosis of ASD, scoring above the cutoff points on both the ADOS-G and the ADI-R. A further three children from the assessment sample were given a consensus diagnosis of an ASD; all of these children scored above 15 on the CAST.

At a cut-point of 15 using the consensus diagnosis as the gold standard, the sensitivity was 100% (95% CI: 74–100%), the specificity 97% (95% CI: 95–99%), and the positive predictive value 50% (95% CI: 28–72%). Taking the assessment diagnosis as the gold standard at a cut-point score of 15, the sensitivity and specificity remained high, but the positive predictive value was somewhat lower at 33%. Using a higher cut-point score to identify children given an assessment diagnosis maintained a high sensitivity and specificity, and increased the positive predictive value. It is possible that a lower cut-point is more suitable for wider spectrum disorders, and a higher cut-point for identifying autism.

This validation study demonstrated that the CAST has high sensitivity and is effective at identifying cases of ASD. The drawback of the CAST is the low positive predictive value, manifest in the high number of false positives. This is primarily due to using the test in a population with very low prevalence (O'Toole, 2000).

Further studies of the validation of the CAST are now required to address some limitations of this study. The findings should be replicated in a larger sample. The time lag between screening and the diagnostic assessment should be minimized. Every effort should be made to maximize the response rate to screening, to ensure that the sample is representative of the general population.

Reliability of the CAST

The test–retest reliability of the CAST was investigated in two studies, one in a population sample and the other in a selected sample enriched with high scorers on the CAST.

In the first study, parents of 1,000 children aged 5–11 years were asked to complete the CAST (J. Williams et al., 2006). After two weeks, the same parent was asked to complete an identical copy of the questionnaire. Agreement above and below the cut-point of 15 was investigated. The kappa statistic for agreement (<15 versus ≥ 15) was 0.70. 97% (95% CI: 93–99) of children did not move across the cut-point. The correlation between the two test scores was 0.83 (Spearman's rho). Despite a disappointing response rate of 28% to both mailings (although not unusual for a population-based study), this study showed that the CAST has good test–retest reliability in a population sample. This is broadly comparable to that of other autism tests: for example, the correlation coefficient in clinical samples between tests using the Autism-Spectrum Quotient in adults was found to be 0.7 (Baron-Cohen, Wheelwright, Skinner, Martin, & Clubley, 2001), and the ASSQ (parent version) had a correlation of 0.96 between scores two weeks apart (Ehlers et al., 1999).

The second CAST reliability study examined the important question of the stability of scores around the screening cut-point. This study was nested within the previously described study of validity, and included children who formed the assessment sample (n = 65), and therefore had a relatively high proportion of higher scorers on the CAST. The test–retest reliability of the CAST was examined between the screening and assessment phases of the study when the questionnaire was completed a second time by the parent. In this sample of children scoring higher on the CAST, the test–retest reliability was found to be moderate (Allison et al., 2007).

Teacher version of the CAST

Ehlers and colleagues (1999) have observed that teachers and parents tend to select different children for further assessment for ASD. Consequently, a teacher screen may be desirable. Teachers may have more opportunities than parents to observe children interacting with their peers and may therefore notice difficulties in a group setting, in particular in the area of social skills (Verhulst & Van der Ende, 1991). To increase the sensitivity of a potential screening program it may be valuable to have both a parent and a teacher complete a questionnaire on a child (Szatmari, Archer, Fisman, & Streiner, 1994). Furthermore, in population studies, teachers may be asked to identify children, and tests are needed for this purpose (Webb, Lobo, Hervas, Scourfield, & Fraser, 1997).

A teacher version of the CAST (TCAST) was developed, altering two of the scoring questions and adding two questions, such that the total score was 33 (Williams, 2003). The TCAST was piloted and evaluated in a small sample of 65 children, the assessment sample of the validation study described above. The response rate was high at 70%, but only 40% of the questionnaires were fully complete. As might be expected, teachers had difficulty answering questions about a child's history of language delay or history of difficulties in pretend play. Due to these missing data it was not possible to establish the discriminant validity of the test, but some questions discriminated well between children with and without an ASD. The findings from this preliminary study can contribute to a revision of the TCAST.

Recommendations for the use and further development of the CAST

In these studies, the CAST has been shown to be effective in identifying the subtler manifestations of ASD, including Asperger syndrome, in 5–11-year-olds in a population setting. It has been shown to have good sensitivity, specificity, and test–retest reliability. The positive predictive value in a population setting is moderate. The high number of "false positives" is a concern if anxiety is unnecessarily evoked, as well as the resource implications of diagnostic assessments. However, it is possible that children identified as "false positives" may have other conditions which need further clinical investigation. Therefore follow-up of such children is important in order to identify other developmental difficulties that may be emerging (Bryson, Zwaigenbaum, & Roberts, 2004). The identification of other developmental difficulties with similarities to autism may also be valuable when using the CAST in a research context.

There are three potential applications of the CAST: in population screening; in individual testing where there are existing concerns about a child's development; and in epidemiological research.

As described, the NSC criteria have not been met due to gaps in the evidence relating to the condition, to treatment options, and to a screening program as a whole. As a result, the CAST cannot currently be recommended for population screening.

The CAST may be an additional valuable test where there are concerns about a child's development in a primary school-age group (5–11 years). The NAPC (Le Couteur et al., 2003) recommends the CAST for use in this context, by staff in health and education. The CAST can be used early on in the diagnostic process to indicate whether a child's difficulties may be due to ASD and to inform the choice of later diagnostic tools and assessments.

The CAST can be strongly recommended as a screening test for ASD in population studies: for example, to identify children in the first phase of a prevalence study. Such applications can continue to inform our understanding of ASD and contribute to the body of evidence required to decide whether population screening may be appropriate in the future.

Further research on the CAST can continue to develop a teacher version. Preliminary work has investigated the construct validity of the test and its dimensionality. This may lead to a more precise scoring algorithm. In addition to previous work of this type (Scott et al., 2002), quantitative comparison of the CAST to other screening tests would clarify their relative merits. The CAST has been translated into German (ARC, 2006). Further development and research in other languages or cultures would ensure the stability of the CAST in different settings.

Integration Section: Relationship to Current and Future Research

The examination of evidence relevant to screening has exposed a number of gaps in autism research. Many of the chapters in this book describe work that is pertinent to the screening debate and to the development of screening tests. Their ideas and research findings are considered in turn in relation to the condition, the test, the treatment options, and the screening program.

The condition

Disagreement still exists around appropriate case definitions for ASD. Leekam and McGregor (Chapter 16) discuss how a shift in perspective may be required away from using diagnostic criteria based on descriptions of static behaviors, such as those in the international psychiatric classification systems, to take fuller account of the developmental nature of autistic conditions.

Another gap in the evidence is in our understanding of the natural history of ASD. Maestro and Muratori's research using home movies of infants later diagnosed with autism (Chapter 9) provides an insight into the early stages of autism prior to the full manifestations of symptoms sufficient for a diagnosis. Such research can help us to understand the developmental trajectory and the natural history of autism, the times at which there is divergence from typical development, and may provide clues for earlier identification of the condition, or potential for earlier intervention.

Bruno Wicker's research using neuroimaging (Chapter 2) draws valuable links between neurobiological models and behavioral symptoms of ASD—in particular, difficulties in processing emotional stimuli. Although research of this type cannot contribute directly to screening programs, it can contribute indirectly, by building our understanding of the causation and natural history of ASD.

The test

The CAST includes questions on a wide range of symptoms. As neurocognitive research continues to develop, manifestations of impairments may be described in more specific terms, which could result in detection of impairments in screening tests being more precise. For example, Jones and Klin (Chapter 4) comment on how their eye-tracking studies can identify subtle features of altered visual salience. The ability to identify such features might have future applications as early diagnostic indicators. Aspects of clinical research may have similar potential. Work by McCann and colleagues (Chapter 11) refines distinctions in the prosody–language relationship in children with high-functioning autism. The CAST already includes a question that relates to prosodic impairment, question 20: "Is his/her voice unusual (e.g., overly adult, flat, or very monotonous)?" As research defines areas of impairment such as prosody and the relationship to other areas of language more precisely, it may be possible to devise more sensitive questions to identify these aspects of the condition in screening tests.

The treatment options

The NSC criteria (National Screening Committee, 2003) state that evidence of the effectiveness of interventions must be available. The lack of systematic evidence for the effectiveness of interventions in autism has been highlighted here. The problem is examined in Chapter 14, where Jones and Jordan explain that a major reason for this lack of evidence is the different emphases of intervention research in educational or family settings compared to in medical settings. For example, in educational or family settings, outcomes are often assessed in terms of measuring change within individuals, whereas in medical settings outcomes are typically assessed in RCTs with the aim of detecting differences between treatment groups.

In Chapter 16, Leekam and McGregor discuss how the independent research paths of medical science and developmental science have, in part, led to separate research cultures in education and medicine. The difficulties with intervention research exemplify this issue. The NSC criteria in general, and the criteria for interventions specifically, are firmly grounded in the "evidence-based medicine" approach. The educational methods as described by Jones and Jordan are rarely, if ever, designed to fit this model. The NSC criteria put pressure on the autism field to produce evidence of effectiveness of a type and standard comparable to that from other fields, but there are inevitably difficulties of adapting methodology to behavioral approaches to intervention.

In spite of these difficulties in intervention research, three further chapters in this volume do contribute to the evidence base. Much research has previously focused on typical autism. Research into interventions for individuals with subtler manifestations of ASD are clearly important in relation to this discussion of screening in mainstream schools. Golan and Baron-Cohen (Chapter 12) present an evaluation of the "mind-reading" software designed to facilitate individuals with Asperger syndrome in acquiring deeper understanding of emotions. Dunlop and colleagues (Chapter 13) also build evaluation into their intervention, which examines ways to develop social interaction and understanding for children and adolescents with ASD. Richard Hastings's studies (Chapter 15) on the effect of intensive interventions on families are focused on children with typical autism, but the issues are likely to be similar across the ASD spectrum. The findings highlight the importance of taking a wider perspective on interventions, to understand not just their effectiveness and cost-effectiveness, but their acceptability to the individual and the family. These topics and the research findings are highly relevant to the debate on interventions in the context of screening.

The screening program

When reviewing the evidence relevant to screening, possible harms of screening identified included anxiety and stress for parents. Chapter 15 highlights the importance of considering parental stress in all aspects of provision of services for families, and contributes to our understanding of the factors that trigger or protect from stress in families.

Research and audit into current practice in identification

Population screening for ASD is not currently recommended due to gaps in the evidence. Ongoing research contributes to this body of evidence, such that screening policy can be reviewed regularly in the future. In the absence of screening, the model of effectively responding to concerns, as outlined in the NAPC (Le Couteur et al., 2003), is being implemented. In the NAPC each local area is advised to audit the age of detection and diagnosis of all developmental difficulties. It is hoped that these data will expose unnecessary delays in the process of the identification and diagnosis of children with an ASD such that these delays can be addressed and reduced.

Acknowledgments

Much of the research described was carried out within a research team at the Autism Research Centre, University of Cambridge, as a collaboration between the Section of Developmental Psychiatry and the Department of Public Health and Primary Care. Acknowledgment is due to members of the team, as reflected in the citations: Prof. Simon Baron-Cohen, Dr Fiona Scott, Dr Carol Stott, Prof. Patrick Bolton, Prof. Carol Brayne, and Ms Carrie Allison. I am grateful to the Medical Research Council and the Shirley Foundation for their financial support.

References

Allison, C., Williams, J., Scott, F., Stott, C., Bolton, P., Baron-Cohen, S., et al. (2007). The Childhood Asperger Syndrome Test (CAST): Test–retest reliability in a high scoring sample. *Autism, 11*, 173–185.

American Psychiatric Association (1994). *Diagnostic and statistical manual of mental disorders (DSM-IV).* (4th ed.) Washington, DC: APA.

ARC (2006). Autism Research Centre. Download of the Childhood Asperger Syndrome Test (CAST) and scoring key. www.autismresearchcentre.com/tests/cast_test.asp. Accessed 25/10/06.

Baird, G., Charman, T., Baron-Cohen, S., Cox, A., Swettenham, J., Wheelwright, S., et al. (2000). A screening instrument for autism at 18 months of age: A 6-year follow-up study. *Journal of the American Academy of Child and Adolescent Psychiatry, 39*, 694–702.

Baird, G., Charman, T., Cox, A., Baron-Cohen, S., Swettenham, J., Wheelwright, S., et al. (2001). Current topic: Screening and surveillance for autism and pervasive developmental disorders. *Archives of Disease in Childhood, 84*, 468–475.

Baron-Cohen, S., Wheelwright, S., Skinner, R., Martin, J., & Clubley, E. (2001). The autism-spectrum quotient (AQ): Evidence from Asperger syndrome/high-functioning autism, males and females, scientists and mathematicians. *Journal of Autism and Developmental Disorders, 31*, 5–17.

Bassett, K., Green, C. J., & Kazanjian, A. (2000). *Autism and Lovaas treatment: A systematic review of effectiveness evidence* (BCOHTA 00:1T ed.). Vancouver: British Columbia Office of Health Technology Assessment, University of British Columbia.

Berument, S. K., Rutter, M., Lord, C., Pickles, A., & Bailey, A. (1999). Autism screening questionnaire: Diagnostic validity. *British Journal of Psychiatry, 175*, 444–451.

Bishop, D. V., & Norbury, C. F. (2002). Exploring the borderlands of autistic disorder and specific language impairment: A study using standardised diagnostic instruments. *Journal of Child Psychology and Psychiatry, 43*, 917–929.

Bölte, S., Crecelius, K., & Poustka, F. (2000). The Questionnaire on Behaviour and Social Communication (VSK): An autism screening instrument for research and practice. *Diagnostica, 46*, 149–155.

Bryson, S., Zwaigenbaum, L., & Roberts, W. (2004). The early detection of autism in clinical practice. *Pediatrics and Child Health, 9*, 219–221.

Charman, T. (2002). The prevalence of autism spectrum disorders. Recent evidence and future challenges. *European Child and Adolescent Psychiatry, 11*, 249–256.

Dietz, C., Swinkels, S., van Daalen, E., van Engeland, H., & Buitelaar, J. K. (2006). Screening for autistic spectrum disorder in children aged 14–15 months. ii: Population screening with the early screening of autistic traits questionnaire (ESAT). Design and general findings. *Journal of Autism and Developmental Disorders, 36*, 713–722.

Diggle, T., McConachie, H. R., & Randle, V. R. L. (2002). Parent-mediated early intervention for young children with autism spectrum disorder. *Cochrane Database of Systematic Reviews, Issue 2*. Art. No.: CD003496. DOI: 10.1002/14651858.CD003496.

Eaves, L. C., Wingert, H., & Ho, H. H. (2006a). Screening for autism: Agreement with diagnosis. *Autism, 10*, 229–242.

Eaves, L. C., Wingert, H. D., Ho, H. H., & Mickelson, E. C. (2006b). Screening for autism spectrum disorders with the social communication questionnaire. *Journal of Developmental and Behavioral Pediatrics, 27*, S95–S103.

Ehlers, S., & Gillberg, C. (1993). The epidemiology of Asperger syndrome. A total population study. *Journal of Child Psychology and Psychiatry, 34*, 1327–1350.

Ehlers, S., Gillberg, C., & Wing, L. (1999). A screening questionnaire for Asperger syndrome and other high- functioning autism spectrum disorders in school age children. *Journal of Autism and Developmental Disorders, 29*, 129–141.

Filipek, P. A., Accardo, P. J., Ashwal, S., Baranek, G. T., Cook, E. H. Jr., Dawson, G., et al. (2000). Practice parameter: Screening and diagnosis of autism: Report of the Quality Standards Subcommittee of the American Academy of Neurology and the Child Neurology Society. *Neurology, 55*, 468–479.

Fombonne, E. (2002). Epidemiological trends in rates of autism. *Molecular Psychiatry, 7*, Supplement 2, S4–S6.

Fombonne, E. (2003). Epidemiological surveys of autism and other pervasive developmental disorders: An update. *Journal of Autism and Developmental Disorders, 33*, 365–382.

Gillberg, C., & Steffenburg, S. (1987). Outcome and prognostic factors in infantile autism and similar conditions: A population-based study of 46 cases followed through puberty. *Journal of Autism and Developmental Disorders, 17*, 273–287.

Gold, C., Wigram, T., & Elefant, C. (2006). Music therapy for autistic spectrum disorder. *Cochrane Database of Systematic Reviews, Issue 2.* Art. No.: CD004381. DOI: 10.1002/14651858.CD004381.pub2.

Gray, K. M., & Tonge, B. J. (2001). Are there early features of autism in infants and preschool children? *Journal of Paediatrics and Child Health, 37,* 221–226.

Gray, K. M., & Tonge, B. J. (2005). Screening for autism in infants and preschool children with developmental delay. *Australian and New Zealand Journal of Psychiatry, 39,* 378–386.

Hall, D. M. B. (1996). *Health for all children. The report of the Joint Working Party on Child Health Surveillance* (3rd ed.). Oxford, UK: Oxford University Press.

Hall, D., & Elliman, D. (2003). *Health for all children* (4th ed.). Oxford, UK: Oxford University Press.

Howlin, P., & Asgharian, A. (1999). The diagnosis of autism and Asperger syndrome: Findings from a survey of 770 families. *Developmental Medicine and Child Neurology, 41,* 834–839.

Hwang, B., & Hughes, C. (2000). The effects of social interactive training of early social communicative skills of children with autism. *Journal of Autism and Developmental Disorders, 30,* 331–343.

Kadesjo, B., Gillberg, C., & Hagberg, B. (1999). Brief report: Autism and Asperger syndrome in seven-year-old children: A total population study. *Journal of Autism and Developmental Disorders, 29,* 327–331.

Krug, D. A., Arick, J., & Almond, P. (1980). Behavior checklist for identifying severely handicapped individuals with high levels of autistic behavior. *Journal of Child Psychology and Psychiatry, 21,* 221–229.

Kurita, H., Koyama, T., & Osada, H. (2005). Autism-spectrum quotient—Japanese version and its short forms for screening normally intelligent persons with pervasive developmental disorders. *Psychiatry and Clinical Neurosciences, 59,* 490–496.

Le Couteur, A., Baird, G., & National Initiative for Autism Screening and Assessment (2003). *National Autism Plan for Children: Plan for the identification, assessment, diagnosis and access to early intervention for pre-school and primary school aged children with autism spectrum disorders.* London: National Autistic Society.

Lord, C., Risi, S., Lambrecht, L., Cook, E. H., Jr., Leventhal, B. L., DiLavore, P. C., et al. (2000). The autism diagnostic observation schedule-generic: A standard measure of social and communication deficits associated with the spectrum of autism. *Journal of Autism and Developmental Disorders, 30,* 205–223.

Lord, C., Rutter, M., & Le Couteur, A. (1994). Autism Diagnostic Interview—Revised: A revised version of a diagnostic interview for caregivers of individuals with possible pervasive developmental disorders. *Journal of Autism and Developmental Disorders, 24,* 659–685.

Lotter, V. (1974). Factors related to outcome in autistic children. *Journal of Autism and Child Schizophrenia, 4,* 263–277.

Medical Research Council (2001). *MRC review of autism research.* London: Medical Research Council.

Mesibov, G. B., Fuentes, J., Prior, M., & Wing, L. (2006). The past decade. *Autism, 10,* 7–10.

Millward, C., Ferriter, M., Calver, S., & Connell-Jones, G. (2004). Gluten- and casein-free diets for autistic spectrum disorder. *Cochrane Database of Systematic Reviews, Issue 2.* Art. No.: CD003498. DOI: 10.1002/14651858.CD003498.pub2.

National Screening Committee (1998). *First report of the National Screening Committee.* London: Health Departments of the United Kingdom.

National Screening Committee (2003). *Criteria for appraising the viability, effectiveness and appropriateness of a screening programme.* http://www.library.nhs.uk/screening/ Accessed 06/22/06.

National Screening Committee (2006). *National Screening Committee policies.* http://www.library.nhs.uk/screening/ Accessed 06/22/06.

Nye, C., & Brice, A. (2005). Combined vitamin B6–magnesium treatment in autism spectrum disorder. *Cochrane Database of Systematic Reviews, Issue 4.* Art. No.: CD003497. DOI: 10.1002/14651858.CD003497.pub2.

O'Toole, B. I. (2000). Screening for low prevalence disorders. *Australian and New Zealand Journal of Psychiatry, 34,* Supplement S39–S46.

Robins, D. L., Fein, D., Barton, M. L., & Green, J. A. (2001). The modified checklist for autism in toddlers: An initial study investigating the early detection of autism and pervasive developmental disorders. *Journal of Autism and Developmental Disorders, 31,* 131–144.

Sand, N., Silverstein, M., Glascoe, F. P., Gupta, V. B., Tonniges, T. P., & O'Connor, K. G. (2005). Pediatricians' reported practices regarding developmental screening: Do guidelines work? Do they help? *Pediatrics, 116,* 174–179.

Scott, F. J., Baron-Cohen, S., Bolton, P., & Brayne, C. (2002). The CAST. (Childhood Asperger Syndrome Test): Preliminary development of a UK screen for mainstream primary-school-age children. *Autism, 6,* 9–31.

Sinha, Y., Silove, N., Wheeler, D., & Williams, K. (2004). Auditory integration training and other sound therapies for autism spectrum disorders. *Cochrane Database of Systematic Reviews 2004, Issue 1.* Art. No.: CD003681. DOI: 10.1002/14651858.CD003681.pub2.

Skuse, D. H., Mandy, W. P., & Scourfield, J. (2005). Measuring autistic traits: Heritability, reliability and validity of the Social and Communication Disorders Checklist. *British Journal of Psychiatry, 187,* 568–572.

Stone, W. L., Coonrod, E. E., & Ousley, O. Y. (2000). Brief report: Screening tool for autism in two-year-olds (STAT): Development and preliminary data. *Journal of Autism and Developmental Disorders, 30,* 607–612.

Stone, W. L., Coonrod, E. E., Turner, L. M., & Pozdol, S. L. (2004). Psychometric properties of the STAT for early autism screening. *Journal of Autism and Developmental Disorders, 34,* 691–701.

Szatmari, P., Archer, L., Fisman, S., & Streiner, D. L. (1994). Parent and teacher agreement in the assessment of pervasive developmental disorders. *Journal of Autism and Developmental Disorders, 24,* 703–717.

Verhulst, F. C., & Van der Ende, J. (1991). Four-year follow-up of teacher-reported problem behaviours. *Psychological Medicine, 21,* 965–977.

Volkmar, F., Klin, A., & Cohen, D. (1997). Diagnosis and classification of autism and related conditions: Consensus and issues. In D. J. Cohen & F. R. Volkmar (Eds.), *Handbook of autism and pervasive developmental disorders* (2nd ed., pp. 5–40). New York: John Wiley and Sons, Inc.

von Knorring, A., & Hagglof, B. (1993). Autism in Northern Sweden. A population based follow-up study: Psychopathology. *European Child and Adolescent Psychiatry, 2,* 91–97.

Webb, E. V., Lobo, S., Hervas, A., Scourfield, J., & Fraser, W. I. (1997). The changing prevalence of autistic disorder in a Welsh health district. *Developmental Medicine and Child Neurology, 39,* 150–152.

Williams, J., Allison, C., Scott, F., Stott, C., Bolton, P., Baron-Cohen, S., et al. (2006). The Childhood Asperger Syndrome Test (CAST): Test–retest reliability. *Autism, 10,* 415–427.

Williams, J., & Brayne, C. (2006). Screening for autism spectrum disorders: What is the evidence? *Autism, 10,* 11–35.

Williams, J., Scott, F., Stott, C., Allison, C., Bolton, P., Baron-Cohen, S., et al. (2005). The CAST. (Childhood Asperger Syndrome Test): Test accuracy. *Autism, 9,* 45–68.

Williams, J. G. (2003). *Screening for autism spectrum disorders.* PhD thesis: University of Cambridge.

Williams, J. G., Higgins, J. P., & Brayne, C. E. (2006). Systematic review of prevalence studies of autism spectrum disorders. *Archives of Disease in Childhood, 91,* 8–15.

Williams, K. W., Wray, J. J., & Wheeler, D. M. (2005). Intravenous secretin for autism spectrum disorder. *Cochrane Database of Systematic Reviews, Issue 3.* Art. No.: CD003495. DOI: 10.1002/14651858.CD003495.pub2.

Wing, L., & Potter, D. (2002). The epidemiology of autistic spectrum disorders: Is the prevalence rising? *Mental Retardation and Developmental Disabilities Research Review, 8,* 151–161.

Wong, V., Hui, L. H., Lee, W. C., Leung, L. S., Ho, P. K., Lau, W. L., et al. (2004). A modified screening tool for autism (Checklist for Autism in Toddlers [CHAT-23]) for Chinese children. *Pediatrics, 114,* e166–e176.

World Health Organization (1993). *The ICD-10 classification of mental and behavioural disorders: Diagnostic criteria for research.* Geneva: World Health Organization.

11

The Prosody–Language Relationship in Children With High-Functioning Autism

Joanne McCann, Sue Peppé, Fiona Gibbon, Anne O'Hare, and Marion Rutherford

Introduction

Kanner included unusual prosody as part of his original description of autism in 1943: many of the children spoke in a monotonous, abrupt, or singsong way, or with a voice "peculiarly unmodulated, somewhat hoarse" (p. 241). A simple definition of prosody is that it refers to the manner in which things are said, not the content of what is said. The manner is conveyed by a number of different factors: variations in the relative pitch and duration of syllables, loudness of voice, pauses, intonation, speech rate, stress, and speech rhythm. Disordered expressive prosody is widely reported to occur in the speech of people with autism (e.g., Baltaxe, 1984; Fine, Bartolucci, Ginsberg, & Szatmari, 1991; Shriberg et al., 2001) but very little empirical or clinical research has been conducted on this aspect of autism. A recent review (McCann & Peppé, 2003) found only 16 studies between 1980 and 2002 on the topic. Of these, only two considered receptive prosodic disorder, which may not only account, at least in part, for expressive disorder, but also be related to the language disorders so frequently seen in autism. This chapter provides an overview of prosodic skills in autism and how these may link with language development more broadly. It then goes on to describe our recent research, which aimed to develop methods of prosodic assessment and provide finer-grained information on the links with aspects of language development. Two case studies are included to further illustrate this relationship.

Background

Language in autism

Impairment in language skills is one of the diagnostic features of autism (ICD-10, World Health Organization, 1993; DSM-IV, American Psychiatric Association, 2000) but there is a considerable range of impairment. While in low-functioning autism there can be a complete absence, at least of expressive language, high-functioning autism can present intact phonological, grammatical, and semantic systems, frequently with fluent speech and large vocabularies. Lord and Paul (1997) identify some 20 common communication/language problems found in autism, but one key area of difficulty is the metaphorical and social use of language. For example, words are used with their literal meaning: "on the wall" might be interpreted as on top of the wall rather than hanging on it, and pronouns fail to change reference according to the speaker (e.g., children with autism often refer to themselves as "you"). Echolalia occurs frequently; for example, answering a question can sometimes take the form of echoing the question, together with its intonation. In conversation such use of language can be disconcerting and require some adjustment by an unfamiliar listener, thus resulting in social difficulties. As language develops in children with autism, skills such as pronoun reversal, question construction, and requests for clarification are usually mastered, but with delay.

Kjelgaard and Tager-Flusberg (2001) investigated the communication ability of school-aged children with autism using standardized language measures similar to those used in our research described below, and concluded that the language impairment in children with autism is very variable (but that articulation skills are spared). For some children, expressive skills were in advance of receptive skills, but the majority of children had equal receptive and expressive skills. They draw various parallels with the speech and language profiles of children with specific language impairment (SLI), suggesting genetic links between the two conditions. An earlier study by Tager-Flusberg (1981) suggested that children with autism had more severe comprehension and pragmatic deficits than children with SLI, and in particular that semantics was more impaired than grammar in the children with autism.

In broad agreement with Kjelgaard and Tager-Flusberg (2001), Rapin and Dunn (2003) note that children with autism have types of language disorder similar to those seen in children with SLI: the most frequently occurring profile of language impairment in both groups of children was a mixed receptive/expressive disorder with impairments in both syntax (with similar patterns of grammatical errors) and phonology. In their cohort of preschool children with autism, however, comprehension appeared to be universally impaired, whereas in many of the children with language disorders there were expressive language impairments but intact comprehension. Bishop (2003) discusses the complexity of the differences of language impairment in SLI and autism and suggests that they derive from etiological continuities between SLI and autism.

Tager-Flusberg and Joseph (2003) and Happé (1995) note that the severity of autism is linked to disproportionate language impairment, and the former study demonstrated that children with high non-verbal ability and low verbal ability were more impaired on social interaction (and thus more severely autistic) than those with good verbal ability and poor non-verbal skills. In addition, a longitudinal study by Astington and Jenkins (1999) showed strong correlation in young typically developing children between language development and theory of mind (ToM) skills. These are the skills required to postulate mental states in others and to understand that these differ from one's own, and they have been proposed to account for some of the behavioral characteristics of autism (for an overview see, e.g., Baron-Cohen, Tager-Flusberg, & Cohen, 2000).

Prosody in autism

Research in this area has been sparse, as noted above, and somewhat conflicting (see McCann & Peppé, 2003). Like Kanner (1943), other authors have noted that expressive prosody can be atypical in autism, but the terms used are vague and unquantifiable e.g., "wooden," "singsong," and "bizarre" (Baltaxe & Simmons, 1985; Fay & Schuler, 1980). The terms can also be apparently contradictory, e.g., "monotonous" as well as "exaggerated" (Baron-Cohen & Staunton, 1994), suggesting a wide variability in the kinds of atypical expressive prosody found in autism. More concretely, some early studies of both children and adults found that prosodic stress was often wrongly placed (Baltaxe 1984; Baltaxe & Simmons, 1985; Fine, Bartolucci, Ginsberg, & Szatmari, 1991) with a tendency to occur early in utterances (Baltaxe & Guthrie, 1987). The use of stress is, however, only one aspect of prosody; a few studies (e.g., Baltaxe & Simmons, 1985; Fosnot & Jun, 1999) also examined intonation, which is important for distinguishing types of utterances (such as questions/statements) and speakers' feelings, but did not produce conclusive results. In recent years there have been more large-scale studies and a more comprehensive approach to prosody. Shriberg et al. (2001) examined stretches of continuous speech in young adults with high-functioning autism and Asperger syndrome, and judged them to have inappropriate or dysfluent phrasing as well as disordered placement of stress (i.e., prominence, as in "failing to emphasise a contrastive word in an utterance"). In a later study by the same team (Paul, Shriberg, et al., 2005) stress and resonance (hypernasality) were shown to correlate with communication and socialization ratings, albeit weakly. Paul, Augustyn, Klin, and Volkmar (2005) examined receptive

skills as well as expressive skills, again in young adults, in several aspects of prosody: stress, the intonation that distinguished utterance types (such as statements
versus questions), and phrasing (verbal punctuation). These prosodic phenomena
are used both for grammatical distinctions and for affective/pragmatic purposes.
However, although this study supported previous findings suggesting that receptive
and expressive stress, and both grammatical and pragmatic aspects of stress, are particular areas of difficulty, significant differences between the people with autism and
the unimpaired controls were not found in relation to intonation or phrasing. Both
these recent studies included people with Asperger syndrome (AS) as well as those
with high-functioning autism (HFA), and it is possible that the broad diagnosis and
older age range may account for the ceiling effects and findings of few significant
group differences in Paul et al.'s study. The use of prosody as verbal punctuation (important for knowing, for example, whether a speaker has finished a turn) was also
examined by Paul, Augustyn, et al. (2005) but no significant difference was found.

Prosody and language

For some time now, receptive prosody has been thought to have primary importance in language acquisition. In a theory known as the "prosodic bootstrapping
hypothesis" (Morgan & Demuth, 1996) it is thought that infants need to be sensitive to prosodic differences to be able to segment the continuous speech-stream
that is their first experience of language. Various studies (e.g., Jusczyk, Cutler, &
Redanz, 1993; Jusczyk et al., 1992) have demonstrated an association between a
lack of sensitivity to prosody in infants and disorders of developmental language.
Chiat (2001) argues convincingly for the importance of infants' sensitivity to the
frequency of co-occurrence of prosodic patterns, syllables, and segments in speech
input, and consequent recognition of word units and subsequent lexical and syn-
tactic development. Siegal and Peterson (2006) review much of the research in this
area and view auditory processing as a "key gatekeeper" (p. 378) for later development of both language and ToM skills. As receptive prosody skills in children
who have acquired verbal skills have been studied only recently, however, it is not
known whether this relationship persists or what its nature is in later development.

A Study of Prosody and Language in Children With Autism

In order to address some of the problems of previous studies of prosodic skills
in autism, we conducted a large study of prosody and language skills in children

with HFA. We will describe this research and further illustrate the relationship between prosody and language using two case studies. This study aimed to determine the nature and relationship of expressive and receptive language in school-aged children with HFA and to determine how aspects of prosody relate to these abilities.

Participants

The present study focused on a large, tightly defined diagnostic group and a closely matched control group, in order to avoid issues such as heterogeneity, which made findings in some earlier prosody studies difficult to interpret.

The experimental group consisted of 31 children with autism, conforming to a narrow diagnosis of high-functioning autism (HFA): i.e., children with normal non-verbal cognitive ability and receptive language age-equivalent >4 years but with a history of preschool language delay. The sample, therefore, did not include children with a diagnosis of Asperger syndrome, where preschool language delay is not apparent. The children were also younger than those in previous studies, which we hoped would allow us to extend earlier findings. The children were in the age range 6–13 years (mean age 9.75 years, 25 boys and 6 girls). The children's verbal mental age, assessed with the British Picture Vocabulary Scale (BPVS-II: Dunn, Dunn, Whetton, & Burley, 1997), ranged from 4.3 to 11.7 years (mean 6.9 years). All of the children had undergone multidisciplinary assessment of their communication disorder and a consultant pediatrician had diagnosed the children during their preschool years as having autism, with normal cognitive ability and early delay in speech/language development. The diagnostic criteria included those described by Gillberg and Coleman (2000), ICD-10 (World Health Organization, 1993), and a range of other autism assessment tools: the Childhood Autism Rating Scale (Schopler, Reichler, & Renner, 1988), Gilliam Autism Rating Scale (Gilliam, 1995), and Autism Diagnostic Observation Schedule (Lord et al., 2000).

The prosody assessment used in the study, Profiling Elements of Prosodic Systems in Children (PEPS-C: Peppé & McCann, 2003), is not standardized, so a control group of 72 typically developing children matched to the children with HFA on verbal mental age, sex, and socio-economic status were recruited. These children were aged 4–11 years (mean age 6.75 years) with verbal mental ages between 4 and 12 years (mean 7.5 years). This group comprised 54 boys and 18 girls.

Language, speech, and non-verbal assessments

The children with autism completed a battery of standardized speech, language, and non-verbal assessments, a subset of which are reported here. Standardized language assessments have been shown by Condouris, Meyer, and Tager-Flusberg (2003) to be a good indication of the ability of children with autism. This may seem surprising given the social and behavioral difficulties of children with autism, but Condouris et al. demonstrated that in their sample of 44 children with autism (ages 4 to 14 years) standardized language measures correlated with analyses of spontaneous speech, showing relationships with lexical-semantic measures and grammatical measures. This enables us to be confident that the standardized measures used in the present study give a good indication of the actual level of functioning in the children with autism.

Receptive language was measured using the BPVS-II and the Test for Reception of Grammar (TROG: Bishop, 1989). Expressive language was measured using the three expressive sub-tests of the Clinical Evaluation of Language Fundamentals-3UK (CELF-3UK, Semel, Wiig, & Secord, 2000). To confirm the children's normal non-verbal ability, the Raven's Progressive Matrices were used (RM: Raven, Court, & Raven, 1986).

Prosody assessment

Until now there has been no easy way to assess prosody. Prosody operates in conjunction with core linguistic skills such as lexis, syntax, and phonology, and it has been difficult to isolate. Moreover, it is difficult to design prosodic minimal pairs (pairs of words/phrases which can be distinguished entirely by prosody), which can be presented in simple concrete terms that a child can understand. The PEPS-C tasks (see Appendix) were designed on lines similar to those used in the study by Paul, Augustyn, et al. (2005); i.e., multiple-item tasks with binary option responses, assessing a range of prosodic functions, but have been designed with school-aged children in mind. It consists of twelve prosodic sub-tests plus a vocabulary check test and follows a psycholinguistic framework, incorporating receptive and expressive tasks which are further divided into form (bottom-up processing where no meaning is involved) and function (top-down processing involving meaning). The test assesses the ability to understand and express prosody as used in four communicative functions in which prosody has a crucial role (Roach, 2000): Turn-end, Affect, Chunking, and Contrastive Stress. "Turn-end" denotes the way speakers end a conversational turn, indicating by their intonation what sort of response they expect.

"Affect" refers to the attitudinal or emotional inflections conveyed by non-linguistic aspects of speech. "Chunking" is the oral equivalent of punctuation, indicating how speech is delimited into meaningful units. "Contrastive Stress" encompasses the notion of emphasis on important parts of utterances, i.e., the use of stress for con-trastive purposes; the studies referred to above examined this as well as other uses of stress. A detailed description of the PEPS-C tasks can be found in the Appendix.

A new computerized version of PEPS-C was used here (Peppé & McCann, 2003); the computerized version of the test has the advantage of making the audi-tory stimuli easy to administer, and responses are recorded directly onto computer. Additionally, there is evidence to suggest that some individuals with autism may favor a computerized environment (see, e.g., Golan & Baron-Cohen, Chapter 12). Most children, with or without autism, are able to complete the PEPS-C assess-ment in 50 minutes and enjoy using the computer. The stimuli were recorded in a Scottish-English accent, likely to be familiar to all the children.

As all of the items in the reception tasks are binary choice, a pass criterion was set at 75% (i.e., 12 out of 16 items), below which the element of chance in the scores would be considerable. All expression tasks require the tester to rate responses as either right (1 point), wrong (zero), or ambiguous (zero). The pass criterion here was again set at 75%, because quite often children with autism, particularly at younger ages, will produce all test items with the same prosodic form, resulting in 50% cor-rect because each expressive function task has two prosodic function targets. For example, in the Turn-end Expression task it was common for young children to produce all the items with prosody suggesting that all the items were statements. As half the stimuli were statements and half were questions, this resulted in a score of 50% correct, but clearly a child who performs in such a way has not yet acquired the prosodic skills required to complete this task. Expressive tasks were scored by a second judge, blind to diagnosis, whose ratings were compared with those of the tester using Cronbach's alpha: the mean intraclass correlation coefficient was .82 ($p<.001$), minimum .78 (Chunking Task), maximum .98 (Short-Item Imitation).

Results: Language profiles of children with HFA

Although there was heterogeneity among the HFA group, all of the children except one had a score outwith the normal range on one or more of the language measures (BPVS-II, TROG, and CELF-3UK). Table 11.1 shows the group results for all measures. For each standardized measure we calculated the percentage of children performing within normal limits (standard score 85 or more), with mild impairment (scores between 70 and 84), and with more significant impairment (scores of 69 or less). Paired t-tests were used to determine which aspects of language were most impaired.

Table 11.1 Group results

Measure	Children with HFA					TD children	
	BPVS-II	TROG	CELF[a]	RM[b]	PEPS-C%	BPVS-II	PEPS-C%
Mean (SD)	81.4	79.6	69.8	96.4	64.6	107.5	75.0
	(16.2)	(17.9)	(8.5)	(15.9)	(11.0)	(9.3)	(9.5)
% within normal limits SS<85[c]	48	39	10	84.5		100	
% mild impairment 70<SS<84	26	32	26	12.5		0	
% moderate to severe impairment SS<69	26	29	58	0		0	

[a] N = 29

[b] N = 30

[c] SS = standard score

Note: Numbers are in standard scores unless otherwise stated.

In the HFA group the BPVS-II scores and TROG scores were not significantly different, showing that receptive vocabulary and grammar skills were equivalent. In contrast, performance on the CELF-3UK was significantly lower than on both the BPVS-II and TROG ($p<.001$ in both cases), suggesting that in general, expressive language is more severely impaired than receptive language. For some children this was a dramatic discrepancy of two standard deviations, or in one case three standard deviations.

This is contrary to Kjelgaard and Tager-Flusberg's (2001) finding that children with autism show either the opposite pattern, or equal expressive and receptive skills. However, their study included children with a wider diagnosis of autism, and it may be that an expressive deficit is a particular characteristic of children with high-functioning autism; that is, children with intellectual disabilities may have additional language comprehension difficulties that result in similar expressive/receptive abilities. Indeed, Kjelgaard and Tager-Flusberg found a significant relationship between IQ and language ability, suggesting that children with additional intellectual disabilities do indeed have additional language difficulties. Alternatively, the discrepancy in findings may relate to the fact that in the present

Table 11.2 Prosody results

	Children with HFA (N = 31)a	TD children (N = 72)b
PEPS-C task	mean % scores (SD)	mean % scores (SD)
Turn-end Reception	65.9 (21.4)	64.8 (18.1)
Turn-end Expression	68.1 (21.8)	74.2 (18.1)
Affect Reception	71.2 (21.6)	84.5 (11.4) **
Affect Expression	63.3 (26.3)	79.4 (19.2) **
Chunking Reception	67.5 (15.7)	69.0 (15.6)
Chunking Expression	66.5 (26.4)	71.2 (11.8)
Contrastive Stress Reception	59.6 (19.0)	65.9 (19.1)
Contrastive Stress Expression	61.6 (26.4)	84.0 (15.0) **
Short-Item Discrimination	68.8 (22.0)	80.1 (17.4) *
Short-Item Imitation	64.7 (20.6)	79.9 (18.0) **
Long-Item Discrimination	63.5 (23.1)	79.0 (13.3) **
Long-Item Imitation	65.7 (22.0)	85.4 (11.4) **

[a] HFA: N = 29 for Contrastive Stress Expression

[b] TD: N = 71 for Contrastive Stress Reception and Contrastive Stress Expression

** statistically significantly higher than the group with autism at $p<.0038$ to take account of Bonferroni adjustment; * = $p<.01$

study we chose not to use the receptive sub-tests of the CELF-3UK, instead choosing the TROG, which tests only understanding of grammar, whereas the type of receptive language skills involved in the CELF-3UK may be more difficult for children with autism. For example, in addition to the "sentence structure" sub-test, which is similar to the TROG, the CELF-3UK assesses "concepts and directions," a task which places heavy demands on auditory memory, and "word classes/semantic relationships" which taps into semantics, a known area of difficulty for children with autism. However, the children in Kjelgaard and Tager-Flusberg's study actually found the sentence structure task the most difficult of the receptive sub-tests, thus refuting such an interpretation of the results. It therefore seems likely that the difference is due to difference in the participants.

The results of the language assessments do, however, partially support Kjelgaard and Tager-Flusberg's (2001) suggestion that the language impairment in autism is similar to that in SLI. For example, children with SLI show better vocabulary than grammar skills. Although this was not demonstrated by our HFA group's performance in the BPVS-II and TROG (statistically not different, although there was a trend), performance in the CELF-3UK (production of grammatically correct utterances) demonstrated that this was a greater area of difficulty for these children. Moreover, like children with SLI, language skills were independent of non-verbal cognitive skills.

Results: Prosody

The performance of children with HFA was significantly lower than that of language matched peers ($p<.001$, for mean overall PEPS-C raw score). At sub-test level, Affect Reception, Affect Expression, Contrastive Stress Expression, Short-Item Imitation, Long-Item Discrimination, and Long-Item Imitation scores were all significantly lower (see Table 11.2).

As PEPS-C is not standardized, it was not possible to determine if there was a more significant deficit in prosody than in the standardized language assessments. However, because the groups were matched on the BPVS-II and the HFA group scored lower than the TD group on the PEPS-C, prosodic ability overall does appear to be more impaired than receptive vocabulary. This suggests that children with HFA have a specific difficulty with some aspects of prosody, which is more severe than their deficit in receptive vocabulary. The majority (74%) of the HFA group scored below the pass criterion of 75%, again suggesting a significant difficulty with prosody. However, these results must be interpreted with caution, as almost half the younger children in the TD group also scored below this level (of children aged <7 years, 47.7% scored below 75%). Most of the children in the HFA group showed a significant deficit in prosody, and all of them had difficulty with at least one of the PEPS-C sub-tests. Had the experimental groups been matched on chronological age, rather than receptive vocabulary, the difficulty with prosody would have been much more pronounced.

Comparing language and prosody

In order to explore the relationship between language measures and aspects of prosody in the HFA group, a series of correlations were conducted. This revealed that total prosody scores correlated highly ($p<.01$) with receptive vocabulary (BPVS-II), receptive grammar (TROG), expressive language (CELF-3UK) but not with chronological age or non-verbal mental age (Raven's matrices). The PEPS-C composite receptive scores correlated with all language measures, and also with chronological age and non-verbal mental age. In contrast, the PEPS-C composite expressive score correlated only with the TROG and the CELF-3UK.

The PEPS-C function tasks, which assess the ability to understand and use prosody meaningfully, correlated with all of the language measures, whereas the imitation form tasks, that assess the ability to produce prosody without reference to meaning, did not correlate with any of the measures. This latter finding suggests that the ability to imitate prosodic forms is unrelated to language skills or chronological age. However, the discrimination form tasks did correlate with the BPVS-II and with chronological age. This might relate to increased attention and auditory memory in older children, making it easier for them to meet the demands of these particular tasks.

Prosodic Impairment With and Without Language Impairment

Since prosody correlates strongly with language, it is tempting to conclude that prosodic impairment is simply a manifestation of the severe language impairment that many children with autism have. Why this may or may not be the case is explored with two case studies of children with high-functioning autism. Fiona has a language impairment, typical of children with autism, whereas Ian has age-appropriate language skills. Both of the children took part in the project described above investigating prosody and language skills in children with HFA.

Fiona

Fiona was aged 10.58 years when she took part in the project. She attends a language unit attached to a mainstream school for children with autism spectrum disorders. Fiona has normal non-verbal ability for her age, but her language is severely impaired: she scored more than two standard deviations below the mean for all the language measures.

Fiona presented with disordered prosody, in that her speech sounded unusual. Her scores in the PEPS-C sub-tests were all below the "pass-mark" of 75% (12 out of 16) suggesting that she has not mastered any of the prosody functions or forms assessed in PEPS-C. By comparing Fiona's performance with a group of typically developing children with a similar verbal mental age, we can see a probable asso-

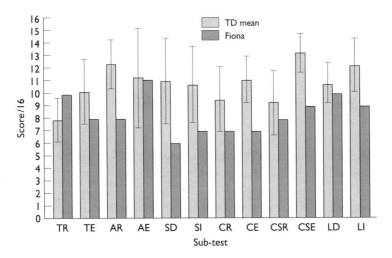

Figure 11.1 Prosody results for Fiona and TD controls

Note. TR = Turn-end Reception, TE = Turn-end Expression, AR = Affect Reception, AE = Affect Expression, SD = Short-Item Discrimination, SI = Short-Item Imitation, CR = Chunking Reception, CE = Chunking Expression, CSR = Contrastive Stress Reception, CSE = Contrastive Stress Expression, LD = Long-Item Discrimination, LI = Long-Item Imitation.

Error bars show +/– 1 SD from TD mean.

ciation between language impairment and prosodic impairment. Fiona's score on the BPVS-II translates to an age equivalent of 5.83 years, so her performance on the PEPS-C was compared with a control group of 18 typically developing children with a mean BPVS-II age equivalent of 5.89 years (SD = 0.84). Figure 11.1 shows a comparison between Fiona's scores on the PEPS-C and the scores of the control group.

Fiona scored more than one standard deviation below the typical children on three sub-tests and more than two standard deviations below the typical children on a further three sub-tests. This marks a very significant deficit in Fiona's prosodic ability, which is not wholly accounted for by her receptive language impairment (since she has a BPVS-II score similar to that of the control group). In contrast, Fiona actually scored more than one standard deviation above the typical children in the Turn-end Reception task, but both Fiona and the typically developing children failed to meet competence (a score over 12 or 75%, see above) in this sub-test, which appears to tap into a skill which develops relatively late in typically developing children.

If Fiona's performance had been compared to that of a chronological age-matched group, then the deficit in her prosodic skills would be even more pronounced.

However, it is clear that Fiona has the disadvantage of both a language and a prosodic impairment and that impaired prosody may therefore be associated to some extent with impaired language. If we look at the results of the group study above, we can see that Fiona's results are quite typical of children with high-functioning autism.

Ian

Ian was aged 13.5 years when he took part in the project. He attends a special school for children with autism spectrum disorders. Ian has normal non-verbal ability for his age, and his language is within normal limits: he scored within the normal range for all the assessments with the exception of the BPVS-II, where he scored slightly above the normal range (standard score of 117), suggesting a relative strength in receptive vocabulary. Since Ian has normal language ability, his prosodic performance was compared with that of children of a similar chronological age. The typically developing children had BPVS-II scores within the normal range, so these were slightly lower than Ian's BPVS-II score. Figure 11.2 shows a comparison of his scores on the PEPS-C and those of a group of 9 children of a similar age.

Ian did not present with perceptually disordered expressive prosody; i.e., he sounded much like his peers; but he scored more than one standard deviation below them on three sub-tests and more than two standard deviations below them on a further four sub-tests. This marks a very significant deficit in his prosodic ability, which is not in line with his language ability. He also scored below the "pass-mark" of 75% (12 out of 16) in four of the PEPS-C sub-tests (all expressive ones), while the control group achieved the pass criterion in all of the PEPS-C sub-tests, suggesting that prosody is usually well developed by age 13 years. Ian achieved scores at or near ceiling in some of the prosody tasks, however, suggesting an uneven profile of prosodic development.

The cases where Ian performed differently in parallel expressive and receptive tasks are perhaps the most interesting: for example, he scored 14/16 (an adult-like score) on understanding of affect, but had great difficulty expressing affect. This suggests that although Ian can understand the way other people use prosody to express emotions, he cannot reliably do so himself. Although Ian's BPVS score was above his expressive language score, this does not wholly account for a discrepancy in receptive and expressive prosody skills. Ian did not show a discrepancy between receptive and expressive grammatical skills (as measured by TROG and CELF-3UK). Moreover, the expressive prosodic skills tested are usually acquired at a much lower language level than Ian's (e.g., Affect Expression is usually mastered before the age of 6 years). A similar dissociation occurred on the Contrastive

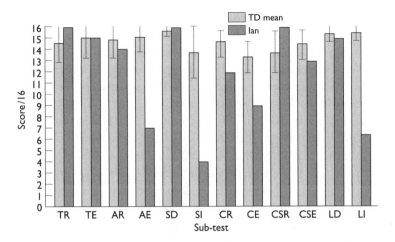

Figure 11.2 Prosody results for Ian and TD controls.

Note. TR = Turn-end Reception, TE = Turn-end Expression, AR = Affect Reception, AE = Affect Expression, SD = Short-Item Discrimination, SI = Short-Item Imitation, CR = Chunking Reception, CE = Chunking Expression, CSR = Contrastive Stress Reception, CSE = Contrastive Stress Expression, LD = Long-Item Discrimination, LI = Long-Item Imitation.

Error bars show +/– 1 SD from TD mean.

Stress tasks: Ian outperformed his peers in perceiving contrastive stress (a skill that appears to be acquired late in typically developing children), but his score was relatively low (although above the competence level) on the parallel expressive task, which requires no metaprosodic skill and is one where typically developing children aged 5 years frequently score at ceiling.

Although these two children demonstrate the wide variability in the HFA group, and Ian's profile is very different from Fiona's, it is interesting that they both show weaknesses in the areas where the majority of the HFA group had difficulty: i.e., in the expression of Affect and Contrastive Stress and in Imitation tasks.

Implications for communication, socialization, and therapy: Fiona and Ian

Disordered expressive prosody (unusual-sounding speech) may make it difficult for speakers to integrate with their peers. In the case of Fiona this is indeed likely, compounding the problems of socialization that are a defining feature of autism.

On the other hand, Ian had perceptually normal prosody but a covert difficulty with tasks in which messages were differentiated by prosody alone, as required by an assessment such as PEPS-C. That is, although his prosody sounded normal in conversational speech, he was not able to make use of prosody to express some of the functions when specifically asked to do so. This would make it difficult for Ian to use prosody for clarification in conversation.

One of Fiona's main areas of difficulty was using and understanding affective prosody, and she may therefore be unable to judge another person's feelings from intonation alone. This has implications for understanding emotions, beliefs, and intentions generally, perhaps suggesting that this PEPS-C sub-test involves aspects of theory of mind (ToM), known to be disordered in people with autism (see Golan & Baron-Cohen, Chapter 12).

The clinical management implications of prosodic deficits in children with autism have not been well explored. Clinicians (speech and language therapists) have felt under-equipped to assess and treat prosody. Although not yet standardized, the prosody assessment described above is one way that clinicians can gain some information about a child's prosody to determine if children like Ian have covert prosodic difficulties, or if, as in Fiona's case, unusual expressive prosody extends to receptive prosodic problems. There exist, however, few therapy approaches for treating prosodic disorders in autism. One approach to treating receptive affective prosody in adults is described by Golan and Baron-Cohen (Chapter 12), and it is possible that this could be extended to other types of prosody.

Although prosodic therapy approaches are scarce, clinicians can provide carers with advice to ensure that a child with autism is not disadvantaged by a receptive prosodic impairment by advising that speakers do not rely on prosody to get their message across. Similarly, if a child has difficulty using prosody functionally, then listeners should take care not to rely on the child's prosody skills: for example, if a child has difficulty using affective prosody, then the listener cannot rely on prosody to interpret a child's attitude but must ask explicitly what or how the child is feeling.

Integration Section: Understanding the Prosody–Language Relationship in the Context of Autism Research

It is notable that in this volume there are few chapters that deal with impaired communication skills in autism, although this constitutes one of the three main diagnostic features of autism (Wing & Gould, 1979). It is also true that the study of prosody and language in autism has not been well explored in the context of cognitive theories, with most investigations of prosody in autism focusing on the behavioral aspects only. The limited work that has been carried out in this field nonetheless suggests that the integration of research on prosody, language, and cognition in autism may be beneficial in furthering understanding of autism and developing appropriate interventions.

Work by Rutherford, Baron-Cohen, and Wheelwright (2002), for example, suggests that the understanding of at least one aspect of prosody can be considered to be an advanced test of ToM. They investigated the ability of 19 adults with HFA or AS to judge the affective meaning of 40 phrases. Results showed that the HFA and AS group were impaired on this task compared with the performance of a large number of typical adults, and that the impairment did not correlate with verbal or performance IQs. The authors concluded that affective prosody can be viewed as a ToM skill.

The relationship between affective prosody and language skills more broadly remains unclear. Although language correlated closely with prosody in the large study of prosodic skills in children with autism described above, Ian's performance is a good illustration of how children with normal language skills can still have covert prosodic difficulties, suggesting the possibility of dissociation between prosody and language in at least some children with autism. Ian's difficulty expressing affect in the absence of a language impairment is particularly noticeable. While research by Rutherford, Baron-Cohen, and Wheelwright (2002) focuses on understanding of affect, Ian's difficulties highlight a need to investigate ToM and affect in both receptive and expressive modalities. Similarly, Golan and Baron-Cohen (Chapter 12) focus on remediating receptive prosodic difficulties without focusing on how this might impact on the ability of a person with autism to express affect through prosody.

The relationship between language impairment and ToM also remains unclear: it is generally accepted that ToM correlates highly with language skills (Astington & Jenkins, 1999), but Leslie and Frith (1988) demonstrated that deficits in ToM are associated with factors other than language impairments: in matching children with autism to children with SLI, they found that school-aged children with autism had severe difficulty with ToM tasks whereas the children with SLI performed at ceiling.

In addition to ToM, the theory of weak central coherence (WCC: see López, Chapter 6; Ropar, Mitchell, & Sheppard, Chapter 7) may have much to offer to the study of prosody in autism. The WCC theory proposes that people with autism have a bias toward local rather than global processing. This predicts that individuals with autism will have difficulty integrating information in a verbal context to resolve ambiguous messages. Prosody is nearly always one of several strands of communication making up an oral message, and it is therefore possible that it may be omitted from the integration process. The likelihood of this happening might be increased by the fact that prosody has a lack of transparency similar to non-literal reference, which is known to be problematic for people with autism. Whereas most studies of WCC focus on the visual rather than the auditory modality, it would be possible to explore WCC in the auditory domain using prosody. If children with autism are processing at a local rather than a global level, and if prosody were particularly vulnerable to being omitted from the integration process, then we would expect that they would not succumb to misleading prosody. For example, people without autism are usually more persuaded by prosody than content when they are at odds, for example in sarcasm; but if people with autism are unable to integrate prosody with other information because of a deficit in central coherence then this might explain why they find sarcasm so difficult to interpret. This would have implications for intervention, suggesting that people with autism need to improve their auditory central coherence in order to improve their understanding of prosody. Additionally, as Ropar, Mitchell, and Sheppard (Chapter 7) suggest, although children with autism tend not to rely on prior knowledge when categorizing stimuli, they can do so if prompted. This suggests that children with autism might also use taught knowledge about different types of prosody if prompted.

It is important to understand the relationships between prosody, language, and cognition within a developmental perspective. As discussed earlier in this chapter, receptive prosody is important from the first year of life, in order for infants to be able to meaningfully segment the stream of speech that they hear (Morgan & Demuth, 1996). This, together with Maestro and Muratori's findings of signs of autism in the first six months of life (Chapter 9), raises the concern that prosodic difficulties may also be present in autism at a very early stage, contributing to later language difficulties. This would of course be problematic to investigate, although preferential listening paradigms may be of use. Intervention for prosody difficulties should ideally be in place as early as possible, and prosody research at younger age ranges is therefore desirable.

Investigation of prosody at the neural level has also been under-researched to date, and again an integration of research in this area may be beneficial. Wicker (Chapter 2) looked at explicit and implicit perception and labeling of emotions, and suggested that the core autism deficits in emotional/social behavior relate to abnormal modulation of activity within a distributed network of cerebral structures. Wicker's work focused on visual aspects of emotion, but affect is usually expressed in several modalities. His work raises the possibility that there may also be atypical pathways of connectivity in relation to affective prosody, and perhaps other aspects of prosody. Ideally, more work is needed which utilizes fMRI and other scanning techniques to investigate prosody. Unfortunately, it is not always practical to use these techniques with children, and it can be difficult to conduct experiments which require participants to listen and respond verbally while they are in a scanner.

In terms of prosody intervention, it is of relevance that Golan and Baron-Cohen (Chapter 12) note that cognitive theories of autism are beginning to impact on clinical practice but that generalization of skills remains a major area for concern in people with autism. Therapy for prosodic disorders is particularly problematic, as prosody is expressed in countless different ways (e.g., various types of intonation can be used to express a question). It is probably not possible to teach people with autism every aspect of prosody and its many uses. Any rules taught about prosody will be suggestions and guidelines rather than absolutes, and this is obviously at odds with a systemizing (see Chapter 12) way of learning. However, one possible model of prosody intervention would be to include aspects of prosody in social skills groups such as those suggested by Dunlop, Knott, and MacKay (Chapter 13). In their social skills groups adolescents were taught to think about interaction, rather than simply instructed what to do. This kind of meta-approach would be useful for prosody: rather than giving children examples of different types of prosody, it might be useful to draw their attention to the communicative value of prosody and develop their metaprosodic skills so that they can think about how prosody might affect the meaning of an utterance. Moreover, prosody could help with intervention targeting turn-taking (usually a target in social skills groups) by emphasizing that there are prosodic cues at the end of a turn.

Conclusions

The widely reported unusual expressive prosody in people with autism spectrum disorders has been quantified by the findings of the above study and extended to show that children with autism also have difficulty understanding prosody. Furthermore, the results of the group study show that prosody relates closely to language skills, with receptive skills appearing to have the greatest relationship. The case studies illustrate that the relationship is not straightforward, with covert prosodic deficits still observable in children without language impairments. More research is therefore needed to clarify whether the prosodic impairments shown by children with HFA are directly associated with language impairments or are an autism-specific difficulty. Research has begun on understanding affective prosody in autism, with some work cutting across disciplines and approaches. However, other aspects of prosody such as pragmatic and linguistic prosody (such as that used in the Turn-end task above) have not yet been well explored across domains. There is much scope, therefore, for further research in this area.

Appendix

Profiling Elements of Prosodic Systems in Children (PEPS-C) (Peppé & McCann, 2003)

	Mode*	Task name	Description
FUNCTION	R	Turn-end Reception (TR)	Understanding questions and statements. Stimuli are single words with intonation suggesting items are being offered ("Carrots?") or read ("Carrots").
	E	Turn-end Expression (TE)	Producing single words with intonation suggesting either questioning or stating.
	R	Affect Reception (AR)	Comprehending liking or disliking as expressed by intonation on single words (food-items).
	E	Affect Expression (AE)	Producing affective intonation to suggest either liking or disliking on single words.
	R	Chunking Reception (CR)	Comprehending prosodic phrase boundaries. Items are syntactically ambiguous phrases, e.g., "chocolate-biscuits and jam" versus "chocolate, biscuits and jam."
	E	Chunking Expression (CE)	Producing prosodic phrase boundaries in phrases similar to those above, from picture stimuli.
	R	Contrastive Stress Reception (CSR)	Comprehension of contrastive stress: identifying the stressed color in, e.g., "blue and WHITE socks."
	E	Contrastive Stress Expression (CSE)	Production of contrastive stress: stressing the word to be corrected, e.g., (Stimulus) "The white cow has it" (Response) "No the BLACK cow."
FORM	R	Short-Item Discrimination (SD)	Auditory discrimination of prosodic forms without reference to meaning. Stimuli consist of laryngograph recordings (which sound like a hum) of items from the Affect and Turn-end Reception tasks (single words).
	E	Short-Item Imitation (SI)	Assesses whether an individual has the voice skills required to imitate various prosodic forms. Stimuli are similar to those in Affect and Turn-end function tasks.
	R	Long-Item Discrimination (LD)	Discrimination of long prosodic forms without reference to meaning. Stimuli consist of laryngograph recordings of the Chunking and Contrastive Stress Expression tasks (short phrases).
	E	Long-Item Imitation (LI)	Imitation of long prosodic forms. Stimuli are items similar to those in Chunking and Contrastive Stress Function tasks.

* R = Reception E = Expression

Note: Task names have been revised since first publication (Peppé & McCann, 2003). Names in parentheses refer to original name: Contrastive Stress (Focus); Short-Item (Intonation); Long-Item (Prosody); Reception (Input); Expression (Output).

References

American Psychiatric Association (2000). *Diagnostic and statistical manual of mental disorders, text revision DSM IV-TR*. (4th ed.). Washington, DC: APA.

Astington, J. W., & Jenkins, J. M. (1999). A longitudinal study of the relation between language and theory-of-mind development. *Developmental Psychology, 35*, 1311–1320.

Baltaxe, C. A. M. (1984). Use of contrastive stress in normal, aphasic, and autistic children. *Journal of Speech and Hearing Research, 27*, 97–105.

Baltaxe, C. A. M., & Guthrie, D. (1987). The use of primary sentence stress by normal, aphasic and autistic children. *Journal of Autism and Developmental Disorders, 17*, 255–271.

Baltaxe, C. A. M., & Simmons, J. Q. (1985). Prosodic development in normal and autistic children. In E. Schopler & G. B. Mesibov (Eds.), *Communication problems in autism* (pp. 95–125). New York: Plenum Press.

Baron-Cohen, S., & Staunton, R. (1994). Do children with autism acquire the phonology of their peers? An examination of group identification through the window of bilingualism. *First Language, 14*, 241–248.

Baron-Cohen, S., Tager-Flusberg, H., & Cohen, D. J. (Eds.) (2000). *Understanding other minds: Perspectives from developmental cognitive neuroscience* (2nd ed.). Oxford, UK: Oxford University Press.

Bishop, D. V. M. (1989). *Test for reception of grammar* (2nd ed.). Manchester, UK: University of Manchester, Author, Age and Cognitive Performance Research Centre.

Bishop, D. V. M. (2003). Autism and specific language impairment: Categorical distinction or continuum? In G. Bock & J. Goode (Eds.), *Autism: Neural bases and treatment possibilities*, Novartis Foundation Symposium 251 (pp. 213–234). Chichester, UK: Wiley.

Chiat, S. (2001). Mapping theories of developmental language impairment: Premises, predictions and evidence. *Language and Cognitive Processes, 16*, 113–142.

Condouris, K., Meyer, E., & Tager-Flusberg, H. (2003). The relationship between standardized measures of language and measures of spontaneous speech in children with autism. *American Journal of Speech-Language Pathology, 12*, 349–358.

Dunn, L., Dunn, L., Whetton, C., & Burley, J. (1997). *British Picture Vocabulary Scale* (2nd ed.). Windsor, UK: NFER-Nelson.

Fay, W., & Schuler, A. L. (1980). *Emerging language in autistic children*. London: Edward Arnold.

Fine, J., Bartolucci, G., Ginsberg, G., & Szatmari, P. (1991). The use of intonation to communicate in pervasive developmental disorders. *Journal of Child Psychology and Psychiatry, 32*, 771–782.

Fosnot, S. M., & Jun, S. (1999). Prosodic characteristics in children with stuttering or autism during reading and imitation. *Proceedings of the 14th International Congress of Phonetic Sciences*, 1925–1928.

Gillberg, C., & Coleman, M. (2000). *The biology of the autistic syndromes* (3rd ed.). London: MacKeith Press.

Gilliam, J. E. (1995). *Gilliam Autism Rating Scale (GARS)*. Austin, TX: PRO-ED.

Happé, F. (1995). The role of age and verbal ability in the theory of mind task performance of subjects with autism. *Child Development, 66,* 843–855.

Jusczyk, P. W., Cutler, A., & Redanz, N. J. (1993). Infants' preference for the predominant stress patterns of English words. *Child Development, 64,* 675–687.

Jusczyk, P. W., Hirsh-Pasek, K., Kelmer Nelson, D. G., Kennedy, L. J., Woodward, A., & Piwoz, J. (1992). Perception of acoustic correlates of major phrasal units by young infants. *Cognitive Psychology, 24,* 252–293.

Kanner, L. (1943). Autistic disturbances of affective contact. *Nervous Child, 2,* 217–250.

Kjelgaard, M., & Tager-Flusberg, H. (2001). An investigation of language impairment in autism: Implications for genetic subgroups. *Language and Cognitive Processes, 16,* 287–308.

Leslie, A., & Frith, U. (1988). Autistic children's understanding of seeing, knowing, and believing. *British Journal of Developmental Psychology, 6,* 315–324.

Lord, C., & Paul. R. (1997). Language and communication in autism. In D. J. Cohen & F. R. Volkmar (Eds.), *Handbook of autism and pervasive developmental disorders* (2nd ed., pp. 195–225). New York: Wiley.

Lord, C., Risi, S., Lambrecht, L., Cook, E. H., Leventhal, B. L., & DiLavore, P. C. (2000). The Autism Diagnostic Observation Schedule–Generic: A standard measure of social and communication deficits associated with the spectrum of autism. *Journal of Autism and Developmental Disorders, 30,* 205–223.

McCann, J., & Peppé, S. (2003). Prosody in autism spectrum disorders: A critical review. *International Journal of Language and Communication Disorders, 38,* 325–350.

Morgan, J., & Demuth, K. (1996). *Signal to syntax: Bootstrapping from speech to grammar in early acquisition.* Mahwah, NJ: Erlbaum.

Paul, R., Augustyn, A., Klin, A., & Volkmar, F. (2005). Perception and production of prosody by speakers with autistic spectrum disorders. *Journal of Autism and Developmental Disorders, 35,* 205–220.

Paul, R., Shriberg, L., McSweeny, J., Cicchetti, D., Klin, A., & Volkmar, F. (2005). Brief report: Relations between prosodic performance and communication and socialization ratings in high functioning speakers with autism spectrum disorders. *Journal of Autism and Developmental Disorders, 35,* 861–869.

Peppé, S., & McCann, J. (2003). Assessing intonation and prosody in children with atypical language development: The PEPS-C test and the revised version. *Clinical Linguistics and Phonetics, 17,* 345–354.

Rapin, I., & Dunn, M. (2003). Update on the language disorders of individuals on the autistic spectrum. *Brain and Development, 25,* 166–172.

Raven, J., Court, J., & Raven, J. (1986). *Raven's progressive matrices and Raven's coloured matrices.* London: H. K. Lewis.

Roach, P. (2000). *English phonetics and phonology.* Cambridge, UK: Cambridge University Press.

Rutherford, M. D., Baron-Cohen, S., & Wheelwright, S. (2002). Reading the mind in the voice: A study with normal adults and adults with Asperger syndrome and high functioning autism. *Journal of Autism and Developmental Disorders, 32,* 189–194.

Schopler, E. C., Reichler, R., & Renner, B. (1988). *The Childhood Autism Rating Scale (CARS)*. Los Angeles: Western Psychological Services.

Semel, E., Wiig, E. H., & Secord, W. (2000). *Clinical evaluation of language fundamentals* (3rd ed UK [CELF-3UK]). London: Psychological Corporation.

Shriberg, L. D., Paul, R., McSweeney, J. L., Klin, A., Cohen, D. J., & Volkmar, F. R. (2001). Speech and prosody characteristics of adolescents and adults with high-functioning autism and Asperger's syndrome. *Journal of Speech, Language, and Hearing Research, 44,* 1097–1115.

Siegal, M., & Peterson, C. (2006). Language and theory of mind in atypically developing children: Evidence from studies of deafness, blindness, and autism. In C. Sharp, P Fonagy, & I. Goodyer (Eds.), *Social cognition and developmental psychopathology.* New York: Oxford University Press.

Tager-Flusberg, H. (1981). On the nature of linguistic functioning in early infantile autism. *Journal of Autism and Developmental Disorders, 11,* 45–56.

Tager-Flusberg, H., & Joseph, R. M. (2003). Identifying neurocognitive phenotypes in autism. *Philosophical Transactions of the Royal Society London, Ser. B., 358,* 303–314.

Wing, L., & Gould, J. (1979). Severe impairments of social interaction and associated abnormalities. *Journal of Autism and Developmental Disorders, 9,* 11–29.

World Health Organization (1993). *The ICD-10 classification of mental and behavioural disorders: Clinical descriptions and diagnostic guidelines.* Geneva: World Health Organization.

12

Teaching Adults With Autism Spectrum Conditions to Recognize Emotions

Systematic Training for Empathizing Difficulties

Ofer Golan and Simon Baron-Cohen

The study of autism spectrum conditions (ASC) has seen a shift in focus from solely describing and explaining the deficits in autism to nowadays investigating strengths as well as difficulties (Baron-Cohen, 2000; Happé, 1999; Hill, Chapter 8; Jones & Klin, Chapter 4; López, Chapter 6). Awareness of the strengths that individuals with ASC possess could lead to novel interventions, harnessing strengths to compensate for difficulties. This chapter describes an attempt to use such compensatory principles, based on the Empathizing-Systemizing (E-S) model of ASC.

Empathizing Difficulties in ASC

Empathizing is defined as the ability to identify emotions and mental states in others and to respond to these with an appropriate emotion (Baron-Cohen, Wheelwright, Lawson, Griffin, & Hill, 2002). The centrality of an empathy deficit in autism spectrum conditions is well established (Gillberg, 1992; Hobson, 1993; Wing, 1981). The empathy deficit accounts for the social and communication difficulties, and for the limited imagination and pretence (due to difficulties in imagining others' minds) seen in ASC. The deficit is seen in both understanding of others' intentions, emotions, and beliefs, and the ability to produce an appropriate response (Baron-Cohen et al., 2002). Many studies confirm an empathizing deficit in ASC, finding reduced joint attention (Charman, 2003), difficulties in "theory of mind"

(Baron-Cohen, Leslie, & Frith, 1985; Baron-Cohen, Tager-Flusberg, & Cohen, 2000), difficulties in recognizing and understanding emotions and mental states in others, and altered brain activation in regions related to empathy, including in the "mirror neuron" system (e.g., Dapretto et al., 2006). Reduced levels of empathy are also found in adults with ASC on self-report questionnaires, such as the Empathy Quotient (Baron-Cohen & Wheelwright, 2004).

Systemizing Strengths in ASC

In contrast to these empathizing difficulties, the E-S model argues that individuals with ASC show good and sometimes even superior skills in "systemizing" (Baron-Cohen, 2003). Systemizing involves the understanding and the creation of rule-based, predictable systems. A systemizer seeks to analyze the system down to its lowest level of detail, in order to understand its underlying rules and regularities. Systems can be technical (e.g., the workings of a machine), natural (e.g., the process of coastal erosion), abstract (e.g., a mathematical model), taxonomic (e.g., criteria for arranging birds), and even social (e.g., the structure of a social class system).

Individuals with ASC are hyper-attentive to detail (López, Chapter 6) and prefer predictable, rule-based environments, features intrinsic to systemizing. When tested on different tasks tapping such skills, individuals with ASC perform as well as or better than controls from the general population. Individuals with ASC also perform better than controls on tasks that require an intuitive understanding of physics (Lawson, Baron-Cohen, & Wheelwright, 2004). Finally, on a self-report questionnaire, the Systemizing Quotient, which taps systemizing related interests and abilities (e.g., "I can easily visualize how the motorways in my region link up," or "When I read something, I always notice whether it is grammatically correct"), adults with ASC score higher than those in the general population (Baron-Cohen, Richler, Bisarya, Gurunathan, & Wheelwright, 2003). The strong drive to systemize may also underlie the circumscribed interests seen in children and adolescents with ASC, in topics (systems) such as trains, geography, electronics, etc. (Attwood, 2003; Baron-Cohen & Wheelwright, 1999). Later in life, high-functioning individuals with ASC (or their first-degree relatives, for genetic reasons) may use these good systemizing skills in professional fields such as mathematics, physics, engineering, and computers (Baron-Cohen, 2003; Baron-Cohen, Wheelwright, Stott, Bolton, & Goodyer, 1997).

From the perspective of intervention, the good systemizing skills that individuals with ASC possess may provide a route to compensate for the empathizing difficulties. However, these two domains are quite distinct: whereas systemizing is exact, rule-based, and predictable, people's actions are open "systems"—there is always some ambiguity, or factors we cannot control or predict. Empathizing can cope with such open systems because it is less precise and more flexible than systemizing. However, despite this caveat, if empathizing principles were presented and taught systematically, systemizing strengths could be harnessed more easily, to help individuals with ASC learn aspects of empathizing.

One aspect of empathizing is emotion recognition (ER). Emotions have been systematically analyzed through different models and taxonomies (e.g., Ortony, Clore, & Foss, 1987; Russell, 1980). Similarly, facial expressions have been analyzed and presented systematically in terms of facial muscle configuration both in psychological research (Ekman, Friesen, & Hager, 2002) and in computer science studies, attempting to decipher human expressions (el Kaliouby & Robinson, 2005). Therefore, we selected emotion recognition as the empathy component to be systematically presented to individuals with ASC.

Emotion Recognition in ASC

Emotion and mental state recognition are core difficulties for individuals with ASC (Baron-Cohen, 1995; Hobson, 1994). Such difficulties have been identified through cognitive, behavioral, and neuroimaging studies, and across different sensory modalities (Frith & Hill, 2004). Below we review findings of studies with adults and children with ASC, testing emotion recognition (ER) from faces, voices, context, and their integration.

Emotion recognition in faces

Most ER studies have focused on facial expressions and have tested recognition of the so-called basic emotions: happiness, sadness, fear, anger, surprise, and disgust, which are universally recognized (Ekman & Friesen, 1971). Some studies reveal ER deficits among children and adults with ASC, compared to typical or clinical control groups (e.g., Hobson, 1986a, 1986b). For example, Celani, Battacchi, and Arcidiacono (1999) found that participants with autism performed significantly worse than matched typically developing and Down's syndrome controls on matching of facial emotional expressions, but not on identity matching, suggesting that the face-processing difficulties in autism are specific to ER.

However, other studies have found no difference in the ability of children and adults with ASC to recognize basic emotions from pictures (Adolphs, 2001; Piggot et al., 2004) or films of facial expressions (Loveland et al., 1997). For example, Castelli (2005) found that children with autism were as able as controls to recognize the six basic emotions with different intensity levels, and that they made the same type of errors as controls. These inconclusive findings may be explained by developmental and methodological factors: Recognition of basic emotions is found in typical development by the age of 4–5 years (Herba & Phillips, 2004). Therefore, it is possible that individuals with ASC, despite their developmental delay, learn to recognize these basic emotions, or to compensate for their face-processing deficits using alternative strategies. Another possible explanation for these inconclusive findings relates to attentional factors, as shown in a recent study by Begeer, Rieffe, Terwogt, and Stockmann (2006): when asked to sort photos of emotional expressions, children with ASC performed worse than matched controls. However, when given instructions that called for socio-emotional processing (e.g., "Which of these faces is likely to give you a sweet?"), no group differences were found, suggesting that when given the appropriate context, basic ER of children with ASC may be intact. Wicker (Chapter 2) reports similar results, with supporting neuroimaging evidence, suggesting that explicit recognition of emotion calls for a compensatory, conscious, frontally controlled ER process in individuals with ASC, instead of the automatic sub-cortical face processing seen in the general population. These findings suggest that individuals with ASC who show intact basic emotion recognition on explicit ER tasks in lab settings may still have difficulties recognizing the same basic emotions in real life.

Compared to the inconclusive findings from basic ER tasks, studies testing recognition of "complex" emotions and mental states show more consistent difficulties in people with ASC.[1] High-functioning adults with ASC, who can label basic emotions, as well as controls, have difficulties recognizing complex emotions from photos of facial expressions (Baron-Cohen, Wheelwright, & Jolliffe, 1997) and judging whether people are trustworthy, based on photos of their faces (Adolphs, Sears, & Piven, 2001). Capps, Yirmiya, and Sigman (1992) asked children with ASC to label emotions from photographs and to provide examples of situations that made them feel this way. Compared to matched controls, children with ASC found it harder to recognize and explain complex emotions such as pride and embarrassment. No group difference was found in recognizing basic emotional expressions such as sadness or happiness. In addition, high-functioning children and adults with ASC perform worse than controls from the general population when asked to attribute a complex emotion or mental state to a person based on a photo of the eye region only or from silent video clips of the face area (Baron-Cohen, Wheelwright, Hill, Raste, & Plumb, 2001; Golan, Baron-Cohen, & Hill, 2006). These findings suggest that even when recognition of basic emotions is preserved among high-functioning individuals with ASC, they still show difficulties recognizing more complex emotional and mental states.

ER difficulties from facial expressions in ASC are also mirrored in neuroimaging studies. Individuals with ASC show less activation in brain regions central to face processing, such as the fusiform gyrus (e.g., Critchley et al., 2000). There is also evidence of reduced activation and altered connectivity between "social brain" areas that play a role in processing of emotion (Baron-Cohen et al., 1999; Critchley et al., 2000; Wicker, Chapter 2). In addition, gaze-tracking studies show that individuals with ASC tend to focus on the mouth region when looking at faces and miss the more salient eye region (see Jones & Klin, Chapter 4).

Emotion recognition in voices

Individuals with ASC have difficulties using intonation and pragmatic/emotional stress in speech to make socio-emotional judgments, such as telling whether a speaker is calm or excited, or whether s/he is talking to a child or to an adult (Paul, Augustyn, Klin, & Volkmar, 2005; McCann, Peppé, Gibbon, O'Hare, & Rutherford, Chapter 11). As with ER studies from faces, studies of basic ER from vocal stimuli in ASC show inconclusive findings. Some studies report difficulties (e.g., Boucher, Lewis, & Collis, 2000; Hobson, 1986a), whereas other studies found no deficits (e.g., Boucher et al., 2000). However, a consistent deficit is reported in vocal recognition of complex emotions and mental states (Golan, Baron-Cohen, & Hill, 2006; Golan, Baron-Cohen, Hill, & Rutherford, in press).

ER deficits from vocal stimuli in ASC are again mirrored by a few neuroimaging studies. For example, Gervais et al. (2004) found that areas in the superior temporal sulcus which typically respond to voices showed no response to vocal sounds in adults with ASC, whereas a normal activation pattern was found in response to non-vocal sounds. These findings suggest that the autistic brain does not specialize in processing the human voice and does not prioritize it as more salient than other sounds.

Emotion recognition from context

Emotions and mental states are felt and expressed in context, which provides information about their causes and consequences. Studies assessing the ability of individuals with ASC to identify emotions and mental states from context have also shown deficits relative to control groups. For example, adult participants with ASC had difficulties judging whether a story contained a potentially upsetting utterance and why this utterance would have upset the character concerned (Lawson et al., 2004). Adolescents and adults with ASC also have difficulties answering questions on the Strange Stories Test (Happé, 1994; Jolliffe & Baron-Cohen, 1999), which assesses the ability to provide context-appropriate mental state explanations for non-literal statements (e.g., ironic or sarcastic statements).

When using this task in a neuroimaging study, reduced activation of the left medial prefrontal cortex was found in people with ASC compared to matched controls (Happé et al., 1996).

Multimodal emotion recognition

Judging complex emotions requires integration of multimodal information, including contextual information, prosody, and non-verbal visual cues (body postures and facial expressions) into a coherent holistic picture (Herba & Phillips, 2004). Studies assessing complex emotion and mental state recognition from such multimodal sources of information, show a deficit in individuals with ASC (Golan, Baron-Cohen, Hill, & Golan, 2006; Klin, Jones, Schultz, Volkmar, & Cohen, 2002; see also Jones & Klin, Chapter 4). For example, Golan et al. (2006) found that adults with ASC, compared to matched typical controls, focused on using the content of characters' speech in order to label the emotions they felt, often ignoring contradictory messages in the facial expression or intonation. In a study assessing the effect that the number of social cues from different perceptual channels had on integrative socio-emotional understanding, children with autism, children with intellectual disabilities, and typically developing children were shown videotapes of child–child interactions in which the number of cues leading to a correct interpretation varied from one to four (these being prosody, verbal content, non-verbal, or non-verbal with object). The children were asked whether the behavior shown was a good way to make friends, whether the child was mean or nice, how the recipient of the behavior was feeling, and why. Children with ASC performed as well as both control groups on scenes containing one cue, but performed worse on scenes containing multiple cues. This suggests that multiple cues in different channels do not facilitate better ER among individuals with ASC (Pierce, Glad, & Schreibman, 1997).

To summarize, although ER deficits in ASC are life-long, some high-functioning individuals may develop compensatory strategies that allow them to recognize basic emotions. However, when recognition of more complex emotions and mental states is required, either from faces, voices, context, or the integration of these, many find them hard to interpret. This deficit has considerable implications for the ability of children and adults with ASC to function socially.

Teaching Emotion Recognition in ASC

The skills of emotion and mental state recognition are intuitive and automatic for most people, making it difficult to imagine life without them. However, individuals with ASC have to be taught these skills, and work hard to bridge this gap. Given the centrality of ER, there have been different attempts to train children and adults with ASC on recognition of emotions and mental states. These attempts have often focused only on recognition of basic emotions (Hadwin, Baron-Cohen, Howlin, & Hill, 1996; Howlin, Baron-Cohen, & Hadwin, 1999). Hadwin et al. (1996) taught children with autism to recognize basic emotions from schematic drawings and photographs of facial expressions. They were then taught to recognize situation-based emotions from drawings of emotion-eliciting situations (e.g., a big dog chasing a child as a fear-eliciting example). Children improved in their performance on the kind of tasks they were trained on, but not on other related tasks. A follow-up assessment two months later yielded the same results.

Other attempts to teach complex ER have been part of social skills training courses, usually run in groups (Barry et al., 2003; Howlin & Yates, 1999; Ozonoff & Miller, 1995; and see Dunlop, Knott, & MacKay, Chapter 13). For example, Ozonoff and Miller trained children with ASC in conversation skills, expression of non-verbal cues and emotional expressions, recognition of emotions in others, and false belief understanding. Role modeling by facilitators, and feedback on children's videotaped role playing, were used throughout the training. However, after 14 weekly sessions, there were no changes in parents' and teachers' ratings of social skills out of the course environment, suggesting poor generalization of learnt material to everyday social functioning (Ozonoff & Miller, 1995). Other evaluation studies of social skills training have reported improved results (Bauminger, 2002; Howlin & Yates, 1999). However, due to reliance only on participants' self-report with regards to improvement, or the absence of a control group, these studies remain methodologically limited.

Unfortunately, social skills groups are not widely available (Rogers, 2000), especially for adults with ASC (Howlin & Yates, 1999). Group interventions also require trained staff to facilitate the groups, and these are not always available. Furthermore, group-based interventions may be too socially demanding for people with ASC, and may therefore deter more socially anxious participants (Tantam, 2000). Finally, in such groups it is difficult to target the individual's specific level and pace of learning, potentially leaving some participants challenged and others bored. Using computers to teach ER may address these needs.

Using Computers to Teach Emotion Recognition to Individuals With ASC

In the last two decades, attempts to teach individuals with ASC have increasingly used computer-based training due to its unique advantages: Individuals with

ASC favor the computerized environment, since it is rule-based, predictable, and consistent. This fits well with their good systemizing skills. The computer is also free from social demands, which they typically find stressful. On the computer, information can be presented in a way that reduces the potentially confusing and anxiety-inducing, multimodal inputs that characterize "real-world" social situations. Computer users can work at their own pace and level of understanding, immediate feedback is provided, and lessons can be repeated over and over again, until mastery is achieved. Interest and motivation can be maintained through different and individually selected computerized rewards (Moore, McGrath, & Thorpe, 2000). In addition, computer-based training is easily available commercially, and can therefore serve a wider audience. High-functioning children and adults can use it on their own, with little support required from professionals.

Several studies have evaluated software attempting to enhance socio-emotional understanding in individuals with ASC. Bernard-Opitz, Sriram, and Nakhoda-Sapuan (2001) created a computer-training program that presented users with social problems around themes of turn-taking, requesting help and objects, giving in, and negotiating. Animated scenarios were played on the computer, followed by a selection of solutions, encouraging users to produce additional solutions of their own. Children with autism, who used the software for 10 sessions, showed a steady increase in the number of solutions they initiated. However, generalization into real life settings was not assessed.

Another program trained children with ASC on basic emotion recognition, using still photos of faces, situation-based context, and belief-based context. Children with ASC who used the software for 10 daily sessions over a period of 2–3 weeks improved significantly more than an ASC control group who did not use the software, on ER from situation-based and belief-based context, and on a generalization task of ER from context. However, no significant improvement was found on ER from facial expressions, possibly due to participants being old and high functioning enough to successfully recognize basic emotions from facial expressions (Silver & Oakes, 2001).

A third computer program teaching ER was evaluated by Bölte et al. (2002). The program taught recognition of the six basic emotions using whole face and eye region only still photos. Adults with ASC who used the software for 10 hours over a period of 5 weeks improved on ER from faces and eyes photos included in the training program, but not on ER from the generalization task.

The examples above demonstrate the utility of using computers to teach individuals with ASC, though all found similar generalization problems, as have the non-computerized programs. However, the computer-based interventions above used drawings or photographs for training, rather than more life-like stimuli. This might have made generalization harder than if more ecologically valid stimuli were used. In addition, the programs teaching ER focused on basic emotions, and only on facial expressions. No reported program to date has systematically trained complex ER in both visual and auditory channels, with life-like faces and voices. In our research, summarized next, we evaluated such a program. The question tested was: Can the good systemizing skills that individuals with ASC possess be used to teach them to improve their recognition of complex emotions?

Mind Reading: A Systematic Guide to Emotions

In the remainder of this chapter we focus on *Mind Reading* (Baron-Cohen, Golan, Wheelwright, & Hill, 2004), an interactive guide to emotions and mental states, and its value as an ER teaching tool for learners on the autism spectrum. *Mind Reading* is based on a taxonomic system of 412 emotions and mental states, systematically arranged into 24 emotion groups, and six developmental levels (from age 4 years to adulthood). Each emotion group is introduced and demonstrated by a short video clip. Every emotion is defined and demonstrated in six silent films of faces, six voice recordings, and six written examples of situations that evoke this emotion. The resulting library of emotional "assets" (video clips, audio clips, or brief stories) comprises of $412 \times 18 = 7,416$ units of emotion information to learn to recognize or understand.

The face videos and voice recordings comprise actors of both sexes, various ages and ethnicities, to facilitate generalization. Faces and voices are presented separately for each emotion (i.e., silent face films and faceless voice recordings) to encourage analysis of the emotion in each modality, and to facilitate the learning process by avoiding over-burdening the user perceptually and cognitively. All face video clips and voice recordings were validated by a panel of ten independent judges, and were included in *Mind Reading* if at least eight judges agreed that the emotional label given described the face/voice. Through three different zones (an Emotion Library, a Learning Centre with lessons, quizzes, and rewards, and a Games Zone), the software offers children and adults of various levels of functioning the opportunity to systematically study emotional expressions in a predictable and enjoyable environment.[2] Figure 12.1 shows some screen shots from the software.

A Study of Adults with ASC, Using *Mind Reading* Over 10–15 Weeks

We tested for any improvement in adults with ASC in ER skills following independent use of the software, and the extent to which these users could generalize

The Emotions Library: an emotion page

The 24 emotions groups

The Learning Centre: a quiz question

The Game Zone: "Famous face"

Figure 12.1 Screen shots from *Mind reading, the interactive guide to emotions* (Baron-Cohen, Golan, Wheelwright, & Hill, 2004).

their acquired knowledge. The intervention took place over a period of 10–15 weeks, to assure a meaningful period for training (whilst assuming that a longer duration might have led to individuals dropping out).

Participants were tested before and after the intervention. A no-computer-intervention control group of adults with ASC was matched to the intervention group. This control group was also tested before and after a similar period of time, but had no intervention. The purpose of a no-intervention ASC group was to assess whether any improvement was related to the intervention or merely due to taking the tasks twice, or to time passing. A third control group of adults from the general population was matched to the ASC groups. This group was tested only once, to obtain baseline measures.

Participants with ASC were randomly allocated into the first two groups below:

1 Software home-users: 19 participants (14 males) were asked to use the software (provided free of charge) at home by themselves for 2 hours a week over a period of 10 weeks, a total of 20 hours. Participants were included in the study

if they completed a minimum of 10 hours of work with the software. If they did not complete this minimum, participants were given an extension of up to 4 weeks to do more work with the software. Out of 24 participants originally recruited to this group, 3 withdrew during the 10-week period and 2 others were excluded at the end, as they failed to reach the 10-hour minimum.

2 ASC control group: 22 participants (17 males) attended the assessment meetings with a 10–15-week period between them, during which they did not take part in any intervention related to ER.

In addition, we included a third group as controls:

3 Typical control group: 24 participants (19 males) were recruited for this group from a local employment agency.

The three groups were matched on age, verbal and performance IQ, handedness, and sex. They spanned an equivalent range of employment and educational levels.

Assessment of Generalization

In order to test whether software users could generalize their acquired knowledge to other situations, we compared the groups' performance at three different levels of generalization, using stimuli in two perceptual modalities (visual and auditory):

1 *Close generalization*: This level tested ER from stimuli that are included in *Mind Reading*, so that participants may have been exposed to them while using the software. This was tested by playing face video clips and voice recordings that were included in *Mind Reading* on a different computer program, with more answers to choose from and with no feedback or support as is provided in *Mind Reading*. The battery used to test facial and vocal ER at this level, *The Cambridge Mindreading (CAM) Face-Voice Battery* (Golan, Baron-Cohen, & Hill, 2006), includes a face task and a voice task, with 50 items in each, to test recognition of 20 different complex emotions and mental states (e.g., *intimate, insincere, nervous*), all taken from *Mind Reading*. In both tasks four adjectives are presented after each stimulus is played, and participants are asked which adjective best describes how the person feels. The battery provides an overall facial and an overall vocal ER score, as well as individual scores for each of the 20 emotions assessed (pass/fail) and an overall number of the emotions correctly recognized. Individuals with ASC have been found to score significantly lower than controls on all three scores of the battery (Golan et al., 2006a).

2 *Feature-based distant generalization*: This level tested the ability to transfer ER skills separately in faces and voices, using faces and voices which were not included in *Mind Reading*. This was tested in the visual channel using the *"Reading the Mind in the Eyes"* task [Revised, Adult version] (Baron-Cohen, et al., 2001). The task includes 36 items, in which participants are presented with a photograph of the eyes region of the face and must choose one of four adjectives or phrases to describe the mental state of the person pictured. In the auditory channel, we used the *"Reading the Mind in the Voice" task* [Revised] (Golan et al., in press), which includes 25 speech segments, taken from BBC drama series. After each segment is played, participants are asked to choose out of four adjectives which one best describes how the speaker is feeling. Adult participants with ASC score significantly lower than matched controls from the general population on both tasks.

3 *Holistic distant generalization*: This level comprised multimodal socio-emotional stimuli, including faces, voices, body language, and context. It used the *"Reading the Mind in Films"* task (Golan et al., 2006b), which comprises 22 short social scenes taken from feature films. Participants are presented with four adjectives and are asked to choose the one that best describes the way a target character feels at the end of the scene. Participants with ASC performed significantly worse on this task compared to matched controls. This level was tested only at time 2.

In addition to the two assessment meetings, follow-up questionnaires were sent to participants a year after the intervention, to assess long-term effects of using the software on broader socio-emotional functioning.

The Procedure of the Study

Participants in the intervention group were asked to help in the evaluation of a new piece of software by attending two assessment meetings and using *Mind Reading* for 10 weeks between these meetings. At the first meeting, *Mind Reading* was introduced to them in detail, including a presentation of the emotion taxonomy, the different zones, and a demonstration of a systematic analysis of an emotion, comparing different faces and voices to identify the unique facial/intonation features of this emotion. Participants were encouraged to analyze the stimuli systematically. They were asked to use the Emotions Library and Learning Centre as they pleased, but not to use the Games Zone for more than a third of the usage time (to ensure that significant time was dedicated to systematic learning rather than random game playing). Participants in the ASC control group were asked to come to two assessment meetings, separated by a 10–15-week period.

Table 12:1 Means (and standard deviations) of the three groups on all tasks at time 1 and time 2

	Software home users		ASC controls		Typical controls
	Time 1	Time 2	Time 1	Time 2	
CAM face task	31.3	37.5[1]	32.5	34.8[1]	42.0[2]
(Max score = 50)	(8.8)	(7.8)	(8.4)	(8.2)	(5.2)
CAM voice task	33.8	38.9[1]	35.2	36.6	42.1[2]
(Max score = 50)	(6.6)	(6.2)	(7.4)	(7.9)	(4.2)
CAM no. of concepts recognized	9.8	13.6[1]	10.5	11.3	16.1[2]
(Max score = 20)	(5.2)	(4.8)	(5.2)	(5.4)	(3.0)
Reading the Mind in the Eyes	23.1	23.8	23.9	23.0	28.5[2]
(Max score = 36)	(6.7)	(4.7)	(6.7)	(7.3)	(3.1)
Reading the Mind in the Voice	16.1	16.7	16.1	17.4	18.6[2]
(Max score = 25)	(2.9)	(3.9)	(3.9)	(3.5)	(2.4)
Reading the Mind in Films		11.8		12.8	15.5[2]
(Max score = 22)		(3.8)		(3.4)	(2.4)

[1] The within-group difference between time 2 and time 1 scores is significant at the $p<.01$ level.

[2] Time 1 scores are significantly higher in the typical control group, compared to the two ASC groups ($p<.01$).

Results of the Evaluation

The results of the evaluation are presented in Table 12.1. Following 10–20 hours of using the software over a period of 10–15 weeks, users with ASC improved their ability to recognize complex emotions and mental states from both faces and voices significantly more than controls with ASC. This finding is encouraging, considering the short usage time and the large number of emotions included in the software, and since participants were not asked to study these particular emotions. Though the performance of both ASC groups was significantly lower than the typical control group on all ER tasks at time 1, no such differences were found between the clinical groups. Hence, any difference between clinical groups at time 2 can be attributed to the intervention.

The intervention group improved significantly on close generalization measures, including emotional faces and voices that individuals with ASC have particular difficulties with (Golan et al., 2006a). These findings, together with participants' reports of greater attention to faces and emotions and improved eye contact following the use of the software, suggest that the analysis of emotions using *Mind Reading* allows people with ASC to improve ER skills from both faces and voices.

Follow-up Results

Follow-up questionnaires were sent to participants with ASC a year after the time 2 assessment. Questionnaires included a general feedback questionnaire and the Friendship and Relationship Questionnaire (FQ: Baron-Cohen & Wheelwright, 2003), which assesses the need for and enjoyment of close, empathic, supportive and caring friendships, interest in people, and perception of friendship as important. Eighteen participants (9 from each group) returned the questionnaires. An analysis of participants' FQ scores showed a significant decrease in the FQ scores of participants who belonged to the ASC control group, and a marginally significant increase in the FQ scores of participants with ASC who originally belonged to the intervention group.

This finding suggests that using the software might affect one's interest and perceived ability to form friendships and relationships. Participants' feedback revealed the positive impact that *Mind Reading* had in increasing their awareness of the importance of emotions and emotional expressions in everyday life, improving their understanding of emotions and their corresponding expressions, and affecting their ability to function socially. Though these results were obtained from a partial sample, and relied on self-report, they offer some evidence for the long-term positive effects that the systematic analysis of emotional expressions may have on the socio-emotional functioning of adults with ASC.

Generalization Issues

Despite the encouraging effects described above, improvement on ER tasks following the use of the software was limited to different presentation and variations on taught stimuli, i.e., to faces and voices taken from *Mind Reading*. As Table 12.1 shows, participants found it hard to generalize their knowledge to other tasks of ER from voices and eyes, and did not perform better than controls on a task involving integration of facial, vocal, and contextual cues. Similar findings of poor generalization have been found in other studies teaching theory of mind, ER, and social skills to individuals with ASC (Bölte et al., 2002; Hadwin et al., 1996; McGregor, Whiten, & Blackburn, 1998; Swettenham, 1996; see also Dunlop, Knott, & MacKay, Chapter 13). Software usage time was, however, positively correlated with the holistic distant generalization task scores, suggesting that using the software for a longer period may assist with generalization to multimodal, life-like situations.

Generalization difficulties are reported to be common amongst those with ASC (Rimland, 1965). A number of explanations have been put forward for this, including focusing on small details at the expense of the larger picture (Frith, 1989), difficulties with complex information processing (Minshew & Goldstein, 1998), an inability to recognize the similarities between stimuli (Plaisted, 2001), or adherence to rule-based categories while failing to use prototype-based categories (Klinger & Dawson, 1995). In terms of socio-emotional stimuli, if each social situation experienced or emotional expression perceived is seen as unique, there will be no way to form social rules or emotional categories, resulting in poor generalization of taught material.

According to the systemizing model, the ability to generalize from learned material depends on two factors: The centrality of systemizing in the individual's cognitive style, and the degree to which the information is systemizable, i.e., relies on clear rules which allow accurate predictions (Baron-Cohen, 2006). Strong systemizers who study a well-defined rule-based system would be able to successfully generalize their knowledge and apply its rules to examples that were not present in the learning process (e.g., in mathematics, engineering etc.). However, if strong systemizers are faced with variable, loosely structured, and less predictable information, their attempts to structure ("systemize") this information may result in a multitude of single information units, which cannot be grouped further. With no grouping of information or clear rules, generalization for the strong systemizer is hard, if not impossible. The socio-emotional domain is an example of such an open system: although it includes some rules (e.g., a smiling person is happy), these are often context-dependent (e.g., a person who has just realized that his socks don't match may be smiling in embarrassment) or culture-dependent (e.g., a smiling person could be being polite), and leave lots of room for error. Since individuals with ASC are strong systemizers, the likelihood of learning from direct encounters with socio-emotional phenomena is predicted to be low. What *Mind Reading* attempted to do is to insert a level of systematic structure into this open system of emotions, to improve the chance of learning and generalizing it. Although perhaps less close to real-life emotions, the imposed "closure" of the emotional domain in *Mind Reading* made it easier for strong systemizers to access this domain, and increased awareness of its importance, as participants reported.

Integration Section: How Could Findings of This Study Integrate With Current and Future Autism Research?

The majority of studies to date of ER in ASC focus on the recognition of basic emotions from still photographs of facial expressions. The tasks created for the present study, as well as *Mind Reading* itself, can be used to extend the range of ER research in ASC with more complex and ecologically valid stimuli. For example, our tasks allow the study of recognition of complex emotions from facial *and* vocal expressions, an area which, as McCann et al. (Chapter 11) suggest, has hardly been studied.

The results of our study call for neuroimaging studies to examine possible intervention-related changes in the functioning and connectivity between "social brain" areas, such as the amygdala, fusiform gyrus, superior temporal sulcus, and prefrontal cortex. The reports of Wicker (Chapter 2) show that people with ASC have atypical connectivity patterns between these brain areas, related to emotional processing from faces. This could be associated with difficulties integrating emotional stimuli from perceptual channels, as seen in our study. Studying intervention-related changes at a neurological level might show improvement in functioning and connectivity between these regions in individuals with ASC. Alternatively, it might show that improvement on ER abilities at the behavioral level may be associated with increased activation and connectivity between alternative brain regions, used to compensate for the deficit in the standard socio-emotional brain network. Wicker found strong influence of the right dorso-lateral prefrontal cortex on activity of the fusiform gyrus amongst participants with ASC when they were explicitly asked to process emotion from facial expressions. Such "top-down" influence suggests that individuals with ASC may consciously enhance their processing of emotional expressions from faces (and arguably from other channels) if prompted and trained to do so.[3] Though this activity pattern of the social brain differs from that of the people in the general population, it might provide individuals with ASC with an alternative channel for more successful emotion recognition.

Such an increase in use of compensatory brain areas has been reported by Bölte et al. (2006). Contrary to the researchers' hypothesis, improvement in facial ER at the behavioral level was associated with increase in the activation not in the fusiform face area, but in the right medial occipital gyrus, a region involved in object and face recognition, and in the right superior parietal lobule, which is involved in visuo-spatial processing and in visual attention.

Our findings suggest that improvement in recognition of emotion in the auditory channel is also possible with appropriate training (although generalization of skills remains a difficulty). Further research of intervention into prosody processing difficulties in ASC (McCann et al., Chapter 11) could make use of the systemizing model (and the vocal emotional material included in *Mind Reading*) through systematic analysis of spectral diagrams of prosody with individuals with ASC, while pointing out characteristic prosodic patterns. As with the questions raised with regard to emotional face processing in the brain, it would be interesting to find the impact of such vocal and prosody interventions upon activation of typical or compensatory brain areas.

Participants in our study reported looking more at faces and engaging in more eye contact following the use of *Mind Reading*. Such reports need to be experimentally confirmed. Using gaze-tracking technology before and after the intervention could be useful to verify our participants' reports (Jones & Klin, Chapter 4), i.e., to test if they show more attention to relevant facial features (e.g., eyes), and decreased attention to irrelevant features (e.g., objects), following the intervention. Our findings on the holistic film task suggest that explicit instructions may be needed for participants with ASC to improve their attention to the right cues. However, our follow-up findings suggest that participants who used *Mind Reading* with no specific instructions may have become more aware of the importance of facial and vocal expressions of emotion without further prompting. This awareness of emotional expressions and their meanings may have differentiated them from the control ASC group on their self-reported friendship skills.

In our study, *Mind Reading* trained recognition of emotions in faces and voices separately. This may have encouraged an atomized learning style and lack of generalization to holistic stimuli. Hence, we recommend that *Mind Reading* should be viewed as a first step in a training program. The next steps should deal with the systematic introduction of context and integration of different socio-emotional cues into one (flexible) picture. After acquiring sufficient understanding of how emotions look and sound, individuals with ASC could practice integrating these and adapting them according to contextual cues (López, Chapter 6) and cultural knowledge (Loth, Chapter 5). The limited generalization found in our study may be due to our exclusive focus on ER, with no reference to the association of ER to other social skills. Hence, it might be best if the mediation between computer-based systematic training and real-life flexibility is included in the curriculum of social skills groups for children (Dunlop, Knott, & MacKay, Chapter 13) and for adults (Howlin & Yates, 1999), as these groups offer a semi-natural and tutor-supported setting for socio-emotional interaction.

For children, integration of principles learned using *Mind Reading* with real life context could also be supported by teachers in school settings, and/or by parents at home. Indeed, we found that parent-supported use of *Mind Reading* at home could bring improvement in children with ASC on distant, as well as close, generalization measures (Golan, 2006; Golan & Baron-Cohen, submitted). Findings reported by Maestro and Muratori (Chapter 9), of signs of reduced social attention in the first few months of life in children who later receive a diagnosis of ASC, suggest that drawing the attention of such children to the salience of emotional expressions at an early stage may have a strong impact on the development of their socio-emotional skills (Dawson & Zanolli, 2003).

Such young children may be unable to use computers, but could be exposed to emotional expressions by "passively" watching multimedia. We are currently evaluating the effectiveness of *The Transporters* animation series aimed at toddlers with ASC, which uses mechanical vehicles to draw the children's attention to emotions and facial expressions (www.transporters.tv). Such early stimulation could also be of use for children's developing perception of gaze directed "to me" vs. "elsewhere" (Williams, Chapter 3). As with *Mind Reading*, strengths that individuals with ASC possess can be harnessed to support areas of difficulty. Here, the use of stimuli children with ASC are drawn to (i.e., mechanical motion of vehicles) is used to draw their attention to emotions and facial expressions that they tend to naturally ignore.

With the rapid advances of assistive technology, similar interventions for individuals with ASC are likely to be developed (Golan, LaCava, & Baron-Cohen, 2007). If they lead to successful generalization of learnt skills, such interventions may be an important source of support for children and adults on the autistic spectrum.

Acknowledgments

Ofer Golan was supported by the National Alliance for Autism Research (NAAR), the Corob Charitable Trust, the Cambridge Overseas Trust and B'nai B'rith Leo Baeck scholarships. Simon Baron-Cohen was supported by the Shirley Foundation, the Medical Research Council, and the Three Guineas Trust.

Notes

1   Complex emotions involve attributing a cognitive state as well as an emotion, and are more context- and culture-dependent (Griffiths, 1997). They may be belief- rather than situation-based emotions (Harris, 1989), e.g., disappointed or insincere, or social emotions, e.g., embarrassed, intimate (Kasari, Chamberlain, & Bauminger, 2001). Typically developing children can recognize complex emotions like embarrassment, pride, and jealousy by the age of 7 (Harris, 1989), and complex emotion and mental state recognition skills continue to develop across the lifespan.

2   The software is described in detail in Golan & Baron-Cohen, 2006 and at www.jkp. com/mindreading

3   See also Adolphs et al., 2005 for an example of the effectiveness of drawing attention to essential facial features for recognition of emotion in a patient with amygdalae lesions.

References

Adolphs, R. (2001). The neurobiology of social cognition. *Current Opinions in Neurobiology*, *11*(2), 231–239.

Adolphs, R., Gosselin, F., Buchanan, T. W., Tranel, D., Schyns, P., & Damasio, A. R. (2005). A mechanism for impaired fear recognition after amygdala damage. *Nature, 433*(7021), 68–72.

Adolphs, R., Sears, L., & Piven, J. (2001). Abnormal processing of social information from faces in autism. *Journal of Cognitive Neuroscience, 13*, 232–240.

Attwood, T. (2003). Understanding and managing circumscribed interests. In M. R. Prior (Ed.), *Learning and behavior problems in Asperger syndrome* (pp. 126–147). New York and London: Guilford Press.

Baron-Cohen, S. (1995). *Mindblindness: An essay on autism and theory of mind.* Boston: MIT Press/Bradford Books.

Baron-Cohen, S. (2000). Is Asperger syndrome/high-functioning autism necessarily a disability? *Development and Psychopathology, 12*(3), 489–500.

Baron-Cohen, S. (2003). *The essential difference: Men, women and the extreme male brain.* London: Penguin.

Baron-Cohen, S. (2006). Two new theories of autism: Hyper-systemizing and assortative mating. *Archives of Disease in Childhood, 91*(1), 2–5.

Baron-Cohen, S., Golan, O., Wheelwright, S., & Hill, J. J. (2004). *Mind Reading: The interactive guide to emotions.* London: Jessica Kingsley Limited.

Baron-Cohen, S., Leslie, A. M., & Frith, U. (1985). Does the autistic child have a "theory of mind"? *Cognition, 21*(1), 37–46.

Baron-Cohen, S., Richler, J., Bisarya, D., Gurunathan, N., & Wheelwright, S. (2003). The Systemizing Quotient (SQ): An investigation of adults with Asperger syndrome or High Functioning Autism and normal sex differences. *Philosophical Transactions of the Royal Society, Series B., Special issue on "Autism: Mind and Brain," 358*, 361–374.

Baron-Cohen, S., Ring, H. A., Wheelwright, S., Bullmore, E. T., Brammer, M. J., Simmons, A., et al. (1999). Social intelligence in the normal and autistic brain: An fMRI study. *European Journal of Neuroscience, 11*, 1891–1898.

Baron-Cohen, S., Tager-Flusberg, H., & Cohen, D. J. (2000). *Understanding other minds: Perspectives from developmental cognitive neuroscience* (2nd ed.). Oxford, UK: Oxford University Press.

Baron-Cohen, S., & Wheelwright, S. (1999). "Obsessions" in children with autism or Asperger syndrome: Content analysis in terms of core domains of cognition. *British Journal of Psychiatry, 175*, 484–490.

Baron-Cohen, S., & Wheelwright, S. (2003). The Friendship Questionnaire: An investigation of adults with Asperger syndrome or high-functioning autism, and normal sex differences. *Journal of Autism and Developmental Disorders, 33*(5), 509–517.

Baron-Cohen, S., & Wheelwright, S. (2004). The empathy quotient: An investigation of adults with Asperger syndrome or high functioning autism, and normal sex differences. *Journal of Autism and Developmental Disorders, 34*(2), 163–175.

Baron-Cohen, S., Wheelwright, S., Hill, J. J., Raste, Y., & Plumb, I. (2001). The "Reading the Mind in the Eyes" Test revised version: A study with normal adults, and adults with Asperger syndrome or high-functioning autism. *Journal of Child Psychology and Psychiatry, 42*, 241–251.

Baron-Cohen, S., Wheelwright, S., & Jolliffe, T. (1997). Is there a "language of the eyes"? Evidence from normal adults, and adults with autism or Asperger syndrome. *Visual Cognition, 4*, 311–331.

Baron-Cohen, S., Wheelwright, S., Lawson, J., Griffin, R., & Hill, J. J. (2002). The exact mind: Empathizing and systemizing in autism spectrum conditions. In U. Goswami (Ed.), *Handbook of childhood cognitive development* (pp. 491–508). Malden, MA: Blackwell Publishers.

Baron-Cohen, S., Wheelwright, S., Stott, C. M., Bolton, P., & Goodyer, I. (1997). Is there a link between engineering and autism? *Autism, 1*(1), 101–109.

Barry, T. D., Klinger, L. G., Lee, J. M., Palardy, N., Gilmore, T., & Bodin, S. D. (2003). Examining the effectiveness of an outpatient clinic-based social skills group for high-functioning children with autism. *Journal of Autism and Developmental Disorders, 33*(6), 685–701.

Bauminger, N. (2002). The facilitation of social-emotional understanding and social interaction in high-functioning children with autism: Intervention outcomes. *Journal of Autism and Developmental Disorders, 32*(4), 283–298.

Begeer, S., Rieffe, C., Terwogt, M. M., & Stockmann, L. (2006). Attention to facial emotion expressions in children with autism. *Autism, 10*(1), 37–51.

Bernard-Opitz, V., Sriram, N., & Nakhoda-Sapuan, S. (2001). Enhancing social problem solving in children with autism and normal children through computer-assisted instruction. *Journal of Autism and Developmental Disorders, 31*(4), 377–398.

Bölte, S., Feineis-Matthews, S., Leber, S., Dierks, T., Hubl, D., & Poustka, F. (2002). The development and evaluation of a computer-based program to test and to teach the recognition of facial affect. *International Journal of Circumpolar Health, 61 Suppl 2*, 61–68.

Bölte, S., Hubl, D., Feineis-Matthews, S., Prvulovic, D., Dierks, T., & Poustka, F. (2006). Facial affect recognition training in autism: Can we animate the fusiform gyrus? *Behavioral Neuroscience, 120*(1), 211–216.

Boucher, J., Lewis, V., & Collis, G. M. (2000). Voice processing abilities in children with autism, children with specific language impairments, and young typically developing children. *Journal of Child Psychology and Psychiatry and Allied Disciplines, 41*(7), 847–857.

Capps, L., Yirmiya, N., & Sigman, M. (1992). Understanding of simple and complex emotions in non-retarded children with autism. *Journal of Child Psychology and Psychiatry, 33*, 1169–1182.

Castelli, F. (2005). Understanding emotions from standardized facial expressions in autism and normal development. *Autism, 9*(4), 428–449.

Celani, G., Battacchi, M. W., & Arcidiacono, L. (1999). The understanding of the emotional meaning of facial expressions in people with autism. *Journal of Autism and Developmental Disorders, 29*(1), 57–66.

Charman, T. (2003). Why is joint attention a pivotal skill in autism? *Philosophical Transactions of the Royal Society, Series B., 358*(1430), 315–324.

Critchley, H. D., Daly, E. M., Bullmore, E. T., Williams, S. C., Van Amelsvoort, T., Robertson, D. M., et al. (2000). The functional neuroanatomy of social behaviour: Changes in cerebral blood flow when people with autistic disorder process facial expressions. *Brain, 123 (Pt 11)*, 2203–2212.

Dapretto, M., Davies, M. S., Pfeifer, J. H., Scott, A. A., Sigman, M., Bookheimer, S. Y., et al. (2006). Understanding emotions in others: Mirror neuron dysfunction in children with autism spectrum disorders. *Nature Neuroscience, 9*(1), 28–30.

Dawson, G., & Zanolli, K. (2003). Early intervention and brain plasticity in autism. In G. Bock & J. Goode (Eds.), *Autism: Neural bases and treatment possibilities*, Novartis Foundation Symposium 251 (pp. 266–280). Chichester, UK: John Wiley & Sons.

Ekman, P., & Friesen, W. V. (1971). Constants across cultures in the face and emotion. *Journal of Personality and Social Psychology, 17*, 124–129.

Ekman, P., Friesen, W. V., & Hager, J. C. (2002). *The facial action coding system* (2nd ed.). London: Weidenfeld & Nicolson.

el Kaliouby, R., & Robinson, P. (2005). Real-time inference of complex mental states from facial expressions and head gestures. In B. Kisacanin, V. Pavlovic, & T. S. Huang (Eds.), *Real-time vision for human–computer interaction* (pp. 181–200). New York: Springer-Verlag.

Frith, U. (1989). *Autism: Explaining the enigma*. Oxford, UK: Blackwell.

Frith, U., & Hill, E. (2004). *Autism: Mind and brain*. Oxford, UK: Oxford University Press.

Gervais, H., Belin, P., Boddaert, N., Leboyer, M., Coez, A., Sfaello, I., et al. (2004). Abnormal cortical voice processing in autism. *Nature Neuroscience, 7*(8), 801–802.

Gillberg, C. L. (1992). The Emanuel Miller Memorial Lecture 1991. Autism and autistic-like conditions: Subclasses among disorders of empathy. *Journal of Child Psychology and Psychiatry, 33*(5), 813–842.

Golan, O. (2006). *Systemising emotions: Teaching emotion recognition to people with autism using interactive multimedia*. Unpublished PhD thesis, University of Cambridge.

Golan, O., & Baron-Cohen, S. (2006). Systemizing empathy: Teaching adults with Asperger syndrome and High Functioning Autism to recognize complex emotions using interactive multimedia. *Development and Psychopathology, 18*(2), 591–617.

Golan, O., & Baron-Cohen, S. (submitted). *Teaching children with Asperger syndrome and high functioning autism to recognize emotions using interactive multimedia*.

Golan, O., Baron-Cohen, S., & Hill, J. J. (2006a). The Cambridge Mindreading (CAM) Face–Voice Battery: Testing complex emotion recognition in adults with and without Asperger syndrome. *Journal of Autism and Developmental Disorders, 36*(2), 169–183.

Golan, O., Baron-Cohen, S., Hill, J. J., & Golan, Y. (2006b). The "Reading the Mind in Films" task: Complex emotion recognition in adults with and without autism spectrum conditions. *Social Neuroscience, 1*(2), 111–123.

Golan, O., Baron-Cohen, S., Hill, J. J., & Rutherford, M. D. (in press). The "Reading the Mind in the Voice" test—Revised: A study of complex emotion recognition in adults with and without Autism Spectrum Conditions.

Golan, O., LaCava, P. G., & Baron-Cohen, S. (2007). Assistive technology as an aid in reducing social impairments in autism spectrum conditions. In R. L. Gabriels & D. E. Hill (Eds.), *Growing up with autism: Working with school-age children and adolescents* (pp. 124–142). New York: Guilford Press.

Griffiths, P. (1997). *What emotions really are: The problem of psychological categories*. Chicago: University of Chicago Press.

Hadwin, J., Baron-Cohen, S., Howlin, P., & Hill, K. (1996). Can we teach children with autism to understand emotions, belief, or pretence? *Development and Psychopathology, 8*(2), 345–365.

Happé, F. G. (1994). An advanced test of theory of mind: Understanding of story characters' thoughts and feelings by able autistic, mentally handicapped, and normal children and adults. *Journal of Autism and Developmental Disorders, 24*, 129–154.

Happé, F. G. (1999). Autism: Cognitive deficit or cognitive style? *Trends in Cognitive Sciences, 3*(6), 216–222.

Happé, F. G., Ehlers, S., Fletcher, P., Frith, U., Johansson, M., Gillberg, C., et al. (1996). "Theory of mind" in the brain: Evidence from a PET scan study of Asperger syndrome. *Neuroreport, 8*(1), 197–201.

Harris, P. L. (1989). *Children and emotion: The development of psychological understanding*. Oxford, UK: Blackwell.

Herba, C., & Phillips, M. (2004). Annotation: Development of facial expression recognition from childhood to adolescence: Behavioural and neurological perspectives. *Journal of Child Psychology and Psychiatry, 45*(7), 1185–1198.

Hobson, R. P. (1986a). The autistic child's appraisal of expressions of emotion. *Journal of Child Psychology and Psychiatry, 27*, 321–342.

Hobson, R. P. (1986b). The autistic child's appraisal of expressions of emotion: A further study. *Journal of Child Psychology and Psychiatry, 27*, 671–680.

Hobson, R. P. (1993). *Autism and the development of mind*. Hove, UK: Lawrence Erlbaum.

Hobson, R. P. (1994). Understanding persons: The role of affect. In S. Baron-Cohen, H. Tager-Flusberg, & D. J. Cohen (Eds.), *Understanding other minds* (pp. 204–227). Oxford, UK: Oxford University Press.

Howlin, P., Baron-Cohen, S., & Hadwin, J. (1999). *Teaching children with autism to mindread: A practical guide for teachers and parents*. Chichester, UK: J. Wiley.

Howlin, P., & Yates, P. (1999). The potential effectiveness of social skills groups for adults with autism. *Autism, 3*(3), 299–307.

Jolliffe, T., & Baron-Cohen, S. (1999). The Strange Stories Test: A replication with high-functioning adults with autism or Asperger syndrome. *Journal of Autism and Developmental Disorders, 29*, 395–406.

Kasari, C., Chamberlain, B., & Bauminger, N. (2001). Social emotions and social relationships: Can children with autism compensate? In J. A. Burack, T. Charman, N. Yirmiya & P. R. Zelazo (Eds.), *The development of autism: Perspectives from theory and research* (pp. 309–323). Mahwah, NJ: Lawrence Erlbaum Associates.

Klin, A., Jones, W., Schultz, R., Volkmar, F., & Cohen, D. J. (2002). Visual fixation patterns during viewing of naturalistic social situations as predictors of social competence in individuals with autism. *Archives of General Psychiatry, 59*, 809–816.

Klinger, L. G., & Dawson, G. (1995). A fresh look at categorization abilities in persons with autism. In E. Schopler & G. B. Mesibov (Eds.), *Learning and cognition in autism* (pp. 119–136). New York: Plenum Press.

Lawson, J., Baron-Cohen, S., & Wheelwright, S. (2004). Empathising and systemising in adults with and without Asperger syndrome. *Journal of Autism and Developmental Disorders, 34*(3), 301–310.

Loveland, K. A., Tunali Kotoski, B., Chen, Y. R., Ortegon, J., Pearson, D. A., Brelsford, K. A., et al. (1997). Emotion recognition in autism: Verbal and non-verbal information. *Development and Psychopathology, 9*, 579–593.

McGregor, E., Whiten, A., & Blackburn, P. (1998). Teaching theory of mind by highlighting intention and illustrating thoughts: A comparison of their effectiveness with three-year-olds and autistic subjects. *British Journal of Developmental Psychology, 16*(3), 281–300.

Minshew, N. J., & Goldstein, G. (1998). Autism as a disorder of complex information processing. *Mental Retardation and Developmental Disabilities Research Reviews, 4*(2), 129–136.

Moore, D., McGrath, P., & Thorpe, J. (2000). Computer-aided learning for people with autism—a framework for research and development. *Innovations in Education and Training International, 37*, 218–228.

Ortony, A., Clore, G., & Foss, M. (1987). The referential structure of the affective lexicon. *Cognitive Science, 11*, 341–364.

Ozonoff, S., & Miller, J. (1995). Teaching theory of mind: A new approach to social skills training for individuals with autism. *Journal of Autism and Developmental Disorders, 25*(4), 415–433.

Paul, R., Augustyn, A., Klin, A., & Volkmar, F. R. (2005). Perception and production of prosody by speakers with autism spectrum disorders. *Journal of Autism and Developmental Disorders, 35*(2), 205–220.

Pierce, K., Glad, K. S., & Schreibman, L. (1997). Social perception in children with autism: An attentional deficit? *Journal of Autism and Developmental Disorders, 27*(3), 265–282.

Piggot, J., Kwon, H., Mobbs, D., Blasey, C., Lotspeich, L., Menon, V., et al. (2004). Emotional attribution in high-functioning individuals with autistic spectrum disorder: A functional imaging study. *Journal of the American Academy of Child and Adolescent Psychiatry, 43*(4), 473–480.

Plaisted, K. C. (2001). Reduced generalization in autism: An alternative to weak central coherence. In J. A. Burack, T. Charman, N. Yirmiya, & P. R. Zelazo (Eds.), *The development of autism: Perspectives from theory and research* (pp. 149–169). Mahwah, NJ: Lawrence Erlbaum Associates.

Rimland, B. (1965). *Infantile autism: The syndrome and its implications for a neural theory of behavior*. London: Methuen.

Rogers, S. J. (2000). Interventions that facilitate socialization in children with autism. *Journal of Autism and Developmental Disorders, 30*(5), 399–409.

Russell, J. A. (1980). A circumplex model of affect. *Journal of Personality and Social Psychology*, *39*, 1161–1178.

Silver, M., & Oakes, P. (2001). Evaluation of a new computer intervention to teach people with autism or Asperger syndrome to recognize and predict emotions in others. *Autism*, *5*, 299–316.

Swettenham, J. (1996). Can children with autism be taught to understand false belief using computers? *Journal of Child Psychology and Psychiatry*, *37*, 157–165.

Tantam, D. (2000). Psychological disorder in adolescents and adults with Asperger syndrome. *Autism*, *4*(1), 47–62.

Wing, L. (1981). Asperger's syndrome: A clinical account. *Psychological Medicine*, *11*(1), 115–129.

13

Developing Social Interaction and Understanding in High-Functioning Individuals With Autism Spectrum Disorder

Aline-Wendy Dunlop, Fiona Knott, and Tommy MacKay

The nature of the social impairments that lie at the heart of the autism spectrum is highlighted throughout this volume (see, e.g., Golan & Baron-Cohen, Chapter 12; Loth, Chapter 5; Jones & Klin, Chapter 4; Maestro & Muratori, Chapter 9; Wicker, Chapter 2; Williams, Chapter 3). These impairments are considered to be the primary deficit (Fein, Pennington, Markowitz, Braverman, & Waterhouse, 1986) and can be seen across the lifespan. They reflect difficulties in understanding others' minds, engaging in interaction which is truly reciprocal, and understanding concepts such as friendship. For individuals with autism spectrum disorder (ASD), the impact of these difficulties is severe, affecting the ability to make and sustain satisfying friendships and other relationships, and contributing to difficulties accessing education and later employment. The need to provide appropriate and effective intervention is therefore paramount. In this chapter, we therefore describe and reflect on a two-year project which aimed to develop and assess social interaction and understanding groups for children and adolescents with ASD. The design, implementation, and outcomes of the project are discussed, together with reflections from practical experience on the running of such groups.

Social Interaction in ASD

In very young children with ASD, interaction with a caregiver is particularly impaired in the social behaviors which are the keystones for all later social and communicative skills: collectively joint attention. These difficulties are shown by lack of mutual eye-gaze, pointing, and requesting (Charman, 1997) and a lack of enjoyment of early social games. In early childhood, children with ASD show less interest in other children and often fail to imitate others' movements, to play cooperatively with one or a group of children, to follow simple rule-based games, or to play imaginatively (Stone & Lemanek, 1990). In older children, while interaction with adults may improve, there remain gross difficulties in play with peers. In particular, there is a marked lack of cooperative play, little reciprocity, and a tendency to spend much time in solitary or stereotypic play (Howlin, 1986).

Across the lifespan, more able individuals on the autism spectrum, who are the subject of the study reported here, have difficulty using communication appropriately for social purposes, even when functional language is good (Attwood, 1998; Landa, 2000). They may, for instance, not use eye-gaze to monitor conversational turn-taking or may talk in a flat monotonous voice without using pitch and tone to communicate emotions (see McCann, Peppé, Gibbon, O'Hare, & Rutherford, Chapter 11). Conversations often lack reciprocal flow, and individuals with ASD may "monologue" about a favorite subject, without picking up cues from the listener about lack of comprehension, boredom, or the inappropriateness of their comments. They also have difficulty with peer interaction, but with age are often acutely aware of the difficulties they experience in making and sustaining friendships.

The consequences of these impairments are far-reaching. In adulthood, high-functioning individuals with ASD are less likely than their typically developing counterparts to live independently away from home, to marry or have friendships, to complete college courses or to work independently (Howlin, Goode, Hutton, & Rutter, 2004). Mood disorders such as anxiety and depression are common (Green, Gilchrist, Burton, & Cox, 2000; Stewart, Barnard, Pearson, Hasan, & O'Brien, 2006), and this may relate to their ability to understand accurately their social difficulties (Capps, Sigman, & Yirmiya, 1995).

Interventions for Social Impairments in ASD

Social skills training has often been used for children with ASD (for review see Rogers, 2000). However, most studies report difficulties with the generalization of skills from those learned in one setting to other areas of the individual's life. This was particularly true of early approaches which focused on the teaching of "splinter skills" (Howlin, 1998), such as the use of appropriate positive and negative assertions during games to facilitate peer interaction (McGee, Krantz, & McClannahan, 1984). As one of the key features of autism is a difficulty understanding and generalizing, teaching splinter skills without considering the need to facilitate generalization may be of value only within a restricted set of circumstances.

Other approaches to social intervention have taken a more theoretical perspective, attempting to address directly the difficulties relating to the psychological underpinnings of ASD, as opposed to the acquisition of new behaviors per se. These have included, for example, interventions drawing on a theory of mind model, designed to enhance children's perspective-taking skills (McGregor, Whiten, & Blackburn, 1998; Swettenham, Baron-Cohen, Gómez, & Walsh, 1996), and those drawing on a systematizing-empathizing model to teach understanding of emotions (see Golan & Baron-Cohen, Chapter 12). Again, maximizing generalization of acquired skills can be a source of difficulty within such interventions (see Jones & Jordan, Chapter 14). Other interventions drawing on theories of autism have been aimed at teaching developmentally earlier social and communication skills, such as eye-gaze and joint attention. In a review of 16 such intervention studies, Hwang and Hughes (2000) reported that teaching these skills, using a variety of behavioral approaches, led to increases in these social behaviors, but with limited generalization.

Another approach to intervention involves the use of non-socially impaired peers or siblings as skill trainers, usually in naturalistic settings, focusing on the key area of impaired peer relationships. These studies tend to be based on sound behavioral principles and to utilize rigorous single-case methodology. A long history of work in this area has demonstrated that the use of peer trainers yields considerable benefit to children with autism (e.g., Celiberti & Harris, 1993; Kamps et al., 2002). In general, there are increases in positive social behavior when peers are trained to initiate and reinforce social interaction, but there are ongoing difficulties with the generalization of skills, which tend to revert back to baseline at the end of the intervention. Using several peer trainers in naturalistic settings with opportunities to practice skills in novel settings, however, appears to aid generalization (Kamps et al., 2002).

A method of enhancing social skills of most relevance to the study reported here concerns the use of social skills groups. Group work is used particularly when individuals are relatively able and have good verbal language skills, such as those who have a diagnosis of Asperger syndrome or who attend mainstream schools. However, while group work may have clinical validity, there is currently only a small evidence base demonstrating the utility of such an approach (Attwood, 2000).

Groups which run for a considerable time (e.g., Howlin & Yates, 1999) report improvement in participants' skills levels. Williams (1989) described a four-year project in which 10 children participated weekly for varying lengths of time. The mixed format included role play, games, and modeling. Outcomes were generally favorable in areas such as initiating conversation with staff and use of facial expression, but perhaps more importantly, the children themselves reported that they had made friends during the group. Short-term groups lasting only a matter of weeks tend to find negligible change in skills, but are nevertheless reported to be useful by participants and their families (Marriage, Gordon, & Brand, 1995; Mesibov, 1984). However, a more recent short-term group (Webb, Miller, Pierce, Strawser, & Jones, 2004) demonstrated that high-functioning adolescents with ASD made significant gains in five targeted social skills over a 10-week period.

Although there is evidence for the benefits of social skills groups, there are a number of problems with existing studies. First, until recently, as described above, few social skills interventions have been based on a theoretical understanding of the mechanisms underpinning ASD but instead focused on the splinter skills. Good understanding of the theoretical underpinnings of ASD will be a key factor in developing effective interventions (Attwood, 2000; but see also Jones & Jordan, Chapter 14). The recent shift in the focus of interventions from the teaching of splinter skills to teaching skills that take account of more fundamental deficits and their psychological bases is a welcome development. Second, most interventions suffer from a lack of generalization of skills from the intervention setting to the day-to-day environment. For instance, Barry et al. (2003) found that children were able to develop skills such as appropriate play in a clinic setting but were reported by parents not to use them outside this setting. In their review, Hwang and Hughes (2000) argue cogently that social interaction skills cannot be successfully developed in isolation from daily life.

A third limitation is that few existing studies use a control group to examine the effects of intervention systematically, though there is a small number of exceptions such as Solomon, Goodlin-Jones, and Anders (2004), who used a wait-list control to examine a social adjustment enhancement curriculum. Furthermore, most studies are based on small numbers of participants (e.g., Marriage et al., 1995; Timmler, Olswang, & Coggins, 2005). Lack of a control group is particularly important when sample sizes are small or if the intervention lasts a long time. As Williams (1989) points out, although his study produced improvements in some areas, the children were involved for considerable periods of time, and change could have resulted from maturation or other educational methods being used at the same time. Finally, the assessment measures used are another source of concern. Research can be undermined if the pre- and post-intervention measures are not appropriate (Greenway, 2000) or are lacking in rigor. Parent- and self-reports can add to the broader picture of intervention effects, but there is a danger that these will be subject to the effects of social desirability (see Jones & Jordan, Chapter 14, for a further discussion of the issues surrounding the use of assessment measures in intervention research).

The Social Interaction and Understanding Study

Addressing limitations of previous research

The methodology adopted in the social interaction and understanding study (Dunlop, Knott, & MacKay, 2002) sought to address the principal criticisms made of previous research. In terms of the content of the intervention, the focus was on social interaction and understanding, with a significant focus on the latter rather than on individual social skills. A sound theoretical knowledge base informed not only the intervention but also the assessment strategies devised to support it. Knowledge of the mindblindness and empathizing theories of autism (e.g., Baron-Cohen et al., 2005), for instance, highlights the need to examine what the children understood about others' perspectives, how they obtained this information, and how they responded to it. Similarly, understanding the implications of weak central coherence (e.g., Happé, 2005) meant that the focus on social understanding as a way of assisting generalization of skills was paramount. Teaching therefore focused on "how" to think about interaction, rather than simply instructing the participants in what to do. Furthermore, formal assessment measures were sufficiently robust to allow quantitative data analysis and comparison with standardization data drawn from a normative population. Confidence in the outcome measures obtained was further enhanced by the assessment process, in which neither of the first two authors, who were running the groups and in one case also clinically involved with the sample, was responsible for gathering the data for evaluation. This was undertaken by the third author, who had no direct involvement with the "helping process," thus reducing the "social desirability" factor.

The size of the sample was also a significant strength of this study. The small number of existing studies in this area have been based on groups with very few participants, usually in single figures. Indeed, the 16 studies cited by Hwang and Hughes (2000) in their more general review of social interaction training in autism had a total combined sample size of only 64. By comparison, this was a large sample for a single study, with reliable pre–post data for 32 of the participants. This greatly increased the weight that can be given to the consistent findings obtained.

Perhaps the most difficult criticism to address in work in the area of ASD is the lack of generalization of skills from the intervention setting to everyday life. In the current study, a number of steps were taken to assist this process. First, attention was paid to the development of broad social understanding rather than to splinter skills throughout all the activities. Secondly, parents were seen as key players in encouraging the practice of skills outside the group. Basing group themes on areas of concern raised by parents aimed to increase their motivation to work with their children; furthermore, groups were structured such that parents and team members had weekly opportunities for mutual feedback.

Profile of sample

The participants in this study were recruited from 51 children and young people of the appropriate age known to education or health services. All had a diagnosis of ASD or were awaiting confirmation of that diagnosis. Diagnoses were made by specialist multidisciplinary teams or, in those areas where a team was not available, by experienced professionals with responsibility for ASD diagnosis. All but one of the participants attended mainstream schools. Of this group, 46 attended one of six groups with up to eight participants in each. Allocation to groups was determined by age, by geographical location, and by availability at different times over the course of 20 months of group meetings. Ages ranged from 6 to 11 years in the primary groups, and from 12 to 16 years in the secondary groups. Of the participants, 39 were boys and 7 were girls, giving a ratio of approximately 5:1, in line with general expectations for an able group of this kind (Ehlers & Gillberg, 1993). For inclusion in the evaluation, a cutoff point of attendance at a minimum of 50% of sessions was used. This criterion was met by 38 participants, with most attending all or almost all the sessions.

The Vineland Adaptive Behavior Scales (VABS), Survey Form was used to provide an overall assessment profile of the participants prior to the intervention (Sparrow, Balla, & Cicchetti, 1984). A representative sample (in terms of age) of 50% (N = 23) of those attending the groups was assessed individually, with parents as informants. This clearly demonstrated two features of this group. First, when compared with the overall population with autism (Carter et al., 1998), their scores for adaptive behavior confirmed that, as a predominantly Asperger group, they were at the high-functioning end of the autism spectrum. Their average percentile rank was 80, with 43% scoring at or above the 90th percentile. However, when compared with the general population, the extent of impairments present in this group became apparent. Only three had scores above the first percentile, while 48% were at or below percentile level 0.1. The scores for each of the separate domains—communication, daily living skills, socialization, and motor skills—all highlighted the key impairments in this high-functioning group. As might be expected, the scores on socialization were lowest. Motor impairments, most commonly in the gross motor areas such as hopping and running, were also clearly apparent in most of the sample.

Assessment measures

Three procedures were adopted: the Spence Social Skills and Social Competence Questionnaires (Spence, 1995), individual parent ratings, and follow-up interviews.

The Spence Questionnaires were completed by parents, and also by participants where possible, prior to the start of the intervention and after its completion. These questionnaires comprise a series of statements that assess whether particular skills and competences are fully, partly, or not at all established. The Social Skills Questionnaire evaluates the core skills needed to engage in social interactions such as eye-gaze and the ability to make requests appropriately (Spence, 2003), while the Social Competence Questionnaire measures the outcome of such skills, such as ease of making friends. The information gathered can be used qualitatively and quantitatively. Good standardization data are provided, and alpha coefficients for reliability range from 0.75 for the Social Competence (Pupils) Questionnaire to 0.91 for the Social Skills (Parents) Questionnaire (Spence, 1995).

The individual parent ratings involved a novel procedure, the "three things" measure, which was individualized to each participant. All parents were asked to identify three key social skill areas which represented a particular difficulty for their child. This then became a specific focus for intervention during the group work. Ratings were made on an 11-point Likert scale (Oppenheim, 1992) for the same three items before and after the intervention.

At the end of the intervention, follow-up interviews were held with the parents of all participants. These semi-structured interviews provided qualitative commentary on the parents' perceptions of their child's experience of the groups, and whether or not they felt that progress in social interaction skills had been made. Parents were also asked at this stage for qualitative comments in relation to progress with the "three things."

The intervention

The intervention was designed to assist in the development of skills in social interaction and understanding, and consisted of six groups of up to eight children. Groups met weekly, the first two groups (one primary and one secondary) for 12 weeks and the remaining four for 16 weeks. Groups were staffed by a mix of professionals with ASD experience, including teachers, clinical psychologists, nurses, and student volunteers. The social skills themes explored within the intervention sessions were derived from pre-group assessment, in particular the "three things to change" and thus varied from group to group. The process by which themes were developed and operationalized is described later in this chapter.

As with the themes, the structure and content of the sessions varied from group to group, depending on the needs and strengths of the participants as well as our understanding of the theoretical underpinnings of ASD. A variety of activities were used to develop and practice skills, including small and large group discussion, stories, activity sheets, role play, and games. Free time was always included via a snack break or "choice time." Some children, notably those who had prior experience of speech and language therapist-led groups, were quickly able to take responsibility for designing the program and producing a relevant visual timetable. Identifying individual interests which could contribute to a common theme (e.g., for a puppet play or a photographic exhibition) became a useful mechanism to develop skills such as negotiation, listening, and perspective taking. Other children, especially those who had only recently received a diagnosis of ASD, on the other hand, needed a clearly structured program to allow them to understand and predict what was to happen each week. Small group work based around the theme for the week was followed by collaborative activities such as group games, or arts and crafts activities for the older children. These provided opportunities to practice skills such as emotion recognition or eye contact in a less structured setting.

Results

Social Skills and Social Competence Questionnaires

Correctly completed pre- and post-questionnaires were returned by parents for 24 of the 38 participants in the final sample. Of the participants themselves, 19 were able to complete a pre–post Social Skills Questionnaire, while 21 completed the Social Competence Questionnaire. In terms of pre-test scores, the results of all four questionnaires confirmed the social impairments in this group. There were significant differences in the estimations of skills provided by parents and their children, with the latter reporting fewer difficulties in social interactions. Nonetheless, participants still reported their scores to be at least one standard deviation below the norm (Knott, MacKay, & Dunlop, 2006). Following the intervention, significantly higher scores were obtained on all four questionnaires.

Although the groups were short-term (12–16 weeks), it was recognized that developmental changes might have taken place over that period, and that it would be necessary to show that these improvements did not reflect the effects of increased age and developmental maturity. Two factors are of relevance here. First, the standardization data for all four questionnaires showed no significant differences in scores across the age range (Spence, 1995). Second, for the sample in this study, when the parents' pre-test data were analyzed, social skills and social competence scores were found not to vary systematically on the basis of the child's age.

Also, there was no systematic relationship between the pre–post test gains and the child's adaptive behavior levels as measured by the VABS.

Individual parent ratings (the "three things")

Pre–post parent ratings were available for 31 participants whose parents were able to generate three key social skill areas to be addressed for their child, and to provide numerical ratings on these items before and after the intervention. The items selected by the parents were recurrent, and taken together they almost present a clinical description of Asperger syndrome. The main areas raised in order of frequency were: ability to initiate, maintain, and finish a conversation appropriately; showing an interest in other people's interests, rather than going on repetitively about one's own interests; turn-taking skills, rather than being unable to wait or constantly butting in; refraining from making embarrassingly frank or inappropriate statements about people; ability to mix appropriately with a group. Other recurrent but less frequently occurring items related to overreacting, not observing personal space, volume or tone of voice, and reading the body language of others. This part of the assessment produced the most significant—sometimes dramatic—results. Of the 93 items generated, 65% were reported to have improved, often to a notable degree.

Follow-up interviews

Of the 38 participants, the parents of 31 contributed to the follow-up interviews at the end of the intervention. Many reported specific and substantial gains which they attributed directly to the group work. The consistent message was that the intervention had been helpful, that the most helpful aspect was addressing the "three things," that skills taught in the groups had generalized into relevant, real-life situations, and that observable change had taken place. Individual comments repeatedly confirmed that the outcomes were meaningful in terms of real change: "He listens more to what's going on in general conversation. It has been a big surprise to us. He's more interested in what other people have to say now." "Before he would have been distraught and throwing books around. Now he is saying, 'I need help with this.'" For one parent the main outcome was: "Not coming home from school desperately upset."

The Capacity of Group Work to Support the Development of Effective Social Interaction and Understanding

This study demonstrated significant gains in social interaction and understanding following the intervention program. This was clearly shown on all of the assessment measures used. On each of the questionnaires both parents and participants reported significantly enhanced levels of functioning for both social skills and social competence. Changes in individual parent ratings supported these findings, which were further confirmed in the semi-structured follow-up interviews. A key feature of this study was that it not only developed effective intervention strategies at a practical level, but also adopted a robust, research-based model underpinned by theoretical understanding of autism spectrum disorders and supported by statistical analysis using formal assessment measures. It was therefore successful both in the development of practical applications for enhancing social interaction and in contributing to the currently small evidence base in this field of study.

These successes notwithstanding, there are a number of limitations of the study. The most pressing is the lack of a control group. In fact, attempts were made to run a wait-list control, but practical and ethical reasons prevented this. Therefore, we cannot be sure that the effects we observed were directly attributable to the group. Furthermore, although the researcher who carried out the interviews did not take part in the groups themselves, social desirability might still have played a part. Triangulating the evidence by including reports from teachers would have improved our assessment of the effectiveness of the group, as would long-term follow-up of participants. Finally, given that one of the key strengths of the work was that it was individualized to group members, it is not easy to compare groups or to evaluate which aspects of the group work were responsible for change. Indeed, it is difficult even to evaluate which children this type of approach is most suited to, although the participants were nearly all those of a suitable age known to health and education in a particular geographical area.

Running Social Interaction and Understanding Groups: Reflections From Practical Experience

In the next section of this chapter, reflections on a number of the practical aspects of the project are presented. In particular, we explore the areas that we felt contributed most highly to the success of the groups: developing cogent and coherent themes, involving parents, and encouraging generalization.

Table 13.1 Sample parent reports of the "three things"

Stephie*

1 To be able to have an appropriate conversation without reference to fantasy figures as if they were real (2)

2 Accepting other people's views if they are different from your own (and without extreme reactions) (2)

3 Giving appropriate responses to questions (especially if the question is seen as being in any way threatening—like being asked who it was that did something) (3)

Davie

1 To be able to mix with children in his own age group (no friends; no one calls, no one phones) (2)

2 Not to speak inappropriately about others (e.g., using vulgar terms inappropriately to describe girls) (0)

3 To show an interest in other people's interests and not just to talk about his own all the time (0)

Oskar

1 To have confidence to initiate a conversation with peers and not just wait till others speak to him (0)

2 To develop the skill of taking an interest in other people's interests (2)

3 Not to say things inappropriately (like asking people straight off how old they are) (2)

Danny

1 To be more forthcoming (e.g. "with Mum"– described as "well beyond the unforthcomingness of other teenagers") (2.5)

2 To show an interest in other people's interests and not just his own (3)

3 To be able to understand other people's emotions—"he's blinkered" (2)

Jack

1 To answer questions appropriately (e.g., he answers adults in authority, like teachers, in inappropriate ways) (3)

2 To have awareness of other people's feelings and not just his own (3)

3 To learn how not to be over-influenced/set up by his peers (2.5)

Notes: Numbers in parentheses indicate baseline rating given by parents on an 11-point Likert scale where 0 = skill effectively not present, 5 = average for age, 10 = skill developed to highest level.

* Pseudonyms are used throughout.

Moving from assessment to themes for the groups

Information about participants' interests, social skills and social competence, and social learning priorities were collected through interviews with parents and participants, which along with the standardized measures and the "three things" provided ample information from which to devise appropriate starting points with the group (Knott & Dunlop, 2003, 2006). As outlined earlier, this latter approach involved asking families to identify three things that they would like to be achieved through group participation. The skills chosen need to be clearly defined, realistic for a short-term group, and related to the arena of social interaction skills. For instance, a target of "making a friend" is too broad to act as a focus for work. It is also more than likely to fail, as there are no guarantees that even with better skills participants will meet others with whom they desire to become friends. Shaping a realistic target of "coping better with losing during a board game" is clearly within the same arena and is a key skill which will ultimately aid achievement of the wider aim. By working on elements where parents were motivated toward a good outcome, we hoped to increase the commitment to sharing in the activities their children would bring home and to practicing skills in day-to-day situations. Table 13.1 provides a sample of responses to the "three things" measure for one of the older groups.

The priorities given to us by parents in the "three things" measure led to three distinct themes in group work to enhance social interaction and understanding: these were social and emotional perspective taking, conversation skills, and friendship skills. Subsequently, the materials generated by the project were based on these three areas: they provide a bank of flexible resources which have been informally piloted with a range of different groups. Feedback confirms the importance of these areas of work in the effort to increase the understanding of social interaction that remains so elusive for people with ASD.

Social and emotional perspective taking

Focusing on the processes that would allow the children to participate in the group was the starting point for theme one. Noticing and interpreting cues to others' thoughts and feelings, as well as being able to recognize and describe their own, contributed to engagement in both conversation and group activities. Social and emotional perspective-taking activities such as detecting feelings through personal experience, researching the feelings of others in the group and at home, and carrying out social problem-solving activities enabled the group to begin to manage conversations better, to give and listen to information and opinions of others, and to negotiate with each other in play situations.

Example: In one of the primary groups, Rick took part in making paper plate faces for the puppet characters. He had been very active in thinking about the story line in the play: he decided it should be a journey through time, with a central character called Tragic Magic. The planning session led to a discussion of how the characters might feel as the events of the plot unfolded. Rick displayed great excitement about the sequence of events, and drew a picture to illustrate this; but his puppet character's face was without any expression, and he found it very hard to relate to how Tragic Magic might feel as his precious time machine disappeared. He was encouraged to try out different voices, and was then able to decide that Tragic Magic would feel angry. On the day of the puppet play Rick took the role of three different characters and varied their moods successfully.

Conversation skills

The need to foster and develop conversation skills was paramount and developed accordingly into theme two. In one of the secondary groups, roleplay was a useful mechanism to work on the aspects of conversation skills which participants had determined were important (eye contact, facial expression, posture, distance, choice of words). Role plays centered on activities commonly experienced by teenagers, such as buying candy or returning damaged clothes to a shop. The older group also chose to practice job interviews and saying "no" to drugs.

Example: Nancy had great difficulty joining in ordinary conversations, usually choosing to monopolize a member of staff in any free time. However, she roleplayed a job interview with great care, and through this structured medium, took on board suggestions about eye contact and the speed at which she talked. By the end of the intervention, Nancy was observed talking for short periods to some of the group members as well as staff.

Friendship skills

Difficulties with friendships and peer relationships were mentioned by nearly all of the families, and relevant activities were therefore collated into a third theme. The "Social Code Breaker" (a set of social problem-solving tools developed for the project) was used to aid young people in one of the groups determine what was happening in complex social interactions. Two of the older group members, for instance, wished to think about opposite sex relationships, and used the Code Breaker to think about situations such as working out if a girl likes you, what to do if someone likes you but you do not like them, and how to deal with rejection.

Example: Despite assurances from his mother that Gavin had never had a girl-friend (and indeed never went out at night except with his family), Gavin used the Social Code Breaker to talk about social relationships in a way that was very insightful. Relating his answers to his "prior experience" of relationships, we believed, allowed him to try out his ideas in a safe venue while preserving his self-esteem. Most interestingly, he was able to engage his friend Derek in this task when Derek would not talk directly to adults about this subject.

Encouraging parental involvement

The importance of collaborating with parents in interventions is indisputable (e.g., Marcus, Kunce, & Schopler, 2005). In the social interaction and understanding study, parental contact was achieved in three ways. Initial assessment allowed parents' own goals for their children to be incorporated into group work, thereby, we hoped, increasing their motivation to participate as well as identifying the most relevant targets for their children. Contact was maintained through face-to-face time at the start and finish of each meeting and through the planned home activities. A folder system was used to record information about the session as well as keep all the activity sheets that the children had completed. This was particularly helpful if families were unable to attend, but also enabled all children and their parents to think about the themes covered that week. At the end of each session, feedback was sought on the practice tasks, and new ones were explained before the families left each day. The young people in the older groups either came to the group independently, worked toward that during the project, or came by taxi. Where children and young people came by taxi, the folder system played an important part in maintaining contact, as did the telephone. Feedback to parents in these groups was done on a one-to-one basis with the project staff and, toward the end of the project, increasingly by the young people themselves.

The Challenge of Generalization to Everyday Life

It is possible to develop skills, and indeed a logical and abstract understanding, for example, of how friendships form, and still leave the individual with ASD with profound difficulties in putting this knowledge into practice in everyday life (Green et al., 2000). Acknowledging that the teaching of social skills risks becoming a context-specific exercise brings an obligation to work from the interests of participants and the priorities for change offered by the parents (and sometimes the participants themselves). A recent review of approaches to autism also concluded that, where possible, a gradual reduction of structure and an increasing focus on teaching understanding, reflection, and internal cognitive control of skills needs to be developed for individuals with ASD so that they can benefit from inclusion by generalizing beyond the immediate environment of the group (Marwick, Dunlop, & MacKay, 2005).

The results of this study suggested that the systematic steps taken to ensure the generalization of skills were largely successful. Both the quantitative measures and the feedback from parents indicated that the skills being taught in the group sessions had not been developed in isolation from the day-to-day environment but were being used within the home and the community. However, it was clear that the role of parents in encouraging practice and reflection in the time between groups was vital. For some children, especially those who traveled by taxi and whose parents thus did not participate in the weekly feedback, home activity sheets tended not to be completed, and it was harder to develop social understanding by building from one week to the next.

Choice, Ownership, Imagination, and Flexibility

Participants feel a greater sense of belonging to a group when they see their interests responded to and their own ideas absorbed into the program for the group as a whole. Increased confidence that they can affect what goes on can lead to being able to make genuine choices. It is likely that older group participants may not be experiencing the sort of independence that they see their peers enjoying: supporting and developing their ideas and interests is an important step toward a greater sense of autonomy and effectiveness. For this reason we aimed to involve participants as far as possible in the day-to-day planning of the groups. In one of the secondary groups the chance to plan the group activities resulted in a rush to arrive first: very quickly, however, others in the group insisted on negotiation of the day's agenda. This in itself highlights the importance of activities being relevant to the day-to-day interests of members of the group.

The Importance of Adult Team Skills

One of the more informal outcomes of the project was reflection on the qualities needed by team members if they were to work successfully with people with ASD. The generalization of skills is less likely if the group ethos is very hierarchical. The adults in our teams took a very active part in all activities: a blurring of status and the feeling of equal participation was especially important in the teenage groups.

At the same time we needed to find appropriate ways of offering praise and encouragement. Direct praise can be hard for some individuals on the spectrum to cope with, and so tackling what makes people feel good about themselves may be an important part of such group work. Understanding that individuals may vary in the approaches to which they respond best helps team members to tune the timing of responses, consider best seating arrangements, give a little advance notice of a change of activity, or write down what will happen next, so as to support each member of the group to feel and be included.

Conclusions: The Development of Social Interaction With Understanding

In some ways, teaching of social interaction skills has face validity. The underpinning principles are already generally recognized. In general, teaching is the foundation of a great deal of learning, and, in relation to autism, structured educational approaches have long been established as the most effective intervention (Jordan & Powell, 1995). The focus of this research has therefore been to demonstrate specifically that social interaction skills, leading to understanding, can effectively be developed within a specific group—children and young people with ASD. This research did not consider the development of social interaction skills at one-to-one level. There are many situations in schools where one-to-one will be the main form of additional support available to a particular child or young person, and the materials developed for this program will be of value in these circumstances.

The short-term value of developing social interaction skills as demonstrated by this study provides a basis, as with intervention in general, for longer-term approaches. Therefore, it is recognized that the development of social interaction skills should be built in methodically to the curriculum for all children and young people with ASD, and it is hoped that the materials produced as a result of this project provide an effective resource for longer-term approaches.

Integration Section

This chapter opened by recognizing that social impairments lie at the heart of autism and are considered to be the primary deficit (Fein et al., 1986). If that is indeed the case, then social impairments are also central to a view of autism that integrates neurocognitive, clinical/diagnostic, and social-educational perspectives. Social-educational interventions must be thoroughly grounded in psychological theories of autism, and these theories in turn must articulate fully with neuro-biological models.

Wicker (Chapter 2) has highlighted anomalies that point to early structural and functional abnormalities of the "social brain." These anomalies are found in the network of areas associated with socio-emotional processing, and include the amygdala, the orbitofrontal cortex, the temporal poles, and the superior temporal sulcus. Neurobiological models have been proposed on the basis of many aspects of brain structure and functioning, leading to difficulties in social processing, impairments in theory of mind, and in language and social skills.

Neurobiological models such as these inform, and in turn are informed by, psychological theories. It is crucial that any intervention aimed at enhancing social function should reflect the key insights arising from the theoretical frameworks discussed throughout this book—theory of mind, as discussed in the studies by Golan and Baron-Cohen on emotion recognition and mental state recognition (Chapter 12), central coherence theory as discussed by López (Chapter 6) and Ropar, Mitchell, and Sheppard (Chapter 7), executive function as discussed by Hill (Chapter 8) and affective theories as discussed by Wicker in his insights arising from neuroimaging of the emotional brain in autism (Chapter 2).

Golan and Baron-Cohen (Chapter 12) have reviewed the emotion recognition and mental state recognition difficulties that underlie the social impairments in the autism spectrum. In contrast with these difficulties, those with ASD show good skills in systemizing: that is, in the drive to analyze or build systems and to understand rules and regularities. They are attentive to detail and prefer predict-able and rule-based environments (Baron-Cohen, 2003). This combination of specific difficulties and strengths has clear implications for interventions in social interaction and understanding. It is important on the one hand to design inter-ventions that address the theory of mind difficulties of recognizing the emotions and mental states of others. On the other hand, good systemizing skills can be used to compensate for these difficulties by helping to build systems that foster a better understanding of the unpredictable world of social interaction.

This study, in highlighting what the children understood about others' perspec-tives, sought to promote social understanding rather than isolated social skills. Activities such as reflecting on feelings through personal experience, researching the emotions of others, and engaging in social problem solving helped the par-ticipants in the key area of social and emotional perspective taking. The study focused on the difficulties the participants experience in recognizing feeling and mental states in others. However, it also built on the strengths of the participants in relation to rules and systems. For example, the use of the "Social Code Breaker" allowed the systematic application of problem-solving tools to help to understand what was happening in the complex social environment.

López (Chapter 6) and Ropar et al. (Chapter 7) discuss developments in central coherence theory since its early conception. It is generally recognized that individuals with ASD show weak central coherence in the processing of both visual and verbal information, while often being superior to controls in tasks that involve scanning for details, such as the Embedded Figures Test. Ropar et al. approach the issue of central coherence by focusing on weaknesses in conceptual as opposed to perceptual processing in autism (see Plaisted, 2001). López proposes that only tasks that require a higher level of integration, with the requirement to establish relationships that link all, and not just some, of the elements in the information to be processed would present a problem for those with ASD.

Weaknesses in central coherence were emphasized in this study as a significant element in the difficulties people with ASD have in the generalization of skills from one context to another. This has been noted as a consistent feature across most studies. While isolated social skills can be learnt in one situation, they do not transfer well to dealing with the same social scenario in a new setting, or to a slightly different scenario arising in the same setting. Rules and skills are learned in a rigid way, but without the ability to integrate them coherently into a wider conceptual framework. Again the focus on conceptual understanding was central to this study. The emphasis was on how to think about social interaction, rather than simply acquiring a number of specific skills. This is clearly a complex area and one that requires considerable further study in terms of both the theoretical mechanisms that govern it and the most effective ways of addressing it to foster generalization.

Executive function anomalies are likely to affect both abilities in social interaction and also the generalization of appropriate social behavior from one context to another. Hill (Chapter 8) discusses executive function in relation to its main elements and its neuroanatomical correlates. Difficulties with the initiation and monitoring of action, lack of cognitive flexibility, and weaknesses in inhibition and impulse control lead to inappropriate social responses, while difficulties with generativity have implications for carrying out previously learned responses where changed circumstances occur.

The impact of executive function difficulties was apparent in the items generated by parents in this study for the "three things," with many items reflecting poor ability to monitor and respond to social information, and lack of inhibition and impulse control in a wide variety of situations, such as in attempts at engaging in appropriate conversation. The intervention was structured to allow these difficulties to be addressed. For example, the management and monitoring of conversations was fostered, together with strategies to generate appropriate social interaction in new contexts through a focus on social understanding.

Finally, the centrality of social and emotional perspective taking in this study touches on a key theme developed by Wicker (Chapter 2) in his discussion of impairments in the biologically based capacity to appreciate the emotional signifi-cance of incoming stimuli. This gives recognition to the place not only of cognitive theories but also of underlying affective impairments in autism and their impact on social development.

Acknowledgments

This study was carried out in collaboration with the National Autistic Society and was funded by the Scottish Executive Education Department under its Special Educational Needs Innovation Grants Programme. When this research was car-ried out, Fiona Knott was at the University of Glasgow.

References

Attwood, T. (1998). *Asperger's syndrome: A guide for parents and professionals*. London: Jes-sica Kingsley.

Attwood, T. (2000). Strategies for improving the social interaction of children with Asperger syndrome. *Autism, 4*, 85–100.

Baron-Cohen, S. (2003). *The essential difference: Men, women and the extreme male brain*. London: Penguin.

Baron-Cohen, S., Wheelwright, S., Lawson, J., Griffin, R., Ashwin, C., Billington, J., et al. (2005). Empathising and systematising in autism spectrum conditions. In F. Volkmar, R. Paul, A. Klin, & D. Cohen (Eds.), *Handbook of autism and pervasive developmental disorders* (3rd ed., pp. 628–639). New York: John Wiley & Sons.

Barry, T., Klinger, L., Lee, J., Palardy, N., Gimore, T., & Bodin, S. (2003). Examining the effectiveness of an outpatient clinic-based social skills group for high-functioning chil-dren with autism. *Journal of Autism and Developmental Disorders, 33*, 685–701.

Capps, L., Sigman, M., & Yirmiya, N. (1995). Self competence and emotional understanding in high functioning children with autism. *Development and Psychopathology, 7*, 137–149.

Carter, A., Volkmar, F., Sparrow, S., Wang, J., Lord, C., Dawson, G., et al. (1998). The Vine-land Adaptive Behaviour Scales: Supplementary norms for individuals with autism. *Journal of Autism and Developmental Disorders, 28*, 287–302.

Celiberti, D., & Harris, S. (1993). Behavioural interventions for siblings of children with autism: A focus on skills to enhance play. *Behaviour Therapy, 24*, 573–599.

Charman, T. (1997). The relationship between joint attention and pretend play in autism. *Development and Psychopathology, 9*, 1–16.

Dunlop, A.-W., Knott, F., & MacKay, T. (2002). *Developing social interaction and under-standing in individuals with autism*. Glasgow: University of Strathclyde and London: The National Autistic Society. [www.strath.ac.uk/autism-ncas]

Ehlers, S., & Gillberg, C. (1993). The epidemiology of Asperger syndrome: A total popula-tion study. *Journal of Child Psychology and Psychiatry, 34*, 1327–1350.

Fein, D., Pennington, B., Markowitz, P., Braverman, M., & Waterhouse, L. (1986). Towards a neuropsychological model of infantile autism: Are the social deficits primary? *Journal of the American Academy of Child Psychiatry, 25*, 198–212.

Green, L., Gilchrist, A., Burton, D., & Cox, A. (2000). Social and psychiatric functioning in adolescents with Asperger syndrome compared with conduct disorder. *Journal of Autism and Developmental Disorders, 30*, 279–293.

Greenway, C. (2000). Autism and Asperger syndrome: Strategies to promote prosocial behaviours. *Educational Psychology in Practice, 16*, 469–486.

Happé, F. (2005). The weak central coherence account of autism. In F. Volkmar, R. Paul, A. Klin, & D. Cohen (Eds.), *Handbook of autism and pervasive developmental disorders* (3rd ed., pp. 640–649). New York: John Wiley & Sons.

Howlin, P. (1986). An overview of social behaviour in autism. In E. Schopler & G. Mesibov (Eds.), *Social behaviour in autism* (pp. 103–131). New York: Plenum Press.

Howlin, P. (1998). Psychological and educational treatments for autism. *Journal of Child Psychology and Psychiatry, 39*, 307–322.

Howlin, P., Goode, S., Hutton, J., & Rutter, M. (2004). Adult outcomes for children with autism. *Journal of Child Psychology and Psychiatry, 45*, 219–229.

Howlin, P., & Yates, P. (1999). The potential effectiveness of a social skills group for adults with autism. *Autism, 3*, 299–307.

Hwang, B., & Hughes, C. (2000). The effects of social interactive training on early social communicative skills of children with autism. *Journal of Autism and Developmental Disorders, 30*, 331–343.

Jordan, R., & Powell, S. (1995). *Understanding and teaching children with autism.* Chichester, UK: John Wiley & Sons.

Kamps, D., Royer, J., Dugan, E., Kravits, T., Gonzalez-Lopez, A., Garcia, J., et al. (2002). Peer training to facilitate social interaction for elementary students with autism and their peers. *Exceptional Children, 68*, 173–187.

Knott, F., & Dunlop, A.-W. (2003). *Developing social interaction and understanding in individuals with Autistic Spectrum Disorders: A resource pack.* Glasgow: University of Strathclyde; London: The National Autistic Society.

Knott, F., & Dunlop, A.-W. (2006). *Developing social interaction and understanding in individuals with autistic spectrum disorders: A resource pack* (2nd ed.). London: The National Autistic Society.

Knott, F., MacKay, T., & Dunlop, A.-W. (2006). Living with ASD: How do children and their parents assess their difficulties with social interaction and understanding? *Autism, 10*, 603–611.

Landa, R. (2000). Social language use in Asperger syndrome and high-functioning autism. In A. Klin, F Volkmar, & S. Sparrow (Eds.), *Asperger syndrome* (pp. 125–155). New York: Guilford Press.

Marcus, L., Kunce, L., & Schopler, E. (2005). Working with families. In F. Volkmar, R. Paul, A. Klin, & D. Cohen (Eds.). *Handbook of autism and pervasive developmental disorders* (3rd ed., pp. 1055–1086). New York: John Wiley & Sons.

Marriage, K., Gordon, V., & Brand, L. (1995). A social skills group for boys with Asperger's syndrome. *Australian and New Zealand Journal of Psychiatry, 29*, 58–62.

Marwick, H., Dunlop, A.-W., & MacKay, T. (2005). *Literature review of autism*. Livingstone: HMIe, available at http://www.hmie.gov.uk/publication.asp

McGee, G., Krantz, P., & McClannahan, L. (1984). Conversational skills for autistic adolescents: Teaching assertiveness in naturalistic settings. *Journal of Autism and Developmental Disorders, 14*, 319–330.

McGregor, E., Whiten, A., & Blackburn, P. (1998). Teaching theory of mind by highlighting intention and illustrating thought: A comparison of their effectiveness with 3-year-olds and autistic individuals. *British Journal of Developmental Psychology, 16*, 281–300.

Mesibov, G. (1984). Social skills training with verbal autistic adolescents and adults: A program model. *Journal of Autism and Developmental Disorders, 14*, 395–402.

Oppenheim, A. (1992). *Questionnaire design, interviewing and attitude measurement*. London: Pinter.

Plaisted, K. (2001). Reduced generalization in autism: An alternative to weak central coherence. In J. Burack, T. Charman, N. Yirmiya, & P. Zelazo (Eds.), *The development of autism: Perspectives from theory and research* (pp. 149–169). Mahwah, NJ: Lawrence Erlbaum Associates.

Rogers, S. (2000). Interventions that facilitate socialization in children with autism. *Journal of Autism and Developmental Disorders, 30*, 399–408.

Solomon, M., Goodlin-Jones, B., & Anders, T. (2004). A social adjustment enhancement intervention for high functioning autism, Asperger's syndrome, and pervasive developmental disorder NOS. *Journal of Autism and Developmental Disorders, 34*, 649–668.

Sparrow, S., Balla, D., & Cicchetti, D. (1984). *The Vineland Adaptive Behaviour Scales*. Circle Pines, MN: American Guidance Service.

Spence, S. (1995). *Social skills training: Enhancing social competence with children and adults*. London: NFER Nelson.

Spence, S. (2003). Social skills training with children and young people: Theory, evidence and practice. *Child and Adult Mental Health, 8*, 84–96.

Stewart, M., Barnard, L., Pearson, J., Hasan, R., & O'Brien, G. (2006). Presentation of depression in autism and Asperger syndrome: A review. *Autism, 10*, 103–116.

Stone, W., & Lemanek, K. (1990). Parental report of social behaviours in autistic preschoolers. *Journal of Autism and Developmental Disorders, 20*, 513–522.

Swettenham, J., Baron-Cohen, S., Gómez, J., & Walsh, S. (1996). What's inside someone's head? Conceiving of the mind as a camera helps children with autism acquire an alternative to a theory of mind. *Cognitive Neuropsychiatry, 1*, 73–88.

Timmler, G., Olswang, L., & Coggins, T. (2005). "Do I know what I need to do?" A social communication intervention for children with complex clinical profiles. *Language Speech and Hearing Services in Schools, 36*, 73–85.

Webb, B., Miller, S., Pierce, T., Strawser, S., & Jones, W. (2004). Effects of social skill instruction for high-functioning adolescents with autism spectrum disorders. *Focus on Autism and Other Developmental Disorders, 19*, 53–62.

Williams, T. (1989). A social skills group for children with autism. *Journal of Autism and Developmental Disorders, 19*, 143–155.

14

Research Base for Intervention in Autism Spectrum Disorders

Glenys Jones and Rita Jordan

Introduction

With the greater understanding of the nature of autism spectrum disorders (ASD) and their effects, derived from the research described in this book, has been a growth in interventions aimed at enhancing learning and development in this group and/or aiming to offer remediation. In this chapter we consider interventions for children with ASD that fall within psychological or educational models, rather than the biological or medical.

The research base for interventions can come from one (or both) of two sources: there may be a research-based rationale for the intervention and/or there may be research evidence of its efficacy. Those that have a research rationale often stem from psychological theories on the nature of ASD. Those that rely on research evidence of effectiveness frequently arise from the application of a broader model of intervention (e.g., interventions deriving from general learning theory). This chapter reflects these two aspects of the relationship between research and intervention. It considers the seminal psychological theories on the nature of ASD in terms of their influence on interventions, and also examines the research evidence for the effectiveness of interventions.

When reflecting on the relationship between research and interventions, it is important to consider the nature of the population. Individuals with ASD have a wide range of intellectual ability, and although they share core behavioral characteristics, the extent to which each is manifested varies across individuals; it is a very heterogeneous group. The medical model on which the diagnostic categories are based is a necessary construction for clinical diagnosis, research, and theory building, but is not the most effective guide for education and treatment (Jordan,

2005b; Volkmar, 1998). However, there is a growing recognition that there are distinct needs common to this group and that individual needs have to be considered within the framework of understanding the nature of ASD (Jordan, 2005a).

The Research Rationale for Interventions

There are seminal theories on the nature of ASD that have influenced the development of interventions and often provide a rationale for them. Here we review several key theories, their origins, and their influence on interventions. In principle, interventions will change as theories are refined. It is interesting to note, however, that some interventions survive even when their rationale has been discredited through discrediting of the theory on which they were based.

Psychogenic theories

These theories are associated with Bettelheim (1967). His views stemmed from erroneous reasoning based on his experience of a concentration camp where he witnessed severely traumatized behavior in the inmates. When he later saw similarly disturbed and disturbing behavior in children with autism, he ascribed the same causation. Clearly these children had not been exposed to the same severe experiences as those in the concentration camp, so, he reasoned, their trauma must have originated in the home, from the emotional neglect of their mothers. This proposition (in spite of a complete lack of direct evidence) chimed with contemporary views of the effects of maternal deprivation (Bowlby, 1969) and became a widely accepted and influential theory, which still has credence in some countries.

The main treatment approach deriving directly from this theoretical position was psychotherapy. Most often this was treatment provided through forms of psychoanalysis (when the child was verbal) or forms of play therapy (when not). Sometimes the child was removed from the home for this therapy as a form of "parentectomy": removing the supposed source of the child's difficulties. Other treatments involved psychotherapy for the parents or therapy for the entire family, but the rationale always stemmed from this psychogenic view of ASD. It was also the origin of the clinical rather than the educational approach to treating children with ASD. A further treatment sharing this rationale was Holding Therapy (Welch, 1988), whereby the "bonding" between the child and his/her mother was forced in a prolonged session of provoking and forcefully holding a child through an emotional outburst, until the moment of "resolution" when the child was thought to establish a bond with the holder.

The demise of the theory (at least in the scientific community) came about through the overwhelming evidence that ASD was a biological disorder (Bauman & Kemper, 1994; Gillberg & Coleman, 2000; Rimland, 1964; Rutter, 1968) with a largely genetic base. The growth of cognitive research in the 1970s and 1980s also contributed to this demise, offering more coherent and scientifically verifiable theories on the nature of ASD (Jordan, 1999a). On the treatment front, educational interventions were developed in which parents were seen as co-therapists (part of the solution rather than the problem) and which showed that children with ASD could learn if they were given structured teaching matched to their abilities (Mesibov, 1997).

Theory of mind and weak central coherence

These cognitive theories proposed that the brain comprises specialized systems for different aspects of functioning. The impairments in ASD were seen as a consequence of the malfunctioning of a particular cognitive module or modules. In the case of the theory of mind (ToM) theory of autism, this was postulated as a deficit or delay in the development of a specialized "ToM" module for processing mental representations (Baron-Cohen, Leslie, & Frith, 1985; Frith, 1989, 2003), leading to difficulties in attributing mental states to oneself and others (see Golan & Baron-Cohen, Chapter 12). The theory of weak central coherence (WCC: Frith, 1989, 1998, 2003; Happé, 1994) proposed that people with ASD had a bias in cognitive style such that details were perceived at the expense of the meaningful whole (for details of recent developments in this field see Happé & Frith, 2006; López, Chapter 6; Ropar, Mitchell, & Sheppard, Chapter 7). Both ToM and WCC theories came from experimental findings and led to a substantial body of further research aiming to consolidate, disconfirm, or refine the theories. The growth of biological investigations and the new technology allowing brain functioning to be visible, provided further opportunities for testing psychological theories, by mapping cognitive processing at the neurological level. It is notable here that a recent MRC report (Medical Research Council, 2001) suggested that the aim of research should be to trace the causal pathways from the brain through to behavior, and that such understanding would be necessary to develop preventative and appropriate interventions. (However, see Leekam & McGregor, Chapter 16, for the need to give greater attention to developmental processes.)

The greatest influence of these theories on treatment has been in the insight they have provided on what might underlie the behavior seen in ASD and the growth of treatments addressing these hypothesized deficits. Programs have been developed to teach individuals with autism ToM understanding, for example (Baron-Cohen, Golan, Wheelwright, & Hill, 2004; Howlin, Baron-Cohen, & Hadwin, 1998;

McGregor, Whiten, & Blackburn, 1998), or a functional alternative to a ToM (Swettenham, Baron-Cohen, Gómez, & Walsh, 1996), and educational approaches have been designed which take account of these cognitive and learning styles. Weak central coherence theory in particular has been influential in recognizing that ASD may be associated with certain strengths in learning as well as weaknesses, and that effective education might take advantage of those strengths. Research findings in this area have also been a counterbalance to interventions directed solely at changing (modifying) behavior, recognizing that typical strategies may not be the best approach for those whose learning and development are atypical.

Computer-assisted learning, especially virtual reality and augmentative reality techniques, have proved valuable for teaching directed at these cognitive constructs (Herrera et al., in press; Parsons, Mitchell, & Leonard, 2005). The biggest influence, however, has been in the area of social skills teaching more broadly, and the growth of tools to teach social understanding such as Social Stories (Gray, 1994b) and Comic Strip Conversations (Gray, 1994a). Extension of the ToM theory by Baron-Cohen (1995) into precursors of ToM understanding has led to the development of tests for early screening (CHAT: Baron-Cohen, Allen, & Gillberg, 1996; M-CHAT: Robins, Fein, Barton, & Green, 2001) and recognition of the importance of early interventions targeting these "missing" skills such as joint attention (Charman et al., 2001); such interventions have links to social and emotional theories as well as to the ToM research.

Research has shown that the problems identified in relation to ToM and WCC are neither unique to those with ASD (they are apparent in other disabilities) nor common throughout the spectrum, although Happé (1994) and Bowler (1992) have both demonstrated that there is often still a difficulty for able people with ASD, in some situations and with more complex processing. It has also been suggested that passing ToM tests might be accomplished by different cognitive routes in ASD (theory rather than intuition), and interventions have followed some of the techniques found successful in research, demonstrating the need for these compensation strategies to achieve success in ToM tasks. Nonetheless, the difficulty with these interventions remains that while it is possible to teach the skills required to pass particular ToM tasks, this may do little to improve "real-life" functioning; the generalization of these skills remains problematic.

Executive functioning

"Executive function" refers to a collection of skills necessary to reach a goal, including inhibition, planning, and impulse control. Experimental evidence of difficulties with a number of aspects of executive functions has been reported in ASD, associated with the frontal lobes in the brain (for an overview, see Hill, 2004). A well-argued and research-supported case for deficits in social agency (an aspect of executive functioning that involves understanding of intentional acts in both the self and others) in ASD is made by Russell (1996), and the notion of agency has clear links with social-emotional theories on the development of a sense of the self and other. Hill (Chapter 8) discusses the current evidence and formulation of executive function theory.

The biggest challenge to the executive function theory of ASD has been its non-specificity to ASD, except in the case of social agency. However, while it may not relate to fundamental causation, this theory has led to useful insights into the difficulties underlying the behavior seen in ASD and the need to take account of these processing difficulties in designing and implementing interventions. This can be seen most clearly in approaches to managing and pre-empting challenging behavior in ASD (Whitaker, 2001), where the need to train alternatives, rather than to necessarily expect behavior inhibition, is recognized. An educational approach which also dovetails with executive function theory is TEACCH (Treatment and Education of Autistic and related Communication handicapped Children) (Schopler, Mesibov, & Hearsey, 1995). This is probably the most widely used intervention in ASD and involves providing individualized structured teaching supports (in the form of visual schedules, cueing of appropriate responses, good work habits, distraction-free work stations) leading to "autism-friendly" prosthetic environments. This kind of structure has clear links to research related to executive function theory, showing the need for "replacement" of internal structures with external ones.

Social/emotional theories

Social and emotional theories are based on an understanding of ASD as representing a failure or difficulty in developing "intersubjectivity" upon which human social, emotional, and, to a large extent, cognitive, development depends (Hobson, 2002; Trevarthen, Aitken, Papoudi, & Robarts, 1996). Although focusing on failure in the initial bonding process, as do psychogenic theories, these theories differ in that they see the problems as originating within the child's difficulty in responding appropriately to the opportunities for social and emotional engagement with caregivers (parents) rather than any rejection by parents. Research-led support has come from studies demonstrating that individuals with ASD do not find social signals as salient as do typically developing individuals (Klin, 1991; Klin, Jones, Schultz, Volkmar, & Cohen, 2002; Jones & Klin, Chapter 4).

It is not necessarily the case that the undoubted growth of interventions designed to develop early social and emotional engagement with others has resulted from the influence of these theories, rather than as a direct response to the problems witnessed in the individuals themselves. Interventions have involved attempts to make social stimuli emotionally salient and engaging (Son Rise: Kaufman, 1994), as well as to slow down and emphasize interaction to make it accessible (Developmental, Individual-Difference, Relationship-based (DIR): Greenspan & Wieder, 1999; Relationship Development Intervention (RDI): Gutstein & Sheely, 2002; More than Words: Sussman, 1999; Frameworks for Communication: Chandler, Christie, Newson, & Prevezer, 2002; Social Communication, Emotional Regulation and Transactional Supports (SCERTS): Prizant, Wetherby, Rubin, Laurent, & Rydell, 2002); Child's Talk: Aldred, Phillips, Pollard, & Adams, 2001). Research has continued to support the validity of social and communicative problems lying at the heart of ASD and the development of interventions addressing these.

Evaluating the Effectiveness of Interventions

Current status of evaluation research

There is still little scientific research on the effectiveness of different interventions in ASD. In the relative absence of such evidence, Rutter (1999) argues that "false claims, mistaken inferences and misleading enthusiasms" (p. 169) have developed. Practitioners, providers, and parents can be overwhelmed by the information available on interventions, and misled by some of the claims. Considerable human, financial, and emotional resources can be expended in exploring and engaging in particular interventions, and the progress and well-being of individuals and families may suffer more than they gain in their pursuit. Outcome research has been conducted on some of the interventions, but the design and methodologies of these studies have often been flawed and the claims overstated (Jordan, Jones, & Murray, 1998).

It is not likely that a single intervention will meet all the needs of an individual or that a particular approach will be appropriate for all kinds of goals or situations. Currently, decisions on interventions in ASD are often based on beliefs, tradition, and assumptions, rather than on research data (Jones, Meldrum, & Newson, 1995; Jordan et al., 1998; Trevarthen et al., 1996; Webster, Webster, & Feiler, 2002). Teachers, for example, may prefer to rely on their experience of using an intervention rather than on reported research findings, which they may not value (Stephenson, 2002). Some interventions make big claims on the basis of small samples or studies with design flaws, and the effects, when replicated, are found to be weaker or not substantiated (Connor, 1998; Freeman, 1997; Jordan et al., 1998; Prizant & Rubin, 1999; Schuler, 2001; Shea, 2004).

The impact of an intervention might also be the result of a placebo effect in some studies in autism, especially when those who carry out the intervention also evaluate it (Lord, 2000). In addition, children with developmental disorders do improve over time, independent of input, and certain factors (such as high cognitive ability and good structural language ability) can outweigh the impact of a particular intervention (Piven, Harper, Palmer, & Amdt, 1996). An uneven and erratic profile of development in ASD also means that there may be dramatic changes that are coincidentally linked to the onset of intervention, and if proper controls are missing, parents, and professionals can then understandably become powerful advocates for that intervention.

Parents also may fight for an intervention as a coping strategy in dealing with their child's disability (Fleischmann, 2005), and indeed many interventions offer a powerful and supportive structure for parents, aside from any direct benefits to the child. Although some interventions demand large commitments of time, finance, and energy on the part of parents, involvement in them does not appear to increase parental stress levels (see Hastings, Chapter 15).

Although the research base for interventions remains incomplete, recent reviews and critiques of evaluation research have led to ideas on more robust methodologies and sampling and on the areas where research needs to be conducted (Bristol et al., 1996; Jordan et al., 1998; Schuler, 2001; Webster et al., 2002).

Difficulties in conducting intervention research in ASD

Measuring progress and outcomes in ASD is not straightforward. Particular difficulties arise because of the heterogeneity of the population, changing diagnostic criteria and practice, the relatively small number of children engaged in a particular intervention, the lack of appropriate standardized measures, problems in assessing children with ASD (see Baker, 1983; Koegel, Koegel, & Smith, 1997), and the fact that individuals may be engaged in more than one intervention simultaneously. There may also be inconsistencies and contradictions in the way that interventions are carried out, with community-based research showing fewer mechanisms for ensuring treatment fidelity and preventing "therapist drift" (Jordan & Powell, 1996). Lovaas (2002) has commented that he would expect his finding of 47% "successful" outcome for his university-based ABA study to fall to 20% for community studies. The knowledge and competence of practitioners also varies and will affect how the approach is implemented. Additionally, interventions may be consciously adapted to better suit the needs of the child.

Deciding on what counts as success, and from whose perspective, is complex. In intervention there is a tension between the concern of parents and practitioners for the effectiveness of the approach with a particular individual in a particular context and that of service planners and theoreticians (and advocates of specific interventions) who are more concerned with issues of the *general* effectiveness of an intervention. General indicators of good scientific research, such as a large sample size, can obscure the details needed to judge the value for the individual. Thus there may be statistical evidence of effectiveness in a large experimental group, relative to controls, but the individual, developmental, or performance change may be small; alternatively, some individuals may have made substantial gains under treatment whereas others have made none or have regressed. Equally, an intervention may be considered broadly ineffective when in fact it has worked very well, but only for a minority. Evaluating interventions, then, is a complex process for which crucial factors are the purpose of the evaluation and those for whom it is intended.

Measurement of intervention-related change is also a complex area. Often easily measured variables are chosen, such as school placement or number of words/symbols used, when others, which are harder to measure, such as emotional well-being or self concept, may be more important to the individual in both the short and the longer term (Dawson, 2004). Rutter (1996) has suggested that outcome measures should concentrate on variables that are significant in the development of ASD (such as social and emotional development) rather than on measures such as IQ, which are more likely to be measuring changes in testability. In addition, most studies look at relatively short-term gains, with few studies on long-term outcomes. Schuler (2001) concluded that there is no proper research base to guide families or others in designing home, school, or community-based interventions.

Intervention research is complicated by the heterogeneity within the spectrum. There is a possibility for under- and over-identification of ASD and individuals may be wrongly assigned to a particular sub-group (Bishop, 1989; Gagnon, Mottron, & Yves, 1997; Kugler, 1998). Diagnostic instruments have only recently been developed with good levels of validity and reliability, so confidence in past research studies is not as high. Researchers need to confirm diagnosis, but this is not always done or reported. Attributing effects only to the nature of the ASD or the intervention is questionable, as many factors will influence progress. Establishing which individuals do well, under which circumstances, and the characteristics of those who do less well, is therefore important.

In addition to the effects of ASD, intellectual disabilities or specific learning difficulties may also be associated with ASD. Intellectual ability is an important prognostic indicator (Howlin, Goode, Hutton, & Rutter, 2004), yet measuring IQ in young children with ASD is problematic. The validity of tests can vary for different age or ability groups. Assessing the skills and abilities of those with ASD is a challenge, due to their difficulties in communication and social understanding (Dawson, 1996; Howlin, 1998b; Parks, 1983). Few assessment instruments are designed for, or standardized on, children with ASD. Most standardized, cognitive tests require the individual to understand verbal instructions and to give a verbal response. Non-verbal tests (e.g., Leiter International Performance Scale—Revised, Roid & Miller, 1997) may require pointing, which may also be problematic.

Where psychometrics are used as a measure of progress, practice effects may skew the results, as these tend to be greater for the non-verbal, the more able child, and for timed tests (Jensen, 1980). Scores on these tests may also reflect the child's "testability" rather than the dimension concerned. Koegel et al. (1997) demonstrated that when standard procedures were modified for children with autism, without altering the essence or ease of the tasks, their chances of success were enhanced.

Another challenge to intervention research is that documents may exist on some interventions, but these vary in terms of the detail given on the rationale, practice, target group, aims, and evaluative data. It is often difficult for practitioners and parents to access and to review this information to aid decision making. Nor is it always clear in research accounts which exact procedures or versions of an intervention are being followed. This is particularly evident in comparison groups, where the non-targeted interventions are often given non-specific and unhelpful descriptions such as "an eclectic curriculum" or an "autism-specific" setting, without any details.

In the UK, it is rare for just one intervention to be followed. Practice is influenced and develops as a result of the experience and expertise of staff, parents, and visiting professionals. This may be the case even in settings that market themselves on the basis of a single approach but then incorporate other interventions as "strategies" or "tactics." Siegel (1999) recommends systematic eclecticism to emphasize different treatment models at different times, in response to the individual's changing needs. This depends on knowing the individual and understanding the rationale and aims of the interventions. Eclectic "packages" need to offer a coherent program. There is a danger of adopting a collection of interventions based on the most recent or most accessible. If practitioners do not fully understand the rationale and principles, they may be unable to adapt and individualize the intervention. This difficulty was highlighted by a parent, in relation to the work done with his son (Lubbock, 2001). When the intervention being used started to fail, the therapists had no suggestions or alternatives to offer.

An additional consideration in intervention research is that there are a number of ethical issues to consider, which include gaining informed consent and the withholding of interventions in randomized, controlled designs. The latter is only ethical where a "good enough" service is being delivered to all, and the intervention is additional. It would also need to be one where the parents and evaluators would somehow not be aware that their children (or the children not be aware themselves) were or were not receiving the intervention, and so there would also need to be a "dummy" intervention of some kind. A "waiting list" model could be used, but such models have proved difficult to operate when parents or services are anxious to start a program (Magiati & Howlin, 2003).

Research evidence on interventions in autism spectrum disorders

A past review of the research evidence on interventions in ASD (Jordan et al., 1998) found that studies were often limited to those conducted by the proponents of the intervention, and the majority did not include a comparison or control group. The studies were therefore open to bias and difficult to interpret. Sample size was often small (20 or fewer), there was a focus on short-term effects, and few identified the characteristics of the children who did best or least well. There were often no details given as to how the diagnoses were confirmed, or of which children were excluded from the study. Other reviews of research into interventions have also concluded that studies suffer from shortcomings in relation to experimental design, participant selection, outcome measures, fidelity of implementation, and the interpretation of results (Freeman, 1997; Prizant & Rubin, 1999; Schuler, 2001; Webster et al., 2002). Furthermore, these limitations are rarely made explicit in published reports of the research.

A review conducted on the diagnostic methods used in 142 research papers published in the *Journal of Autism and Developmental Disorders* between 1993 and 1997 by Waller, Armstrong, McGrath, and Sullivan (1999) found that many studies did not report on how the diagnostic criteria were applied and gave few data on inclusion or exclusion criteria or co-morbidity. They called for improved reporting in this area. There is often a lack of detail about methodology in the studies reviewed (Jordan et al., 1998). It is then difficult for professionals and parents to assess the strength of the claims made and their applicability. However, if the goal is to find out what is best for an individual child, rather than to evaluate an intervention in general (as discussed above), then Jordan (1999b) suggests a range of small-scale individual case study designs that are fit for that purpose. Combining the results of such studies might produce a valuable "bottom-up" approach to the inherent value of interventions.

Other sources of guidance apart from research evidence

Research evidence is only one source of information that a professional or parent might use to decide on how to work with a child. Practical knowledge of the individual and his/her response to previous interventions, ideas from current theories (e.g., on ASD, child development, and learning), previous experience with others and current social and cultural values are important and will all contribute to the decisions made (Prizant & Rubin, 1999). Expert opinion is another source of guidance. Many of the recommendations in the literature are based on what appears to make good sense, by those with experience in the field, rather than on empirical evidence. For example, of the 28 recommendations from a working party convened to investigate practice in ASD in relation to diagnosis and assessment, 25 were based purely on "the expert Working Group advice" (NIASA, 2003, p. 9), and not on research findings. This was also the case in the Department for Education and Skills (DfES) Good Practice Guidance on ASD (Department for Education and Skills, 2002). Very few research studies could be identified to support the recommendations made.

Some people with ASD have developed strong views on particular interventions (Dawson, 2004). Many more are now able to write about their experiences, and many describe the very unhappy and traumatic times they have experienced trying to fit into unadapted mainstream services (Gerland, 1997; Grandin, 1995; Jackson, 2002; Lawson, 1998; Sainsbury, 2000). These are valuable accounts, but the heterogeneity of the spectrum makes it difficult to simply apply the experience and views of one person with an ASD to another. Parents also write accounts extolling the benefits of particular interventions, but, as with the individuals themselves, these views arise from particular, and limited, experiences. It may also be the case that the parents' reactions are to the first attempt to support them, rather than to the intervention itself.

Future Research Directions

Several authors have written on the research priorities in relation to ASD and interventions (Bristol et al., 1996; Freeman, 1997; Howlin, 1998a; Jordan, 1999b; Lord, 2000; Rutter, 1996; Schuler, 2001; Webster et al., 2002). Schuler (2001) suggests that research needs to ascertain the extent to which intervention gains can be predicted by individual characteristics and how much should be attributed to environmental variables such as family involvement, school placement, sibling and peer relationships, resources, and parental beliefs. In addition, the most appropriate research methods need to be explored and used. Given the challenges of conducting research in the real world, those research methods that are likely to yield the strongest data should be employed. Schuler (2001) argues for multiple measures that build on each other, including more qualitative data, which note differences in context and interaction effects (e.g., family characteristics and input; school and center variables), as opposed to those that solely focus on child variables as related to child outcomes.

Parental involvement has been identified as an important variable in the success of interventions, but this is often loosely defined. Details on the nature and extent of parental engagement; the training and support required and offered; and the potential physical and emotional costs (or benefits) of this to the parents and other family members need to be explored (see Hastings, Chapter 15).

Future research also needs to study process as well as outcome. This might focus on how the intervention is implemented, the resource, training, and supervision requirements and processes, and the degree of fit with the existing style and competence of the parents and practitioners. It is necessary to consider the views of all stakeholders, including the individual, in terms of what counts as success, and to identify the factors which promote well-being and competent functioning outside the intervention, and which acknowledge any potential biases in the research team. It is also important, but rarely done, to ask the participants in the research for feedback on the research process. This can add to the knowledge base on the effects of the research process and address or identify any ethical issues.

Researchers also need to work more collaboratively. Some research funders now state a preference for collaborative work across disciplines and/or institutions, which will promote this; but there are still barriers to sharing ideas, samples, and data across the research community. The creation of a database with scores of individuals with ASD at different ages, on commonly used instruments such as the Vineland Adaptive Behavior Scales (Sparrow, Balla, & Cicchetti, 1984), which was available to all researchers, would be extremely useful.

Finally, although there is a body of research on interventions for ASD (often specific named interventions for preschool children), relatively little research has been conducted on education per se (Jordan, 2005a). There are a series of issues unique to education which are relevant to explore: How are different interventions adapted for use within different educational settings? How can interventions in educational settings promote social inclusion? How can the educational experience of children with ASD best be assessed? There will also be unique challenges to researching in this area, not least the fact that since education is very much a cultural activity, it will be far more difficult to generalize findings from one country to another.

Ways Forward for Practice

It is useful to have a framework to highlight key questions for parents, providers, practitioners, and researchers to guide decision making. From a thorough assessment of the child, identifying strengths, weaknesses, interests, communicative competence, personality, learning style, and parental wishes (and capacities), initial decisions can be made on interventions, which then need to be monitored and reviewed. On the basis of the individual's responses to interventions, decisions can be made on whether to amend, alter, or abandon particular interventions.

In the absence of more robust research data and clear and detailed descriptions of the rationale and practice of interventions, it is often necessary for parents and professionals to collect their own information to make informed decisions. Strengths and weaknesses of different interventions need to be considered, rather than just adopting or rejecting an intervention as a total approach (Jordan, 2004). Key areas to consider are the rationale of the intervention and how this fits with current understandings of ASD; clear information on what practitioners and parents are required to do, and whether this fits their philosophy and personal style; information on expected outcomes and the nature of the evidence on these; whether the skills taught are used in other everyday situations; and details on the financial and emotional costs of the intervention. The proponents and practitioners engaged in interventions rarely have answers to all these questions, and some questions can be answered only in relation to a particular individual, the parents, and the social context. It is necessary to know whether parental participation is expected or essential, and what might be offered to parents who are unable to be engaged.

Interventions offered to parents should not greatly alter their parenting style, but evolve from it. Parents can be encouraged to identify aspects of their interactions that are beneficial and develop these, whilst replacing aspects that are less successful. The same is true for professionals. It is also important to ask what the intervention would replace in terms of time and resources, how easy it is to access, whether the same results could be obtained in a less costly manner, and whether the outcomes are worth the emotional and financial costs involved. Ideally, the intervention chosen should be evaluated from the start, to determine its impact. On the basis of the data collected, informed decisions can be made as to whether the intervention should continue.

Professionals working in education, health, and social services need to be encouraged to conduct more research themselves (Webster et al., 2002), rather than merely being the subjects of research designed by others. At the same time, academic researchers have often been distanced from the reality of the classroom, the home setting, and policy making. More staff are engaging in evaluative work, and researchers are collaborating and sharing research methods and data. Case-study approaches and action research methods are being promoted and are likely to provide a better basis for supplying data to practitioners than the results of experimental, clinic-based studies (Webster et al., 2002). With the increasing need for evidence-based practice, it might be possible to collect more data on the effects of interventions in the future.

There have been several reviews of interventions (Bristol et al., 1996; Connor, 1998; Dawson & Osterling, 1997; Freeman, 1997; Harris & Handleman, 1994; Howlin,

1998a; Jordan & Jones, 1996, 1999; Prizant & Rubin, 1999; Rutter, 1996). There is a consensus on the features of interventions that are thought to be effective: early intervention; parental involvement; acknowledging sensory issues; developing joint attention, communication, and social understanding; gaining the individual's perspective; acknowledging differences in attention, perception, and processing; using the individual's special interests; involving typically developing children; adopting a functional approach to behavior; and treating co-morbid conditions such as high anxiety (e.g., obsessive compulsive disorder, phobias) and depression. In the absence of a research base for all of the interventions currently available, these features are likely to prove useful in guiding work with children with ASD.

Conclusions

When considering the research base for interventions in ASD, there may be evidence for the rationale of the intervention or its efficacy, or both. This chapter has explored the issues in gaining such evidence. Exploring the rationale of an intervention requires an examination of the theories and understandings of ASD on which it is based. The influence of the seminal psychological theories of ToM, WCC, executive functioning, and a failure to develop intersubjectivity has been examined. Interventions arising from these theories still need to be evaluated, particularly in terms of whether such teaching has any effect on the everyday functioning and understanding of individuals with ASD.

In terms of outcome evaluations, many studies have been conducted, but there are inherent difficulties in doing such research. Key challenges are the heterogeneity of individuals with ASD, diagnostic and assessment issues and co-morbidity, and the fact that more than one intervention is often being followed simultaneously. There are methodological issues in terms of sample size, research design, assessment measures, and fidelity of implementation, all of which can call into question the evidence produced. Future research needs to have independent evaluators, and larger samples, to look at process as well as outcome, to produce detailed case studies, and to explore long-term effects. Increased collaboration between researchers and encouraging practitioners to evaluate practice will refine and improve the methods used and strengthen the research base on interventions in ASD.

Integration Section

As indicated in this chapter, and demonstrated in Dunlop, Knott, and MacKay (Chapter 13), cognitive theories of ASD have been a direct inspiration for interventions. Neuroscience, however, while influencing theories of ASD, has not yet had much direct influence on interventions. For example, Wicker (Chapter 2) suggests abnormal connectivity between the brain structures of the socio-emotional network in ASD, but interventions on emotions (Golan & Baron-Cohen, Chapter 12) tend to be based primarily on cognitive theories rather than these findings. Similarly, Jones and Klin (Chapter 4) show that individuals with autism process faces using neural areas that typically developing individuals use to process objects, and although there are interventions aimed at increasing the saliency of human interaction, many of these pre-date these neuroscientific findings (based on theories of causation: e.g., *Son-Rise*: Kaufman, 1994, or educational priorities: e.g., *Intensive Interaction*: Nind & Hewett, 1994). Part of the explanation for this may lie in the time lag between scientific research and practical applications. However, using Morton and Frith's (1995) model of developmental disorders, as is done by Hill (Chapter 8), we can see a further factor in that "making sense" of neuroscientific findings seems to happen at the cognitive level, and thus it is this level from which interventions are derived. Thus findings from neurology can (and do) inform the research basis for intervention, but indirectly, through effects on cognitive theories of processing differences. Knowledge of brain function may help the design of interventions in terms of both content and process, but this will need careful programs to model the differences revealed and make processes accessible. It may be that professional training of practitioners in ASD will put them in touch with mediators of neuroscientific findings and make them more directly accessible and of practical relevance.

The two chapters on central coherence (López, Chapter 6; Ropar, Mitchell, & Sheppard, Chapter 7) and Hill's chapter on executive functions (Chapter 8) outline some of the developments in theories since their initial description and illustrate the points made in this chapter about the process of theory adaptation being as valuable to practitioners as the theories themselves. Ropar et al. suggest that integration of information at a *perceptual* level may be intact in ASD, whereas there may be difficulty integrating information at the *conceptual* level, leading to the decreased influence of conceptual knowledge in autism processing. López suggests that superior local processing in autism is not likely to be a reflection of a global processing impairment, and Hill gives the state of play with respect to research on many executive functions. It is not directly evident that the theory modifications are themselves responsible for influences on interventions. However, the findings derived from these "tests" of the theory do appear to have had an impact (see, e.g., Jordan's (2005c) suggestions of ways of developing conceptual understanding and teaching approaches in ASD). López's work is part of a broader phenomenon, coming in part from such findings but coming also from the voices of people with ASD themselves: the recognition and valuing of difference and the teaching to strengths rather than deficits. Golan and Baron-Cohen (Chapter 12) also make this point and show how their own intervention is clearly based on research on differences in processing.

Maestro and Muratori (Chapter 9) report findings of lower levels of social attention at 0–6 months in ASD, at a stage when the child is vulnerable, but not yet with a clear deficit. They suggest that the study of atypical developmental trajectories could help create appropriate early interventions, which could limit consequences of the dysfunction of brain regions and help to develop compensatory strategies. This raises important dilemmas with respect to both the ethics of early intervention and the evaluation of interventions. The NIASA group (2003) suggested a way round the first ethical dilemma by proposing services based on need rather than diagnosis, while operating on the "least damaging assumption" that the child *may* have an ASD and that ways of making social information salient and structured (for example) will not do harm even if the diagnosis is not confirmed later. The dilemma over evaluation remains; how can the success of the intervention be distinguished from the possibility of misdiagnosis at this early age? There are research designs that could attempt to control for these variables but it is a problem (at least ethically) to demonstrate the value of an early screening instrument if the way the child is treated (even without specific interventions) alters as a result of the screening. This resonates with issues raised by Williams (Chapter 10) in her review of the National Screening Committee (NSC) criteria, which must be met before an ASD screening program could be introduced in the UK. In particular, it states that there should be effective treatment or interventions available, with evidence of effectiveness from randomized controlled trials. As indicated in this chapter, this is only possible where interventions are "additional to" or different from an equally valued general intervention, and this is often far from the case, especially in early intervention. Nor is it yet clear whether any approach can be judged as "effective" without indicating for whom, in what circumstances, and to achieve what end (see also Dunlop et al., Chapter 13).

A further factor in the evaluation of interventions lies in the effects on families, an issue dealt with by Hastings (Chapter 15). In reviewing the work of Hastings and Johnson (2001) regarding "protective factors," he suggests that parents' belief in the efficacy of an intervention may be a protective factor, but is also aware of other "mediator variables" (e.g., maternal self-efficacy) that may be important. In that respect, approaches that empower parents, while offering personally relevant but unbiased information, are an encouraging development from ones that insist on adherence to a single approach. The concern is that even these eclectic interventions need to be purchased (unless they are developed by professionals as part of a service), and they may then depend for effectiveness on parental capacity— further disadvantaging those without such capacities. These interventions need to be evaluated empirically not just in terms of the effect on the child, and on the families that use them, but also in social policy terms with regard to who is excluded and what professional support is needed.

Dunlop et al. (Chapter 13) and Golan and Baron-Cohen (Chapter 12) also raise the issue of generalization of results of interventions, both over time and across situations. Most interventions are still presented as discrete entities, whereas what is likely to be needed is an approach that is integrated into the daily teaching and learning situations of the child. The issue is one that is evidenced by this book: how can ecologically valid approaches be evaluated? Most "scientific" evidence is assumed to be of the medical model involving RCTs, but it may be that the science of detailed particular observation is a better model at present. Single-case designs can produce "evidence" that might be more accessible, and useful to practitioners. Generalization can come from the detailed case descriptions that allow case matching. Eventually there may be generalizations to be made about particular interventions, but the variables (of child, setting, procedure, intensity, interventions, goals, etc.) need to be fully acknowledged rather than submerged in large "quasi-scientific" evaluations.

References

Aldred, C., Phillips, R., Pollard, C., & Adams, C. (2001). Multidisciplinary social communication intervention for children with autism and pervasive developmental disorder: The Child's Talk project. *Educational and Child Psychology, 18*, 76–87.

Baker, A. F. (1983). Psychological assessment of autistic children, *Clinical Psychology Review, 3*, 41–59.

Baron-Cohen, S. (1995). *Mindblindness: An essay on autism and theory of mind.* Cambridge, MA: MIT Press.

Baron-Cohen, S., Allen, J., & Gillberg, C. (1996). Can autism be detected at 18 months? The needle, the haystack and the CHAT. *British Journal of Psychiatry, 161*, 839–843.

Baron-Cohen, S., Golan, O., Wheelwright, S., & Hill, J. J. (2004). *Mind Reading: The interactive guide to emotions.* London: Jessica Kingsley.

Baron-Cohen, S., Leslie, A., & Frith, U. (1985). Does the autistic child have a theory of mind? *Cognition, 21*, 37–46.

Bauman, M. L., & Kemper, T. L. (Eds.) (1994). *The neurobiology of autism.* Baltimore: Johns Hopkins University Press.

Bettelheim, B. (1967). *The empty fortress: Infantile autism and the birth of the self.* New York, London: The Free Press.

Bishop, D. V. M. (1989). Autism, Asperger's syndrome and semantic-pragmatic disorder: Where are the boundaries? *British Journal of Disorders of Communication, 24*, 107–121.

Bowlby, J. (1969). *Attachment and loss: Vol. 1. Attachment.* London: Hogarth Press.

Bowler, D. M. (1992). "Theory of Mind" in Asperger's syndrome. *Journal of Child Psychology and Psychiatry, 33*, 877–893.

Bristol, M. M., Cohen, D. J., Costello, E. J., Denckla, M., Eckberg, T. J., Kallen, R., et al. (1996). State of the science in autism: Report to the National Institute of Health. *Journal of Autism and Developmental Disorders, 26*, 121–154.

Chandler, S., Christie, P., Newson, E., & Prevezer, W. (2002). Developing a diagnostic and intervention package for 2 to 3 year olds with autism: Outcomes of the Frameworks for Communication approach. *Autism: The International Journal of Research and Practice, 6*, 47–69.

Charman, T., Baron-Cohen, S., Swettenham, J., Baird, G., Cox, A., & Drew, A. (2001). Testing joint attention, imitation and play as infancy precursors to language and theory of mind. *Cognitive Development, 15*, 481–498.

Connor, M. (1998). A review of behavioural early intervention programmes for children with autism. *Educational Psychology in Practice, 14*, 109–117.

Dawson, G. (1996). Neuropsychology of autism: A report on the state of the science. *Journal of Autism and Developmental Disorders, 26*, 179–184.

Dawson, G., & Österling, J. (1997). Early intervention in autism. In M. Guralnick (Ed.) *The effectiveness of early* intervention (pp. 307–326). Baltimore: Brookes.

Dawson, M. (2004). Autism and ostracism in Paul Martin's Canada: Not the usual autism letter. *Good Autism Practice, 5*, 68–70.

Department for Education and Skills (2002). *Autistic spectrum disorders: Good practice guidance*. London: DFES.

Fleischman, A. (2005). The hero's story and autism: Grounded theory study of sites of parents. *Autism: The International Journal of Research and Practice, 9*, 299–316.

Freeman, B. J. (1997). Guidelines for evaluating intervention programs for children with autism. *Journal of Autism and Developmental Disorders, 27*, 641–645.

Frith, U. (1989). *Autism: Explaining the enigma* (1st ed.). Oxford, UK: Blackwell.

Frith, U. (1998). Cognitive deficits in developmental disorders. *Scandinavian Journal of Psychology, 39*, 191–198.

Frith, U. (2003). *Autism: Explaining the enigma* (2nd ed.). Oxford, UK: Blackwell.

Gagnon, L., Mottron, L., & Yves, J. (1997). Questioning the validity of the semantic pragmatic syndrome diagnosis. *Autism: The International Journal of Research and Practice, 1*, 37–55.

Gerland, G. (1997). *A real person*. London: Souvenir Press.

Gillberg, C., & Coleman, M. (2000). *The biology of the autistic syndromes* (2nd ed.). Cambridge, UK: Cambridge University Press.

Grandin, T. (1995). *Thinking in pictures and other reports from my life with autism*. New York: Doubleday.

Gray, C. (1994a). *Comic strip conversations*. Arlington, TX: Future Horizons.

Gray, C. (1994b). *The new social stories book*. Arlington, TX: Future Horizons.

Greenspan, S. L., & Wieder, S. (1999). A functional developmental approach to autism spectrum disorders. *Journal of the Association for Persons with Severe Handicaps, 24*, 147–161.

Gutstein, S. E., & Sheely, R. K. (2002). *Relationship development intervention with young children*. London: Jessica Kingsley.

Happé, F. (1994). *Autism: An introduction to psychological theory*. London: UCL Publications.

Happé, F., & Frith, U. (2006). The weak coherence account: Detailed-focused cognitive style in autism spectrum disorders. *Journal of Autism and Developmental Disorders, 36*, 5–25.

Harris, S. L., & Handleman, J. S. (1994). *Preschool education programs for children with autism.* Austin, TX: PRO-ED.

Hastings, R. P., & Johnson, E. (2001). Stress in UK families conducting intensive home-based behavioral intervention for their young child with autism. *Journal of Autism and Developmental Disorders, 31*, 327–336.

Herrera, G., Alcantua, F., Jordan, R., Blanquer, A., Labajo, G., & De Pablo, C. (in press). Development of symbolic play through the use of Virtual Reality tools in children with autistic spectrum disorders: Two case studies. *Autism: The International Journal of Research and Practice.*

Hill, E. L. (2004). Evaluating the theory of executive dysfunction in autism. *Developmental Review, 24*, 189–233.

Hobson, R. (2002). *The cradle of thought: Exploring the origins of thinking.* Basingstoke: Macmillan.

Howlin, P. (1998a). *Children with autism and Asperger syndrome.* London: Wiley.

Howlin, P. (1998b). Practitioner review: Psychological and educational treatment for autism. *Journal of Child Psychology and Psychiatry, 39*, 307–322.

Howlin, P., Baron-Cohen, S., & Hadwin, J. (1998). *Teaching children with autism to mind-read: A practical guide for teachers and parents.* Chichester, UK: John Wiley & Sons.

Howlin, P., Goode, S., Hutton, J., & Rutter, M. (2004). Adult outcome for children with autism. *Journal of Child Psychology and Psychiatry, 45*, 212–229.

Jackson, L. (2002). *Freaks, geeks and Asperger syndrome: A user guide to adolescence.* London: Jessica Kingsley.

Jensen, A. R. (1980). *Bias in mental testing.* New York: Free Press.

Jones, G., Meldrum, E., & Newson, E. (1995). *A descriptive and comparative study of current interventions for children with autism.* Unpublished research report, Nottingham University, UK.

Jordan, R. (1999a). *Autistic spectrum disorders: An introductory handbook for practitioners.* London: David Fulton.

Jordan, R. (1999b). Evaluating practice: Problems and possibilities. *Autism: The International Journal of Research and Practice, 3*, 411–434.

Jordan, R. (2004). Meeting the needs of children with autistic spectrum disorders in the early years. *Australian Journal of Early Childhood, 29*, 1–7.

Jordan, R. (2005a). Autistic spectrum disorders. In A. Lewis & B. Norwich (Eds.), *Special teaching for special children? Pedagogy for special educational needs* (pp. 110–123). Milton Keynes: Open University Press.

Jordan, R. R. (2005b). Diagnosis and the identification of special educational needs for children at the "able" end of the autism spectrum: Reflections on social and cultural influences. *Autism News: Orange County & the Rest of the World, 2*, 13–16.

Jordan, R. (2005c). Managing autism and Asperger's syndrome in current educational provision, *Paediatric Rehabilitation, 8*, 104–112.

Jordan, R., & Jones, G. (1996). *Review of provision for children with autism in Scotland:*

Report of research for the Scottish Office. Birmingham, UK: School of Education, University of Birmingham.

Jordan, R., & Jones, G. (1999). Review of research into educational interventions for children with autism in the UK. *Autism, the International Journal of Research & Practice, 3,* 101–110.

Jordan, R., Jones, G., & Murray, D. (1998). *Educational interventions for children with autism: A literature review of recent and current research, Report 77.* Sudbury, UK: DfEE.

Jordan, R., & Powell, S. (1996). Therapist drift: Identifying a new phenomenon in evaluating therapeutic approaches. In G. Linfoot and P. Shattock (Eds.), *Therapeutic intervention in autism* (pp. 21–30). Sunderland, UK: Autism Research Unit, University of Sunderland.

Kaufman, B. (1994). *Son-Rise: The miracle continues.* Tiburon, CA: H. J. Kramer.

Klin, A. (1991). Young autistic children's listening preferences in regard to speech: A possible characterisation of the symptoms of social withdrawal. *Journal of Autism and Developmental Disorders, 23,* 15–35.

Klin, A., Jones, W., Schultz, R., Volkmar, F., & Cohen, D. (2002). Visual fixation patterns during viewing of naturalistic social situations as predictors of social competence in individuals with autism. *Archives of General Psychiatry, 59,* 809–816.

Koegel, L. K., Koegel, R. L., & Smith, A. (1997). Variables related to differences in standardised test outcomes for children with autism. *Journal of Autism and Developmental Disorders, 27,* 233–240.

Kugler, B. (1998). The differentiation between autism and Asperger syndrome, *Autism, 2,* 11–32.

Lawson, W. (1998). *Life behind glass.* Lismore, NSW: Southern Cross University Press.

Lord, C. (2000). Commentary: Achievements and future directions for intervention research in communication and autism spectrum disorders. *Journal of Autism and Developmental Disorders, 30,* 393–398.

Lovaas, O. I. (2002). *Teaching children with developmental delays: Basic intervention techniques.* Austin, TX: Pro-Ed.

Lubbock, J. (2001). In the balance: The Lovaas experience. In J. Richer & S. Coates (Eds.), *Autism: In search of coherence* London: Jessica Kingsley.

Magiati, I., & Howlin, P. (2003). A pilot evaluation study of the Picture Exchange Communication System (PECS) for children with autistic spectrum disorders. *Autism: The International Journal of Research and Practice, 7,* 297–320.

McGregor, E., Whiten, A., & Blackburn, P. (1998). Teaching theory of mind by highlighting intention and illustrating thoughts: A comparison of their effectiveness with three-year-olds and autistic subjects. *British Journal of Developmental Psychology, 16,* 281–300.

Medical Research Council (2001). *Review of autism research: Epidemiology and causes.* London: MRC.

Mesibov, G. (1997). Formal and informal measures of the effectiveness of the TEACCH program. *Autism: The International Journal of Research and Practice, 1,* 25–35.

Morton, J., & Frith, U. (1995). Causal Modeling: A structural approach to developmental psychopathology. In D. Cichetti & D. J. Cohen (Eds.), *Manual of developmental psychopathology* (Vol. 1, pp. 357–390). New York: John Wiley.

NIASA. (2003). *National autism plan for children.* London: National Autistic Society.

Nind, M., & Hewett, D. (1994). *Access to communication.* London: David Fulton.

Parks, S. L. (1983). The assessment of autistic children: A selective review of available instruments. *Journal of Autism and Developmental Disorders, 13,* 255–267.

Parsons, S., Mitchell, P., & Leonard, A. (2005). Do adolescents with autistic spectrum disorders adhere to social conventions in virtual environments? *Autism: The International Journal of Research and Practice, 9,* 95–117.

Piven, J., Harper, J., Palmer, P., & Amdt, S. (1996). Course of behavioural change in autism: A retrospective study of high-IQ adolescents and adults. *Journal of the American Academy of Child and Adolescent Psychiatry, 35,* 523–529.

Prizant, B. M., & Rubin, S. A. (1999). Contemporary issues in interventions for autism spectrum disorders: A commentary. *Journal of the Association for Persons with a Severe Mental Handicap, 24,* 199–208.

Prizant, B. M., Wetherby, A. M., Rubin, E., Laurent, A. C., & Rydell, P. (2002). The SCERTS model: Enhancing communication and socioemotional abilities of children with autism spectrum disorders. *Jenison Autism Journal, 14,* 2–19.

Rimland, B. (1964). *Infantile autism.* New York: Appleton-Century-Crofts.

Robins, D. L., Fein, D., Barton, M. L., & Green, J. A. (2001). Modified checklist for autism in toddlers. *Journal of Autism & Developmental Disorders, 31,* 131–144.

Roid, G. H., & Miller, L. J. (1997). *The Leiter International Performance Scale–Revised Edition.* Lutz, FL: Psychological Assessment Resources.

Russell, J. (1996). *Agency: Its role in mental development.* London: Taylor & Francis.

Rutter, M. (1968). Concepts of autism. *Journal of Child Psychology and Psychiatry, 9,* 1–25.

Rutter, M. (1996). Autism research: Prospects and priorities. *Journal of Autism and Developmental Disorders, 26,* 257–275.

Rutter, M. (1999). Autism: Two-way interplay between research and clinical work. *Journal of Child Psychology & Psychiatry, 40,* 169–188.

Sainsbury, C. (2000). *Martian in the playground.* Bristol, UK: Lucky Duck Publishers.

Schopler, E., Mesibov, G. B., & Hearsey, K. (1995). Structured teaching in the TEACCH system. In E. Schopler & G. B. Mesibov (Eds.), *Learning and cognition in autism* (pp. 243–268). New York: Plenum Press.

Schuler, A. (2001). Editorial. *Autism: The International Journal of Research and Practice: Special Issue on Early Interventions, 5,* 331–340.

Shea, V. (2004). A perspective on the research literature related to early intensive behavioural intervention (Lovaas) for young children with autism. *Autism: The International Journal of Research and Practice, 8,* 349–368.

Siegel, B. (1999). Autistic learning disabilities and individualising treatment for autistic spectrum disorders. *Infants and Young Children, 12,* 27–36.

Sparrow, S. S., Balla, D., & Cicchetti, D. (1984). *Vineland Adaptive Behavior Scales.* Circle Pines, MN: American Guidance Service.

Stephenson, J. (2002). Characterization of multisensory environments: Why do teachers use them? *Journal of Applied Research in Intellectual Disabilities, 15,* 73–90.

Sussman, F. (1999). *More than words: Helping parents promote communication and social skills in children with autism spectrum disorder.* Toronto: The Hanen Centre.

Swettenham, J., Baron-Cohen, S., Gómez, J. C., & Walsh, S. (1996). What's inside a person's head? Conceiving of the mind as a camera helps children with autism develop an alternative theory of mind. *Cognitive Neuropsychiatry, 1*, 73–88.

Trevarthen, C., Aitken, K., Papoudi, D., & Robarts, J. (1996). *Children with autism: Diagnosis and intervention to meet their needs.* London: Jessica Kingsley.

Volkmar, F. (1998). Categorical approaches to the diagnosis of autism: An overview of DSM-IV and ICD-10. *Autism: The International Journal of Research and Practice, 2*, 45–60.

Waller, S. A., Armstrong, K. J., McGrath, A. M., & Sullivan, C. L. (1999). A review of the diagnostic methods reported in the *Journal of Autism and Developmental Disorders. Journal of Autism and Developmental Disorders, 29*, 485–490.

Webster, A., Webster, V., & Feiler, A. (2002). Research evidence, polemic and evangelism: How decisions are made on early intervention in autistic spectrum disorder. *Educational and Child Psychology, 19*, 54–67.

Welch, M. (1988). *Holding time.* New York: Simon & Schuster.

Whitaker, P. (2001). *Challenging behaviour and autism*, London: NAS.

15

Stress in Parents of Children With Autism

Richard P. Hastings

The majority of the chapters in this volume describe research evidence relating to an understanding of children with autism. Especially during childhood, individuals with autism typically live in the family home with one or both parents and potentially with other family members. Thus, it is important to consider the potential impact of having a child with autism on the functioning of the family. In the present chapter, I provide a review of some of the key issues in research focused on parents of children with autism and identify some areas for future research. Specifically, I consider the evidence that parents of children with autism may be at increased risk for stress and discuss the question of demonstrating causality here. I also explore the limitations of group design studies in helping us to understand families and advocate instead longitudinal research, studies of psychological processes and parental resilience, and an explicit focus on the family system. I then draw on research literature that addresses the impact of child and also parent-focused interventions on parental well-being. Within this discussion, I include an analysis of the putative impact of early intensive behavioral intervention on parents. Finally, I consider how issues of family functioning relate to other areas of autism research.

Parents at Increased Risk for Stress

Research over several decades has suggested that parents of children with developmental disabilities report more stress and other psychological problems than parents of children with no known disabilities. The results of group comparison studies are largely consistent, and show higher levels of parenting stress and mental health problems in both mothers and fathers of children with developmental disabilities (Baker, Blacher, Crnic, & Edelbrock, 2002; Beckman, 1991; Dyson, 1991; Emerson, 2003; Friedrich & Friedrich, 1981). This pattern of results is robust, in that it also holds when studies are summarized using meta-analytic methods. For example, Singer (2006) found evidence across 18 studies that mothers of children with developmental disabilities were at increased risk for the symptoms of depression (overall weighted effect size d = .39, 95% CI = .31, .47). Overall, this effect size represents a small to moderate overall increased risk.

Parents of children with autism have often been studied in family research within broader developmental disability samples, where their experiences are not distinguished from those of other parents. Thus, it is difficult to establish what may be similar and different about the experiences of parents of children with autism. However, in some research, families of children with autism have also been studied separately. When compared with parents of children with no known disabilities, parents of children with autism report poorer psychological well-being, following the same pattern as parents of children with disabilities generally (Duarte, Bordin, Yazigi, & Mooney, 2005; Koegel et al., 1992; Rodrigue, Morgan, & Geffken, 1990; Weiss, 2002). Interestingly, parents of children with autism have often been found to have more or more severe psychological problems. Thus, when compared with parents of children with other disabilities they typically have the highest scores on measures of negative adjustment. Such results have been found in comparisons with groups of parents of children with other disabilities, mixed etiology intellectual disabilities, and other syndromes related to intellectual disability such as Down's syndrome and Fragile X syndrome (Abbeduto et al., 2004; Bouma & Schweitzer, 1990; Dumas, Wolf, Fisman, & Culligan, 1991; Konstantareas, Homatidis, & Plowright, 1992; Rodrigue et al., 1990; Sanders & Morgan, 1997; Wolf, Noh, Fisman, & Speechley, 1989). This increased risk is also supported by meta-analytic evidence. Singer (2006) found that studies focusing on mothers of children with autism reported significantly larger effect sizes for depression differences than those focusing on intellectual disability or other disabilities.

By way of further illustration of these research findings, I returned to a longitudinal data set of mothers of children with developmental disabilities that included a sub-set of mothers of children with autism (Hastings, Daley, Burns, & Beck, 2006). In this research, we gathered data on maternal well-being primarily indexed using the Parental Distress sub-scale of the short form of the Parenting Stress Index (PSI: Abidin, 1990). Seventy-five mothers of school-age children with developmental disabilities were recruited, including 26 mothers of children with autism. Two years later, we assessed maternal distress again and were able to gather data from 20 of these mothers of children with autism. At the first data collection point, mothers of children with other intellectual disabilities had a high risk for clinically significant levels of parenting stress (56% of them scored above the PSI clinical cutoff), but the mothers of children with autism were at an even higher level of risk (75% scored above the PSI clinical cutoff). This difference was also reflected in the mean scores for the mothers of children with autism on the PSI Parental Distress scale being significantly higher than those of the other mothers (effect size of difference, Cohen's d = .69). Furthermore, the stress scores of the mothers of children with autism were highly stable over the two years of the study (r = .93).

The data from the Hastings et al. (2006) sample represent a classic pattern of findings in research focusing on parents of children with autism. First, these mothers reported considerably more stress than mothers of another high-risk group (mothers of children with intellectual disabilities)—not far off an effect classified as large in size (Cohen, 1992). Second, a large proportion of these mothers were reporting stress at a clinically significant level. Third, stress remained very stable over time. Thus, not only might parents of children with autism be at considerably increased risk of stress, but this is chronic, persisting over several years at least.

Moving Beyond the Group Design Study

Although there appears to be compelling evidence that parents of children with autism are at increased risk for chronic stress, repeated research findings of this nature are not in themselves particularly useful. Specifically, there is an underlying assumption that group design studies might somehow constitute evidence that children with autism cause their parents to become stressed. Regrettably, comparisons of parents of children with autism to other parents do not meet the basic standard for inferring causality of a "true" experimental design (Cook & Campbell, 1979). The key criterion defining an experimental design is the random allocation of participants to research conditions. Examples are common in the field of medicine, where randomized controlled trials are used as the gold standard research design to evaluate the evidence for the efficacy of new treatments such as new drugs for cancer and other major diseases. Controlled trials of this kind have also been used to evaluate the impact of interventions for children with autism (e.g., Lovaas, 1987). However, it is not the case, nor would it be practically or ethically possible to randomly assign some parents a child with autism and some parents another child. Thus, group design family research studies in the field of autism do not provide causal evidence that raising a child with autism leads to stress in their parents.

If we want to demonstrate that it is indeed autism, or something associated with autism, that causes stress in parents, we need to move to consider the core criteria that underpin research to establish causal pathways in psychopathology research. Three core criteria are often described: (1) association; (2) non-spuriousness; and

(3) temporal precedence (Haynes, 1992; Kazdin, Kraemer, Kessler, Kupfer, & Offord, 1997). The first of these, I have already discussed in the previous section: there is plenty of evidence of an association between autism, increased stress, and other psychological difficulties in parents. The second—non-spuriousness—refers to the fact that an association found between autism and parental stress might be due to an additional variable associated with both of these. For example, it may be that intellectual disability is the active ingredient. Poor intellectual functioning and autism are associated, as are intellectual disability and parental stress. However, several studies (including the example of data from my own research above) have shown that parents of children with autism are at further increased risk for stress than parents of children with other disabilities, including intellectual disability.

In terms of the potential for a spurious association between autism and parental stress, perhaps a more direct challenge emerges from the literature on the broader phenotype of autism. Some of the family members of children with autism who do not meet the diagnostic criteria for the disorder nonetheless display some of the phenotypic characteristics of autism (e.g., Fombonne, Bolton, Prior, Jordan, & Rutter, 1997; Hughes, Plumet, & Leboyer, 1999; Piven & Palmer, 1997). It may be the case that some parents report more stress at least partly because they have psychological problems related to a genetic risk that is associated with autism. Thus, their problems may not be due specifically or entirely to the difficulties of raising a child with autism.

In a recent meta-analysis, Yirmiya and Shaked (2005) showed that parents of children with autism were at increased risk for psychiatric disorders when compared with other parents (overall effect size, Cohen's $d = .26$). This effect was strongest when parents were compared in studies with parents of children who have disorders with no current known genetic liability. An increased risk for psychiatric problems could partly explain the findings of an association between childhood autism and parental stress, because there is longitudinal evidence that parents with mental health problems tend to experience more parenting stress (Hastings et al., 2006). Clearly, the effect size from this meta-analysis is relatively small. Thus, by no means the majority of parents of children with autism have psychiatric problems. Although it may be a part of the picture, shared genetic vulnerability seems unlikely to be the full explanation for the experiences of parents reported in the research reviewed thus far.

There is a further candidate variable that may explain the association between autism and parental stress. Children with autism are also at increased risk for significant behavior problems, especially aggressive behaviors, self-injury, and, by definition, repetitive behaviors (e.g., Hastings & Mount, 2001; McClintock, Hall, & Oliver, 2003). Behavior problems in children with developmental disabilities have been found to be associated with increased stress and mental health problems in parents (Baker et al., 2002; Baxter, Cummins, & Yiolitis, 2000; Beck, Hastings, Daley, & Stevenson, 2004; Blacher, Shapiro, Lopez, Diaz, & Fusco, 1997; Hastings, 2002; Orr, Cameron, Dobson, & Day, 1993; Quine & Pahl, 1985, 1991; Sloper, Knussen, Turner, & Cunningham, 1991; Stores, Stores, Fellows, & Buckley, 1998). This association has also been found specifically for parents of children with autism (Bromley, Hare, Davison, & Emerson, 2004; Hastings & Johnson, 2001; Konstantareas & Homatidis, 1989; Tobing & Glenwick, 2002; Tomanik, Harris, & Hawkins, 2004).

Thus, it may be that parents of children with autism report more stress because their children also have more behavior problems. Autism is diagnosed by one type of behavior problem (repetitive behaviors), but otherwise the key features relate to social behavior and communication. Other behavior problems are also not unique to autism. Is it the case that it is not autism per se, but associated behavior problems, that may explain parental psychological adjustment? To address this question, I returned to the data described above because the study also included a measure of the child's behavior problems as reported by the mothers (Hastings et al., 2006). There was initially a significant difference in stress reported by the mothers of children with autism compared with mothers of children with intellectual disabilities ($F(1, 73) = 7.94$; $p = .006$), but this difference became non-significant once the child's behavior problem scores were controlled in an ANCOVA design ($F (1, 72) = 1.82$; $p = $ ns). We have also shown previously that behavior problems, rather than adaptive skills or symptoms of autism, are the strongest predictors of maternal stress (Hastings et al., 2005b).

Using the label "non-spurious" is probably misleading in the present context, because it implies a less interesting or important relationship. The possibility that the behavior problems of children with autism may be the key variable in explaining parents' stress is actually extremely important at a practical level, as there may be potential for remediation using various intervention techniques (see below). However, we have not yet demonstrated that behavior problems do cause stress in parents of children with autism. To do this, we also need evidence of our third causality criterion—that of temporal precedence. Thus, we need to demonstrate that behavior problems, or changes in them, predict parental stress over time. What is needed is a longitudinal study where data on both parental stress and children's behavior problems are measured at more than one point in time.

Lecavalier, Leone, and Wiltz (2006) have carried out one such study. Eighty-one children and adolescents with autism spectrum disorders and their parents were assessed one year apart with measures of behavior problems and parenting stress. Using longitudinal data in regression analyses, Lecavalier et al. (2006) showed that the child's behavior problems at time 1 were associated with increased parental stress at time 2 after controlling for stress at time 1. However, the reverse temporal path was also supported, such that high parenting stress predicted children's behavior problems over time. The relationship between child behavior problems and parental stress was thus found to be bi-directional. This pattern of results is not unique to autism, as several other studies of parental stress in families of children with developmental disabilities have also found evidence of a bidirectional relationship between child and parent functioning (Baker et al., 2003; Hastings et al., 2006; Nihira, Mink, & Meyers, 1985; Orsmond, Seltzer, Krauss, & Hong, 2003).

The preceding review of research studies suggests that behavior problems are important in understanding the increased experience of stress in parents of children with autism. Associations have been found between child behavior problems and parental stress in families of children with autism. In addition, there is evidence of a temporal relationship such that behavior problems seem to predict parental stress over time (and vice versa). Perhaps less clear is whether these relationships are non-spurious. Very few data are available to show that behavior problems and not classic autism features or symptoms are the key predictor of parental stress. Thus, more research of this kind especially employing longitudinal designs is needed to more fully explore the hypothesis that behavior problems are the key driver of parental stress.

Resilience and Psychological Mechanism

One of the dangers with the preceding discussion about the evidence for a causal relationship between childhood autism, or an associated feature of the disorder, and parental stress is that it might appear to imply that all parents of children with autism will develop problems. Although a high proportion of mothers from the Hastings et al. (2006) sample scored above a clinical cutoff on the PSI, there was a group who did not report problems at this level. Thus, some parents appear to "cope" well with the difficulties typically associated with raising a child with autism. An important question to ask is what might distinguish those parents that appear to be negatively affected from those parents who are not. This is essentially a question about resilience: What stops some parents from becoming stressed?

Variables that act to reduce the risk associated with parenting a child with autism are likely to be of two main types, and it is crucial to distinguish between them. First, a variable might share a main effect relationship with better adjustment or less stress. Main effects represent simple associations between one variable and another without the complications of interactions between factors. Such variables are probably best labeled as compensatory factors (Luthar & Zigler, 1991). For example, positive coping strategies (e.g., seeing the positive aspects of the situation, accepting the situation) have been found to be positively associated with well-being in both mothers and fathers of children with autism (Hastings et al., 2005a).

The second type of variable of interest is the protective factor. Protective factors are a special type of moderator variable:

> A moderator is a qualitative . . . or quantitative . . . variable that affects the direction and/or strength of the relation between an independent or predictor variable and a dependent or criterion variable (Baron & Kenny, 1986, p. 1174).

Thus, protective variables *interact* with risk variables to influence outcomes (Rutter, 1985). Under conditions of low risk (e.g., low levels of child behavior problems), they will have little impact on outcomes (e.g., parental stress). However, under conditions of high risk (e.g., high levels of child behavior problems), the presence of the protective factor (or more of it) will tend to reduce the risk of negative outcomes. Thus, those without the protective factor (or little of it) will be at the highest risk for negative outcomes.

Hastings and Johnson (2001) identified a putative protective factor that may be important in understanding parental stress in contexts where parents are involved with intensive early intervention programs for their child with autism. Under conditions of relatively lower risk (children with less severe autism), parents' beliefs in the efficacy of the intervention program did not affect their psychological well-being, measured in this study in terms of their pessimism about the future. However, under conditions of relatively higher risk (children with more severe autism), parents who had positive views about the efficacy of the intervention had higher levels of well-being than parents who had less positive beliefs about the intervention. Thus amongst these families, beliefs in intervention efficacy seemed to serve as a protective factor. However, in this study, belief in the efficacy of the intervention also had a significant main effect (cf. compensatory) relationship with parental pessimism. This illustrates how important it is to search for interaction effects that might clarify the function of a variable and potentially identify protective effects.

Another danger with a focus on demonstrating causality is the lack of psychological meaning conveyed. Specifically, we need to be asking *how* or *why* one variable might cause another. If we want to be able to intervene to help parents, it is not enough to show that behavior problems might cause parents of children with autism to become stressed. Rather, we need to show how or why this might happen, and to design interventions that directly address the identified processes. Thus, in addition to the criteria of association, non-spuriousness, and temporal precedence outlined earlier in the chapter, a fourth causality criterion in the field of psychopathology has been identified: that a plausible psychological mechanism needs to be demonstrated (Haynes, 1992; Kazdin et al., 1997). Identifying psychological mechanism is a search for a class of variables that are called mediators:

> A given variable may be said to function as a mediator to the extent that it accounts for the relation between the predictor and the criterion. Mediators explain how external physical events take on internal psychological significance ... mediators speak to how or why such effects occur (Baron & Kenny, 1986, p. 1176).

Baron and Kenny (1986) identify four steps to establish the presence of a mediator variable: (1) a significant association between a predictor and a criterion variable (e.g., behavior problems of the child with autism, and parental stress); (2) a significant association between the predictor variable and the putative mediator; (3) a significant association between the putative mediator variable and the criterion variable; and (4) that the association at step 1 is removed or significantly reduced when the relationship is explored whilst controlling for the mediator. The fourth step is typically achieved using a hierarchical regression model. Thus, the predictor variable initially predicts the criterion variable, but when the putative mediator is added to the model, it becomes a significant predictor, whereas the initial predictor variable now does not make an independent contribution to the prediction of the criterion variable.

Hastings and Brown (2002) explored the role of maternal self-efficacy (beliefs in their own ability) as a mediator of the relationship between behavior problems in children with autism and mothers' mental health. Twenty-six mothers of school-age children with autism completed measures of their mental health (anxiety and depression), teachers reported on the child's behavior problems, and mothers also rated their feelings of efficacy specifically in managing their child's behavior problems. Regression analyses showed that the child's behavior problems were a strong predictor of both maternal anxiety and depression. However, when self-efficacy was entered into the models, behavior problems ratings were no longer a significant predictor, and instead self-efficacy made a significant independent contribution to the prediction of both anxiety and depression. Thus, higher levels of child behavior problems tended to reduce mothers' feelings of self-efficacy, and it was this reduced self-efficacy that primarily accounted for raised anxiety and depression.

The identification of compensatory factors, protective factors, and also mediator variables (or mechanisms) is significant at a practical level. These variables point to factors that could be addressed directly in interventions designed to reduce parental stress. One may be able to increase resilience by developing characteristics that are protective. Similarly, one could boost mediator factors that could have positive effects (e.g., increase self-efficacy) and work to reduce mediator factors that may have negative effects (e.g., decrease feelings of hopelessness). The development of interventions for parents of children with autism are discussed later in the chapter.

The Family System

Thus far, our discussion has focused on the dyadic relationship between parent and child. Specifically, I have drawn on literature that addresses the relationship between some characteristics of the child with autism and the well-being of one parent. In most cases, research literature has focused on mothers of children with autism. However, in many families there will also be a father present and often also other family members such as siblings and grandparents. This raises at least two significant questions. The first is whether parents experience the stresses of raising children with autism similarly. The second is whether there is a way to develop our understanding from the basic dyadic relationship to one that involves three or more family members.

Although studies comparing the experiences of mothers and fathers of children with autism are less prevalent in the literature than studies of only one parent, several researchers have analyzed within-family differences and found that mothers typically report more problems with stress and mental health than fathers (Bristol, Gallagher, & Schopler, 1988; Gray & Holden, 1992; Hastings & Brown, 2002; Hastings et al., 2005b; Konstantareas et al., 1992; Moes, Koegel, Schreibman, & Loos, 1992). Some studies have reported no differences in maternal and paternal stress (e.g., Bebko, Konstantareas, & Springer, 1987; Factor, Perry, & Freeman, 1990; Wolf et al., 1989), but I have found no studies reporting data from a sample where fathers report more stress than mothers. Despite these typical within-family differences, maternal and paternal stress generally seem to be related to similar variables. For example, coping styles may correlate similarly with well-being outcomes for mothers and fathers of children with autism (Hastings et al., 2005a), and stress for both mothers and fathers is lower when they hold more positive attitudes toward their child (Honey, Hastings, & McConachie, 2005).

Simple comparisons between mothers and fathers of children with autism, whilst informative, are a relatively unsophisticated way of addressing the impact of autism more broadly on the family system. It is important to widen research to consider the family system more explicitly. We have adopted such an approach in our own research, in which we look separately for mothers and fathers at whether the functioning of the child with autism and/or their partner is associated with psychological well-being. In the first small scale study Hastings (2003) assessed 18 married couples with a school-age child with autism. Partial correlation analyses were used to demonstrate that maternal stress was associated with both their child's behavior problems (as rated by teachers) and their partner's anxiety and depression. In contrast, paternal stress was associated with neither their child's behavior problems nor maternal anxiety. Furthermore, there was only a marginal association between maternal depression and paternal stress (although this was a small sample).

In a second study designed to replicate and extend the Hastings (2003) results, Hastings et al. (2005b) collected data from 41 mothers and fathers of preschool children with autism. Regression analyses again showed that maternal stress was affected positively both by their child's behavior problems and their partner's depression. Paternal stress, in contrast, was not associated with child characteristics but was positively predicted by their partner's depression. Data were also available on the positive perceptions of parents of children with autism (about their child, and his or her impact on the parent and the wider family). In the systems analyses, neither child nor father variables were predictive of maternal positive perceptions. Thus, mothers' positive perceptions appear to be determined by variables other than those measured in the study. In contrast to the maternal analyses, paternal positive perceptions were negatively predicted by maternal depression. Thus, these data suggest that paternal positive perceptions are affected by similar variables to those that affect stress (i.e., maternal depression).

The preceding discussion goes some way to exploring aspects of the family system and recognizing that family members may affect each other's well-being. However, the conceptual approach adopted to date is very simple. It is important to remember that the definition of family can be complex, and that even if we consider a classic pattern, there may be siblings in the family and also extended family members such as grandparents. Research on siblings of children with autism suggests that they too may be at increased risk for psychological problems (Bågenholm & Gillberg, 1991; Fisman et al., 1996; Gold, 1993; Howlin, 1988; Rodrigue, Geffken, & Morgan, 1993), although this is certainly not always the case (e.g., Pilowsky, Yirmiya, Doppelt, Gross-Tsur, & Shalev, 2004). Again, it is difficult to establish whether these findings are related to the impact of the child with autism on an unaffected sibling, indirectly because of increased parental stress, or whether there is a genetic effect relating to the broader autism phenotype. However, there is some evidence that a temporal relationship exists such that the behavior problems of children with autism predict sibling adjustment over time (Hastings, in press).

In contrast, there is very little research on grandparents of children with autism. Research suggests that grandparents may estimate the ability of children with autism more positively than do parents (Harris, Handelman, & Palmer, 1985). It is impossible to say whether grandparents are realistic and parents underestimate their child's abilities, but the key problem may be the opportunity for disagreements about the child with autism and their care. In other research, parent–grandparent disagreements about children with disabilities have been found to be associated with maternal stress but not with paternal stress (Hastings, Thomas, & Delwiche, 2002). Thus, it may be worth exploring grandparent involvement with families of children with autism and how they might support parents.

Research on the broader family systems of children with autism has also been cross-sectional to date. Longitudinal studies are needed to establish the putative causal relationships that may be in place. Furthermore, there is a need to identify the psychological mechanisms through which the effects discussed above operate. In particular, why might fathers be affected only by their spouse's mental health, whereas mothers seem to be affected both by their child's behavior problems and their partner's depression?

The Impact of Intervention on Parents

Following on from the observation that characteristics of the child with autism, especially their behavior problems, are associated with parental stress (especially, and perhaps specifically, for mothers), we might expect that interventions designed to teach parents to manage their child's behavior would impact positively on parental well-being. In a recent study, Tonge et al. (2006) compared the impact of a 20-week education and skills training program for parents of preschool children with autism to a parent education and counseling intervention, and also to a control condition. The main feature that distinguished the two interventions was the focus on practical behavior management skills in the former. Overall, effects on a broad spectrum of parents' mental health were not observed at post-treatment, but at six month follow-up both interventions were superior to the control condition, although they did not differ from each other. For both interventions, there was evidence that parents who were more distressed pre-treatment benefited most from intervention.

In addition to shorter-term parent training, autism has attracted a great deal of research and practical interest relating to the use of intensive early intervention focused on directly teaching the child basic adaptive and educational skills using applied behavior analysis methods. Debate has often centered on the findings of Lovaas who showed that around one half of children with autism receiving home-based early intensive behavioral intervention (EIBI) improved to the extent that they were indistinguishable from typically developing peers, effects that maintained over several years (Lovaas, 1987; McEachin, Smith, & Lovaas, 1993). Critics have noted that as EIBI typically involves 52-week-per-year intervention, delivered for 40 hours per week, involving paid staff working in the family home, and a large financial cost to families, it is likely to cause considerable stress to the family system. However, one might also expect such intervention to positively affect children's behavior and skills and thus help to reduce parental stress. What do the data tell us?

A small number of published studies have provided data on the functioning of family members in the context of EIBI. Several researchers have reported that parental stress may decrease over time when families are engaged in EIBI (Birnbrauer &

Leach, 1993; Smith, Buch, & Gamby, 2000; Smith, Groen, & Wynn, 2000). However, these studies typically do not include comparison groups and also typically involve very small samples. In a cross-sectional study of 141 parents whose children with autism were engaged in various stages of EIBI, Hastings and Johnson (2001) found that mothers in the sample (N = 130) reported similar levels of stress to mothers of children with autism in other research studies. Hastings and Johnson (2001) also explored predictors of stress within the sample of parents. Intervention variables (e.g., child's age when EIBI was started, length of time the child had been engaged on EIBI, whether parents were also therapists for the child) did not predict parental stress, but other psychological variables did so (e.g., social support, positive reframing coping strategies, and parents' beliefs about the efficacy of the EIBI methods).

The Hastings and Johnson (2001) study did not include a separate control group recruited for the research and also did not involve assessment of families over time. However, a recent evaluation of the Southampton Childhood Autism Programme (SCAmP) used a controlled design where maternal and paternal well-being were assessed at baseline, at 12 months, and at 24 months through an EIBI program (Remington et al., 2006). Data for mothers showed that their stress, mental health, and positive perceptions of their child with autism did not differ between the EIBI group and the comparison group ("treatment as usual") over time. An identical pattern of results was found for paternal stress, anxiety, and positive perceptions. However, there was some indication that paternal depression increased more over time in the EIBI group than in the comparison group. The Remington et al. (2006) data confirm that parents whose children with autism are engaged in EIBI may be no more stressed than other parents of children with autism. There is some suggestion that fathers report more depression symptoms during EIBI, but this result is yet to be replicated, and research is needed to address why this might be the case. For example, it may be that the financial pressures of the program weigh heavily on fathers rather than any more direct impact of the presence of the EIBI program within the home.

There have also been a small number of studies aimed at intervening to directly remediate stress in parents of children with autism, in addition to the Tonge et al. (2006) study described above. Although the evidence base is small, there are some controlled studies that support the use of cognitive behavioral therapy (CBT) group interventions for parents of children with developmental disabilities, including parents of children with autism (Gammon & Rose, 1991; Greaves, 1997; Nixon & Singer, 1993; Singer, Irvin, & Hawkins, 1988; Singer, Irvin, Irvine, Hawkins, & Cooley, 1989). However, data specifically on parents of children with autism are rare in the literature. Bitsika and Sharpley (2000) described positive outcomes of a stress management group intervention for parents of children with autism, and Bristol, Gallagher, and Holt (1993) reported the results of a psycho-educational intervention that putatively reduced stress and symptoms of depression. Other data on a general support group fail to support a positive impact on maternal mental health (Shu & Lung, 2005).

Encouraging data relating to the effects of modern behavior therapy have been reported recently. Blackledge and Hayes (2006) used Acceptance and Commitment Therapy (ACT: Hayes, Strosahl, & Wilson, 1999) as a group intervention for reducing depression and stress experienced by parents of children with autism. In this intervention, parents were taught to accept their feelings of stress rather than battle to try to reduce and avoid these feelings, as this can be counter-productive to well-being. Instead, parents were encouraged to clearly identify the values important to them and the care of their child, and to develop actions for their lives consistent with these values. The intervention was delivered during 14 hours of workshop-based intervention. Using a single-group comparison design, data were collated for parents in three of these treatment groups. Parents were assessed pre-, during, and post-intervention. Both depression and stress were significantly reduced post treatment and at three month follow-up, and mothers also showed significantly increased levels of general acceptance across these time periods. The data were suggestive of a mediational relationship between acceptance and psychological distress (i.e., the intervention may have had its main effect by increasing acceptance), though these findings are not conclusive, since no control group was used.

A particular problem with the scant literature on direct stress interventions for parents of children with autism is that there is no clear link between basic family research in the field and the design of interventions (Hastings & Beck, 2004). This may be due in part to the lack of data on psychological processes/mechanisms in the research literature on parental stress and adjustment. The Blackledge and Hayes (2006) research is significant in this respect, as ACT is very much a process-focused intervention, and the mechanism of change was explored in the analyses. Acceptance is the ability to take what is offered without trying to avoid experience (Hayes et al., 1999), and evidence that avoidant coping is associated with stress for both mothers and fathers of children with autism (Hastings et al., 2005a) may provide some support that these are processes that should be the target of interventions for parents. ACT requires further research as an intervention for parents, and further study of the processes responsible for parent stress is also needed.

Conclusions and Integration Section

This chapter has evolved from the perspective of research being conducted with family members of children with autism, especially parents. A broad summary of the relevant literature suggests that there are sufficient data to be concerned that parents of children with autism are at increased risk for stress and other outcomes such as mental health problems. To date, an exploration of what it might be about autism that causes parents this increased stress suggests that behavior problems are the most important factor. However, few studies have explored variation in the underlying deficits in autism as a potential explanation for variation in parental outcomes, and at present such explorations have been at a relatively gross level (e.g., overall total scores on autism rating scales). Thus, there is a great deal more work to do in identifying features of autism that might place parents at significant risk of problems themselves. A particular challenge for researchers exploring the putative impact of autism on family members is to disentangle the contribution made by the broader phenotype of autism. Of most relevance here is that parents and other family members seem to be at a genetic risk for psychiatric problems.

Although these research questions may be interesting, the focus on what it is about autism that leads to increased stress for parents might detract from some more fundamental questions for families. Autism is clearly associated with a variety of cognitive and social deficits as well as behavioral excesses. Thus, children with autism are likely to be a challenge to parents in parenting terms. Perhaps the most important questions about parental adjustment are about how or why some family members become significantly stressed whilst others seem to cope perfectly well. Data on these processes at an individual level, but also in terms of the family system, are extremely thin on the ground. This is despite the fact that building a research-based model of parental adjustment could inform the development of support interventions for parents. There are encouraging data that psychological interventions at an individual or group level might be useful in helping parents to adjust, but interventions tested so far are more focused on a best guess about what might be useful rather than being grounded in a research evidence base.

There are four additional observations that may be important to make and that provide some context for the work described in other chapters in this book. First, it is crucial when developing interventions aimed at children, young people, or adults with autism that the potential involvement of and impact on family members are considered. I have already discussed research that addresses whether intensive interventions focused on children with autism impact negatively on parents and other family members. However, there is a further dimension that is important to consider. There is some evidence that the family environment may be a key factor in the success of interventions for children with disabilities. For example, intervention for children may be more successful when parents are less stressed (Robbins, Dunlap, & Plienis, 1991). Several chapters in this book emphasize the need to involve parents in intervention for children (and potentially adults) as a way of improving outcomes for the individual with autism (Golan & Baron-Cohen, Chapter 12; Jones & Jordan, Chapter 14). Furthermore, generalization of skills developed in intervention is a particularly challenging clinical issue, and

parents might play a key role in supporting individuals with autism to generalize what they have learnt within the family and outside (Golan & Baron-Cohen,
Chapter 12; Dunlop, Knott, & MacKay, Chapter 13).

My second observation is that the implications for families of research on the
early identification of autism must be addressed. This is significant at a number of
levels. One level is the impact, negative or positive, on receiving a diagnosis and the
best way to deliver a diagnosis. It is also important to consider the potential impact
of both false positive and false negative screening results on families (Williams,
Chapter 10). The psychological ramifications may be considerable, and it is imperative to include these concerns as a part of the ethical discussion surrounding the
benefits and problems of screening. A second is how parents are then best supported to consider how the family will go forward and integrate this information
into their future. It is likely that early support for families in these circumstances
would help to prevent later adjustment problems for parents, siblings, and potentially also for the extended family. However, this is clearly a prediction that requires
further research. A third implication is what to offer parents by way of advice about
intervention approaches for their child with autism. The evidence base relating to
outcomes for children is an important part of this, but what is needed is some way
of clarifying what might suit particular families and at what times (Jones & Jordan,
Chapter 14). For example, an intensive program like ABA may not be suitable for
some families, and others may need additional family support to ensure the most
beneficial outcomes for the children.

In terms of how best to support families, if we can identify signs of autism early
(perhaps as young as 6 months—Maestro & Muratori, Chapter 9), we actually
know little about what might be efficacious. The problem is the lack of research
evidence on family experiences when children who later develop autism are this
young. By the preschool years, for example, an association between stress and the
child's behavior problems is already established. However, behavior problems are
unlikely to dominate parents' experience of stress before this time. An integration
of early screening and family research is needed to begin to address parents' support needs at this stage, which could be then addressed with family interventions.

The third general observation about future questions relates to early developmental processes in autism (Leekam & McGregor, Chapter 16). Given that many of the
key difficulties in autism are associated with social behavior and social cognition, the
family context must be important to our understanding of interaction effects. Thus,
children at risk of developing problems in the social domain might well be most
disadvantaged in family environments that, for whatever reason, are less supportive of their needs. Ultimately, children might be helped by very early interventions
focused on parent–child interactions. Although early social behavior has been studied extensively in autism, there is a lack of analysis of the variables that might help us

to understand the parent side of the interaction equation. Thus, a broader research analysis is needed to put some of these developmental problems into context.

The fourth general observation relating to the integration of material discussed in this volume builds further on the previous question about the role of the family environment, and specifically parents, in the development or exacerbation of the symptoms of autism. Psychogenic theory (Jones & Jordan, Chapter 14) was clearly not helpful, but the historical backlash may have had an impact on the kinds of questions that family researchers ask about autism. Much existing research has focused on the impact that the child with autism can have on parents. One implication of research showing the bi-directional relationships between child behavior problems and parental stress (Lecavalier et al., 2006) is that we need more of a research focus on parents of children with autism and their parenting (i.e., their interactions with their children). A good example of a point that needs to be considered here is that several of the executive function problems in autism (Hill, Chapter 8), which may be a part of the broader phenotype too, may have implications for parenting. Parenting is a highly complex task, involving planning skills, mental flexibility, creativity, and multitasking. Should research support a link between minor difficulties with such skills and parenting behavior, interventions for parents to help them develop strategies to improve their skills may be warranted. Parents being aware of their own difficulties in these executive domains may also increase their empathy with their child's difficulties, perhaps having an additional positive effect.

These final two discussion points have to be clarified because of the historical context. It is not being argued that parents cause autism by the way in which they parent, but rather that the developmental course of autism and well-being in the family might be related to parental characteristics associated with a broader genetic risk and/or to the psychological impact that characteristics of children with autism can have on parents. Research and clinical knowledge on the relevant processes needs to be expanded significantly to inform parents and clinicians how best to support children with autism and their family life.

References

Abbeduto, L., Seltzer, M. M., Shattuck, P., Krauss, M. W., Orsmond, G., & Murphy, M. M. (2004). Psychological well-being and coping in mothers of youths with autism, Down syndrome, or fragile X syndrome. *American Journal on Mental Retardation, 109,* 237–254.

Abidin, R. R. (1990). *Parenting Stress Index.* Odessa, FL: Psychological Assessment Resources.

Bågenholm, A., & Gillberg, C. (1991). Psychosocial effects on siblings of children with autism and mental retardation: A population-based study. *Journal of Mental Deficiency Research, 35,* 291–307.

Baker, B. L., Blacher, J., Crnic, K., & Edelbrock, C. (2002). Behavior problems and parenting stress in families of three-year-old children with and without developmental delays. *American Journal on Mental Retardation, 107*, 433–444.

Baker, B. L., McIntyre, L. L., Blacher, J., Crnic, K., Edelbrock, C., & Low, C. (2003). Preschool children with and without developmental delay: Behaviour problems and parenting stress over time. *Journal of Intellectual Disability Research, 47*, 217–230.

Baron, R. M., & Kenny, D. A. (1986). The moderator–mediator variable distinction in social psychological research: Conceptual, strategic, and statistical considerations. *Journal of Personality and Social Psychology, 51*, 1173–1182.

Baxter, C., Cummins, R. A., & Yiolitis, L. (2000). Parental stress attributed to family members with and without disability: A longitudinal study. *Journal of Intellectual and Developmental Disability, 25*, 105–118.

Bebko, J. M., Konstantareas, M. M., & Springer, J. (1987). Parent and professional evaluations of family stress associated with characteristics of autism. *Journal of Autism and Developmental Disorders, 17*, 565–576.

Beck, A., Hastings, R. P., Daley, D. M., & Stevenson, J. (2004). Pro-social behaviour and behaviour problems independently predict maternal stress. *Journal of Intellectual and Developmental Disability, 29*, 339–349.

Beckman, P. J. (1991). Comparison of mothers' and fathers' perceptions of the effect of young children with and without disabilities. *American Journal on Mental Retardation, 95*, 585–595.

Birnbrauer, J. S., & Leach, D. J. (1993). The Murdoch Early Intervention Program after two years. *Behaviour Change, 10*, 63–74.

Bitsika, V., & Sharpley, C. (2000). Development and testing of the effects of support groups on the well-being of parents of children with autism, II: Specific stress management techniques. *Journal of Applied Health Behaviour, 2*, 8–15.

Blacher, J., Shapiro, J., Lopez, S., Diaz, L., & Fusco, J. (1997). Depression in Latina mothers of children with mental retardation: A neglected concern. *American Journal on Mental Retardation, 101*, 483–496.

Blackledge, J. T., & Hayes, S. C. (2006). Using acceptance and commitment training in the support of parents of children diagnosed with autism. *Child and Family Behavior Therapy, 28*, 1–18.

Bouma, R., & Schweitzer, R. (1990). The impact of chronic childhood illness on family stress: A comparison between autism and cystic fibrosis. *Journal of Clinical Psychology, 46*, 722–730.

Bristol, M. M., Gallagher, J. J., & Holt, K. D. (1993). Maternal depressive symptoms in autism: Response to psychoeducational intervention. *Rehabilitation Psychology, 38*, 3–10.

Bristol, M. M., Gallagher, J. J., & Schopler, E. (1988). Mothers and fathers of young developmentally disabled and nondisabled boys: Adaptation and spousal support. *Developmental Psychology, 24*, 441–451.

Bromley, J., Hare, D. J., Davison, K., & Emerson, E. (2004). Mothers supporting children with autistic spectrum disorders: Social support, mental health status and satisfaction with services. *Autism, 8*, 409–423.

Cohen, J. (1992). A power primer. *Psychological Bulletin, 112*, 155–159.

Cook, T. D., & Campbell, D. T. (1979). *Quasi-experimentation: Design and analysis issues for field settings*. Boston: Houghton Mifflin.

Duarte, C. S., Bordin, I. A., Yazigi, L., & Mooney, J. (2005). Factors associated with stress in mothers of children with autism. *Autism, 9*, 416–427.

Dumas, J. E., Wolf, L. C., Fisman, S. N., & Culligan, A. (1991). Parenting stress, child behavior problems, and dysphoria in parents of children with autism, Down syndrome, behavior disorders, and normal development. *Exceptionality, 2*, 97–110.

Dyson, L. L. (1991). Families of young children with handicaps: Parental stress and family functioning. *American Journal on Mental Retardation, 95*, 623–629.

Emerson, E. (2003). Mothers of children and adolescents with intellectual disability: Social and economic situation, mental health status, and the self-assessed social and psychological impact of the child's difficulties. *Journal of Intellectual Disability Research, 47*, 385–399.

Factor, D. C., Perry, A., & Freeman, N. (1990). Stress, social support, and respite care use in families with autistic children. *Journal of Autism and Developmental Disorders, 20*, 139–146.

Fisman, S., Wolf, L., Ellison, D., Gillis, B., Freeman, T., & Szartmari, P. (1996). Risk and protective factors affecting the adjustment of siblings of children with chronic disabilities. *Journal of the American Academy of Child and Adolescent Psychiatry, 35*, 1532–1541.

Fombonne, E., Bolton, P., Prior, J., Jordan, H., & Rutter, M. (1997). A family study of autism: Cognitive patterns and levels in parents and siblings. *Journal of Child Psychology and Psychiatry, 38*, 667–683.

Friedrich, W. N., & Friedrich, W. L. (1981). Psychosocial assets of parents of handicapped and non-handicapped children. *American Journal of Mental Deficiency, 85*, 551–553.

Gammon, E. A., & Rose, S. D. (1991). The Coping Skills Training Program for parents of children with developmental disabilities: An experimental evaluation. *Research on Social Work Practice, 1*, 244–256.

Gold, N. (1993). Depression and social adjustment in siblings of boys with autism. *Journal of Autism and Developmental Disorders, 23*, 147–163.

Gray, D. E., & Holden, W. J. (1992). Psycho-social well-being among parents of children with autism. *Australia and New Zealand Journal of Developmental Disabilities, 18*, 83–93.

Greaves, D. (1997). The effect of rational-emotive parent education on the stress of mothers of young children with Down syndrome. *Journal of Rational-Emotive and Cognitive-Behavior Therapy, 15*, 249–267.

Harris, S. L., Handleman, J. S., & Palmer, C. (1985). Parents' and grandparents' view the autistic child. *Journal of Autism and Developmental Disorders, 15*, 127–137.

Hastings, R. P. (2002). Parental stress and behaviour problems of children with developmental disability. *Journal of Intellectual and Developmental Disability, 27*, 149–160.

Hastings, R. P. (2003). Child behaviour problems and partner mental health as correlates of stress in mothers and fathers of children with autism. *Journal of Intellectual Disability Research, 47*, 231–237.

Hastings, R. P. (in press). Longitudinal relationships between sibling behavioral adjustment and behavior problems of children with developmental disabilities. *Journal of Autism and Developmental Disorders*.

Hastings, R. P., & Beck, A. (2004). Stress intervention for parents of children with intellectual disabilities. *Journal of Child Psychology and Psychiatry, 45*, 1338–1349.

Hastings, R. P., & Brown, T. (2002). Behavior problems of autistic children, parental self-efficacy and mental health. *American Journal on Mental Retardation, 107*, 222–232.

Hastings, R. P., Daley, D., Burns, C., & Beck, A. (2006). Maternal distress and expressed emotion: Cross-sectional and longitudinal relationships with behavior problems of children with intellectual disabilities. *American Journal on Mental Retardation, 111*, 48–61.

Hastings, R. P., & Johnson, E. (2001). Stress in UK families conducting intensive home-based behavioral intervention for their young child with autism. *Journal of Autism and Developmental Disorders, 31*, 327–336.

Hastings, R. P., Kovshoff, H., Brown, T., Ward, N. J., degli Espinosa, F., & Remington, B. (2005a). Coping strategies in mothers and fathers of pre-school and school age children with autism. *Autism, 9*, 377–391.

Hastings, R. P., Kovshoff, H., Ward, N. J., degli Espinosa, F., Brown, T., & Remington, B. (2005b). Systems analysis of stress and positive perceptions in mothers and fathers of pre-school children with autism. *Journal of Autism and Developmental Disorders, 35*, 635–644.

Hastings, R. P., & Mount, R. H. (2001). Early correlates of behavioural and emotional problems in children and adolescents with severe learning disabilities. *Journal of Applied Research in Intellectual Disabilities, 14*, 381–391.

Hastings, R. P., Thomas, H., & Delwiche, N. (2002). Grandparent support for families of children with Down syndrome. *Journal of Applied Research in Intellectual Disabilities, 15*, 97–104.

Hayes, S. C., Strosahl, K. D., & Wilson, K. G. (1999). *Acceptance and commitment therapy: An experiential approach to behavior change*. New York: Guilford Press.

Haynes, S. N. (1992). *Models of causality in psychopathology: Toward dynamic, synthetic and nonlinear models of behavior disorders*. New York: Macmillan.

Honey, E., Hastings, R. P., & McConachie, H. (2005). Use of the Questionnaire on Resources and Stress (QRS-F) with parents of young children with autism. *Autism, 9*, 246–255.

Howlin, P. (1988). Living with impairment: The effects on children of having an autistic sibling. *Child: Care, Health and Development, 14*, 395–408.

Hughes, C., Plumet, M. H., & Leboyer, M. (1999). Towards a cognitive phenotype for autism: Increased prevalence of executive dysfunction and superior spatial span amongst siblings of children with autism. *Journal of Child Psychology and Psychiatry, 40*, 705–718.

Kazdin, A. E., Kraemer, H. C., Kessler, R. C., Kupfer, D. J., & Offord, D. R. (1997). Contributions of risk-factor research to developmental psychopathology. *Clinical Psychology Review, 17*, 375–406.

Koegel, R. L., Schreibman, L., Loos, L. M., Dirlich-Wilheim, H., Dunlap, G., Robbins, F. R., et al. (1992). Consistent stress profiles in mothers of children with autism. *Journal of Autism and Developmental Disorders, 22*, 205–216.

Konstantareas, M. M., & Homatidis, S. (1989). Assessing child symptom severity and stress in parents of autistic children. *Journal of Child Psychology and Psychiatry, 30*, 459–470.

Konstantareas, M. M., Homatidis, S., & Plowright, C. M. S. (1992). Assessing resources and stress in parents of severely dysfunctional children through the Clarke modification of Holroyd's Questionnaire on Resources and Stress. *Journal of Autism and Developmental Disorders, 22,* 217–234.

Lecavalier, L., Leone, S., & Wiltz, J. (2006). The impact of behaviour problems on caregiver stress in young people with autism spectrum disorders. *Journal of Intellectual Disability Research, 50,* 172–183.

Lovaas, O. I. (1987). Behavioural treatment and normal educational and intellectual functioning in young autistic children. *Journal of Consulting and Clinical Psychology, 55,* 3–9.

Luthar, S. S., & Zigler, E. (1991). Vulnerability and competence: A review of research on resilience in childhood. *American Journal of Orthopsychiatry, 61,* 6–22.

McClintock, S., Hall, S., & Oliver, C. (2003). Risk markers associated with challenging behaviours in people with intellectual disabilities: A meta-analytic study. *Journal of Intellectual Disability Research, 47,* 405–416.

McEachin, J. J., Smith, T., & Lovaas, O. I. (1993). Long-term outcome for children with autism who received early intensive behavioral treatment. *American Journal on Mental Retardation, 97,* 359–372.

Moes, D., Koegel, R. L., Schreibman, L., & Loos, L. M. (1992). Stress profiles for mothers and fathers of children with autism. *Psychological Reports, 71,* 1272–1274.

Nihira, K., Mink, I. T., & Meyers, C. E. (1985). Home environment and development of slow-learning adolescents: Reciprocal relations. *Developmental Psychology, 21,* 784–794.

Nixon, C. D., & Singer, G. H. S. (1993). Group cognitive-behavioral treatment for excessive parental self-blame and guilt. *American Journal on Mental Retardation, 97,* 665–672.

Orr, R. R., Cameron, S. J., Dobson, L. A., & Day, D. M. (1993). Age-related changes in stress experienced by families with a child who has developmental delays. *Mental Retardation, 31,* 171–176.

Orsmond, G. I., Seltzer, M. M., Krauss, M. W., & Hong, J. (2003). Behavior problems in adults with mental retardation and maternal well-being: Examination of the direction of effects. *American Journal on Mental Retardation, 108,* 257–271.

Pilowsky, T., Yirmiya, N., Doppelt, O., Gross-Tsur, V., & Shalev, R. S. (2004). Social and emotional adjustment of siblings of children with autism. *Journal of Child Psychology and Psychiatry, 45,* 855–865.

Piven, J., & Palmer, P. (1997). Cognitive deficits in parents from multiple-incidence autism families. *Journal of Child Psychology and Psychiatry, 38,* 1011–1022.

Quine, L., & Pahl, J. (1985). Examining the causes of stress in families with severely mentally handicapped children. *British Journal of Social Work, 15,* 501–517.

Quine, L., & Pahl, J. (1991). Stress and coping in mothers caring for a child with severe learning difficulties: A test of Lazarus' transactional model of coping. *Journal of Community and Applied Social Psychology, 1,* 57–70.

Remington, B., Hastings, R. P., Kovshoff, H., degli Espinosa, F., Jahr, E., Brown, T., et al. (in press). A field effectiveness study of early intensive behavioral intervention: Outcomes for children with autism and their parents after two years. *American Journal on Mental Retardation.*

Robbins, F. R., Dunlap, G., & Plienis, A. J. (1991). Family characteristics, family training, and the progress of young children with autism. *Journal of Early Intervention, 15,* 173–184.

Rodrigue, J. R., Geffken, G. R., & Morgan, S. B. (1993). Perceived competence and behavioral adjustment of siblings of children with autism. *Journal of Autism and Developmental Disorders, 23,* 665–674.

Rodrigue, J. R., Morgan, S. B., & Geffken, G. (1990). Families of autistic children: Psychological functioning of mothers. *Journal of Clinical Child Psychology, 19,* 371–379.

Rutter, M. (1985). Resilience in the face of adversity: Protective factors and resistance to psychiatric disorder. *British Journal of Psychiatry, 147,* 598–611.

Sanders, J. L., & Morgan, S. B. (1997). Family stress and adjustment as perceived by parents of children with autism or Down syndrome: Implications for intervention. *Child and Family Behavior Therapy, 19,* 15–32.

Shu, B. C., & Lung, F. W. (2005). The effect of support group on the mental health and quality of life for mothers with autistic children. *Journal of Intellectual Disability Research, 49,* 47–53.

Singer, G. H. S. (2006). Meta-analysis of comparative studies of depression in mothers of children with and without developmental disabilities. *American Journal on Mental Retardation, 111,* 155–169.

Singer, G. H. S., Irvin, L. K., & Hawkins, N. (1988). Stress management training for parents of children with severe handicaps. *Mental Retardation, 26,* 269–277.

Singer, G. H. S., Irvin, L. K., Irvine, B., Hawkins, N., & Cooley, E. (1989). Evaluation of community-based support services for families of persons with developmental disabilities. *Journal of the Association for Persons with Severe Handicaps, 14,* 312–323.

Sloper, P., Knussen, C., Turner, S., & Cunningham, C. (1991). Factors related to stress and satisfaction with life in families of children with Down syndrome. *Journal of Child Psychology and Psychiatry, 32,* 655–676.

Smith, T., Buch, G. A., & Gamby, T. E. (2000). Parent-directed, intensive early intervention for children with pervasive developmental disorder. *Research in Developmental Disabilities, 21,* 297–309.

Smith, T., Groen, A. D., & Wynn, J. W. (2000). Randomized trial of intensive early intervention for children with pervasive developmental disorder. *American Journal on Mental Retardation, 105,* 269–285.

Stores, R., Stores, G., Fellows, B., & Buckley, S. (1998). Daytime behaviour problems and maternal stress in children with Down's syndrome, their siblings, and non-intellectually disabled and other intellectually disabled peers. *Journal of Intellectual Disability Research, 42,* 228–237.

Tobing, L. E., & Glenwick, D. S. (2002). Relation of the Childhood Autism Rating Scale—Parent version to diagnosis, stress, and age. *Research in Developmental Disabilities, 23,* 211–223.

Tomanik, S., Harris, G. E., & Hawkins, J. (2004). The relationship between behaviours exhibited by children with autism and maternal stress. *Journal of Intellectual and Developmental Disability, 29,* 16–26.

Tonge, B., Brereton, A., Kiomall, M., Mackinnon, A., King, N., & Rinehart, N. (2006). Effects on parental mental health of an education and skills training program for parents of young children with autism: A randomized controlled trial. *Journal of the American Academy of Child and Adolescent Psychiatry, 45*, 561–569.

Weiss, M. J. (2002). Hardiness and social support as predictors of stress in typical children, children with autism, and children with mental retardation. *Autism, 6*, 115–130.

Wolf, L. C., Noh, S., Fisman, S. N., & Speechley, M. (1989). Psychological effects of parenting stress on parents of autistic children. *Journal of Autism and Developmental Disorders, 19*, 157–166.

Yirmiya, N., & Shaked, M. (2005). Psychiatric disorders in parents of children with autism: A meta-analysis. *Journal of Child Psychology and Psychiatry, 46*, 69–83.

16

Conclusion

Integrating Neurocognitive, Diagnostic, and Intervention Perspectives in Autism

Susan Leekam and Evelyn McGregor

The aim of this book has been to present differing theoretical and applied perspectives on autism and to promote integration between these perspectives. In this final chapter, we revisit the question raised in the Introduction of why these perspectives should be integrated, and how, in real terms, this goal may be achieved. We start with an historical explanation of why different approaches to autism lack integration in the first place, and why it is important to form connections not only within areas of obvious common interest, but also across disparate ideas, traditions, and fields of expertise. We then consider whether and how it will be possible to create meaningful and productive connections across these different areas of expertise, given the range of difficulties at both theoretical and applied levels. Finally, we look at the question of what it will take at a practical level to consolidate connections across different approaches and disciplines.

Why do Neurocognitive, Clinical/Diagnostic, and Social-Educational Approaches Lack Integration?

The range of topics discussed in the book spans diagnosis, neurocognition, and intervention. Why do these fields tend to work independently of each other? One explanation might be that this is the result of a theoretical/practical divide in which some professionals in autism are working as researchers and others as practitioners, and that each of these professional groups has different priorities and concerns. This is a reasonable proposition, since a theory/practice divide does exist. However, it is not the whole story. The segregation of different research and practitioner areas in autism also can be accounted for in a different way, in terms of the historical origins that have directed research toward either the "developmental" or the "disorder" aspect of developmental disorders. These separate historical roots have, in turn, had an influence in shaping our theorizing and our practitioner expertise.

The historical influence of medical science versus developmental science may have contributed to a lack of integration in research in autism because of fundamental differences in theoretical assumptions and focus (see Burack, 1997, for discussion). Originally the central questions from medical science that applied to autism came from *adult* models of psychiatry, biology, and neuropsychology. These questions concerned the primacy of causal factors, involving the uncovering of the central, underlying nature of neurological and neuropsychological impairments. By explaining these underlying problems at the biological level, it was believed that the resulting psychological and behavioral symptoms could then be explained. This was certainly an approach that could provide clear answers in adult neuropsychology where specific affected areas could be identified through patterns of impaired and spared functioning, thereby supporting a domain-specific model of cognitive functioning. In contrast, traditional developmental models have historically focused on principles of change and on the dynamic nature of development across all areas of functioning. Within the framework of typical development, questions about finite causes have been less important than understanding the process of change (illustrated, for example, in the works of Piaget and Vygotsky [Piaget, 1955; Piaget & Inhelder, 1941; Vygotsky, 1962, 1966]). Up until now, perhaps because the identification of autism took place within medicine, it is the traditional assumptions from medical science that have been most influential in the field of autism.

The assumptions that dominate scientific thinking do not only affect research. They also become foundational in the training of practitioners. These assumptions go on to pervade everyday work for the practitioner and influence the development of policy. Theoretical scientific knowledge and assumptions from medical science transfer to the training of clinicians and health-care workers, while assumptions from traditional theories in developmental psychology may potentially infiltrate training in the practice of education and childcare. These divisions are instantiated by government policy and politics in the UK with health care "belonging" in a different government sector than education.

While the end points from theory do influence practice through the training of practitioners, there is also a deep *dis*connection between theory and practice. Practitioners and researchers, especially those in the areas of developmental science related to cognitive, language, and emotional development, do not tend to work alongside one another. This can create a real divide in terms of the dissemination of ideas between people who work "on the ground" with children with autism and those who do not. Each of these professionals has different priorities and concerns and access to different resources. The result of all this is that at a professional

Figure 16.1 An illustration of the connections and disconnections among medical and developmental research and practice.

level we are left with demarcation between who researches, who diagnoses, and who provides treatment, an "ethnocentrism" of perspectives.

In summary, historically in the field of autism there has been a double disconnection that has separated "developmental" from "disorder" and has separated research from practice (see Figure 16.1). As a result, different assumptions and questions have guided "medical" and "developmental" research in autism, and research and practice have carried on in parallel with each other, without explicit recognition of the value of integration.

Why Should We Connect?

The case for connecting across different theoretical perspectives was convincingly made at least a decade ago in an excellent review of the field, in which Bailey, Phillips, and Rutter (1996) argued that we should aim to integrate neurobiological, genetic, and psychological perspectives in autism. The opportunity for integration seemed to be especially ripe at this time, because in the 1980s and 1990s the developmental science perspective, previously led by the theories of Piaget and Vygotsky, had become sidelined, and was overtaken by ideas stemming from the information-processing theories of psychology and the neurosciences (Burack, 1997). A number of cognitive models were proposed in the 1980s and 1990s that drew directly from adult neuropsychology and cognitive psychology, including the theories of "theory of mind," executive functioning and weak central coherence. This opened up the possibility of taking up the challenge of integration that Bailey et al. were advocating.

Why, then, has the goal of integration not been achieved, at least ten years after it was proposed by Bailey and others? Why do we still lack connection between perspectives? There seem to have been several related issues that have together worked against this goal of integration as it was originally conceived. The first related to the difficulty of answering empirical questions that were set up with the aim of identifying specific causal mechanisms that would create a direct link between biological, cognitive, and behavioral levels of functioning. The search for candidate genes for autism, the search for specific brain damage at a cellular or functional level, and the search for a specific cognitive deficit all seemed to lead to the same conclusion. Causal mechanisms cannot be identified at the level of specificity that enables us to build a traditional causal model linking different levels of functioning—biological, cognitive, and behavioral. Chapter 1 notes that some limited attempts were made, but the growing realization of the complexity of such an enterprise may have discouraged progress. The call has recently been made once more: Dawson et al. (2002), for example, argue for the need not only to integrate research findings, but also to integrate approaches and concepts. However, now the call is made with recognition of the likely complexity of any integrated modeling.

Meanwhile, developmental science has been undergoing something of a renaissance. For those researching typical development in the 1980s and 1990s, the field was dominated by cognition, to an extent shaped by theories from adult cognition and cognitive neuropsychology. At the end of the 1990s and early 2000s came a resurgence of interest and ideas concerning developmental change. These were drawn from earlier concepts of Piagetian influence but embraced new ideas in neuroscience (Johnson, 2006; Johnson & Munakata, 2005; Karmiloff-Smith, 1997; Lewis, 2000; Thelen, 1992; Van Geert, 1998). These new ideas came from the areas of neuroconstructivism, dynamic systems theory, and microgenetics: theoretical and technical advances have reawakened interest in exploring processes of change and are offering new opportunities to do so, marking a shift from the cognitive research culture that has used static descriptions at different ages (Johnson & Munakata, 2005). Crucially, these new ideas are not only being taken up in research in typical development but have become influential also in some areas of atypical development—in Williams syndrome, language impairments, dyslexia, and emotional disorders (Bishop, 1997; Goswami, 2003; Karmiloff-Smith et al., 1997; Lewis, 2004; Paterson et al., 1999).

So here we have a new opportunity to connect across the former "medical model" and "developmental model" divide, but with a new set of questions that are directed more emphatically toward developmental change and may ultimately find answers to the causal questions by adopting this approach. Again we have the promising opportunity for integration. This work of integrating across perspectives is gaining pace in other areas of typical and atypical development, yet it has not gone very far at all in the field of autism. In fact, much research in autism still continues to proceed within separate, bounded, theoretical, or professional areas.

If research in autism has avoided integration so far, then why should new ideas in developmental science be the best way forward? After all, these new ideas in developmental science are themselves not integrated, and the approaches of subdisciplines in medical science are also quite separate. Can we not just keep to our original assumptions and continue with what we know?

A good reason for taking up the mantle of integration right now is that an integrated approach to autism has more to offer toward progress in the field than it ever has previously. At a theoretical level, progress has already been made to cross the divide between traditional medical models and developmental models. The pioneering work of Karmiloff-Smith and colleagues and Bishop and colleagues and the development of neuroconstructivism as a framework have already been successful in helping to close the theoretical gap between adult models of disorder drawn from neurospsychology and models of childhood disorders (Bishop, 1997; Thomas & Karmiloff-Smith, 2002).

Increasingly, the assumption of similarity with cognitive models taken from adult neuropsychology has been challenged. Karmiloff-Smith (1997) argues that developmental (and especially genetic) disorders are likely to have an extended atypical trajectory, since early impairment can affect all downstream processes, causing patterns of associated impairments, whereas acquired adult disorders are marked by dissociation of impaired and spared functioning. Developmental neuroscience models offer scope to incorporate patterns of associated impairment, allowing for interaction of developmental stages over time and for atypical compensatory strategies (Bishop, 1997). For example, Wimmer et al. (2002) apply a neuroconstructive approach to dyslexia, and Patterson et al. (1999) describe mapping change in Williams syndrome.

At the theoretical level, therefore, progress across the divide has already started, and we need to allow this work that centers on developmental change to continue. Importantly, however, a new call for integration does not limit itself to connecting across perspectives within research alone. Because the more recent theoretical perspectives highlight the importance of focusing on developmental change, this is also good news for practice.

As the dominant position until recently has been to focus on identification of specific underlying causes and specific behaviors, there has been a natural lack of connection with those practitioners who focus on the development of children's behavior and skills in areas of education and intervention. By having a research agenda that already focuses on developmental change at the theoretical level, the potential for narrowing the gap between research and intervention in these fields is greater. So, instead of research being geared toward either causal questions or questions related to developmental change therefore, both research and practice can move together toward tracing the processing and mechanisms of change through either intervention or learning models. As Bishop (1997) commented,

> It is time for researchers to recognise that intervention studies are not just an optional, applied adjunct to experimental work, but that they provide the best method available for evaluating hypotheses and confounding correlated factors (p. 919).

To summarize: the original call for integration across different perspectives remains as strong today as it was ten years ago. What will facilitate that process is to shift the purpose for that integration. While the goal of integrating neurobiological, genetic, and psychological perspectives was originally about understanding causal mechanisms, we argue that it needs now to be about understanding more complex patterns of causal processes via developmental change. We think that this new goal will not only help to connect it to the former medical and developmental divide but also help to bridge the divide between research and practice.

How Should We Connect?

McGregor, Núñez, Cebula, and Gómez proposed in Chapter 1 that the starting point for integration would be the creation of opportunities to share perspectives across diverse areas. The seminar series fostered such an opportunity, and in their chapters, the contributors to this book provide a representative sample of that range of perspectives. Chapter 1 suggested that the next step was to consider the implications of research findings from one area to those of others, incorporating both research and practice. To support this process, each chapter ends with a separate "integration section." In these, contributors have identified links with other chapters within and across research fields and across research and practice, discussing the theoretical, conceptual, and practical issues. One aim of this process is to formalize "cross-talk." A more ambitious one is to prepare the ground for active collaboration as part of a move toward integrated models.

The contributors have approached the task in several ways. In some cases, just a few quite specific links with other chapters were made and discussed at some length (e.g., López, Chapter 6). In others, multiple links have been more broadly suggested (e.g., Jones & Jordan, Chapter 14). Across this wide range of contributions several integration themes emerge. Initially the potential impact of their research on other areas, both research and practice, is considered. Allied to this, the authors in this volume have also speculated about how they might expand their research through within-disciplinary or interdisciplinary collaboration, or through incorporating approaches or theoretical perspectives from others. Importantly, many have posited broader interpretations of their research findings in the light of those reported in other chapters. In particular, Wicker's research on underlying neural processes in autism (Chapter 2) was widely taken into consideration by others from a variety of areas. Most authors, too, speculated about ways in which their research might contribute to intervention. The process of actively locating individual research within the broader arena seemed to clarify the nature of problems or obstacles in several areas. In a practical sense, it drew attention to difficulties in screening, in creating opportunities for early intervention, and in enabling intervention to keep pace with developing theory and research findings. From the theoretical aspect, the integration sections raised questions about the interpretation of research findings and the potential for mapping findings from one area onto those of another. For example, López (Chapter 6) discussed the relevance of Loth's research on event knowledge for her work in central coherence and the potential of Loth's research for reconnecting social and non-social aspects of cognitive processing in autism. Maestro and Muratori (Chapter 9) postulated that the autistic infant's behavior could have an emotional impact on parents, the focus of Hastings's chapter. These sections indicate that there is a broad interest in integrating perspectives, that there are genuine gains to be made in doing so, first in the scope offered for developing research themes, second for research and practice to inform one another. No overarching framework is possible at this point, but a general move toward collaborative working could help plan the foundations.

Other than the willingness of prospective participants, the biggest issue for a process of integration is methodological. The argument put forward in this chapter has been that integration would be achieved to best effect through the adoption of the new methods in developmental science outlined above. Do the integration sections contribute to that in any way? Do they provide any building blocks to help that process? What adaptations might be required to strengthen it? Several contributors wrote about the potential value and relevance of adopting a developmental approach to autism research. As a starting point, both Loth and Wicker argued for the need for longitudinal data in their respective fields. Loth noted the cumulative developmental effect of other aspects of atypical processing, such as social engagement and imitative learning, for the gradual acquisition of cultural knowledge. McCann, Peppé, Gibbon, O'Hare, and Rutherford (Chapter 11) posited that a developmental perspective was necessary to understand the relationships between prosody, language, and cognition. Wicker noted the need for developmental studies to account for the origin of abnormal functional connectivity. In principle, the value of such an approach was supported. The next step is to explore methods of implementing such an approach, something the contributors did not broach directly.

Learning From Other Models

In the study of other childhood disorders, such as SLI and dyslexia, there is evidence of success in bringing development to the forefront and in connecting with neuroscience (Bishop, 1997; Goswami, 2003). But attention to developmental issues also raises problems for the way we think about disorders. Once you start to include a developmental perspective, then you have to ask questions about what you are looking at. Autism is commonly described as a neurodevelopmental disorder, but in accordance with the international psychiatric classification systems, it is identified and diagnosed in terms of non-developmental, static behavioral features. Symptoms change with age, and so do many psychological functions. So, are you looking at the same disorder at different time points or not? With this in mind, we may need to think carefully about whether existing systems of classification and definitions that have been drawn from a medical classification system, and designed for clinical purposes, actually suit our purposes.

The point here is that working within a developmental framework may lead to challenges both to traditional questions about causes of a developmental disorder and to questions about categorization of that disorder. Research on other childhood disorders may be informative here, and we may learn lessons from the study of dyslexia, SLI, schizophrenia, ADHD, and emotional disorders.

As part of the re-emphasis on developmental change, it will help to become more aware of the assumptions that drive research and practice and of the limitations that these assumptions lead to.

Dichotomies are helpful, as they draw attention to a particular distinction, helping to make it clearer. For example, we have emphasized a medical versus developmental distinction and the research versus practice distinction in this chapter by exaggerating the divide between them. In reality, however, such distinctions are rarely simple, and we may need to break down conceptual barriers in order to understand the phenomena more clearly. Our aim for integration should be to move away from the rigid distinctions such as research *versus* clinical questions, cognitive *versus* social psychological processes, explanation *versus* description, deficit *versus* delay.

Several chapters contribute toward the breaking down of conceptual barriers: for example, Jones and Klin's research on linking social and cognitive processes, Jones and Jordan's emphasis on grounded description that may build theory versus current top-down theories (explanation), Wicker's research on the limitations of deficit models, and Maestro and Muratori's hypothesis that deviant pathways need to be considered when taking account of timing of development.

The move toward a greater focus on developmental processes and less rigid area definitions may result in a revision of methodological approaches. This work of integrating across perspectives is gaining pace in other areas of typical and atypical development. If the questions are novel, the methods for answering them may likewise need to be novel, or at least adapted for purpose.

Chapter 2 describes the use of connectionist modeling to map the complexities of the processing of emotion in ASD. This approach to neuropsychological material also enables the authors to identify compensatory mechanisms and the conditions under which those mechanisms break down. Chapter 9, which utilizes naturalistic home movie footage of infants later diagnosed with autism, provides a good example of the microgenetic approach, using close observation over a period of intense developmental change and applying a systematic coding to reveal essential shifts in interest during the first year and the subtle patterns of apparent similarity and underlying difference from typical development over time. The patterns of these socio-cognitive findings are then considered in the neuropsychological context of what is known of cortical and sub-cortical development, thus integrating two research areas to powerful effect.

The microgenetic approach is also adopted by Jones and Klin, described in Chapter 4 in their detailed analysis of a single toddler with autism, in which they explore the developmental course of altered visual salience and how it affects the "emerging sense of self." Their sense of the centrality of the developmental process for illuminating the condition of autism is captured in the reference to a "life lived along an alternate course of relative salience" (p. 76). These authors, too, make links with neuropsychological accounts. In Chapter 11, McCann et al., like Jones and Klin, report standard sample data, then enrich their data with close, descriptive, individual analyses of the prosody of two children with ASD. These examples are an illustration of the opportunities for forming novel methodological frameworks within a developmental model.

Will It Really Happen?

What will it take for us to gain real connections between different perspectives and, from there, to fully integrate neurocognitive, clinical/diagnostic, and social-educational approaches? In order to have impact on both theory and practice as well as across traditionally different approaches, we need simultaneous changes in both thinking and in doing.

On the thinking side, we need to do some strategic planning. There need to be more national and international initiatives to facilitate the debates that are required in order to coordinate assumptions and viewpoints across different disciplines. "Stand-offs" still occur between areas of neuroscience, developmental psychology, and practical work in health and educational intervention. Professionals within these different approaches need to respect each other's expertise and to talk and work together. To some extent these joint ventures are already being put in place through research council initiatives to promote interdisciplinary and international collaboration, and there are some exciting developments in autism at a theoretical level.

On the doing side, we need simply to open up and share on a local level. We need to involve people with autism in our research, and we need to share our data and expertise. Initiatives in developing data banks that can be shared by researchers, initiatives in developing web sites to inform practitioners and parents as well as researchers, and joint initiatives that involve parents and practitioners as stakeholders in research are some of the important new facilitative steps that are beginning to be taken. We need to go further in enabling professionals from different disciplines to discuss and debate and to allow cross-currents in thinking.

A crucial link in the progress chain that affects thinking and doing is training. Here we need to rethink the professional training structure that allows distinctly different pathways for clinical and non-clinical research and different career pathways for research and practice, and medical and educational work. Training in child psychiatry and pediatrics needs to include attention to a developmental perspective and understanding of developmentally relevant questions, while training in academic developmental psychology needs to incorporate theoretical and professional views from clinical and educational perspectives. Some understanding of research methods, previously the domain only of academic research training courses, should be more routinely incorporated into the training of non-academic professions. Addressing these issues through professional and academic training means that at least people working from different perspectives will have some familiarity with one another's language and conceptual frameworks and be in a position to start work together. Finally, we also need to remain part of an international research and professional community, something that is much more apparent in the academic than the non-academic world. Initiatives for these kinds of developments are beginning to be on the agenda for government-funded research councils, and further initiatives of this kind are needed.

To conclude, the need to integrate neurocognitive, diagnostic, and intervention processes in autism is as great as it has ever been. However, we think that the prospects for achieving this integration now look stronger than before. A developmental science framework may open up new opportunities for integration with research in the medical/biological field and for crossing the research/practice divide. New directions still need to be carved out in the work on autism, however, so this is the beginning of a developing, integrated endeavour.

References

Bailey, A., Phillips, W., & Rutter, M. (1996). Autism: Towards an integrated view. *Journal of Child Psychology and Psychiatry, 37*(1), 89–126.

Bishop, D. V. M. (1997). Cognitive neuropsychology and developmental disorders: Uncomfortable bedfellows. *Quarterly Journal of Experimental Psychology, 50*, 899–923.

Burack, J. (1997). The study of atypical and typical populations in developmental psychopathology: The quest for a common science. In S. Luthar, J. Burack, D. Cicchetti, &

J. Weisz (Eds.), *Developmental Psychopathology* (pp. 139–166). Cambridge, UK: Cambridge University Press.

Dawson, G., Webb, S., Schellengerg, G. D., Dager, S., Friedman, S., Aylward, E., et al. (2002). Defining the broader phenotype of autism: Genetic, brain and behavioural perspectives. *Development and Psychopathology, 14*, 581–611.

Goswami, U. (2003). Why theories about developmental dyslexia require developmental designs. *Trends in Cognitive Sciences, 7*(12), 534–540.

Johnson, M. H. (2006). *Developmental cognitive neuroscience* (revised edition). Oxford, UK: Blackwell.

Johnson, M., & Munakata, Y. (2005). Cognitive development: At the crossroads? *Trends in Cognitive Sciences, 9*(3), 91–93.

Karmiloff-Smith, A. (1997). Crucial differences between developmental cognitive neuroscience and adult neuropsychology. *Developmental Neuropsychology, 13*(4), 513–524.

Karmiloff-Smith, A., Grant, J., Berthoud, I., Davies, M., Howlin, P., & Udwin, O. (1997). Language and Williams syndrome: How intact is "intact"? *Child Development, 68*, 246–262.

Lewis, M. D. (2000). The promise of dynamic systems approaches for an integrated account of human development. *Child Development, 71*(1), 36–43.

Paterson, S. J., Brown, J. H., Gsödl, M. K., Johnson, M. H., & Karmiloff-Smith, A. (1999). Cognitive modularity and genetic disorders. *Science, 286*(5448), 2355–2358.

Piaget, J. (1955). Les stades du développement intellectuel de l'enfant et de l'adolescent. [The stages of intellectual development in the child and the adolescent]. In P. Osterrieth, J. Piaget, R. DeSaussure, J. M. Tanner, H. Wallon, R. Zazzo, et al. (Eds.), *Le Problème des stades en psychologie de l'enfant* [The problem of stages in child psychology] (pp. 33–42). Paris: Presses Universitaires de France.

Piaget, J., & Inhelder, B. (1941). *Le Développement des quantités chez l'enfant* [The development of quantities in the child]. Neuchâtel, Switzerland: Delachaux et Niestlé.

Thelen, E. (1992). Development as a dynamic system. *Current Directions in Psychological Science, 1*, 189–193.

Thomas, M., & Karmiloff-Smith, A. (2002). Are developmental disorders like cases of adult brain damage? Implications from connectionist modelling. *Behavioral and Brain Sciences, 5*, 727–788.

Van Geert, P. (1998). A dynamic systems model of basic developmental mechanisms: Piaget, Vygotsky, and beyond. *Psychological Review, 105*, 634–677.

Vygostsky, L. S. (1962). *Thought and language* (E. Hanfmann & G. Vakar, Trans.). Cambridge, MA: MIT Press.

Vygotsky, L. S. (1966). Play and its role in the psychological development of the child. *Voprosy Psikhologii, 12*, 62–76.

Wimmer, H., Hutzler, F., & Weiner, C. (2002). Children with dyslexia and right parietal lobe dysfunction: Event-related potentials in response to words and pseudowords. *Neuroscience Letters, 331*, 211–213.

Index